LECTURES ON PSYCHICAL RESEARCH

International Library of Philosophy and Scientific Method

EDITOR: TED HONDERICH

For list of books in the series see back end paper

LECTURES ON PSYCHICAL RESEARCH

INCORPORATING THE PERROTT LECTURES
GIVEN IN CAMBRIDGE UNIVERSITY
IN 1959 AND 1960

by

charlie dunbar

C. D. Broad

DISCARD

BF
31
.B745
1962A

LONDON

ROUTLEDGE & KEGAN PAUL

NEW YORK : THE HUMANITIES PRESS

First published 1962
by Routledge & Kegan Paul Ltd
Broadway House, 68–74 Carter Lane,
London EC4V 5EL

Second Impression 1966
Third Impression 1971

Printed in Great Britain
by Compton Printing Ltd.,
London and Aylesbury

ISBN 0 7100 3611 6

In honoured Memory of

Fellows of Trinity College, Cambridge,
and among the Founding Fathers of
The Society for Psychical Research

'And these all, having obtained a good report through faith, received not the promise.'

Epistle to the Hebrews, xi, 39

CONTENTS

SECTION C. STUDIES IN TRANCE-MEDIUMSHIP

PREFACE

THIS book came to be written because Trinity College, Cambridge, the trustees of the Perrott Bequest for the furtherance of psychical research, invited me to give, in the Lent term of 1959, a course of lectures in the university on that subject. At my own request I gave a second course in the Lent term of 1960. It is provided in the ordinance governing the Perrott Lectureship that the lecturer shall publish the substance of his lectures, and the present work was written and is now published in fulfilment of that obligation.

I thought that I might as well be hanged for a sheep as for a lamb, and so I have taken the opportunity to embody a great deal besides the substance of the twelve lectures delivered in 1959 and 1960. Some of the additional material is ultimately derived from lectures and articles already published, and some of it is concerned with topics which I have not handled before in my published writings.

In Section B, and particularly in Chapters VI and IX, I have made use of my Presidential Address of 1958 to the S.P.R., entitled 'Dreaming, and some of its Implications', and my lecture of 1953 to the same society, entitled 'Phantasms of the Living and of the Dead'. The Epilogue is based upon two published lectures, viz. the *Foerster Lecture*, 'Human Personality and the Possibility of Survival', delivered at Berkeley, California, in 1954 and published by the University of California Press, and the *Myers Memorial Lecture*, 'Personal Identity and Survival', delivered under the auspices of the S.P.R. in 1958 and published by them. I acknowledge with thanks the kind permission granted to me by the S.P.R., and in particular the Trustees of the Myers Memorial Fund, and by the University of California Press, respectively, to incorporate the substance of these lectures in my book. I am under a continuous obligation to the *Proceedings* and the *Journal* of the S.P.R., as the main source of the materials of almost every chapter.

Then, again, I have to thank the American S.P.R. for kind permission to incorporate in Chapter XI a lecture, entitled 'The Phenomenology of Mrs Leonard's Mediumship', delivered to that society in New York in June 1954 and afterwards published in their *Journal*. Finally, I would like to record here my indebtedness to certain chapters in Signe Toksvig's book, *Emmanuel Swedenborg, Scientist*

ix

and Mystic (London: Faber & Faber, 1948), for information about those of Swedenborg's opinions to which I refer, mainly in Chapter XIV.

Psychical research, and the alleged facts which it is concerned to investigate, tend to stir irrational prejudices and to arouse strong feelings, positive or negative, in the breasts of many persons. It may, therefore, be as well for me to state explicitly my own biases, so far as I am conscious of them. (There may, of course, be others of which I am not conscious; and I may be to some extent mistaken as to the nature or the strength of those of which I am aware.)

In the first place, it appears to me that I have a certain hankering after what I may call the 'mysterious' or the 'magical', and a strong desire that the current orthodoxy of many contemporary professional scientists (in particular experimental psychologists) may prove to be as inadequate as it certainly is arrogant and ill-informed.

On the other hand, unless I am much mistaken in my introspection, I rather strongly dislike (for my own part) the idea of surviving bodily death. That is because I am of a cowardly and unenterprising temperament, and am moved much more by fear of possible misfortune than by energy, curiosity, or hope. If there should be another life, one can judge of its possibilities only by analogy with the actualities of life on earth. Nothing that I know of the lives and circumstances of most human beings in the present and in the past encourages me to wish to risk encountering similar possibilities after death. If death be the end, one knows the worst; and the worst, if it ceases to be bearable, is at any rate evitable. If death be not the end, then one is confined for all sempiternity in what looks unpleasantly like a prison or a lunatic-asylum, from which there is in principle no escape.

I do not suppose for a moment that this attitude of mine is or has been that of the majority. In the first place, most people have always been too much occupied in keeping themselves and their dependents alive, and in propagating their species, to have leisure to reflect on the desirability or otherwise of life after death. And most of them have been too stupid to be capable of making any general reflexions whatever, and too inarticulate to express them clearly if they had made them. But, if one can infer their desires from their behaviour, one would be inclined to ascribe to most of them the sentiments so forthrightly uttered by Maecenas:

Vita dum superest, bene est; hanc mihi, vel acuta si sedeam cruce, sustine.

Moreover, quite apart from this blind 'will-to-live', which we share with other animals, there is in many (perhaps in most) men and women an admirable spirit of courage, enterprise, and endurance, which makes them ready to take risks and to face with fortitude (either for their own ends, or for love of certain others or of humanity, or from self-respect or fear of the contempt of their fellows, or from a mere sense of duty) the certainty of danger and hardship and pain and the possibility of disaster. Those in whom this spirit is strong will, if they envisage the question, desire to survive bodily death, with all its risks, and will very rightly condemn as craven my prudential preference for the safety of annihilation.

It may be said that I have failed to mention one strong motive which makes many a person desire survival, not only for him or herself, but also for others, viz. the longing for reunion with those whom one has loved and has lost through death. I have no doubt that this motive does operate strongly in some of us at certain times in our lives. But, if one reflects in a cool hour, one cannot but make the two following observations. In the first place, survival would be no guarantee of reunion; and there seems to be no particular reason to think that, if survival were a fact, reunions among those who had loved each other on earth would be the rule rather than the exception. Secondly, we are liable to forget, or to conceal from ourselves, the obvious fact that such reunions would often be a source of acute embarrassment rather than of consolation. One shudders with sympathetic apprehension when one thinks of Aeneas's encounter in the underworld with the shade of poor dear Dido, of his tactful attempt at reconciliation, and of her contemptuous rejection of it:

Illa solo fixos oculos aversa tenebat,
nec magis incepto vultum sermone movetur
quam si dura silex aut stet Marpesia cautes.

In any event neither the wishes of the majority nor my personal wishes in these matters can make any difference to the facts, for 'things are what they are, and the consequences of them will be what they will be'. But I think that the reader should be warned of these possible sources of bias in the author, so that he may allow for them. He should remember, however, that I myself have tried my best to do this in writing my book; and that, if he proceeds to allow for them over again, he runs some risk of bending over backwards.

Trinity College,   C. D. BROAD
    Cambridge

INTRODUCTION

'She's a rum 'un is Natur',' said Mr Squeers. . . . 'Natur' is more easier conceived than described'.

DICKENS, *Nicholas Nickleby*

THE NATURE, RELATIONSHIPS, AND METHODS OF PSYCHICAL RESEARCH

I shall define 'psychical research' as the scientific investigation of ostensibly paranormal phenomena. My first business, then, is to amplify and explain that definition.

The key expression in it is the phrase 'ostensibly paranormal', and I will begin by explaining what I mean by it. I do this in terms of what I call 'basic limiting principles'.

There are certain very general principles, mostly of a negative or restrictive kind, which practically everyone who has been brought up within or under the influence of Western industrial societies assumes without question nowadays. They form the framework within which the practical life, the scientific theories, and even most of the fiction of contemporary industrial civilizations are confined. I have enumerated and discussed these principles fairly fully in the paper entitled 'The Relevance of Psychical Research to Philosophy' in my book *Religion, Philosophy, and Psychical Research*. Here I will merely mention four typical examples by way of illustration.

(1) We take for granted that a person A cannot know what experiences another person B is now having or has had, except in one or another of the following three ways. (i) By hearing and understanding sentences uttered by B, or reproductions of such sentences, which describe his experiences; or by reading and understanding such sentences written or dictated by B, or reproductions or translations of them. Or (ii) by hearing and interpreting interjections which B makes; by seeing and interpreting his movements, gestures, facial expressions; and so on. Or (iii) by seeing, and making inferences from, certain persistent material objects, e.g. tools, pottery, pictures, etc., which B has constructed or used, or copies and reproductions of such objects.

(2) We take for granted also that a person cannot foresee (as

3

distinct from inferring, or being led, without explicit inference, to expect on the basis of regularities in his past experience) any event which has not yet happened.

(3) We take for granted, too, that a person cannot *directly* initiate or modify by his volition the movement of anything but certain parts of his own body.

(4) As a final example, we take for granted that, when a person's body dies, the personal consciousness, which has been associated with it and expressed through it during his lifetime, either ceases altogether or, if not, ceases to be able to manifest itself in any way to those still living on earth.

Within the very wide region left open by these and other basic limiting principles there are various regularities, positive and negative. Some of these are extremely well attested, e.g. the law of gravitation and the non-inheritance of acquired characteristics. Others are accepted with various degrees of reasonable conviction. I do not think that it is possible to draw a hard-and-fast line between certain of the most fundamental and best-attested negative principles of physics, e.g. the Second Law of Thermodynamics, and what I have called 'basic limiting principles'. But, at any rate, we can say this. *Most* of the generally accepted laws of nature would *not* count as basic limiting principles, in the sense described and illustrated above. And *all* the basic limiting principles which I have mentioned, and a number of others besides, are *tacitly* assumed, but not often explicitly formulated, in treatises on physics, chemistry, physiology, biology, empirical psychology, and other natural sciences.

I think, therefore, that it is legitimate and useful to distinguish between well attested and generally accepted laws of nature, on the one hand, and basic limiting principles, on the other. But we must remember that at any time there will be marginal cases, e.g. the Second Law of Thermodynamics. And we must realize that, if experience of a certain kind were to accumulate, a certain generalization might in course of time be transferred from the one class to the other.

Abnormal and Paranormal Events. Any event which seems *prima facie* to conflict only with a well-established law of nature, but *not* with any basic limiting principle, may be called an '*abnormal*' phenomenon. It is an abnormal phenomenon if a baby is born with two heads, and it was an abnormal phenomenon when radioactive material was found to be continually giving out energy, with no apparent loss of energy elsewhere in the surroundings to counterbalance it. Very often it can be shown that an abnormal phenomenon does not conflict with any of the accepted laws of nature, but is

4

explicable in terms of them and of certain special conditions which are seldom fulfilled in the ordinary course of events. Sometimes, however, the occurrence of an abnormal phenomenon shows either that some accepted law of nature does not hold without exception, or that the already accepted laws of nature must be supplemented by others which had not before been suspected.

An event which seems *prima facie* to conflict with one or more of the *basic limiting principles*, and not merely with some well-established uniformity of nature, may be called an 'ostensibly *paranormal* phenomenon'. Suppose that, on investigation, it should be found that the alleged event really did happen as described, and that it really did conflict with one or more of the basic limiting principles. Then it would have to be counted as a *genuinely*, and not merely ostensibly, paranormal phenomenon. It is the business of psychical research to investigate ostensibly paranormal phenomena, with a view to discovering whether they are or are not genuinely paranormal.

Now there is no doubt that there are, and always have been, reports of events, which, if they really happened as described, would be paranormal. There are, e.g., accounts of persons foreseeing events which they had no cause to expect and could not possibly have inferred to be going to happen from any data available to them. There are stories of a sane waking person having an hallucinatory *quasi*-perception as of some friend or relative in a certain situation of danger or distress, and of that experience corresponding accurately in the detail of its content with the state and situation of the individual in question at the time. There are accounts of persons receiving, through the lips of a medium in trance, information purporting to come from a certain deceased friend or relative, describing incidents in that individual's past life which were unknown at the time to the sitter and could not possibly have been guessed by the medium, and of this information being afterwards found to be true and highly characteristic of the alleged communicator.

Such stories as these are an essential part of the raw material of psychical research. I think it is true to say that they were never subjected to a continuous critical study, with a view to discovering whether there did or did not lie at the back of them genuinely paranormal phenomena, until the foundation of the *Society for Psychical Research* in England in 1882. Before that time some people swallowed them whole and others rejected them without investigation. To this day most people fall into one or other of those two classes. But since the foundation of the S.P.R. there has been a continuous critical investigation of such stories by a minority of persons who are prepared neither to accept them for gospel nor to reject them out of hand. This work has gone on steadily in England

and the U.S.A., in France and in Holland (to name only the countries in which it has been most actively pursued) ever since 1882. In the course of it an immense amount of material has been collected, sifted, and published. Much experience has been gained about the characteristic pitfalls and difficulties of the subject, and techniques of investigation and standards of evidence have been developed. Anyone who should nowadays start to investigate these subjects, without first mastering the relevant parts of that literature, would be acting very unwisely, laying up trouble for himself which he might have avoided, and running the risk of 'teaching his grandmother to suck eggs'. And anyone who at the present day expresses confident opinions, whether positive or negative, on ostensibly paranormal phenomena, without first making himself thoroughly acquainted with the main methods and results of this careful and long-continued work, may be dismissed without further ceremony as a conceited ignoramus.

Psychical Research and Spiritualism. There is a strong tendency, even among intelligent persons of good general education, to confuse or to identify psychical research with Spiritualism. As that is a serious mistake, I will at this point briefly indicate the relation between the two.

I understand by the word 'Spiritualist' a person who is fully convinced of all the following propositions:

(1) That, after the death of a person's body, there is a persistent stream of conscious experience, continuous with that which he had during the lifetime of his body, in much the way in which his consciousness after awaking in the morning is continuous with his consciousness before going to sleep on the previous night. (2) That, after bodily death, a person takes up a life continuous with and somewhat similar to that which he led upon earth, with a new body or *quasi*-body and in new *quasi*-material surroundings, which are dissimilar in certain important respects to their *ante-mortem* counterparts. (3) That, for a time at least, the deceased can and occasionally do communicate with those still alive on earth, through mediumistic utterances, table-turning, automatic writing, etc. (4) Finally, that the nature and content of these ostensible communications is an adequate guarantee for the truth of the first three propositions and is a sound basis for much detailed knowledge about the life, conditions, and surroundings of those who have survived bodily death. A man's acceptance of these four propositions is, I think, the minimum condition for it to be appropriate to call him a 'Spiritualist'. Many Spiritualists, however, would go further, and would base specifically religious beliefs and worship upon the revelations which

they believe to have been conveyed to them through mediums in trance.

It is plain from the above definition that a Spiritualist is a person who, for reasons good or bad, adequate or inadequate, has made up his mind *in one particular direction* on *one* of the many inter-related questions which psychical research is concerned to investigate critically, viz. the nature and implications of those phenomena which take the form of ostensible communications from the dead.

Evidently, it might happen that a person, who began to pursue psychical research as a non-Spiritualist, would be led, as a result of his enquiries, to accept spiritualistic conclusions. Conversely, it might happen that a person, who had accepted the spiritualistic position uncritically, should decide to embark on psychical research. If so, he might find that his spiritualistic convictions were confirmed or that they were undermined. In any case, if he pursued the subject honestly and with due attention to *all* its aspects, he would almost certainly find that his initial spiritualistic beliefs were far too simple to fit the very complex and *prima facie* conflicting facts. If he remained a Spiritualist, he would be one of a very different kind at the end from what he was at the beginning. For he would have replaced an uncritically accepted belief by one held for definite reasons and in full awareness of the objections to it. And, in order to deal with those objections, he would almost certainly have had to modify the details of his initial belief and to make it far more complex and subtle.

As a matter of historical fact, some few convinced Spiritualists, e.g. the late Mr Drayton Thomas, have been active in psychical research; and a certain number of very distinguished psychical researchers, e.g. the late Mrs Sidgwick, have reached conclusions which may fairly be described as subtly and critically spiritualistic. But I think it is true to say that the usual attitude of Spiritualists towards psychical research in general, and towards the S.P.R. in particular, has been and is one of scornful hostility.

SUB-DIVISIONS AND METHODS

Having now tried to delimit the subject-matter of psychical research, and having explained its relation to Spiritualism, I shall next say something about its sub-divisions and its methods. These two topics are closely interrelated, since some kinds of phenomena are suited to one method of investigation and others to another.

Sporadic and Recurrent Phenomena. In this connexion an important division of ostensibly paranormal phenomena is into *sporadic* and *recurrent.* Such a phenomenon is *sporadic* if it is a unique or almost unique occurrence in the life of the person who is the subject of it or is an essential agent in producing it. Most stories of phantasms of the living or of the dead fall under this heading. An ostensibly paranormal phenomenon is *recurrent* if it occurs in connexion with a person who is frequently the subject of such phenomena or an essential agent in producing them, or if it occurs in a certain place where such phenomena have frequently happened.

The most obvious examples of the first kind of recurrent phenomena are those occurring in connexion with a medium, and the most obvious examples of the second kind are stories of haunted rooms or of poltergeist manifestations. A medium is, almost by definition, a person in connexion with whom ostensibly paranormal phenomena occur with considerable frequency. But this sub-division covers also phenomena which would not commonly be called 'mediumistic' and which have nothing to do with 'haunting'. Take, e.g., the case of Mr Shackleton and of Mrs Stewart, the only two of the many persons tried by Dr Soal in his original experiments in card-guessing who showed any appreciable paranormal powers. Their achievements are conspicuous examples of recurrent phenomena which are *prima facie* paranormal. But it would be misleading to describe them as 'mediums'. For there was no question of their being in an entranced state; no claim to be controlled by or to be in communication with a discarnate personality; and (so far as I am aware) there is no evidence that they had any other paranormal powers or were liable to any paranormal experiences.

The Investigation of Sporadic Phenomena. It is plain that sporadic phenomena cannot be investigated experimentally. There are, I think, just three activities involved in their investigation, and these form a kind of hierarchy. The first and most fundamental may be described as *Critical Appraisal*; the second as *Classification*; and the third as *Synopsis with a view to Generalization*. I will now say something about each of these.

(I) *Critical Appraisal.* When a psychical researcher receives a report of an ostensibly paranormal phenomenon of the sporadic kind, his first business is to raise and try to answer the following questions:

(1) Did the reported event really happen? Was it accurately observed and described? Obviously this question is most important, and most difficult to answer satisfactorily, when the event, if it happened at all, did so spontaneously and unexpectedly under circumstances which were not deliberately prepared and cannot be repeated at will. Examples are stories of an hallucinatory experience,

alleged to have been had by A at the time when B was undergoing a certain crisis and to have corresponded closely in the detail of its content with B's state and situation at the moment.

The question branches out into such questions as these: (i) Is the story told in good faith, or was it deliberately made up or embroidered, either as a hoax or in order to gain money or notoriety, or from some other extraneous motive, good or bad? (ii) If the story is told in good faith, how far is the description given of the event to be trusted? Is the witness a level-headed person, or inaccurate and unstable? Is he deliberately or unwittingly leaving out relevant details which were open to his observation, or adding details which were not in fact present, or distorting details which were present and were noticed?

All that can be done in this connexion is rigorously to test the evidence, as it might be tested in a court of law. The best type of investigator for this purpose would be a person with the training and experience of a judge or a police magistrate. But it would be well if he were better equipped than such persons generally are with a knowledge of the psychology of hysteria and of unconscious motivation, without being a fanatical adherent of any of the rival schools in that controversial subject.

(2) Suppose that the investigator establishes to his own satisfaction, and to that of other critical and instructed persons, that the reported ostensibly paranormal phenomenon really happened, and that it has been adequately and accurately described. The next question for him to raise is whether it was *in fact* paranormal. Did it really contravene one or more of the basic limiting principles? Might it not reasonably be regarded as an odd coincidence, startling but not beyond the bounds of ordinary probability? Or, again, may it not be explicable within the framework of those principles, by assuming, e.g., an abnormal sensitivity for ordinary sensory clues, or abnormal powers of conscious or unconscious inference, or abnormally clever sleight-of-hand, on the part of the relevant person? If any of these questions can reasonably be answered in the affirmative, it is safest to regard the ostensibly paranormal phenomenon as merely *ab-*normal and not as *para*normal. At this stage of the enquiry the best type of investigator would be one who is well acquainted, both practically and theoretically, with the standard techniques of conjurors, 'stage-telepathists', etc.

(3) Suppose that the reported ostensibly paranormal phenomenon passes both the preceding tests. Then we must ask whether it could not be explained by postulating powers or laws, or both, which have not hitherto been recognized, but which would fall within the framework of the accepted basic limiting principles. If a plausible explanation

on such lines can be suggested, it will be safest not to regard the phenomenon as genuinely paranormal. There are plenty of examples, within the orthodox physical sciences, of phenomena which seemed extremely paradoxical when first reported, but which eventually proved to be explicable in this kind of way.

I think that it is only at this third stage of the process of Critical Appraisal that eminent natural scientists, in their professional capacity, can be of much service to psychical research. It is a profound mistake to imagine that they have, as such, any particular competence for stages (1) or (2); or that their opinions, positive or negative, on the answers to the questions investigated at those stages, are entitled to any special respect.

(II) *Classification*. Let us suppose, what I think is in fact true, that quite a number of reported ostensibly paranormal phenomena have passed all three of these tests, and therefore must be regarded as having in all probability really happened and having been genuinely paranormal. Then the next process is to try to classify them into groups, according to certain *prima facie* likenesses and unlikenesses between them. Thus, e.g., we may classify veridical waking hallucinations into those which seem to correspond to a *contemporary experience of another person*, those which seem to correspond to a certain *past event which the subject never experienced or witnessed*, and those which seem to correspond to a certain *future event which he had no reason to expect to happen*. Again, we can group veridical hallucinations concerning a certain person into *singular*, i.e. those which occur in only one subject, and *collective*, i.e. those which occur in several subjects (whether in company or in separate places) at much the same time.

These are only a few examples of what can and should be done in the way of classification. The result of this process, when carried out thoroughly on a large mass of varied material of good evidential quality, is what might be termed a 'Natural History of Sporadic Paranormal Phenomena'. An extremely good instance is provided by the two volumes of the book *Phantasms of the Living*, compiled by Gurney, Myers, and Podmore, and published in 1886.

(III) *Synopsis and Generalization*. When and only when there is an adequate natural history of sporadic paranormal phenomena, it becomes possible and profitable to inspect them as a whole, or to direct one's attention to certain large classes of them, in order to see whether one can detect and formulate any general rules about them. Do certain features always or nearly always accompany each other? Are certain features always or nearly always associated with

10

the absence of certain others? An admirable example of such work, within an important but limited field, is the late G. N. M. Tyrrell's Myers Memorial Lecture of 1943 entitled *Apparitions*, of which the latest edition was issued in 1953 with an excellent introduction by Professor H. H. Price.

Investigation of Recurrent Phenomena. I pass now to recurrent phenomena and the methods of investigating them. Here it is possible and desirable to use experimental methods. Since the phenomenon in question recurs fairly regularly over a considerable period, the investigator knows in outline what to expect. He can therefore arrange all the relevant external conditions beforehand, can vary them one by one at will, and investigate perfectly determinate questions which admit of a definite answer, positive or negative. An excellent example of this kind of investigation is provided by the experiments carried out by Dr Soal on card-guessing by his two subjects, Mr Shackleton and Mrs Stewart. I shall discuss these experiments in some detail in a later chapter. Here it will suffice to give the following general account, by way of illustration.

The person who is to do the guessing, whom we will call the 'patient', knows beforehand that each card used in the experiments has upon its face one or other of a certain set of five symbols. In the course of an experiment another person, whom we will call the 'agent', either successively turns up and looks for a moment at the face of one or another of five such cards, or else successively touches the back of one or another of them without looking at its face. We will cover these two alternative procedures by speaking of the agent as 'focusing' a certain one of the five cards on each occasion. The experimental arrangements are such that the focusing of the cards with the various symbols on them takes place in a purely random order. Immediately after the agent has focused a card a signal is given to the patient. The latter thereupon writes down the particular one of the five symbols which he then feels moved to do.

The question is this: Does the symbol which the patient, under the experimental conditions described above, writes down, agree with the symbol on the card which the agent has just focused, more or less often than it might be expected to do if there were nothing but chance-coincidence between the nature of what he writes down and the nature of that card? And, if so, what are the odds against a deviation, at least as great as that which has actually been noted, occurring in the actual number of trials, on the hypothesis of chance-coincidence? (Of course, a precisely similar question can be raised with regard to the agreement or lack of agreement between what the patient writes down on each occasion and the nature of the card focused by

11

the agent at any assigned number of stages *before* or *after* that one.)

The great advantages here are the following. Given that the experimental conditions secure that the agent must focus the cards with the various symbols on them *in a random order*, we know before-hand what is the most probable proportion of successes on the hypothesis of chance-coincidence. We know also beforehand what is the probability, on the hypothesis of chance-coincidence, of the actual proportion of successes in any given number of trials deviating from the most probable proportion by not less than an assigned amount. Hence we can state numerically the odds, on the hypothesis of chance-coincidence, against so great a deviation as has actually been observed, occurring in the actual number of trials. If these odds are very great, and if they continually mount as the number of trials is increased, there will come a point at which one simply cannot go on accepting the hypothesis of chance-coincidence. And at that stage, provided one is satisfied that the experimental con-ditions were really such as to exclude all possibility of relevant *normal or abnormal knowledge* on the patient's part, that the agent's focus-ing was in a *strictly random order*, and that the experimenter was *neither in collusion with the patient nor deliberately faking the records*, one is forced to regard the results as genuinely paranormal.

Of course, the mere establishment of the fact (if it be a fact) that certain persons have certain paranormal powers is only the first stage, though it is an absolutely essential one, in the experimental investigation of the subject. For, as will be seen on looking back to our definition of 'paranormal', it is the establishment only of the purely *negative* fact that the phenomenon in question cannot be explained by agencies and laws which fall within the boundaries marked out by the accepted basic limiting principles. The next stage is to vary the conditions, using the same patient and the same agent, but of course still keeping the conditions such as to exclude the possibility of relevant normal or abnormal knowledge on the part of the patient. One must then note what changes, if any, increase or diminish or altogether inhibit the patient's paranormal achievement. In that way one may hope to proceed to the positive result of estab-lishing empirical laws, in accordance with which such paranormal phenomena occur and vary.

Another useful line of experimental research at this stage is the following. If one experiments in the way described with a large number of individuals as patients, one is likely to find that most of them do not score significantly above or below chance-expectation, that some few score consistently and significantly above it, and that some few score consistently and significantly below it. It then becomes a matter of great interest to see whether there are any measurable characteristics, psychological or physiological, in the patients concerned, which are correlated positively or negatively, to a significant degree, with the properties of scoring significantly above or significantly below chance-expectation. Very interesting work has been done on these lines, particularly in the U.S.A. One may refer, e.g., to the researches of Dr Gertrude Schmeidler, on students from Harvard and from the City College of New York, the results of which have recently been published in a book entitled *E.S.P. and Personality Patterns.*

Intermediate between non-experimental investigation of sporadic phenomena and such experimental investigation of recurrent phenomena as I have been describing, comes the systematic investigation of certain mediumistic phenomena, whether mental or physical. One can have a series of sittings with the same medium, and in these phenomena of the same kind are likely to recur.

In the case of a medium who gives ostensible communications from definite deceased persons, it is very important to arrange that *everything* said either by the medium or the sitter is automatically recorded at the time. This can now be done very conveniently by a tape-recording apparatus. The record can then be studied at leisure by the sitter and by others. In this way one may be able to judge whether the sitter unwittingly supplied hints, which were worked up deliberately or unconsciously by the medium. Again, one may be able to separate out lucky guesses and chance hits from items which are extremely characteristic of the alleged communicator and quite outside the range of the medium's normal knowledge. One can then consider how far these items were known to the sitter at the time. If there were some which certainly were not, but which can afterwards be verified, one can at least rule out straightforward telepathy from the sitter to the medium as an explanation of the latter's ability to impart these items of information about the person who is alleged to be communicating.

In the case of a medium who claims to produce paranormal *physical* phenomena, such as moving objects without contact, there are many experimental devices which can and should be used. In the first place, arrangements must be made which render it impossible for the medium to produce such results by normal means without detection. Unless a medium for physical phenomena will submit to such controls as the experimenter considers to be necessary, there is a strong presumption that he or she is fraudulent, and in any case it is idle to pursue the investigation further. If this elementary pre-condition be fulfilled, it is also most desirable to arrange apparatus which will automatically and permanently record any phenomenon that may take place. We thus obviate very legitimate doubts as to the accuracy of the sitters' contemporary observations and subsequent recollections. In such investigations it is desirable that the person in control should be one who is well acquainted, not only with the methods used by stage conjurors, but also with the rather different *repertoire* employed by fraudulent mediums. Such an investigator may obtain very valuable help from a skilled physicist; but the latter, unless he acts under the guidance of the former, is almost as likely to be taken in by fraud as the plainest of plain men.

Comparison between Experimental and Non-experimental Psychical Research. I will now make some comparisons between sporadic phenomena and non-experimental investigation, on the one hand, and recurrent phenomena and experimental investigation, on the other. I will begin by pointing out something which is common to both.

It is certainly right to demand a much higher standard of evidence for events which are alleged to be paranormal than for those which would be normal, if unusual, such as a murder or a landslide, or those which would be merely abnormal, such as the birth of a child with two heads. For, in dealing with evidence we have always to take into account the *antecedent* probability or improbability of the alleged event, i.e. its probability or improbability relative to all the rest of our relevant knowledge and well-founded belief *other than* the special evidence adduced in its favour. The more improbable an event would be antecedently, the stronger is the special evidence needed to force a reasonable person to conclude that such an event almost certainly did take place.

Now, it might be said, the antecedent odds against the occurrence of an event which would be *paranormal*, i.e. would conflict with one or more of the basic limiting principles which form the framework of all our practical activities and our scientific theories, are practically infinite. On the other hand, to suppose that intelligent and careful persons, who are known to be honest in general and have no obvious motives for acting out of character, should on certain occasions have been careless or fraudulent or both to an extreme degree, is to suppose something which would be at most *highly abnormal*. Moreover, historical instances can easily be cited, e.g. the elaborate forgeries of the late Mr T. J. Wise,[1] and the painstaking faking of evidence in connexion with the Piltdown skull.[2] Therefore, it might be argued,

[1] See Carter and Pollard: *An Enquiry into the Nature of Certain XIXth-Century Pamphlets*, 1934.
[2] See J. S. Weiner: *The Piltdown Forgery*, 1955.

however strong the evidence for an alleged paranormal event, and however little positive evidence there may be for carelessness, incompetence, or fraud on the part of those concerned, it is always more reasonable to accept the latter alternative than to admit that a genuinely paranormal event has taken place. That is, in effect, the essential contention of Hume in his famous *Essay on Miracles.*

Now this general contention is plainly most formidable when applied, as Hume applied it, to *sporadic* phenomena. Here I think that the utmost we can say is this. There is a considerable number of reports of sporadic cases which have been carefully investigated, and where the evidence that the phenomenon happened as described seems to be about as satisfactory as human testimony, direct and indirect, ever is. But it would always be possible, with regard to any particular sporadic case, however well attested and carefully investigated, to avoid the conclusion that a genuinely paranormal event happened. Provided that one is prepared to stretch the arm of coincidence far enough, to postulate sufficient imbecility and dishonesty on the part of investigators who are known to be in other respects intelligent and truthful, and to suppose that the narrators have gone to considerable trouble in falsifying diaries and forging letters with no obvious motive, it is always possible to suggest a normal, or at worst an abnormal, explanation for any story of an ostensibly paranormal sporadic event. This procedure, which has a certain amount of plausibility when applied to each of even the best-attested sporadic cases taken severally, becomes much less convincing when applied to the sum total of them taken collectively. For it then has to postulate imbecility and dishonesty on a very large scale in a large number of mutually independent reporters and investigators.

I think that it is of some importance here to distinguish between a *general* scepticism, of the kind which I have just indicated, and the attempt to take a fair selection of the best-attested cases and then to show *in detail* actual or probable defects in the evidence for each of them. Even the former cannot be refuted, though I regard it as unprofitable. For, in the end, we have to balance against each other two alternatives, each of which is antecedently extremely improbable; and there are no rules for estimating the antecedent improbabilities of the two. As to the latter, it is an exercise in astringent criticism, which is very desirable from time to time in order to keep psychical researchers up to the mark, and becomes harmful only if it induces in them a state of defeatism. It was practised very extensively by Mr Podmore, who was a most distinguished and valuable member of the S.P.R. in its early days. In more recent years a good example of it has been provided by another valued member, Dr West, in his paper

15

'The Investigation of Spontaneous Cases' in S.P.R. *Proceedings*, Vol. XLVIII, Part 175.

The impression which I get from reading such work as this is that, in order to cast doubt on the evidence for the best-attested sporadic cases, one needs to be so captious in one's criticisms that by these standards hardly any alleged ordinary historical event could be accepted with confidence, and hardly any criminal charge could ever be sustained. But I fully admit that one *needs* much better evidence to establish the occurrence of an event which would be *paranormal* than one needs in the case of an ordinary historical event, such as the alleged murder by Richard III of his nephews in the Tower of London.

Let us now consider how far the *experimental* investigation of recurrent phenomena can escape these difficulties. We will take experiments in card-guessing as an example.

The first advantage is this. We can state numerically exactly what are the odds, on the hypothesis of chance-coincidence, against the actual proportion of hits deviating from the most probable proportion by at least as much as it has in fact been found to do in the actual number of trials. If these odds are enormous, that is *pro tanto* very strong evidence against the hypothesis of chance-coincidence. Now the odds in, e.g., Dr Soal's experiments with Mr Shackleton and with Mrs Stewart are of the order of many millions to one, and any-one in his senses dealing with admittedly normal or merely abnormal phenomena would unhesitatingly reject the hypothesis of chance-coincidence long before the odds had reached a magnitude of that order. In the non-experimental investigation of sporadic phenomena there is no possibility of this numerical precision in the statement of the odds against chance-coincidence.

So far, so good. But the mere rejection of the hypothesis of chance-coincidence is not equivalent to accepting the alternative that the observed deviation was due to the patient possessing and exercising paranormal powers. The other alternative is that there is some explanation in normal or abnormal terms. And here the immense antecedent improbability which, by definition, attaches to any hypothesis involving paranormality, enters again, just as it entered in coming to a decision about allegedly paranormal sporadic phenomena. Many intelligent and fair-minded persons would be inclined to argue as follows: 'I agree that the experimental results are such as to make the hypothesis that the observed deviations are a mere matter of chance-coincidence quite incredible. Either they are explicable *somehow or other* within the framework of accepted basic limiting principles, or they involve faculties and laws which fall outside that framework. The latter alternative is antecedently so improbable that I think it reasonable to reject it and to accept the former, even though I cannot pretend to suggest any plausible explanation in normal or abnormal terms.' Here we are back again, then, in the region of antecedent improbabilities and counter-improbabilities, which cannot be numerically estimated.

It might fairly be objected that it is rather unprofitable just to assert that there must be *some explanation or other* in normal or abnormal terms, whilst admitting that one is unable to suggest any that is in the least plausible. But I think that one who holds the position in question could fairly retort as follows. To allege that a phenomenon is paranormal is to make a purely negative statement about it; it is not, in itself, to offer any kind of explanation of it. Is it not, then, just as unprofitable to assert that the experimental results involve faculties and laws of *some kind or other*, which fall outside the framework of accepted basic limiting principles, as to assert that they must be capable of *some explanation or other* within that framework? If you hold the phenomena to be paranormal, then you ought to proceed to formulate explicit hypotheses, conflicting with some of the accepted basic limiting principles; to deduce consequences from them which could be experimentally tested; and then to test them by suitably designed experiments. So far, it must be admitted, most psychical researchers have conspicuously failed to do anything of the kind.

At the present stage of development of the subject it is of more interest to consider those critics who put forward specific explanatory hypotheses in normal or abnormal terms. It is evident that this can be done in two ways.

(1) The critic may accept the experimenter's statements as to the experimental arrangements which he made, and his assurance that these were always followed. He may then try to suggest specific ways in which, notwithstanding those arrangements, the patient might, by normal sensory cues and abnormal acuity of the senses, have become aware of the nature of the card focused by the agent. This line of criticism is well worth attempting, provided always that the critic bears in mind the conditions under which the particular experiment in question was allegedly done, and the detailed nature of the results reported to have been obtained. Too often normal explanations, e.g. that old favourite 'unconscious whispering', are proposed, which might fit the arrangements and the results of *some* actual or conceivable experiments, but which could not possibly apply to the particular experiment in question, if that has been accurately described.

(2) The second line is explicitly, or by implication, to impugn the experimenter's competence or his honesty or both. I think that, with

regard to the best of the reported experiments, this is the only line left for those to take who reject the view that the results are genuinely paranormal. Since there are quite a number of such experiments, performed in different countries and by persons having little or no connexion with each other except a common interest in psychical research, it involves ascribing, on purely *a priori* grounds, gross incompetence or dishonesty or both to a number of mutually independent research workers of otherwise unimpeached reputation. The antecedent improbability of such an alleged state of affairs is obviously very great indeed, though it is not of course numerically assignable.

In other branches of scientific work it is extremely rare for investigators, of good general reputation and holding responsible academic or other posts, to be accused, explicitly or by implication, of being in collusion with or exposed to blackmail by their experimental subjects, of lying as to the nature of their experimental arrangements, or of deliberately faking their records. Any psychical researcher who claims to have obtained positive results must expect to be made the object of such accusations. It is, of course, unpleasant for a research worker to find himself suspected or accused of imbecility or dishonesty or both; especially if he should happen to know himself to be honest, and to be no more stupid than his accuser and much more expert than he in the subject-matter. Nevertheless, I do not think that anyone who finds himself in that position should adopt too 'hoity-toity' an attitude. He should rather regard it as one of the occupational risks to which psychical researchers, as such, are exposed. He will be well advised to keep the originals or attested copies of all his records; and to allow them, without imposing any condition, to be inspected, extracted from, and commented upon in reputable journals by any critic of decent academic status who may apply; even though he may know that the sole object of the applicant is to produce evidence of the experimenter's incompetence or dishonesty. A psychical researcher who finds himself in this position cannot do better than recall the following words of that most honourable and scrupulously conscientious man, Henry Sidgwick, spoken to the S.P.R. in 1889: 'My highest ambition in psychical research is to produce evidence which will drive my opponents to doubt my honesty or veracity. I think that there is a very small minority of persons who will *not* doubt them, and that, if I can convince them, I have done all that I can do. As regards the majority even of my own acquaintances, I should claim no more than an admission that they were considerably surprised to find *me* in the trick.' That some eminent psychical researchers, when faced with such accusations, have not always shown this sublime patience, but have lost their tempers and talked and acted injudiciously, is no doubt regrettable. I cannot say, however, that I find it particularly surprising.

Returning from this digression to the general question of the relative value of the experimental investigation of recurrent phenomena and the non-experimental investigation of sporadic phenomena, I would summarize my own views as follows:

(1) It is easier, especially for those whose training and interests are scientific rather than literary, historical, or legal, to estimate the weight to be attached to reports of the results of simple and well designed experiments, than to estimate the weight to be attached to well sifted and criticized reports of sporadic phenomena.

(2) Suppose that one is satisfied that the results which have been obtained in the best experimental work conflict with a certain one of the basic limiting principles. Then the antecedent improbability of there being *sporadic* phenomena incompatible with that particular principle is reduced. Now the main difficulty in admitting the occurrence of a reported event which, if it happened as described, would have been paranormal, is its enormous antecedent improbability. This leads us to hesitate to accept the occurrence of such events even when the testimony is such that one would unhesitatingly accept the occurrence of a normal or an abnormal event on such evidence. So anything which reduces the antecedent improbability of the contravention of a particular basic limiting principle strengthens the case for the best-attested sporadic phenomena involving a breach of that principle.

(3) The aim of psychical research is not merely to ascertain whether there are any genuinely paranormal phenomena. If it should be found that there are such, then its business is to try to discover the laws governing them. Now it is true that something on these lines might be done merely by classifying, comparing, and contrasting well-established sporadic phenomena. But all experience in other branches of science suggests that such discoveries are most likely to be made by deliberately varying the conditions under which recurrent phenomena take place and noting concomitant variations in those phenomena.

In conclusion I would add the following remarks. Even in the investigation of recurrent phenomena by experimental methods psychical research has been at a disadvantage, up to the present, as compared with the physical sciences and with many branches of normal psychology, for the following reasons:

(1) Persons gifted with appreciable paranormal powers seem to be very rare in contemporary Western societies; and we do not know how to call such powers forth, if they be latent in ordinary men and women.

19

(2) Even when one has found a subject who frequently exhibits such powers and is willing to have them properly investigated, there is no guarantee that they will manifest themselves at the appropriate time and place, and there is a strong tendency for them to persist for a while and then fade away.

(3) In many types of experiment an agent is needed, besides the patient whose powers are being investigated. It is only with certain agents that a given patient can manifest his or her powers. At present the choice of suitable agents for a given patient is a matter of mere trial and error.

(4) One cannot exclude the possibility that the personality, the beliefs, and the emotions of the *experimenter*, as well as the powers of the patient and the correlated faculty of the agent, may influence the results of the experiment.

All this is extremely tiresome. But there are analogies to it in certain orthodox branches of science; and, in any case, it is quite idle to complain or to try to lay down in advance the kind of conditions which shall be relevant or irrelevant to the phenomena under investigation.

If we compare sporadic cases and recurrent cases which seem to involve a breach of the same basic limiting principle, we notice the following differences. The sporadic cases are generally much more spectacular and exciting than the experimental ones. We might compare the former to occasional thunderstorms, and the latter to the attractions and repulsions of pith-balls by amber or sealing-wax rubbed with silk or cat's-skin.

We should not have got very far in unravelling the laws of electricity if we had been confined to the study of occasional thunderstorms. We should not have got very far, perhaps, if we had been confined to the feeble electric charges which we can produce by rubbing sealing-wax or amber. The scientific study of the laws of electricity first became possible when men invented devices by which, first, small charges at very high potentials, and then steady currents at comparatively low potentials, could be produced at will. It seems to me unlikely that there will be progress in the study of paranormal phenomena, comparable to that which has taken place in the theoretical study and the practical application of electricity and magnetism during the last 150 years, unless and until someone hits upon methods of inducing paranormal powers in ordinary persons and sustaining them thereafter at a high level for some considerable time. The most promising lines of approach would seem to be to investigate the effects of certain drugs, of hypnotic suggestion, and of certain kinds of mental and bodily training which have been used from time immemorial in the Far East or by certain occult orders in the West.

20

SECTION A

Experiments in Guessing

'Near thee a being, passionate and gentle,
  Man's latest teacher, wisdom's pioneer,
Calmly, majestically monumental,
  Stands: the august Telepathist is here.

He could detect that peppermint's existence,
  He read its nature in the book of doom,
Standing at some considerable distance,
  Standing in fact in quite another room.'

J. K. STEPHEN, *Lapsus Calami*
(Parody on F. W. H. Myers's *St Paul*)

I

DR SOAL'S EXPERIMENTS WITH
MR SHACKLETON AND
WITH MRS STEWART

IN this chapter I shall give a fairly full account of the experimental
work in card-guessing carried out by Dr S. G. Soal with two subjects
whose names I have already mentioned, viz. Mr Shackleton and Mrs
Stewart, as patients. Dr. Soal was at the time and for many years
afterwards Lecturer in Mathematics at Queen Mary College in the
University of London. At the time of his recent retirement, on reaching pensionable age, he was Senior Lecturer there in that subject. He
has worked in other branches of psychical research besides experimental card-guessing, having contributed to Vol. XXXV, Part 96, of
the S.P.R. *Proceedings*, an important study of a case of trance-
mediumship under the title 'A Report on some Communications
received through Mrs Blanche Cooper', which I shall refer to in a
later chapter.

It should, I think, be noted, as possibly relevant to the success of
Dr. Soal's experiments with Mr Shackleton and with Mrs Stewart,
that he himself possesses or has possessed the power of automatic
writing. Anyone who reads carefully the Report mentioned above,
and compares it with incidental statements in a paper entitled 'Some
Automatic Scripts purporting to be inspired by Margaret Veley' in
Vol. XXXVIII, Part 110, of *Proceedings*, may (if capable of putting
two and two together) infer with high probability that the automatist
'Mr V.', through whose hand those scripts were written, is no other
than Dr Soal. And it is explicitly stated in the preface to that paper
that this 'Mr V.' is the automatist whose hand wrote the automatic
scripts, purporting to come from Oscar Wilde, which were published
in the *Occult Review* for 1923. These were the subject of an elaborate
critical notice by Mrs Sidgwick in Vol. XXXIV, Part 91, of *Proceedings*. A pseudonym was adopted, as is stated, because it was thought

at the time that it might be an embarrassment to the writer in his profession if it were publicly known that he had practised automatic writing and received through it messages purporting to come from the dead. Such a prejudice would indeed have been absurd; but prejudices, however absurd, if widely held by influential persons, have to be taken into account in practical life.

The experiments with which we are here concerned were originally reported in S.P.R. *Proceedings*, Vols. XLVI and XLVII, and in the Myers Memorial Lecture entitled *The Experimental Situation in Psychical Research*, published as a pamphlet for the S.P.R. in 1947. They are now brought up to the date at which the experiments ended, and they are considerably amplified, in the book *Modern Experiments in Telepathy* by Soal and Bateman, published in 1954.

HISTORY OF THE EXPERIMENTS

The history of Dr Soal's experiments is of some interest. By November 1939 he had been working for five years, had tested 160 persons as patients in card-guessing, and had accumulated in all 128,350 guesses. He had very naturally begun by considering whether each guess corresponded or not with the card which the agent was focusing *while or immediately before* the patient was making and recording his guess. To all appearance the results were not significantly different from those which would have arisen if the connexion between the guesses recorded and the nature of the cards focused simultaneously had been purely a matter of chance coincidence.

But another member of the S.P.R., the late Mr Whately Carington, had been experimenting, quite independently of Dr Soal, with drawings instead of cards. (The report of these experiments appears in S.P.R. *Proceedings*, Vol. XLVI.) Carington had exposed a different drawing on each night over a period of ten successive days in a locked room, and had got his patients to sit down each night in their own rooms and to draw what came into their heads when they tried to guess what picture had been exposed on that night. He did a series of such 10-day experiments, with intervals between them, using the same patients throughout. He had found what seemed to be good evidence for the following conclusion. The drawings made by the patients on any one night in such a 10-day sequence did *not* correspond significantly to the picture exposed *on that night*. But they *did* correspond significantly to the pictures exposed *earlier, simultaneously, or later* in *that particular 10-day sequence*, as contrasted with those exposed in the course of the other 10-day sequences in the same complete series.

Carington therefore advised Dr Soal to re-examine the 128,350 guesses, in order to see whether, perhaps, some of the patients had been scoring significantly, *not* on the card at which the guess had been aimed, but on its *immediate predecessor* or *immediate successor* in the sequence of cards focused by the agent in a complete set of 25 attempts. Dr Soal found that, in the case of two and only two of his subjects, a Mr Shackleton and a Mrs Stewart, this had been happening to an extent which was certainly *prima facie* surprising. He therefore proceeded to conduct a new series of experiments, with these possibilities in view, first with Mr Shackleton and later (when she became available after the Second World War) with Mrs Stewart. It is these experiments, and some of their main results, which I shall describe.

METHOD OF EXPERIMENTATION

I will begin by explaining the way in which the experiments were conducted:

(1) *The Cards.* In these experiments five picture-cards were used. On each different card is depicted in the appropriate colours a different one of the five following animals, viz. Lion (L), Elephant (E), Zebra (Z), Giraffe (G), and Pelican (P). There is also a set of five white cards, each bearing a different one of the integers from 1 to 5.

(2) *General Arrangements.* The two main persons in an experiment are the Agent (A) and the Patient (P). In addition two other persons take part in each experiment. These are the experimenter controlling the agent (EA), and the one controlling the patient (EP). EA and A are together in one room, EP and P are together in an adjoining room. The only communication between the two rooms is a door, which is kept slightly ajar, so that EA may indicate auditorily to P when A has focused a card, and P may then write down his guess. The room in which EA and A sit will be called 'the agent's room' (RA), and that in which EP and P sit will be called 'the patient's room' (RP).

In RA there is a table, 66 cm. square and 69 cm. high, situated at about 3 metres from the wall which divides RA from RP. This table is divided across the middle by a screen 85 cm. wide and 69 cm. high, which stands upon it. At the middle of the upper part of this screen is a little window, 8 cm. square. A sits on the side of the screen furthest from the door into RP and facing towards it, and therefore screened from it, EA sits on the opposite side of the screen and faces in the opposite direction.

On the table in front of A is a box, closed on all sides except that which faces A. The five picture-cards, after having been shuffled, are placed, still *face downwards*, on the floor of this box from left to right. The purpose of the box is to ensure that no confederate, who might be concealed in the room above RA and provided with a hole in the ceiling, could see the cards as they are turned up by A and signal their nature to the patient in RP.

On the same table, in front of EA (and therefore on the opposite side of the screen to A) are the five white number-cards arranged *face upwards* in order from 1 to 5 from left to right.

The arrangements described above are shown in the diagram opposite.

P and EP sit on the opposite sides of a small table in RP. The position of this is such that P could not see either EA or the screen, even if the door into RA were wide open. *A fortiori* P cannot see A or the box in which A's picture-cards are laid out, since they are on the far side of the screen.

(3) *The Scoring-sheets.* The scoring-sheets are arranged as follows. Each is divided vertically into two halves, headed (*a*) and (*b*). Each half is subdivided vertically into two parallel columns, of which the left-hand one is used for P to record his successive guesses, whilst the right-hand one is used for recording the actual card which A had focused just before the guess was made. The former column is headed G (for 'guess') and the latter A (for 'actual'). Each column is divided into 25 rows, numbered 1 to 25.

(4) *Randomization.* It is important, for reasons which will be given later, in order to estimate the significance of the results of such experiments, that the agent shall focus the picture-cards successively in a strictly *random* order. This was secured in the following two stages. (i) The five picture-cards were shuffled before each set of fifty guesses to be recorded on a single scoring-sheet. This shuffling was done either by the agent himself or by some independent person. It was *never* done by, or in sight of, either P or EP or EA. The picture-cards were then laid in the resulting order face downwards from left to right on the floor of the box facing A.

(ii) The other part of the randomization was effected in one or other of the following two alternative ways, viz. (*a*) by means of a list of prepared random numbers (PRN Method), or (*b*) by drawing counters from a bag (Counter Method).

(*a*) *PRN Method.* Dr Soal prepared a random sequence of the numbers 1 to 5 from mathematical tables. On the evening before a day on which an experiment was to be made he would enter these numbers, in their random order, into the successive rows of the

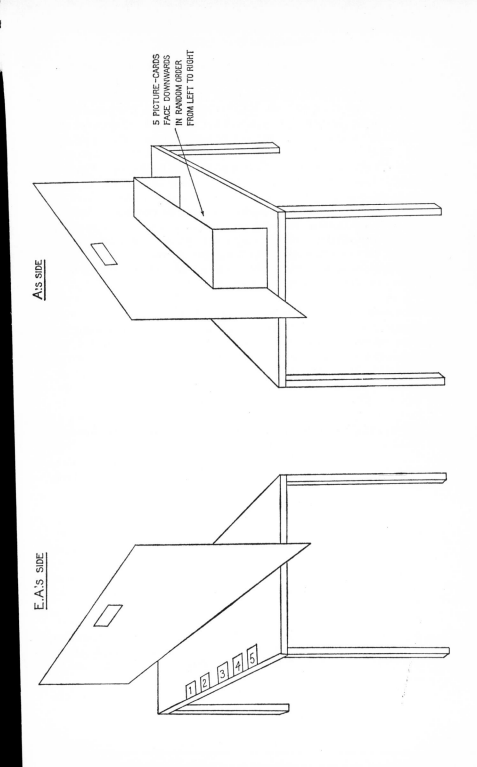

E.A.'s SIDE

A.'s SIDE

5 PICTURE-CARDS FACE DOWNWARDS IN RANDOM ORDER FROM LEFT TO RIGHT

1 2 3 4 5

A-columns of as many scoring-sheets as would be used next day. These prepared sheets would remain in his possession until the experiment was about to begin, when he would hand them to EA.

As an experiment goes on, EA lifts up his five number-cards one by one in the random order in which the numbers 1 to 5 occur in the A-columns of the scoring-sheet before him. As he lifts each number-card he shows it for a moment, through the window in the screen, to A. He then replaces it. A thereupon lifts the picture-card which is lying at that number of places from the left in the row of five such cards in the box in front of him, looks at the picture on the front of it for a moment, and then replaces it face downwards as before. EA does *not* know at the time the order in which the picture-cards are lying in the box facing A. Therefore he does not know which picture-card corresponds to which number. So there can be no complication due to his acting either as a supplementary agent or as a witting or unwitting normal informant.

(*b*) *Counter Method.* The alternative method is for EA to have, instead of a sheet with prepared random numbers, a bag containing equal numbers of counters of five different colours, well mixed up. A different number, from 1 to 5, is arbitrarily associated beforehand with each different colour. A row of five number cards, each with a counter of the associated colour upon it, is laid on the top of the box in sight of A. As an experiment goes on, EA draws a counter from the bag at random, shows it to A through the window in the screen, and then replaces it in the bag. A thereupon notes the number which has been associated with the colour of that counter. He then lifts and looks at the picture-card which lies at that number of places from the left of the row of such cards on the floor of the box before him.

(5) *Focusing, Guessing, and Recording.* The experiments fall into two main groups, viz. (i) those in which A *looks at the picture on the front* of the selected card, whilst P is making his guess as to the nature of that card, and (ii) those in which A merely *touches with his finger the back* of the selected card. We may describe experiments of the first kind as *permitting telepathy*, and those of the second kind as *excluding telepathy*, on the part of the agent. For in the former the agent *does*, and in the latter he does *not*, know at the time by normal means what symbol is on the face of the selected card. Therefore, in the former such knowledge on the part of the agent *may* be a factor influencing the nature of the patient's guess, whilst in the latter it *cannot* be an influencing factor.

The guessing in all cases was conducted as follows. P is provided

28

with some empty scoring-sheets. When EA holds up the number or the counter, which is the signal to A to focus a certain one of the five picture-cards lying before him, he pauses for about one second. Then he calls out ONE!, if it is the first item in a sequence; TWO!, if it is the second; and so on up to TWENTY-FIVE! On hearing EA call the serial number, P writes down, in the corresponding line of the G-column of his scoring-sheet, the initial letter (L, E, Z, G, or P) of the name of the animal whose picture he takes to be on the card which A is looking at the front of or touching the back of, as the case may be. After the completion of the first column of twenty-five guesses on a score-sheet there is a pause of a few seconds before beginning on the second set of twenty-five on the same sheet. EA then calls out NEXT COLUMN!, and the procedure just described is repeated.

Evidently, when P has completed a sheet it will contain in all fifty permutations of the letters L, E, Z, G, and P in the two G-columns, and nothing in either of the two A-columns. The corresponding sheet used by EA will contain fifty permutations of the numbers 1, 2, 3, 4, and 5 in the two A-columns, and nothing in either of the G-columns.

EA now goes round to A's side of the screen and turns up the five picture-cards, which are lying face downwards on the floor of the box in front of A, keeping them in the order in which they were lying. He then finds, for the first time, the correlation between the *ordinal number* of a card from the left of the row and the *picture* on the front of that card. Thus, e.g., it might be

1	2	3	4	5
E	L	G	P	Z

In the meanwhile P and EP remain at their table in RP.

The numbers corresponding to the letters in P's G-column are now entered into the corresponding lines of the G-columns of EA's scoring-sheet, opposite to the numbers which are already in the A-column of that sheet. (The latter are, of course, either the prepared random numbers, or the numbers associated with the colours of the counters successively drawn by EA, as the case may be.) This is done by EA and EP, with A looking on and a witness to check the entries. The correspondences are then noted and counted, and entered on the sheet. Each completed sheet was duplicated in ink, and then signed by both EA and EP. In the experiments with Mr Shackleton as patient the duplicates were put into a stamped envelope addressed to me at Trinity College, Cambridge, in the presence of several witnesses. They were then posted in a nearby pillar-box, also in the presence of witnesses. I kept these duplicates in a drawer in my writing-table in my rooms in College until the end of the Second World

War. At some time after that I forwarded all of them to the offices of the S.P.R. in their original envelopes, and they have been lodged with the S.P.R. from then onwards and were still there at the time of writing these lines. Dr Soal took the originals home with him each time and re-checked all the counts.

It is indeed fortunate that duplicates were made and kept, for Dr Soal has stated (see S.P.R. *Journal*, Vol. XXXVIII, No. 687, p. 216) that early in 1945 the originals were all lost at Cambridge railway station. Presumably they have never been recovered, and most probably they no longer exist.

STATISTICAL TREATMENT

In order to explain this clearly, I will begin by distinguishing what I will call 'direct' and 'deflected' hits. Suppose that the r-th guess in a sequence of 25 guesses agrees with the actual nature of the r-th card focused by the agent in that sequence. Then I say that there was a *direct* hit. If the r-th guess agrees with the actual nature of a card focused earlier or later in the sequence, I say that there was a *deflected* hit. Such a correspondence may be deflected *forwards* on to a card which had *not yet* been focused by the agent at the time when the patient made the guess in question. Or it may be deflected *backwards* on to a card which the agent *had already* focused, and the patient had already responded to, before making the guess in question. Suppose that the r-th guess in a sequence agrees with the $(r + p)$-th card focused by the agent in that sequence. Then I will call it a '$+p$ fore-hit'. Suppose that the r-th guess agrees with the $(r - p)$-th card focused by the agent. Then I will call it a '$-p$ back-hit'. We will now consider in turn direct and deflected hits. Since a good deal of 'clever-silly' comment on the statistical reasoning has been made from time to time, I propose to go into it rather fully. There are two alternative possible ways of dealing with the data. Both are valid, and the two are consistent with each other. The first is simpler and easier to explain, and leads to less laborious numerical calculations. The second makes a fuller use of the detailed information supplied by the experiments. The second is therefore to be preferred in theory, though it is much more troublesome in practice.

(1) *Direct Hits: Method A.* Let the probability that the patient will write down the letter E (for *elephant*) on the r-th occasion be p_{r1}. Let the probability that he will write down the letter L (for *lion*) on that occasion be p_{r2}. And so on for the remaining three symbols, viz. G (for *giraffe*), P (for *pelican*), and Z (for *zebra*). Then, since he

wili certainly write down one or another, and not more than one, of these five letters, we have

$$p_{r1} + p_{r2} + p_{r3} + p_{r4} + p_{r5} = 1.$$

The statement that the order in which the agent focuses a card of one or another of the five kinds on successive occasions is *random* has the following meaning. It means that on each occasion he is *equally* likely to focus any one of them, regardless of *which* of them he may have focused on *each of the previous occasions* in the sequence. Now he will certainly focus one or other, and not more than one, of the five cards on each occasion. Hence, if the order in which he focuses is strictly random, the probability of his focusing any particular one of them on any particular occasion is independent of the nature of the card and of the occasion. It is therefore $\frac{1}{5}$.

On the hypothesis that the hits are nothing but *chance-coincidences*, the probability of the compound event, composed of the agent's focusing a card with an *elephant* on it on the r-th occasion and the patient's writing down E (for *elephant*) on that occasion is (by the definition of 'chance-coincidence') the product of the probabilities of the separate events. It is therefore $\frac{1}{5}p_{r1}$. Similarly, on the same hypothesis, the probability of the agent's focusing a card with a *lion* on it on the r-th occasion and the patient's writing down L (for *lion*) on that occasion is $\frac{1}{5}p_{r2}$. The same holds *mutatis mutandis* for the remaining three symbols.

Now, for there to be a *direct hit* on the r-th occasion is *either* that an *elephant*-card is focused and an E written down, *or* that a *lion*-card is focused and an L written down, *or* so on for the remaining three alternatives, on that occasion. Therefore the probability of a direct hit on the r-th occasion is the probability of the disjunctive event composed of the disjunction of those five alternative compound events. Since these five alternatives are mutually exclusive, its probability is the sum of the probabilities of the five alternatives. It is, therefore, on the hypothesis of chance-coincidence,

$$\tfrac{1}{5}p_{r1} + \tfrac{1}{5}p_{r2} + \ldots + \tfrac{1}{5}p_{r5}$$

But this is simply $\frac{1}{5}$, since

$$p_{r1} + p_{r2} + p_{r3} + p_{r4} + p_{r5} = 1$$

Since the probability of a direct hit, on the hypothesis of chance-coincidence, is the same on every occasion, viz. $\frac{1}{5}$, it follows that the most probable number of direct hits in a sequence of n trials is, on that hypothesis, $n/5$. On the same hypothesis, it follows also that the probabilities of the various possible numbers of direct hits, from 0 to n, in a sequence of n trials is distributed normally with a standard deviation $\sigma = \sqrt{\tfrac{1}{5} \cdot \tfrac{4}{5}n} = \tfrac{2}{5}\sqrt{n}.$

31

The question now is this. Does the actual number of direct hits differ (by excess or by defect) from the number which is most probable on the hypothesis of chance-coincidence by so much as to make that hypothesis quite incredible? In order to test this one has to take the ratio, z, of the actual deviation d to the standard deviation σ. One can then find out, by looking up a table of values of the Error Function, what is the probability, on the hypothesis of chance-coincidence, that *at least as great* a multiple of the standard deviation as that actually observed would occur. If the actual deviation should be more than 2·5 times the standard deviation, the probability of a deviation at least as great as this occurring begins to be very small, on the hypothesis of chance-coincidence. (It should be noted that, for the present purpose, significantly large *negative* deviations are just as important as significantly large positive ones.)

It is often convenient to state the result in terms of the *large odds against* getting so great a deviation as that actually found, rather than in terms of the *small probability* of getting so great a deviation. It is easy to pass from the latter (which is what one finds in tables of values of the Error Function) to the former. Suppose that p is the probability, on the hypothesis of chance-coincidence, of getting a deviation not less than that actually found. Then the odds against this are $(1 - p) : p$, i.e., $(1/p - 1) : 1$. If p be very small, $1/p$ will be very great, and so no appreciable error will be made by stating the odds against as $1/p : 1$. Suppose, e.g., that the actual deviation were 4 times the standard deviation. We should find in the tables that the corresponding value of p is 6×10^{-5}. In that case the odds against could be stated for all practical purposes as $\frac{1}{6} \times 10^5$ to 1, i.e. $1 \cdot 66 \times 10^4 : 1$.

Method B. There is nothing wrong with the reasoning of Method A. But it will be noted that it does not, and does not need to, take account of the *actual* frequencies with which the various kinds of card are focused by the agent in the course of an experiment, or of the *actual* frequencies with which the patient writes down the various letters. Now both these are known from the record-sheets after the experiments; and it is obviously desirable, if we can, to make full use of our data.

Essentially, the method is as follows. We take, as the antecedent probability that a given agent will focus a card of a given kind on any occasion, the ratio of the number of occasions on which he has in fact focused a card of that kind to the total number of occasions on which he has focused a card of any of the five kinds. Similarly, we take, as the antecedent probability that a given patient will write down a given one of the five initial letters on any occasion, the ratio of the number of occasions on which he has in fact written down that letter to the total number of occasions on which he has written down any of the five letters in the course of an experiment. We have then to work out an expression for the most probable number of hits, and an expression for the standard deviation, in a sequence of n trials, on the hypothesis that all the hits are a matter of chance-coincidence.

That problem has been worked out in its most general form by Mr W. L. Stevens, and his paper will be found in Vol. 46 of the *Psychological Review*. I shall content myself here with giving the application of his general results to our special case.

Suppose that, in a sequence of n trials, the agent focuses an *elephant*-card on a_1 occasions, a *lion*-card on a_2 occasions, and so on for the remaining three alternatives. Suppose that, in the same set of n trials, the patient writes down E on b_1 occasions, L on b_2 occasions, and so on for the three remaining initial letters. Obviously we have

$$a_1 + a_2 + \ldots + a_5 = n$$

and

$$b_1 + b_2 + \ldots + b_5 = n$$

On the hypothesis of chance-coincidence the probability of a direct hit on any occasion is

$$\frac{a_1}{n}\cdot\frac{b_1}{n} + \frac{a_2}{n}\cdot\frac{b_2}{n} + \ldots + \frac{a_5}{n}\cdot\frac{b_5}{n}$$

The most probable number of direct hits in n trials, on the hypothesis of chance-coincidence, is n times this, i.e.

$$\frac{a_1b_1 + a_2b_2 + \ldots + a_5b_5}{n}$$

On the same hypothesis the probabilities of the various possible numbers of direct hits from 0 to n are distributed normally. Mr Stevens has shown that the standard deviation is the complicated expression

$$\frac{1}{n^2(n-1)}\left\{\left(\sum_1^5 a_r b_r\right)^2 - n\sum_1^5 a_r b_r(a_r + b_r) + n^2\sum_1^5 a_r b_r\right\}$$

From this point onwards the reasoning is precisely the same as in Method A. The differences in the odds against obtaining, on the hypothesis of chance-coincidence, such large deviations as were actually found, when calculated by the two methods, are not great. Stevens's method gives a somewhat more conservative estimate of them. As we shall see, they are so fantastically high that multiplication or division by a few tens makes no practical difference. It may be remarked that Dr Soal states that he used Stevens's method for calculating the most probable number of hits, and Method A for calculating the standard deviation.

(2) *Deflected Hits.* In a run of 25 trials let us denote the r-th guess by G_r and the $(r + p)$-th actual card by A_{r+p}. Then, for hits at a distance of p cards ahead, we have to consider pairs of the form $G_r A_{r+p}$. The number of such pairs is found by letting r range from 1 to $(25 - p)$. In N sets of 25 trials there will be $N(25 - p)$ such pairs. Therefore (if we use Method A) the most probable number of $+p$ fore-hits in N sets of 25 trials is, on the hypothesis of chance-coincidence, $\frac{1}{5}N(25-p)$. The standard deviation will be $\frac{2}{5}\sqrt{N(25-p)}$. The expressions will be the same for $-p$ back-hits. If we use Method B, we must make similar substitutions, i.e. $N(25 - p)$ for 25N, in the expressions for the most probable number of hits and for the standard deviation. Apart from this, the statistical procedure is precisely the same in dealing with deflected hits as it is for direct hits.

EXPERIMENTS WITH MR SHACKLETON

In the preliminary experiments, in which Mr Shackleton had been one of the 160 persons tested as patients by Dr Soal, he had made 800 guesses. The results may be summarized as follows for direct hits, $+1$ fore-hits and -1 back-hits:

	−1 *back-hits*	*Direct hits*	+1 *fore-hits*
Value of z	+3·74	+0·44	+3·65
Odds against	5,500 : 1	1·51 : 1	3,700 : 1

There was plainly no reason to suspect anything but chance-coincidence in the *direct* hits; but it looked as if there might be something more than this in the deflected ones. It was therefore decided to carry out a special investigation on Mr Shackleton, with particular attention to such hits.

These experiments were conducted in 1941 and 1942. It should be noted that in all of them Dr Soal confined his attention deliberately to just *five* possible kinds of hit, viz. -2 and -1 back-hits, direct hits, and $+1$ and $+2$ fore-hits. Altogether 13 different agents were used, but significantly large deviations in any of these positions were got only with three of them, viz. two women, R. E. and G. A., and one man J. A. The results with J. A. were in certain respects unlike those with the two successful women agents. The experimenters were Dr Soal and another experienced member of the S.P.R., Mrs Goldney. Various persons acted as EA or as EP.

I will begin by remarking that Mr Shackleton finds it most comfortable to work with an interval of about two to three seconds between successive calls. This may be called the 'Normal Rate of Calling'. We will consider first experiments done at that rate, and then those in which the rate fell outside these limits.

(I) *Normal Rate of Calling*

(1) *Conditions permitting of Telepathy*
(a) *With R. E. and the PRN Method of Randomization.* The total number of trials was 3,946. (This is not an exact multiple of 25. The reason is that 4 trials in one set of 25 were cut out because of a mistake in procedure.) There was no significant deviation except for $+1$ fore-hits. Here the deviation was positive and colossal, giving $z = +13 \cdot 2$. The probability, on the hypothesis of chance-coincidence, of getting a deviation not less than this is $8 \cdot 69 \times 10^{-40}$. Since this is only one alternative out of the five under consideration, we must multiply the probability by 5 in order to get the probability that *at least one* of the five categories would deviate by as much as the $+1$ fore-hits did. This makes no practical difference to the enormous odds against obtaining such a result on the hypothesis of chance-coincidence. They are $2 \cdot 3 \times 10^{38}$ to 1 against.

(b) *With R. E. and the Counter Method of Randomization.* The total number of trials was 1,644. (This again is not an exact multiple of 25. Six trials in one series of 25 had to be rejected because of a mistake in procedure.) As before, the only significant deviation was for $+1$ fore-hits, and it was positive, giving $z = 7 \cdot 45$. The corresponding value of the probability is $9 \cdot 27 \times 10^{-14}$. As before, this must be multiplied by 5. That leaves the odds against getting such a result, on the hypothesis of chance-coincidence, in one or other of the five places, at $2 \cdot 15 \times 10^{12}$ to 1.

(c) *With G. A. and the PRN Method of Randomization.* The total number of trials was 450. As before, there was no significant deviation except for $+1$ fore-hits, and there it was positive, giving $z = 6 \cdot 06$. The corresponding value of the probability, multiplied as usual by 5, is $6 \cdot 79 \times 10^{-9}$. The odds against getting such a result in one or other of the five places are $1 \cdot 47 \times 10^8$ to 1.

(d) *Aggregate of above Results.* Taking together all the trials with R.E. and with G.A. at the normal rate of calling and under conditions which permit of telepathy, we have in all 5,799 guesses which *could* have resulted in $+1$ fore-hits. Of these 1,679 *in fact* did so. Using Method A, for the sake of simplicity, the most probable number of such hits, on the hypothesis of chance-coincidence, is

35

one-fifth of 5,799, i.e. 1,160 to the nearest integer. The excess of $+1$ fore-hits over the number that is most probable on the hypothesis of chance-coincidence is therefore 519. Using Method A, the standard deviation is $\frac{2}{5}\sqrt{5,799}$, i.e. 30·46. So z, the ratio of the actual to the standard deviation, is almost exactly 17. The probability, on the hypothesis of chance-coincidence, of getting a deviation not less than this is $8\cdot32 \times 10^{-65}$. Multiplying this by 5, we get $4\cdot16 \times 10^{-64}$. The corresponding odds, on the hypothesis of chance-coincidence, against getting so great a deviation in one or other of the five places under consideration, are $2\cdot4 \times 10^{63}$ to 1. They are about the same as the odds against throwing not less than 82 sixes in succession, when one starts throwing a fair die and proposes to go on until a non-six turns up.

(*e*) *With Mr J. A. and the PRN Method of Randomization.* The number of trials was 750. Here there were significant scores *both* on $+1$ fore-hits and on -1 back-hits, but not on any of the other alternatives under consideration. In the case of the $+1$ fore-hits $z = +5\cdot42$, in that of the -1 back-hits $z = +5\cdot84$. The probability, on the hypothesis of chance-coincidence, of each of these deviations severally is respectively $5\cdot9 \times 10^{-8}$ and $5\cdot16 \times 10^{-9}$. But here we have to notice that there are *two* deviations, of about the same order and in the same direction, in the five alternative places under consideration. Let us suppose, for the sake of simplicity, that the probabilities of these were exactly equal; and, in order to be on the safe side, let us take the *higher* value of the two (corresponding to *smaller* odds against), viz. $5\cdot9 \times 10^{-8}$, as the common value. Then the probability, on the hypothesis of chance-coincidence, of *two* such deviations occurring in the five places under consideration is approximately 10 times the square of the single probability, i.e. it is $3\cdot48 \times 10^{-14}$. The corresponding odds are $2\cdot87 \times 10^{13}$ to 1 against.

(2) *Conditions excluding Telepathy*
Still confining our attention to experiments in which the normal rate of calling was used, we will now consider those in which the agent merely *touched the back of the card*, instead of turning it up and looking at the front of it, and so was unaware at the time by normal means of the picture on it.

In the first series of such experiments two sets of 50 calls made under these conditions were interspersed, more or less at random, among sets of calls made under conditions which would permit telepathy. The patient had no normal knowledge that the change of conditions was being made. In the second series, sets of 50 guesses done under one or other of the two kinds of condition were alter-

36

nated regularly with each other, and the patient was told which was which. The agent in all cases was R. E., and the PRN method of randomization was used throughout.

The results are, on any view, of great interest. In each series the experiments done under conditions which *exclude* telepathy gave *no* significant deviations, whilst those done under conditions which *permit* telepathy gave the usual *highly significant deviations*, viz. excess of +1 fore-hits. The results for the two series together may be summarized as follows.

Thirty-two sets of 25 guesses were made under conditions which *exclude* telepathy. The ratio of the actual to the standard deviation for +1 fore-hits was only +0·47, which is quite insignificant. Thirty-six sets of 25 guesses were made under conditions that would *permit* telepathy. The ratio in this case was +5·86. The probability, on the hypothesis of chance-coincidence, of getting so large a deviation is about $5·16 \times 10^{-9}$. This must, as usual, be multiplied by 5. When that has been done, the odds against getting so large a deviation in at least one of the five places under consideration are found to be $3·88 \times 10^7$ to 1.

This alternation of insignificant and highly significant deviations within the same series of experiments, when one and only one of the experimental conditions is varied, is plainly very important. It strongly supports the view that the high scoring in +1 fore-hits, under conditions which permit telepathy, is a non-fortuitous phenomenon and not a mere statistical freak, and that normal knowledge by the agent of the nature of the card focused by him on each occasion is a necessary condition for success, at any rate in the case of the particular patient Mr Shackleton. Those who hold that the experimenter was reliable, and that the experimental conditions were such as to exclude the possibility of collusion between Mr Shackleton and R. E., will be strengthened in the view that the experiments demonstrate genuine telepathy. Those who harbour doubts on these points will argue that these results strengthen the case for supposing that there was collusion between the patient and the agent, and that this can operate when and only when the latter has normal knowledge of the nature of the card focused on each occasion.

(II) *Abnormal Rates of Calling*

We will next consider experiments in which the rate of calling was either quicker or slower than the normal rate of 2 to 3 seconds per call.

(i) *Quickening*. Here we have two sets of experiments. The first were done with R.E. as agent, using the Counter Method of randomization. The second were done with J. A. as agent, using the PRN Method. There was an effect *common* to both experiments, viz. that the significant excess of +1 fore-hits *vanished* and was replaced by a significantly great excess of +2 fore-hits. With J. A. there were certain additional peculiarities. In each set of experiments the calling was at about *twice* the normal rate, i.e. the average interval was from 1 to 1·5 seconds. The detailed results are as follows.

(*a*) *R. E. as Agent.* 850 trials were made. The ratio of the actual to the standard deviation sank to −1·11 in the case of +1 fore-hits, and rose to +6·77 in the case of +2 fore-hits. The former ratio is quite insignificant; whilst the odds, on the hypothesis of chance-coincidence, against so great a deviation occurring, in one or other of the five places, as actually does occur for +2 fore-hits, are 1·56 × 10^{10} to 1.

(*b*) *J. A. as Agent.* I have already mentioned that there is a peculiarity in the percipient's scoring with this agent at the *normal* rate of calling. With J. A., and with him only, there is a significant excess of −1 *back-hits*, in addition to the usual significant excess of +1 fore-hits. These peculiarities were reflected in a modified form when the experiments were conducted at the rapid rate. In none of these was there any significant excess of either +1 fore-hits or −1 back-hits. But there was a highly significant excess of both +2 fore-hits and −2 back-hits. The ratios in these cases were +4·7 and +5·2 respectively. Thus, the effect of doubling the rate of calling was to push the successful fore-hits one step forward and the successful back-hits one step backwards.

(ii) *Retarding.* When the rate of calling was slowed down, so that the interval between successive calls became five seconds, instead of the normal two to three seconds, Mr Shackleton showed great discomfort, and no significant deviation from chance-expectation occurred in any of the five places under consideration. In one series of trials sets of calls at the *slow* rate were alternated with sets at the *normal* rate. 400 trials at the slow rate gave no significant deviations anywhere. But the same number of trials at the normal rate, alternated with these, gave a ratio of +4·4 for +1 fore-hits, which is a highly significant excess over the most probable number on the hypothesis of chance-coincidence.

It is worth while to remark again that such systematic variation in the number of hits achieved in a given position, when one condition is altered and all the others remain unchanged, is not only interesting in itself. It also strongly reinforces the conclusion that the excess of

+1 fore-hits, at the normal rate of scoring and under conditions which would permit telepathy, is not a mere chance-phenomenon or statistical artifact. It is a genuine causally conditioned phenomenon, either paranormal or due to some normal cause which the experimental conditions have failed to exclude or the experimenter has deliberately concealed.

EXPERIMENTS WITH MRS STEWART

I pass now to Dr Soal's experiments with Mrs Stewart as patient. In the preliminary tests with 160 subjects before the end of 1939 she had made 2,000 guesses, and it looked as if the excess of +1 fore-hits and of −1 back-hits might be significant. During the war she was not available for further experiments. But in August 1945 she returned to London, and Dr Soal started a series of investigations which went on until January 1950. An interim report on these was given in his Myers Memorial Lecture of 1947, entitled *The Experimental Situation in Psychical Research*. The final report on them will be found in the book *Modern Experiments in Telepathy* by Soal and Bateman (Faber, 1954).

The experimental arrangements appear to have been practically the same as those already described in the case of experiments with Mr Shackleton. Mrs Stewart was successful with more agents than he was. With her, twelve persons were tried as agents, and she was successful with eight of them. I will now describe briefly some of the main results.

(1) *General Remarks*. At first no special variations in conditions were introduced. It was now found that the patient was scoring an enormous excess of *direct* hits, but there was no sign of any excess of +1 fore-hits or −1 back-hits. When a total of 37,100 trials had been made, at the normal rate and under conditions permissive of telepathy, the actual number of direct hits had exceeded the number most probable on the hypothesis of chance-coincidence by about 1,990. This is about 25·8 times the standard deviation. The odds against such a result, on the hypothesis of chance-coincidence, are astronomical.

In the preliminary experiments in 1936 Mrs Stewart had scored a significantly large *excess* of +1 fore-hits. In the course of the present experiments it gradually emerged that the number of +1 fore-hits was significantly *smaller* than the most probable number on the hypothesis of chance-coincidence. Of the 35,616 trials which *could* have led to a +1 fore-hit only 6,775 in fact did so. That is *less* by 348 than the number most probable on the hypothesis of chance-coincidence. The ratio to the standard deviation is −4·61. This is a significant result. The odds, on the hypothesis of chance-coincidence, against getting so large a deviation in one or other of the five places under consideration are 50,000 to 1. It also emerged that Mrs Stewart was scoring a significant *defect* in −1 back-hits.

(2) *Effect of increasing the Rate of Calling.* When the rate of calling was doubled, Mrs Stewart ceased to score significantly with direct hits, and began instead to score a highly significant excess of −1 back-hits. This is probably capable of a quite simple explanation. When she made her r-th guess it may still have tended to be a direct hit on the card focused by the agent on the r-th occasion. But, with the quicker rate of calling, she may fail to write down her r-th guess until the agent is focusing the $(r + 1)$-th card. If the guess were correct, it would then count as a −1 back-hit. We may call this explanation the hypothesis of 'delayed response'.

It is interesting to compare and contrast these results with those which were observed in the case of Mr Shackleton when the rate of calling was doubled. It will be remembered that, with one agent (J. A.), he scored significantly highly in −1 back-hits when the calling was at the normal rate. When the rate of calling was doubled he ceased to do this and began to score with significantly high frequency in −2 back-hits. This effect seems to be quite comparable with the effect of doubling the rate of calling with Mrs Stewart, and it is probably susceptible of a similar explanation.

But there was another phenomenon with Mr Shackleton, to which there is no parallel with Mrs Stewart. He had scored significantly highly, both with R. E. and with J. A. as agent, in +1 fore-hits, when the calling was at the normal rate. When the rate was doubled he ceased to do this, but began to score significantly in +2 fore-hits. It has been suggested that Mr Shackleton's 'acts of pre-cognitive awareness' are normally directed upon events at a certain short period ahead, and pass over intermediate events. Suppose, now, that the rate of calling is doubled; so that when he makes his r-th guess the exposure of the $(r + 1)$-th card is a future event in the *middle of this period*, whilst the exposure of the $(r + 2)$-th card is a future event *at the end of it*. Then, on the present hypothesis, his r-th guess would tend to be a pre-cognitive awareness of the $(r + 2)$-th card to be exposed. This may be called the hypothesis of 'a minimal pre-cognitive time-span'.

Now, whilst each of these hypotheses taken separately furnishes an explanation of the facts which it is put forward to explain, it seems to me that they would have to be combined in the case of Mr Shackleton. And, if we combine them, we seem to come into conflict with the facts. Suppose that he is making his r-th guess in a sequence in which the rate of calling is twice the normal rate. And suppose that this guess is an 'act of pre-cognitive awareness'. Then, on the hypothesis of a *minimal pre-cognitive time-span*, the guess will be directed to the $(r + 2)$-th card to be focused, and will pass over the $(r + 1)$-th. But, on the hypothesis of *delayed response*, Mr Shackleton would not record this guess until the $(r + 1)$-th card is being exposed. It will therefore count as a $+1$ fore-hit. So the doubling of the rate of calling should not, as it did, change a significant excess of $+1$ fore-hits into a significant excess of $+2$ fore-hits.

(3) *Conditions excluding Telepathy.* As in the experiments with Mr Shackleton, so too with Mrs Stewart, the subject failed completely to score anything significantly different from what might be expected on the hypothesis of chance-coincidence when the agent merely tapped the back of the card with his fingers without ever having turned it up and looked at its face. Blocks of 50 trials, done under these conditions, were interspersed, without Mrs Stewart being informed, among blocks of normal trials, where the agent looked at the front of the card to be guessed. On the latter she continued to score significantly in direct hits.

It appears, then, that for both Mr Shackleton and Mrs Stewart, working with Dr Soal as experimenter and with the particular agents employed, knowledge by the agent of the nature of the card focused on each occasion is a necessary condition for successful guessing by the patient.

(4) *Effect of attenuating the Conditions permissive of Telepathy.* The next question which Dr Soal investigated was this. Granted that the patient can score significantly only under conditions which would make telepathy from the agent possible, how far can that condition be attenuated without detriment to the scoring?

He found that the following procedure on the part of the agent worked just as well as when the agent actually turned up the card each time and looked at the picture on its face. The agent shuffles the five cards and lays them face downwards on the floor of the box in front of him. At a signal from the experimenter the agent turns them all face upwards, looks at them for 30 seconds, and then turns them over without altering their order. He makes no special effort to remember which is which; and, if asked, it may be found that he cannot answer correctly. In doing the experiment the agent, thus prepared, now simply taps with his finger the back of the card whose position from the left of the row corresponds with the number shown by EA in the window in the screen.

When this method was used by the agent, Mrs Stewart continued

41

to score direct hits at the same rate as before. Reducing the period during which the agent was allowed to look at the cards before turning them over at the beginning of an experiment did no harm, provided the period was not less than five seconds. But success was materially reduced, if the agent was allowed only to glance briefly at the face of each card *severally and in succession*, and was not allowed to see them *all together* lying face upwards. It would seem, then, that the minimal necessary condition is (i) that the agent should have been consciously aware, for a short time just before the beginning of the experiment, of the symbols on the faces of the five cards in the ordered pattern in which they lie, and (ii) that at each call he shall consciously receive a signal (viz. the showing to him of a number) which will direct his attention to the back of a particular one of these cards.

(5) *Use of two Agents together*. I will conclude this account of Dr Soal's work with Mrs Stewart by mentioning the following interesting variations which he tried, viz. (i) *division of functions* between two agents, and (ii) *conjunction or opposition* between two agents.

(i) *Division of Function*. In these experiments one agent, A_1, sits behind the screen and is shown the random numbers in the usual way by EA. But, instead of having five picture-cards face downwards in front of him, he has five *blank* cards. When he is shown a number by EA he touches the back of the corresponding one of these blank cards. Meanwhile the other agent, A_2, sits in *another room*, with the five *picture-cards* before him. He shuffles them, lays them face downwards, turns them all up and looks at them for 30 seconds, and then turns them over in their original order, just as he would do if he were sitting behind the screen and acting as agent in an ordinary experiment. Thus, A_1 has no normal knowledge of the nature and spatial order of the cards, but knows the temporal order in which the random numbers are shown; whilst A_2 knows (or has known) the nature and spatial arrangement of the cards, but has no knowledge of the temporal order in which they are to be made targets in the course of an experiment.

It appeared that a necessary condition for Mrs Stewart to score significantly in such experiments was that she should be informed, at the time, of the arrangements. When that condition was fulfilled she scored an excess of direct hits quite comparable with that which she scored with a single agent working under normal conditions.

This very interesting result may be summarized as follows. We must distinguish between the *occurrent* and the *dispositional* parts of the relevant knowledge possessed by an agent at a given moment.

The *occurrent* part is that which takes the form of actual experience, e.g. sense-perception or recollection, in him at that moment. The *dispositional* part is that which takes the form of a power and a tendency to have certain experiences or to react in certain ways, acquired as the result of past experience of a particular kind, and presumably based upon some kind of persistent organized pattern of traces in the psycho-physical individual in question. Now it appears that Mrs Stewart can score significantly when the relevant information is divided in the following way between two agents. The occurrent part of the necessary knowledge, viz. the awareness of the ordinal number of the card to be focused on each occasion, is possessed by one and only one of the agents, viz. A_1. The dispositional part of that knowledge, viz. the trace left by having seen the cards face upwards in their spatial order and having noted the symbols on each just before the experiment, is present in the other agent, viz. A_2, and only in him. Thus, an *occurrent* factor, present in one agent without its dispositional supplement, and a *dispositional* factor, present in another agent simultaneously without its occurrent supplement, co-operate, as if both were simultaneously present in a single agent, in influencing Mrs Stewart's guesses to give a significant excess of direct hits.

(ii) *Conjunction or Opposition between Agents.* In these experiments it was arranged either (*a*) that the two agents focused similar cards on each occasion, or (*b*) that they focused dissimilar cards on each occasion. The results may be summarized as follows. (*a*) When two agents, with each of whom severally Mrs Stewart had scored significantly, *co-operated*, there was *no significant improvement* in her scoring. (*b*) When two such agents were in *opposition*, what happened was this. Mrs Stewart would score with *one* of them the usual significant excess of direct hits; whilst, with the other, the number of her direct hits would not differ significantly from what might be expected on the hypothesis of chance-coincidence. It is not clear what determines which of the two opposed agents shall be effective in any such experiment. But the upshot of the matter is this. With this patient and those agents, and under these experimental conditions, the influences of the two agents neither reinforce each other when they are in conjunction nor weaken each other when they are in opposition.

43

II

THE PRATT-PEARCE EXPERIMENT
AND MR TYRRELL'S EXPERIMENTS
WITH MISS JOHNSON

IT would be a great mistake to imagine that Dr Soal's experiments with Mr Shackleton and with Mrs Stewart stand alone; and that, if only the results of them could be accounted for in normal or abnormal terms, all would be over except the shouting. In this chapter I will first describe briefly the Pratt-Pearce experiment, and then more fully the experiments made by Mr Tyrrell with his subject Miss Johnson. The results of both these, to whatever causes they may be due, deviated to a fantastic extent from what could reasonably have been expected on the hypothesis of chance-coincidence.

THE PRATT-PEARCE EXPERIMENT

The experiments in question were done at Duke University, North Carolina, in 1933, and described by Professor Rhine in the *Journal of Parapsychology* in the following year. The experimenter was Mr (now Dr) J. G. Pratt, and the subject was Hubert Pearce, then a student at Duke University.

The method used in these experiments was the following. Cards were printed, having one or another of a certain five symbols on the face of each. From such cards packs of 25 were formed, each containing five cards of each kind. Before each experiment a number of such packs were formed by careful and repeated shuffling, and each pack was then cut. In the four series of experiments which I am about to describe Pearce would come to Pratt's room in the university, and they would compare their watches, in order to make sure that they synchronized. Pearce would then leave Pratt's room and cross the quadrangle and walk to a room in another building. Meanwhile, Pratt would shuffle and cut the cards, keeping them all the time with

44

their faces away from him, and finally laying them face downwards on the table before him. At a moment, previously agreed between the two, Pratt would take the top card from the pack in front of him and would lay it (*without* looking at it) face downwards on the table. Exactly one minute later he would do likewise with the second card, and so on until he had run through the pack. Meanwhile Pearce, in his room in the other building, would write down his first guess exactly 30 seconds after the moment at which Pratt had removed and laid down the top card. Thereafter Pearce proceeded to write down his guesses at intervals of one minute, until he had made and recorded 25 guesses. At each sitting two packs were worked through in this way.

After completing a sitting, Pratt would record in duplicate the order of the actual cards used in the experiment, would seal up one copy before leaving his room, and would afterwards hand the sealed copy to Professor Rhine. Pearce did likewise with the record of his guesses. From the copies which they had retained Pratt and Pearce computed Pearce's scores, whilst Rhine made an independent computation from the copies in sealed envelopes which had been handed to him by Pratt and by Pearce. The records were afterwards photostatted, and the photostats remain for inspection.

In three of the four experiments in question the distance between the rooms in which the two men were sitting was 340 feet. In the remaining one it was 740 feet. The total number of trials was 1,850. The most probable number of hits, on the hypothesis of chance-coincidence, is 370. The actual number exceeded this by 188. The standard deviation is 17·2. So z is $+10·9$. The corresponding probability is $1·16 \times 10^{-27}$. In this case there is no need to multiply by 5, since *only* direct hits or misses were under consideration. The odds, on the hypothesis of chance-coincidence, against obtaining so great a deviation as was actually found are $8·62 \times 10^{26}$ to 1.

The Pratt-Pearce experiments, when compared with those of Dr Soal, illustrate an important general fact. It will be noted that the former were done under conditions which would *exclude* telepathy. Pratt was not aware by normal means, at the time when the experiment was taking place, of the actual order of the cards which Pearce was trying to guess. Now it will be remembered that Dr Soal's two subjects *failed* to score results significantly different from what might be expected on the hypothesis of chance-coincidence, when the conditions were such as to exclude the possibility of telepathy. This shows the unwisdom, at the present stage of development of the subject, of generalizing from what has been found to hold of one or more patients investigated by one experimenter to the case of other patients investigated by another experimenter.

45

MR TYRRELL'S EXPERIMENTS WITH MISS JOHNSON

There is plenty of good evidence, apart from the Pratt-Pearce experiments, that some subjects working with some experimenters, under conditions which seem to exclude the possibility of telepathy, can systematically score an excess of hits of such magnitude that the odds against achieving anything comparable, on the hypothesis of chance-coincidence, are colossal. I shall now give another illustration of this fact from a somewhat different angle, viz. some of the experiments carried out by the late Mr G. N. M. Tyrrell with Miss Johnson as patient. These experiments were performed mainly in the years 1935 and 1936, and they are described in a paper entitled 'Further Research in Extra-sensory Perception' in Vol. XLIV, Part 147, of the *Proceedings* of the S.P.R.

I will premise by saying that Mr Tyrrell, who died in 1952 at the age of 73, had been by profession a telegraphic engineer. He was a man of wide general knowledge and interests, who had seen much of men and things in the course of his professional travels. He first joined the S.P.R. in 1908, and, after serving in the First World War, devoted most of the remaining thirty-four years of his life to psychical research and to philosophical problems arising out of it. He was President of the S.P.R. in the years 1945 and 1946. His Myers Memorial Lecture of 1942, published under the title *Apparitions*, became at once and will long remain a classic in the subject; and his books *Science and Psychical Phenomena* (1938) and *The Personality of Man* (1946) have been widely read and greatly admired. For a valuable account of his varied contributions to psychical research and to philosophy the reader may be referred to articles by Mr Salter, Mr Fisk, and Professor H. H. Price in the S.P.R. *Journal*, Vol. XXXVII, No. 674. It may be remarked that Miss Gertrude Johnson had been known to Mr and Mrs Tyrrell for several years, and that she had become a member of their household at the time when the experiments to be described below were performed. In the S.P.R. *Journal* for June 1922 is a report of earlier experiments made by a 'Mr T.' and a 'Miss Nancy Sinclair', who were in fact Mr Tyrrell and Miss Johnson, respectively. These testify to the wide variety of Miss Johnson's *prima facie* paranormal gifts and experiences.

The experiments which I shall now describe were not done with cards, but with small light-tight boxes in which an electric lamp is lighted or not lighted. The patient has to guess the box in which the lamp is alight on each occasion. Tyrrell, whose professional work as a telegraphic engineer had given him great technical skill, designed a most ingenious electrical apparatus. He introduced into it certain devices to secure randomness and to test the patient under conditions which would exclude telepathy. I may add, for what little it may be worth, that I have seen and operated the machine, under Tyrrell's supervision, in his workshop at his home, and have had the details explained to me by him. It was smashed to bits in one of the air-raids on London, and Tyrrell never reconstructed it.

I will first describe the apparatus, omitting the special devices mentioned above, and will then revert to the latter. The essential features of the apparatus were as follows:

(i) *The Boxes.* There were five little square boxes in a row. Each contained a tiny dull electric glow-lamp, which could be switched on and off at will by methods to be described later. Each box was carefully made light-tight, by the lid being faced with red velvet on the inside, revetted, and held down by springs.

(ii) *The Keys and their Connexions.* There were five keys in a row. They, and the operator who uses them, were completely hidden from the patient by a large screen. In the later experiments the patient sat at one table, facing the boxes; the operator sat at another table, facing the keys; and each table was provided with a screen.

Each key was connected with a different one of the five lamps. When the operator presses a key, the lamp in the box connected with it is lighted and stays alight until the key is released. As soon as the operator has pressed a key he indicates to the patient that he has done so by pressing with his left hand on a contact which momentarily lights a lamp visible to her on her side of the screen. She thereupon opens the lid of the box in which she believes that a lamp has been lighted. While any box remains open a lamp is automatically lighted on the operator's side of the screen. So he knows when the patient has responded, and can press on a key for the next trial as soon as he sees this light go out. No word was ever spoken during the whole of an experiment. The five keys worked by means of mercury contacts, so that the making and breaking of the circuit on each occasion was quite silent. After a little practice it was found possible and convenient to work at the rate of about 70 trials per minute, i.e. about three times as fast as the normal rate in Dr Soal's experiments.

(iii) *The automatic Recorder.* The hits or misses were automatically recorded at the time in the following way. The apparatus was provided with a mechanically driven moving band of paper. Each time the patient opened a box a mark would be automatically made on this band. It took the form of a short straight black line parallel to the direction of motion of the paper. Its length would be proportional to the time for which the lid is held open. *If*, and *only if*, the lamp in the box should be alight at the time when the lid is open, a parallel line would be automatically drawn on the paper. Thus, *success* by the patient in locating the box in which the lamp has been lighted by the operator on any occasion is recorded automatically by the appearance of a *pair* of short parallel lines on the moving band; whilst *failure* is recorded by the appearance of a *single* short line with no parallel to it.

(iv) *Devices to prevent Cheating by the Patient*. Though there was no reason whatever to suspect deliberate or unwitting misuse of the apparatus by the patient, the following precautions against such possibilities were embodied in the machine. (*a*) The automatic recording mechanism was so arranged that the slightest attempt to open a box would be recorded on the moving band *before* the patient had raised the lid far enough to be able to see whether the lamp was alight or not. Thus, it was impossible for her to score a success by slightly opening several boxes *in quick succession*, peeping into them and thus discovering which of them contained the lighted lamp, and then opening that one fully. (*b*) It was made impossible for her to score by opening several boxes *at the same time*. The automatic recording mechanism was so arranged that, if more than one box were open at once, *no* record corresponding to a lighted lamp would be made, even if the lamp in one of them should be alight.

I have now described the essential parts of the apparatus. But, as I have said, Mr Tyrrell introduced certain special devices. These were a mechanical selector, a commutator, and a delay-action mechanism, I will now describe these and their uses.

Supplementary Devices

(i) *Mechanical Selector*. It is most unlikely that an operator, pressing down one key after another in rapid succession, will do so in strictly random order. (For one thing he will fairly certainly avoid pressing down the same key several times in immediate succession.) Any pattern that might be characteristic of the operator might happen to agree with a pattern characteristic of the patient. If so, there would be an excess of hits from perfectly normal causes. In order to obviate this, Mr Tyrrell used in certain of his experiments an apparatus which, in effect, mechanically selects numbers from 1 to 5 in a random way. This was tested for randomness from time to time, and was found to be working satisfactorily. This device could be used in two different ways. *Either* it could be used directly for lighting the lamps, instead of employing the keys; *or* it could be used beforehand to give a list of prepared random numbers, and the operator could then press the keys in that order. It was only when it was used in the *latter* way that the subject scored significantly above chance-expectation with it.

(ii) *Commutator*. Instead of each key being directly and permanently connected with the corresponding lamp, i.e. the *r*-th key from the left in the row of keys being connected with the *r*-th lamp from the left in the row of boxes, the connexions in certain experiments were made through a commutator. By means of this the same key can be connected to a different lamp on different occasions. It is obvious that there are 120 ways in which 5 keys can be connected to 5 lamps, one of them being 'straight' and the other 119 'deranged'. Tyrrell's commutator allowed 8 of these possibilities, viz. the straight one and 7 of the deranged ones. It was operated by pressing a button which caused a rotating contact to stop in one position or another.

Unless the operator opened the apparatus, noted where the contact had stopped, and remembered or looked up his diagram of connexions, he had no idea which keys were connected with which lamps on any occasion when the commutator was in use. So any significant excess above chance-expectation which the patient might score under these conditions could not depend on the *operator's knowledge* of which lamps he was lighting at each trial.

(iii) *Delay-action Device*. This was a device which the operator could put into or out of action at any moment in the course of an experiment by merely pressing a button. If a key were pressed while the device was in action, the lamp in the box connected with that key would *not* light until the subject had opened *one or other of the boxes*, no matter which. So, when this device is in operation, success by the patient on any occasion is success in guessing the box in which a lamp *will* be lighted *after* she has made and acted upon her guess.

There are two different cases to be considered, viz. the use of the delay-action device (*a*) *without* the commutator, and (*b*) *with* it. When it is used *without* the commutator, the operator already knows, on pressing key *r* that it is the lamp in box *r* which will eventually be lighted. So this present knowledge of his about the future may be a condition on which the patient's success depends. When it is used *with* the commutator, no one in the world has any normal knowledge as to which lamp will be lighted on any occasion. If the patient scores significantly above chance-expectation under these conditions, her success cannot depend on anyone's normal knowledge at the time.

Quite apart from these uses, the delay-action device is important as a check on the validity of the other experiments. Suppose, e.g., that it should be suggested that the patient is hyperaesthetic to light, radiant heat, or some other kind of radiation from the lamps when alight, and that this is the cause of her scoring so much above chance-expectation in experiments in which the lamp was alight *before* she opened the box containing it. Then it is relevant if we can point out that she scored equally well in experiments to which this explanation cannot possibly apply, since the lamp did not light until *after* she had opened the box which she had guessed.

The Main Results. I will now quote some of the more important results obtained under various conditions. It may be assumed that Mr Tyrrell himself was the operator and the 'agent' (so far as the latter term is appropriate here) in all these experiments. But it should be added that many of them took place in presence of various independent and competent witnesses.

(1) *Experiments with mechanically pre-selected Random Numbers and the Commutator*. I begin with these, because with them, and with them alone, there can be no question of the statistics being possibly vitiated by the order in which the operator presses down the keys not being truly random.

Under these conditions 7,809 trials were made in the period from March 4th to July 2nd, 1936.[1] The actual number of correct guesses exceeded the number most probable on the hypothesis of chance-coincidence by 279. The standard deviation is 35·5, and so $z = 7·9$. The odds, on the hypothesis of chance-coincidence, against getting a deviation not less than this are $3·55 \times 10^{14}$ to 1. Now these experiments were done with the commutator in use. So the operator did *not* know which lamp he was lighting when he pressed down a given key. The results were therefore obtained under conditions which *exclude the possibility of telepathy*.

(2) *Experiments with the Delay-action Device*. I take these next, because here there can be no question of any explanation in terms of physical radiations from the lighted lamp and hyperaesthetic sense-perception of them by the patient. Unfortunately, the keys were *not* in these experiments pressed down in an order whose randomness is guaranteed by mechanical or other pre-selection.

In the results which I am about to quote the experiments were done in blocks of 100 trials each. After the first 50 trials in such a block the operator would change the conditions, either by coupling in or by cutting out the delay-action device. Otherwise the conditions remained the same throughout. The patient had no normal means of knowing whether the delay-action device was on or off; though she could, no doubt, infer, from the click of the key after the 50th trial

[1] See S.P.R. *Proceedings*, Vol. XLIV, p. 151 and footnote to it.

in a block, that a change had been made in the one direction or the other.

The results of 2,195 trials done between October 12th, 1935, and January 25th, 1936, under these conditions are summarized below:

	Number of trials	Deviation	z	Odds against
Delay-action on	1,105	81	6·1	10^9 to 1
Delay action off	1,090	88	6·7	$4·8 \times 10^{10}$ to 1
Aggregate	2,195	169	9	$1·4 \times 10^{19}$ to 1

It will be noted that there is no significant difference between the degree of success under the two conditions, and that it is fantastically above what might be expected on the hypothesis of chance-coincidence.

Before leaving the topic of the two types of experiment described above, I will make the following general comment. It is quite plain that Miss Johnson was able to score, to an extent that would be absurdly improbable on the hypothesis of chance-coincidence, (a) under conditions where no explanation in terms of *non-randomness* in the operator's selection of the sequence of keys pressed down is possible, and (b) under conditions where no explanation in terms of *hyperaesthetic perception of physical radiations* is possible. But there is no *direct* evidence that she can score where conditions (a) and (b) are *both* fulfilled. For, so far as I am aware, Mr Tyrrell did not do any experiments in which *both* a random sequence of numbers was used to determine the order in which the keys were to be pressed, *and* the delay-action device was used. It would therefore be logically possible for an extreme sceptic to suggest that *all* the results are capable of one or another kind of normal explanation, viz. *non-randomness* (when the delay-action device was used, but the order in which the keys were pressed was not mechanically pre-selected), and *hyperaesthesia* to some kind of physical radiation from the lighted lamps (when the order *was* mechanically pre-selected, but the delay-action device was not used).

I do not think that this combination of two quite different alternative normal explanations for different sections of the results is at all plausible; but it is, no doubt, logically possible. It should be noted, moreover, that the use of the commutator, even without the use of prepared random numbers, would neutralize the effect of any similarities which there might be between operator and patient in their preferences for certain numbers or certain sequences of numbers. For, whenever the connexions between keys and lamps are 'scrambled' by means of the commutator, the same sequence of key-depressions lights a different sequence of lamps. On the whole, then, I think that there can be little reasonable doubt that *either* Miss Johnson achieved genuinely paranormal results of a high degree of excellence, *or* that she and Mr Tyrrell were engaged in deliberate fraud and collusion. I have no hesitation whatever in rejecting the latter alternative.

The 'Fisk Effect'. In reference to these experiments mention must be made of an interlude which proved to be of considerable theoretical interest and of some practical importance. Among those whom Tyrrell had invited to witness his experiments and to try their hand with his machine, either as subjects or as operators, was Mr G. W. Fisk. Mr Fisk has been for many years a valued member of the S.P.R., interested in and skilled at experimental work involving guessing, and he is at the time of writing Editor of the S.P.R. *Journal* and *Proceedings*. Now he devised a 'system', by means of which he could score at a rate comparable to Miss Johnson's best efforts, when he acted as 'patient' and Tyrrell operated the machine without using the mechanical selector.

The method was this. Mr Fisk would begin by arbitrarily picking on one of the boxes, and would continue to open this until it happened that the lamp in it was alight. He then arbitrarily picked on another box, and would continue to open that one until it happened that the lamp in it was alight. He repeated this process throughout the whole of a sequence of trials. Mr Fisk first tried this system on October 28th, 1935, not divulging it in detail to Tyrrell until the conclusion of that day's trials. In all 500 trials were made on that day. In the first 300 Tyrrell operated the machine *without* using the mechanical selector. At that point he coupled in the selector, without informing Mr Fisk that he was doing so, and the remaining 200 trials were with the keys being depressed in a mechanically randomized order. The results were as follows:

	Number of trials	Deviation	z	Odds against
Without selector	300	+29	+4·19	$3·3 \times 10^4$ to 1
With selector	200	+18	+3·19	$7·1 \times 10^2$ to 1

It is quite plain that Mr Fisk's system was scoring an excess of hits which would be fantastically improbable on the hypothesis of chance-coincidence. There is, however, a very curious feature here. The results obtained in the 200 trials, where the order in which the keys were depressed was mechanically randomized and where consequently Mr Fisk's system cannot have been relevant, are quite significantly above what might be expected on the hypothesis of chance-coincidence, though they are considerably less improbable than those obtained when the selector was not used. As we shall see, this peculiarity was ironed out when the number of trials was increased.

On December 2nd, 1935, other experiments were done, some with Mr Fisk using his original method, and some to test the effect of other possible systems. I will begin with those in which the original system was used. The results were as follows:

	Number of trials	Deviation	z	Odds against
Without selector	200	+22	+3·88	10^4 to 1
With selector	298	−7·6	−1·10	2·7 to 1

It will be seen that the system continues to score results well above what might be expected on the hypothesis of chance-expectation, when *no* selector is used. Moreover, it now produces an *insignificant negative* deviation, when the order in which the keys are depressed is mechanically randomized.

The aggregate of the results of using this system on both occasions is shown in the table below:

	Number of trials	Deviation	z	Odds against
Without selector	500	+51	+5·7	10^8 to 1
With selector	498	+10·4	+1·16	3·02 to 1

Two things come out quite plainly from these aggregate results. (1) When Tyrrell operated the machine *without* randomly selecting the order in which he depressed the keys, Mr Fisk secured such an excess of hits over the most probable number on the hypothesis of chance-coincidence that the odds, on that hypothesis, against securing so great an excess are colossal. (2) When the order in which Tyrrell depressed the keys was determined by the mechanical selector, Mr Fisk's system was powerless to produce results significantly different from those which might be expected on the hypothesis of chance-coincidence.

On December 2nd, 1935, Tyrrell and Mr Fisk tried also a variation on the latter's original system. As before, the 'patient' starts by arbitrarily picking on one of the boxes and then continuing to open that one until it happens that the lamp in it is alight. As before, he shifts to another box as soon as that has occurred, and continues to open this until it happens that the lamp in it is alight. But now, instead of selecting each fresh box arbitrarily, he does so in a *pre-determined fixed order*. Suppose, e.g., that he began by opening the *first* box to the left of the row. When a light appears in that, he moves on to the *second* from the left and goes on opening it until a light appears in it. Then he moves on to the *third* from the left. And so on, reverting to the first when a light has appeared in the fifth. Tyrrell called this the 'Fisk *rigid* system', as contrasted with Mr Fisk's original method, which he called the 'Fisk *flexible* system'. The results of using the rigid system without the selector are given below:

	Number of trials	Deviation	z	Odds against
Without selector	200	$+19$	$+3·36$	$1·22 \times 10^3$ to 1

It would appear, then, that 'Fisk rigid' worked about as well as 'Fisk flexible' when Tyrrell operated the machine without using the selector to randomize the order in which he depressed the keys.

The explanation of the success of the Fisk method under these conditions is, no doubt, the following. Suppose, e.g., that 10 trials are made in succession. Then there are 5^{10} possible alternative sequences, since any one of the 5 keys may be depressed on any one of the 10 occasions. Now, to say that the keys are depressed in a *strictly random* order implies that *each particular one* of these 5^{10} alternative possibilities is *equally likely* to be realized in a sequence of 10 successive trials. We can represent any particular one of these possibilities in a diagram with 5 columns, representing the 5 keys from left to right, and 10 rows, representing the 10 successive occasions. If on the r-th occasion we suppose that the s-th key from the left was depressed, we put a cross in the r-th row of the s-th column. Let us now consider, e.g., the case in which the first key is depressed on 3 occasions, the second on 2 occasions, the third on 1 occasion, the fourth on 3 occasions, and the fifth on 1 occasion. This covers $\dfrac{10!}{3! \times 2! \times 1! \times 3! \times 1!}$ alternative possible sequences, i.e., 50,400. Each of them is equally likely to be realized, if the keys are depressed in a *strictly random* order. Now contrast, e.g., the two which are represented by the two diagrams opposite.

The first of these diagrams represents one of the numerous possibilities in which a certain two of the keys (1 and 4) are each depressed *3 times in immediate succession*, a certain one other key (2) is depressed *twice in immediate succession*, and the remaining two keys (3 and 5) are each depressed only once. The second diagram represents one of the numerous possibilities in which *no key is depressed *several times in immediate succession*. Each of the two possibilities represented by these two diagrams is equally likely to be realized, if the keys are pressed in a *strictly random* order. But any normal human being, trying to be 'fair', would be most unlikely to press down the keys in the kind of order represented in the first diagram. He would be much more likely to do so in the kind of order represented by some variant or other of the second diagram. He will, in fact, tend to avoid de-

54

Occasion	Key					Occasion	Key				
	1	2	3	4	5		1	2	3	4	5
1	×					1	×				
2	×					2		×			
3	×					3				×	
4					×	4	×			ı	
5			×			5		×			
6		×				6				×	
7		×				7			×		
8				×		8				×	
9				×		9	×				
10				×		10					×

pressing any one key even twice in immediate succession, and he will tend still more strongly to avoid doing so thrice or more.

Thus, the fact that a certain key has been depressed on any one occasion decreases the probability that the operator will depress *that* key on the next occasion, and therefore increases the probability that he will depress one or other of the remaining four keys on the next occasion. But Mr Fisk's method consists in moving to one or another of the remaining four boxes immediately after the occurrence of a light in the one which he has been opening, has informed him that the key connected with that one has just been depressed. So the method ensures that the next box that he will open, after seeing a light in the one that he has just been opening, shall be one of the four for which the probability that a lamp will be lighted in it on the next occasion has been *increased*, and is *greater than one-fifth*. Now the calculation of the most probable proportion of hits, and of the probability of the actual proportion deviating from the most probable by not less than an assigned amount, proceeds on the assumption that the probability of any one key being depressed on any occasion is *the same* (viz. *one-fifth*), regardless of the order in which the keys may have been depressed before. It is plain, then, that anyone who uses the Fisk method, in conjunction with an operator who does not randomize the order in which he depresses the keys, must in the long run score a proportion of hits which seems fantastically high on that assumption.

We can now raise the question: What bearing has all this on the question whether Miss Johnson's scoring is good evidence for paranormality? We must consider separately experiments made (i) *with* mechanically selected random numbers, and (ii) *without* randomization.

(i) It will be remembered that, in the 7,809 trials made from March 4th to July 2nd, 1936, with mechanically selected random numbers, her aggregate score was such that the odds, on the hypothesis of chance-coincidence, were 3.55×10^{14} to 1 against getting a deviation not less than this from the most probable score. Now here the Fisk method would have been useless. And, in general, no explanation in terms of systematic departures from randomness on the part of the operator and complementary departures on that of the patient is possible. Nor is any explanation possible here in terms of the operator conveying information, deliberately or unwittingly, to the patient. For the commutator was in use, and so the operator could not know by any normal means which lamp would be lighted when he depressed any particular key.

(ii) Since Miss Johnson was able, under the above conditions, to score such an extremely improbable excess of hits, it is reasonable to suppose that a *part* at least of her scoring under less rigid conditions was due to the operation of the same cause, whatever that may have been. On the other hand, it may well be that, under conditions where the Fisk method could have been used, it or something analogous to it was used and did *contribute* to the score. In the table on p. 150 of Vol. XLIV of S.P.R. *Proceedings* Tyrrell states that, in the period from May 13th, 1935, to March 30th, 1936, 17,842 trials were made, *without* randomizing mechanically the order in which the keys were depressed and *without* using the commutator. In these the aggregate number of hits was 4,612, so that the rate of scoring was 25.8 per cent. In the 7,809 trials, made *with* mechanical randomization and *with* the commutator in use, the aggregate number of hits was 1,841, and so the rate of scoring was 23.5 per cent.

The first point to notice is that this difference in the percentage rates of scoring, under the two conditions, is highly significant. Let us suppose, for the sake of argument, that the two sets of trials were just two different random selections from a universe of trials in which the proportion of hits is the weighted mean of the two percentages, i.e. 25.086 per cent. Then it can be shown that the odds against the percentages of hits, in two random samples of these two sizes, differing by not less than the amount by which they were actually found to differ (viz. 2.3 per cent) are 1.4×10^{19}. It is obviously not worth while to consider further an hypothesis in terms of which the odds against the occurrence of so great a difference as was actually found are so colossal.

The position, then, is this. Under *each* of the two alternative sets of conditions Miss Johnson scored at rates which were *very significantly high*; but the rate was *very significantly higher* when there was no mechanical randomization and no 'scrambling' of the connexions by means of the commutator than when both those conditions were present. It would, therefore, be plausible to ascribe the additional 2·3 per cent in the rate of scoring under the looser conditions to the use of something like the Fisk method and perhaps of occasional sensory clues, which would have been possible here, but would have been impossible under the stricter conditions. It should be noted, however, that this simple bit of subtraction may easily lead us to underestimate the degree of paranormality displayed in the experiments done under the looser conditions. For, in them, it is possible that 'clairvoyance' might be supplemented by 'telepathy'; whilst, in the experiments done under the stricter conditions, the possibility of telepathy is excluded.

I will conclude the discussion of this question with the following remark. I do not think it in the least likely that Miss Johnson consciously and deliberately used any form of the Fisk method. What seems to me much more likely is that she would naturally tend to avoid opening the same box on several immediately successive occasions, just as Tyrrell tended to avoid depressing the same key on several immediately successive occasions. This tendency in the patient, when combined with the similar tendency in the operator, would produce unintentionally the same kind of effect as Mr Fisk produced deliberately, though the unintended effect might be less in magnitude and more fitful in occurrence.

III

SOME POINTS ARISING OUT OF
THE EXPERIMENTS OF DR SOAL
AND OF MR TYRRELL

IN this chapter I shall consider a number of points arising out of the experiments which I have described in the two previous chapters. Some are factual, others partly terminological and partly philosophical. I shall begin by saying something about the psychological features noted in these experiments.

SOME PSYCHOLOGICAL FEATURES OF THE EXPERIMENTS

(1) Phrases like 'extra-sensory *perception*', 'paranormal *cognition*', etc., have been used to denote the activities involved in these experiments. I think it is important to notice that such phrases may well call up ideas which go beyond anything that the experiments could establish.

If we are to talk of 'cognition' in general, or of 'perception' in particular, or even of 'guessing', in this connexion, we must remember that these words will have to be interpreted purely *behaviouristically*. The patient does not, e.g., have a *mental image* of a particular symbol or of a particular box with a light in it, on each occasion; and he does not, in response to that, write down the initial letter of the name of that symbol or open the lid of that box, as the case may be. The patient simply performs the action without premeditation, and without being moved to it by any specific modification of consciousness which he or she can introspect and describe. If we stick to the known facts, in the case of Mr Shackleton, e.g., all that we are entitled to say is this. What he does on each occasion is to write down automatically the initial letter of the name of one or other of the five animal symbols which he knows to be the distinguishing marks on the cards used in the experiment. What happened enormously more often than could reasonably be expected on the hypo-thesis of chance-coincidence was that the letter which he would write down on any occasion would be the initial letter of the name of the animal depicted on the card which the agent was *going to focus* on the *next ensuing occasion*. Similar remarks apply, *mutatis mutandis*, to Mrs Stewart, to Pearce, and to Miss Johnson.

(2) Dr Soal found that there was no significant correlation between Mr Shackleton's impressions that he had been successful or that he had been unsuccessful in his guesses and the actual degree of success or failure. The patient often had strong 'hunches', and at other times strong feelings that he was altogether off the mark. These emotionally toned experiences seem to have had no correlation, positive or nega-tive, with the actual measure of his achievement at the time.

(3) Tyrrell noted again and again the following fact in the course of his experiments with Miss Johnson. Whenever any new feature was introduced into the experimental set-up, the patient's scoring tended to fall to the level of chance-expectation. As she gradually became used to, and reconciled with, the new feature, the rate of scoring would begin to rise and would thereafter remain at a significantly high level. It will be worth while to give some examples of this.

(i) The electrical apparatus was constructed and introduced after a long series of experiments with a much cruder method, in which a pointer was stuck into one of five alternative holes by the operator on each occasion. Miss Johnson had been consistently scoring at a very high rate with this primitive apparatus. Immediately after the intro-duction of the electrical apparatus, in which her task was essentially the same as before, her scores dropped to about chance-expectation. Tyrrell had to restore confidence by reverting to the pointer method, instead of using keys and lamps. It was not until after 3,100 trials with the electrical apparatus that significantly high scoring started again. Thereafter it continued, with interruptions when any new device was introduced.

(ii) The commutator was first introduced on June 15th, 1935, at a time when Miss Johnson was habitually scoring at a high level of significance with the electrical apparatus. On that date two experi-ments were made, with the commutator coupled in. In both of these Tyrrell *looked into* the commutator-box on each occasion, and saw how the connexions were set. Thus, if the commutator were set so that the keys were connected *straight through* to the lamps, there was no essential difference, either in the physical facts or in the operator's knowledge of them, between a block of trials done under these conditions and the previous experiments *without* the commutator.

There was a relevant difference in the physical facts, when the commutator was set so that the keys were connected with the lamps in a *deranged* order. But even then, in these two experiments, the operator knew which key was connected with which lamp. It is of great interest to note the results of these experiments.

In the first of the two the commutator was set at *straight* for the first three blocks of trials (276 in all), then at *deranged* for the next block of 100, then at *straight* again for the next 100, and finally at *deranged* for the remaining 100. The aggregate results with straight and with deranged connexions showed a most striking difference. 376 trials with *straight* connexions gave an excess of 71·8 hits over the most probable number on the hypothesis of chance-coincidence. The odds, on that hypothesis, against getting a deviation of this size or larger are $2·88 \times 10^{26}$ to 1. Now contrast this with the aggregate results with *deranged* connexions. Here 200 trials were made, and the actual number of hits happened to coincide exactly with the number most probable on the hypothesis of chance-coincidence, viz. 40. (The result was made up of a negative deviation of 6 in the first block of 100 and a positive deviation of 6 in the second.)

In the second of these two experiments the operator did the trials in blocks of 100, and altered the commutator-connexions from straight to deranged, or conversely, after the first 50 trials in a block. The patient would know that a change was being made, because she would hear a click, but she could not know normally in which direction it was. Exactly the same contrast as in the first experiment showed itself between the results with straight connexions and those with deranged connexions. 200 trials with *straight* connexions gave an excess of 38 hits above chance-expectation. The corresponding odds, on the hypothesis of chance-coincidence, against getting at least as great a deviation as this are $4·8 \times 10^{10}$ to 1. Now contrast the results of the 300 trials made with *deranged* connexions. Here the actual number of hits differed from the number most probable on the hypothesis of chance-coincidence by only 1. It will be useful to show the detailed results in the table below.

Block	Number of trials	Deviation	Commutator
I	First 50	−7	Straight
	Second 50	−3	Deranged
II	100	+4	Deranged
III	First 50	+12	Straight
	Second 50	+3	Deranged
IV	100	−3	Deranged
V	100	+33	Straight

It is plain, then, that the patient was in some way strongly inhibited at first by the variation of *deranged connexions*, and scored significantly at that stage only when the keys were connected with the lamps in the straightforward way to which she had been accustomed in the earlier experiments. This inhibition was effective, in spite of the fact that the operator in all these experiments knew in each case which key was connected with which lamp, just as he had done in the previous experiments without the commutator. Moreover, she reacted in these two different ways, even though she had no normal knowledge as to *which* of the two alternative physical conditions was prevailing at the time.

Significant scoring with deranged connexions did not begin until August 22nd, 1935, when it started immediately after the resumption of the experiments on Miss Johnson's return from a holiday. In this and in many subsequent experiments with the commutator the operator was *not*, as in the earlier experiments, aware of the precise way in which the keys were connected with the lamps. He knew only that it was in one or other of the deranged ways permitted by the commutator. The results of the experiment on August 22nd, with *deranged connexions unknown to the operator*, were as follows. In 90 trials an excess of 19 hits above chance-expectation was scored. The odds against a deviation as great or greater than this, on the hypothesis of chance-coincidence, are $1 \cdot 47 \times 10^5$ to 1.

From August 24th to 31st, 1,656 trials were done with *deranged connexions unknown to the operator*, and 700 with *straight connexions known to him*. It seems reasonable to pool these with the results of the experiment on August 22nd. The aggregate results are shown below.

Conditions	Number of trials	Deviation	Odds against
Deranged, unknown	1,746	+58·8	$2 \cdot 4 \times 10^3$ to 1
Straight, known	700	−5	

The odds in the first category are substantial, though not spectacular. Those in the second category are quite insignificant, and the result is no doubt merely a matter of chance-coincidence.

Miss Johnson was away again after this until September 14th, 1935. Experiments were resumed on September 18th, and a comparative table is given below for the results obtained from then up to October 12th under the two alternative conditions.

Conditions	Number of trials	Deviation	Odds against
Deranged, unknown	4,200	+178	$2 \cdot 46 \times 10^{11}$ to 1
Straight, known	1,900	+84	$1 \cdot 34 \times 10^6$ to 1

It is plain that, by this time, Miss Johnson was scoring very significantly above chance-expectation under *both* conditions. The rate of scoring is 24·24 per cent for the 4,200 trials done under the unknown and deranged conditions, and 24·42 per cent for the 1,900 trials done under the known and straight conditions. The difference between these two rates is not statistically significant.

(iii) Miss Johnson was informed on October 28th, 1935, of Mr Fisk's method, and of the fact that it produced by normal means a rate of scoring about equal to the best that she had been achieving. Her rate of scoring *under all conditions* immediately fell to round about the level of chance-coincidence. It remained in that state, except for a brief recovery on February 13th, 1936, until about the middle of May 1936, after which she gradually returned to her previous form.

(iv) When the mechanical selector was connected up with the apparatus, so that the lamps were lighted *directly* by means of it and *not* by the operator depressing the keys with his fingers, Miss Johnson never managed to score significantly great deviations from the number of hits most probable on the hypothesis of chance-coincidence. But, when the mechanical selector was used *before* an experiment to give a random sequence of numbers from 1 to 5, and when the operator subsequently depressed the keys in the random order thus pre-selected, Miss Johnson did (as we have seen above) eventually manage to score very significantly above chance-expectation. She approached this state, however, only very gradually. In the period from May 13th, 1935, to March 30th, 1936, Tyrrell made 3,261 trials under these latter conditions, and the excess of hits had reached only 55. This is a barely significant result, for the odds against a deviation not less than this, on the hypothesis of chance-coincidence, are only 124 to 1. But, in the period from March 4th to July 2nd, 1936 (which partly overlaps the one already mentioned), in 7,809 trials under these conditions she had (as stated in Chapter II) scored so great an excess of hits that the odds had risen to $3·55 \times 10^{14}$ to 1. By that time she was beginning to recover her form after the depressing effect of the Fisk shock.

From all this there emerges one important moral for researchers in this branch of the subject. In doing experiments it is, of course, essential to introduce from time to time new conditions, in order to see what variations, if any, they induce in the patient's performance. If we substitute condition C' for condition C, and the patient thereupon ceases to score significantly, we are inclined to argue without hesitation that C is a necessary condition for success or that C' is an inhibiting condition. It is now plain that it is rash to draw such conclusions without qualification. For it may well be that some subconscious level of the patient's personality resents the change; or simply that the feeling of ease and self-confidence, which has grown up with success in the familiar conditions, is replaced by one of discomfort or diffidence. Either of these causes might inhibit, either the exercise of the paranormal faculty itself (if this be what is in operation in the successful trials), or the expression of the results of its operation in speech, in writing, or in some overt action, such as opening the lid of a box. It is, therefore, always worth while, before deciding that C is necessary or that C' is inhibitory, to spend a good deal of time and trouble, as Tyrrell did, in trying to coax the patient to score significantly in the absence of C and the presence of C'.

'TELEPATHY' AND 'CLAIRVOYANCE' IN REFERENCE TO THESE EXPERIMENTS

Having provided the reader with a reasonable amount of factual information about certain experiments in 'guessing', I shall now say something about the use of the words 'telepathy' and 'clairvoyance' in connexion with such experiments. I have myself made no use of the word 'clairvoyance'. But I have used the word 'telepathy', when I described certain experiments as 'done under conditions which would *exclude telepathy*'. It has not been uncommon to say that such experiments as these, if the scores in them were very significantly above chance-expectation, and if no normal explanation could be suggested, would furnish evidence for *clairvoyance*.

The words 'telepathy' and 'clairvoyance' were originally coined in connexion with certain sporadic cases, and with certain experiments which differed in important respects from those which we have been considering. In the sporadic cases in question an individual A has a dream, or a waking *quasi*-perceptual hallucination, which, it is alleged, corresponds in detail, to an extent that seems to rule out chance-coincidence, with a certain highly specific experience occurring at about the same time in a certain other individual B, at a distance and not in normal communication at the time with A. In the experimental cases in question B calls up a visual image or looks at a picture at a certain time. The distant A at that time describes verbally, or draws, the visual image which then arises before his mind's eye; and it is alleged that, on a significantly large proportion of such occasions, the latter corresponds in detail with the former to a degree which cannot reasonably be ascribed to chance-coincidence or to normal causes.

I am not at present concerned to discuss the evidence for paranormality provided either by such sporadic cases or by such experiments. What I do want to emphasize is this. In both the sporadic cases and these experiments the nature of A's experience and of its correlation with B's experience is *prima facie* of much the same kind. So any evidence for paranormality in either does to some extent strengthen *quite directly* the evidence for it in the other. But that is not so with the experiments of Dr Soal, of Pratt and Pearce, or of Tyrrell. Here the nature of the patient's response, and of its correlation with the agent's actions and experiences on the relevant occasion, seems to be quite unlike that which is common to most of the sporadic cases and to the older kinds of experimental ones.

One consequence is that there is no *direct* relationship of confirmation between the evidence for paranormality in experiments of the Soal-Tyrrell kind and the evidence for it in the sporadic cases. Another point worth noting is this. It seems quite possible that the notions of 'telepathy' and of 'clairvoyance', originally introduced in connexion with sporadic cases and the experimental cases which *prima facie* resemble them, would not be particularly appropriate to those experimental cases, such as we have been discussing, which *prima facie* differ in important features from both. For here the response of the patient A is, not to have a specific *experience*, but to *do* without premeditation something specific with his fingers, e.g. to write down the first letter of the name of a certain one of five animals or to raise the lid of a certain one of five little boxes.

It will be convenient to defer any general discussion of the terms 'telepathy' and 'clairvoyance' until after we have given examples of sporadic cases. In the meanwhile I will try to suggest a more precise and less question-begging terminology for such experimental results as we have already been considering.

It will be remembered that in Dr Soal's experiments five alternative possibilities were considered in reference to the patient's possible response on each occasion, viz. -2 and -1 back-hits, a direct hit, and $+1$ and $+2$ fore-hits. We may say, then, that for any response by the agent in a run of trials (except, of course, the first two and the last two in any run) there were five *potential targets*. These were the card which the agent *was* focusing at the time when the call was given to the patient; the cards which he *had been* focusing on the immediately previous occasion and its immediate predecessor, respectively; and the cards which he *was about to focus* on the immediately subsequent occasion and its immediate successor, respectively.

Now, when I described certain experiments of Dr Soal's or of Tyrrell's as done 'under conditions which *exclude telepathy*', all that I meant by that phrase was this. In these experiments neither the agent nor anyone else was aware by normal means, at the time when the patient made his response, of the nature of any of the five potential targets. Therefore, normal knowledge of the nature of the potential targets by some person other than the patient, at the time when the latter made his response, cannot have been a factor contributing to determine the nature of the response. (It should be noted that I include here under 'normal knowledge' both *purely dispositional* knowledge, such as I have of the rules of Latin grammar even when I am neither thinking of them nor applying them, and *activated* knowledge, such as I have only when I am either thinking of them in theory or applying them in practice.)

Now, in many of the experiments which fulfil that condition, either the agent or the patient or the experimenter or someone else *will*, after the completion of the experiment, acquire normal knowledge of the nature of the potential targets at each stage of it. Let us leave out, for the moment, the case of the *patient himself* afterwards acquiring such normal knowledge, and confine ourselves to the case of *some other person* doing so. Suppose now that we are prepared to admit that a state of affairs, which did not come into existence until *after* a certain event had taken place, may nevertheless have influenced the nature of that event. Then it will not do to say, without qualification, of such experiments, that they were done under 'conditions which exclude telepathy', even when 'telepathy' is used in the special sense which I have been explaining. We must be content to say that they were such as to exclude *simultaneous or progredient* telepathic conditioning.

Let us now turn to the case which I explicitly set aside for the moment, viz. where the *patient himself* will acquire, after the conclusion of an experiment, normal knowledge of the nature of the potential targets at each stage of the experiment. If we are going to allow the possibility that a state of affairs, not yet in being when a certain event happens, may nevertheless influence the nature of that event, we must allow the possibility that the normal knowledge, which the patient will acquire only after the conclusion of the experiment, may influence the nature of his responses during the experiment. But such influence could not properly be called 'telepathic', even in the most extended sense of that word. For 'telepathy' has always been understood to refer to *at least two* individuals, and to a relationship between the state of mind of one of them and the experiences or actions of the other.

We are now in a position to drop further reference to traditional terminology, and to classify for ourselves the various paranormal alternatives which have to be considered in reference to such experiments as Dr Soal's and Tyrrell's.

The nature of the response made by the patient on any occasion might conceivably be influenced by any one or any combination of the following factors. (1) By the *actual nature* of the possible targets to that response, independently of anyone's earlier, contemporary, or later state of knowledge or belief about them. We might describe this as a 'non-subjective' influence. (2) By someone's normally acquired *knowledge or belief* as to the nature of the possible targets to that response. This might be described as a *'subjective'* influence. This possibility divides into two, according as the relevant state of knowledge or belief is (*a*) in the *patient himself*, or (*b*) in some person or persons *other than the patient*. Alternative (*a*) may be described as *'intra*-subjective' influence, and alternative (*b*) as *'inter*-subjective' influence. Case (2*b*) covers three alternatives, according as the relevant state of knowledge or belief, in some person or persons other than the patient, began to exist (α) *before*, or (β) *simultaneously* with, or (γ) *after*, the patient's response. These three alternatives may be described respectively as *'progredient'*, *'simultaneous'*, and *'retrogredient'* inter-subjective influence. In case (2*a*) only the third, i.e. the *retrogredient* variety, needs to be considered. For, suppose that the nature of the patient's response on a given occasion was influenced by *his own* state of knowledge or belief about the nature of the potential targets, acquired in a normal way by him *before or simultaneously with* that response. Then there would obviously be nothing paranormal in the situation. If the nature of a person's response is influenced by *his own* state of normally acquired knowledge or belief as to the nature of the potential targets, the question of paranormality can arise only if he first acquired that knowledge or belief *after* he had made his response. So, in the case of *intra*-subjective influence, we are concerned only with the *retrogredient* variety.

We may sum all this up as follows. Suppose that, in experiments such as those of Dr Soal or of Tyrrell, the patient seems *prima facie* to have scored to a degree beyond anything that can reasonably be ascribed to chance-coincidence, under conditions which seem to cut out any explanation in normal or abnormal terms. Then we may conjecture that any one or any combination of the following kinds of factor are influencing the nature of the patient's response. (1) The *purely objective* facts as to the nature of the possible targets. (2) *Knowledge or belief* as to the nature of the possible targets, acquired normally by some person or persons *other than the patient*, either before, simultaneously with, or after the patient's response. (3) *Knowledge or belief* as to the nature of the possible targets, acquired normally by the *patient himself, after* he had made his response.

It will be noted that every one of these alternatives conflicts with at least one, and some with several, universally accepted basic limiting principles. To suppose, e.g., that the purely objective facts as to the nature of the possible targets could influence the nature of the patient's response conflicts with the principle that a person's reactions to any physical thing or event or process must be *mediated by specific sensations* which it evokes in him by acting directly, or indirectly through transmissive processes, on an appropriate receptor-organ of his body. Again, to suppose that the nature of the patient's response is influenced by knowledge or belief acquired by *another* person *after* the response has been made, conflicts with two basic limiting principles. One is the almost self-evident principle that a state of affairs cannot begin to influence anything until it has come into existence, and therefore cannot influence any event or process which was completed before it had begun to exist. The other is the principle that a state of knowledge or belief in B cannot influence the experiences or the actions of A, unless it be expressed in speech, writing, gestures, or other overt bodily signs by B, and unless these be perceived (directly or indirectly) by A, and interpreted, wittingly or unwittingly, by him. All this is, of course, in accordance with our original definition of 'paranormal'. *Unless* the phenomena under investigation conflicted with one or more of the basic limiting principles, they would be normal or abnormal, and not paranormal, according to our definition.

DELIBERATE VARIATION OF CONDITIONS

Having distinguished and classified the conditions which might conceivably influence the results in guessing experiments, on the assumption that these are paranormal, we can raise the following questions. Taking each of these kinds of paranormal influence in turn, can we design an experiment in which all the others are absent? And will the patient's rate of scoring in such an experiment continue to be such as would be extremely improbable on the hypothesis of chance-coincidence, or will it sink to about the rate that might be expected on that hypothesis?

On the former alternative, we can conclude that none of the other factors is *necessary* to secure a paranormal response from that particular patient, with that particular agent, experimenter, and experimental set-up; and that the one factor which has been retained is *sufficient* to do so. If, on the other hand, the second alternative should be fulfilled, we could conclude that the one factor retained in the experiment is *insufficient* to secure a paranormal response from that particular patient, with that particular agent, experimenter, and experimental set-up; and that one or other or a combination of some of the excluded factors is *necessary*. It would be very rash to extend such conclusions to other patients, or even to the same patient with a different agent or a different experimenter or a different kind of experimental set-up.

Suppose, now, that it were found, with regard to *several* possible factors, that *each of them severally* is sufficient to secure a paranormal response from the patient, with a particular agent, experimenter, and experimental set-up. Then it would be worth while for that experimenter to try experiments, with that patient and that agent, in which *two or more* of these severally sufficient conditions were present together, whilst all the other kinds of possible paranormal influence were cut out. Would the patient, under these circumstances, score at a rate *significantly different* from that at which he had scored when one or other of these sufficient conditions had been present in isolation? Do these various factors reinforce or do they weaken each other? Is there, perhaps, a kind of 'all or none' situation, so that, if several are present together, one and only one of them is operative?

It is not at all easy to design experiments in which all but one of the possible influences shall certainly be absent, and it is harder in the case of some of them than in that of others. I will now say something, first of Dr Soal's experiments and then of Tyrrell's, from this point of view.

(1) *Dr Soal's Experiments with Mr Shackleton.* It will be remembered that, in Dr Soal's experiments with Mr Shackleton, the fantastically high scoring took the form of $+1$ fore-hits with all three of the agents with whom he had any significant degree of success. It will be remembered also that the rate of scoring fell to within the limits which might reasonably be expected on the hypothesis of chance-coincidence, when the agent merely touched the back of the card focused (without having already seen the front of it before the experiment began), and did not turn it up and look at the front. Thus, at the time when the patient was making a response which would turn out to be a $+1$ fore-hit, the agent was *not yet* aware normally of the nature of the relevant target-card. On the other hand, if and only if the agent *did in due course* acquire normal knowledge of the nature of a target-card, the patient's response tended, to a highly significant degree, to be a $+1$ fore-hit on it.

The most plausible conclusion to be drawn is this. In the case of this patient, with Dr Soal as experimenter, and with all the agents with whom this patient had any significant success, a necessary condition for such success was that the agent should, *after* the completion of a response, acquire for the first time normal knowledge of the nature of the card which, at the time of the response, he was *about to focus next.*

Are we, then, absolutely forced to the shocking conclusion that the nature of the response was influenced by the nature of a state of affairs which had not yet come into being at the time when the response was completed? It will be remembered that there were two kinds of experiment. In one of them the order in which the agent would focus the five cards lying face downwards before him, was determined by a *previously prepared list of random numbers.* In the other it was determined by the *nature of the counter drawn from a bag* by the agent's experimenter immediately before each trial. Let us now consider the two kinds of experiment in turn.

In experiments done by the P.R.N. method it is obvious that there *already existed,* at the moment when the patient made his response, all the conditions which would determine, by ordinary simultaneous and progredient causation, the nature of the card which the agent would next focus. For the cards were lying face downwards in an order fixed at the beginning of the run; and the order in which they were to be focused by the agent was determined by that of the numbers on the list already prepared, and by the fixed intention of the agent's experimenter to follow that order. It might, therefore, be argued that these already existing conditions played two parts. (i) They determined by ordinary causation the nature of the card which the agent would next focus. And (ii) they influenced, by causation which was indeed paranormal, but was at any rate simultaneous or progredient and not retrogredient, the nature of the patient's response. On that view, the knowledge which the agent would later acquire was *not* a factor influencing the response which the patient had by then already made. That knowledge was a later, quite normal, *consequence* of factors existing earlier than it, which had themselves paranormally influenced the nature of the patient's response.

Let us now turn to the experiments in which the order in which the agent focuses the cards is determined by the drawing of a counter out of a bag. Can they be dealt with in a similar way?

I do not think that the two cases differ essentially. Suppose that on each occasion the agent's experimenter draws a certain counter from the bag and shows it to the agent, who thereupon focuses on the card whose ordinal number from the left in the row in front of him is the one that has been arbitrarily associated with the colour of that counter. I take it that, on the r-th occasion, there already exist the conditions which will determine, in accordance with the ordinary laws of physics, physiology, and psychology, the precise movements which the experimenter will make on the $(r + 1)$-th occasion. Of course, no one can precisely specify those conditions; but that is *all* that distinguishes this case from experiments done by the P.R.N. method. Now, given that the movements which the experimenter will make with his hand on the $(r + 1)$-th occasion are completely determined by conditions which already exist on the r-th occasion, it follows that the nature of the card which the agent will focus on the $(r + 1)$-th occasion is completely determined by conditions which already exist on the r-th. All that we need to suppose is that those conditions *paranormally* influence the patient's response on the r-th occasion in such a way that he tends to write down the initial letter of the symbol on the card which those same conditions ensure that the agent will focus on the $(r + 1)$-th occasion.

I do not claim for a moment that this kind of suggested account of the facts is either plausible or palatable. I merely offer it as an alternative to another suggestion, viz. the influence of what has not yet happened on what has already happened, which many people find either meaningless, or, if just barely intelligible, still completely incredible.

(2) *Tyrrell's Experiments with Miss Johnson.* I pass now to discuss some of Tyrrell's experiments from the point of view of the possible paranormal influences operating in them. The experiments which I wish to consider are those in which the commutator was used, *without* the operator knowing at the time by normal means how it was set. Under these conditions he could not know by normal means, when he pressed a key, which of the lamps would be lighted. Nor did he come to know this later. For the recording apparatus merely records hits or misses (by parallel or single dashes, respectively, on the paper band); it does not show *which* lamp was alight on any occasion. So normal knowledge by the operator as to which lamp was alight on which occasion, whether acquired before, during, or after the occasion in question, cannot have influenced the patient's responses in these experiments.

The experiments with the commutator may be divided first into (*a*) those in which the delay-action device was *not* used, and (*b*) those in which it *was* used. The former can be subdivided into (α) those in which the signal was given by the operator to the patient *after* pressing the key, and (β) those in which it was given on each occasion *before* pressing the key. Experiments which fall into the sub-class (*a*,β) or the class (*b*) introduce *prima facie* an additional dose of paranormality. Each of them seems *prima facie* to suggest that the nature of the patient's response on a given occasion was influenced by the nature of an event which at the time *had not yet happened*. For in each of them *no* lamp was alight until *after* the patient had decided which box to open and had begun to open it. I will now consider in turn the experiments in the classes (*a*,α), (*a*,β), and (*b*).

In class (*a*,α) the physical event which the patient was trying to locate, viz. the lighting of a lamp in a certain box, had already begun

70

and was still going on at the time when she received the signal, made her choice, and opened the box which she had chosen. The most obvious suggestion here is that the nature of her choice is influenced paranormally by the relevant features in the physical situation *themselves*, as distinct from anyone's knowledge and belief about them, although they are not affecting her sense-organs in any recognized way. When a person's response is supposed to be influenced in this way, it would often be said that he or she is 'exercising *clairvoyance*'. I think that it is best to avoid such expressions altogether in cases where the response is, so far as we know, completely behaviouristic. For it calls up ideas of some kind of non-sensuous *perception* of external physical things or events or processes or states of affairs, which may well be wholly inappropriate.

In classes (a, β) and (b) the lamp is not alight until *after* the patient has made her choice. But in class (b), i.e. where the delay-action mechanism is in use, there is *a* relevant physical event which has already happened, viz. the pressing down of a certain key by the operator. This key has *already* been put in connexion with the particular lamp which it is going to light, although the operator does not know *which* lamp that is, and although the current will not begin to flow until the patient shall open one or another of the boxes.

Suppose, now, that the patient could be influenced directly by the actual arrangement of the connexions in the commutator at the time, although they are not in any known way affecting her senses. And suppose, further, that she were influenced, *either* in a similar direct way by the depressing of the particular key which the operator had in fact pressed, *or* by the operator's state of knowledge that he was pressing that key. Suppose, finally, that these two influences should jointly influence her to open that particular box in which it is *already* determined that the lamp will be lighted no matter which of the boxes she should happen to open. Then she would score, as she was found to do, significantly above chance-expectation in a sequence of such trials.

I do not care to talk of 'unconscious inference' in such cases as this. But it is proper to point out the following facts. Any reasonably intelligent and instructed person, who had normal knowledge of the two kinds of factor which *already* existed in the apparatus at the time when the operator pressed the key, could infer at once, by normal reasoning of the most elementary kind, *which* lamp would be lighted when the current should be switched on by the opening of no matter which of the boxes. Now I am supposing that the patient is influenced *paranormally* by each of the objective factors which this imaginary person would know by normal sense-perception and memory. And I am supposing that the effect on the patient's response, of those two

71

paranormal influences in conjunction, is analogous to the effect which the compresence in one person of two such bits of normally acquired knowledge has, when he infers from them that such and such a lamp will be lighted when he shall open any (no matter which) of the boxes. If anyone cares to describe the account proposed above of these experiments, as ascribing the results to a process of 'unconscious inference' from data obtained by 'clairvoyance', he is welcome to do so. But he should remember that these phrases call up ideas which certainly go beyond anything for which there is experimental evidence and which may give a quite misleading picture of what is happening.

I pass, finally, to the experiments in class (a, β). In these the commutator was used, but not the delay-action device. I will begin by describing the method which was employed.

About half a second *before* depressing a key, the operator would give to the patient the signal to open a box. Thus, at the time when the patient began to open a box, none of the lamps would be alight. Now it will be remembered that, in case of a hit, i.e. opening a box in which the lamp is *already* alight, two parallel lines appear on the moving band of the recording device. If a box is opened, and the lamp in it is lighted *shortly afterwards*, the beginning of the stroke representing the lighting of the lamp will be a little to the right of the beginning of the parallel stroke representing the opening of the box. This was found to be the case in all the hits recorded in this group of experiments. So there can be no doubt that on each such occasion the patient was in fact opening a box *before* the operator had lighted a lamp in any of them. The actual number of hits, under these conditions, exceeded by 88 the number most probable on the hypothesis of chance-coincidence. The number of trials was 2,255. The ratio of the actual to the standard deviation is 4·6. The odds, on the hypothesis of chance-coincidence, against getting a deviation not less than this are $2·44 \times 10^5$ to 1.

What are we to say of the results of such experiments? At the time when the patient makes her response there would seem to be no relevant physical event or state of affairs already in existence. And neither then nor thereafter did any human being know by any normal means which of the lamps would be lighted or had been lighted on any occasion. So one might seem forced to conclude that the nature of the patient's response on certain occasions was influenced by the nature of a *physical event* which *had not yet happened.*

It seems to me, however, that there would be at least two alternative possibilities. Both of them require that the patient should be influenced directly by the state of the connexions in the commutator at the time.

Assuming that to be the case, one possibility is the following. It seems very likely that in most, if not in all, cases the operator would already have formed (consciously or subconsciously) the intention of depressing such and such a key in the immediate future. Suppose that that intention in the operator were paranormally to influence the patient. Plainly, a person who had *normal* knowledge of the state of the connexions in the commutator and *normal* knowledge of the intention of the operator to press down such and such a key in the immediate future, could *infer* that the lamp in such and such a box would be lighted in the immediate future. Suppose, now, that the influences, exerted *paranormally* on the patient by the state of the commutator and by the intention of the operator, co-operate, in a way analogous to that in which two bits of knowledge of those facts, acquired normally by a person, would co-operate in enabling him to infer that such and such a lamp would be lighted in the immediate future. Then the patient would tend on each such occasion to open the box in which the lamp was about to be lighted, and that tendency would reveal itself in a significantly large excess of hits in a long series of trials. It is, therefore, not *necessary* to assume any retrograde influence, of an event still to happen, on the patient's present response.

The other alternative does involve retrogredient influence. Let us now suppose that the operator, at the time when he sent the signal to the patient, had *not* yet formed any intention of depressing such and such a key in the immediate future. Nevertheless, as soon as he shall have depressed a certain key, he will *ipso facto* come to know which one he is depressing. Suppose, now, that the patient's response was influenced *retrogrediently* by this state of knowledge, which the operator would first acquire about half a second *after* her response had been made. Suppose, as before, that the patient was also paranormally influenced directly by the objective state of the connexions in the commutator at the time when she was making her response. Suppose, finally, that these two paranormal influences co-operate, in the way described, by analogy with inference from two bits of normally acquired information, in formulating the first alternative. Then the patient would tend on each such occasion to open the box in which the lamp was about to be lighted.

As I have said, this second alternative does not avoid the perhaps unintelligible talk of an event being retrogrediently influenced by one which had not yet begun until after it had ceased. But, if it be allowed that such talk is intelligible, some people might prefer to think of the response as influenced retrogrediently by a *state of knowledge or belief about to be acquired by the operator* rather than as influenced retrogrediently by a *mere physical event about to happen in the apparatus.* One wishes to cater for all tastes when one is dealing

73

with alternatives all of which seem *prima facie* to be barely intelligible.

The upshot of this discussion of Tyrrell's experiments with the commutator is as follows. The highly significant rate of excess scoring in the three types of experiment of this kind seems to require, in each type, that the nature of the patient's response is influenced paranormally by a certain *contemporary physical state of affairs in the apparatus*, which *is not and never will be known by normal means to any human being*. In case (*a,α*) this might be the contemporary lighting of a certain concealed lamp. In the other cases it could only be the contemporary arrangement of the connexions concealed in the box of the commutator.

Case (*b*) requires nothing further except paranormal influence on the patient's response by the *operator's simultaneous state of knowledge of the key which he has just depressed*. Most experiments which fall under the heading (*a,β*) could probably be accounted for without assuming anything further except paranormal influence on the patient's response by the operator's *already formed intention to depress such and such a key in the immediate future*.

It is only if we have reason to think that no such intention existed until after the patient had begun to act, that we are forced to postulate *retrogredient* influence on the patient's response. And even here we need not ascribe such influence to a mere physical event or state of affairs which had not yet come into being when the response was made. We can, if we prefer, ascribe it to a *state of knowledge* which the operator *would first acquire in the immediate future*, viz. when he shall have depressed such and such a key.

SOME COMMENTS ON THE STATISTICAL ARGUMENT

I shall conclude this chapter by making some comments on the argument, based on statistical grounds, that the numerical results of such experiments as Tyrrell's and Dr Soal's make it unreasonable to accept the hypothesis of chance-coincidence between the nature of the patient's response on a given occasion and the nature of the target focused by the agent on that or a closely adjacent occasion. There are two different points to be considered. The first is concerned with matters of formal logic or pure theory of probability, and the second is mainly empirical.

(1) *The Argument considered from the point of view of Logic and Theory of Probability.* I think that one would be inclined to formulate the principle of the argument roughly as follows. Suppose that a certain hypothesis would, if accepted, render *extremely improbable*

74

certain propositions which are found on observation to be *true*. Then that extreme improbability is reflected back on the hypothesis, and it becomes unreasonable to accept it. This may be compared with the following principle, which is certainly valid. Suppose that a certain hypothesis would logically entail the *falsity* of certain propositions which are found on observation to be *true*. Then the hypothesis must be rejected as *false*.

Unfortunately the situation is not nearly so simple, and the analogy is misleading in certain important respects.

I begin by remarking that the minimal intelligible statement about the probability of a proposition *a* is that it has such and such a degree of probability *in relation to* another proposition *c*. Let us symbolize what is termed 'the degree of probability of *a* in relation to *c*' by $P[a;c]$. It is assumed that such symbols represent quantities which can be added, subtracted, multiplied, divided, etc. Now the argument is based upon an axiom of the calculus of probability concerning the probability of a conjunction of two propositions, say *a*-and-*b*, in relation to a third proposition, say *c*. The axiom may be formulated as follows:

$$P[(a\&b);c] = P[a;c] \times P[b;(c\&a)] = P[b;c] \times P[a;(c\&b)] \quad (I)$$

From this it follows immediately that

$$P[a;(c\&b)] = P[a;c] \times P[b;(c\&a)] \div P[b;c] \quad (II)$$

This is the fundamental formula for our purpose, and we have now to apply it to the special case of considering the probability of an hypothesis relative to the fact that certain experiments have been done and certain results have been obtained from them.

Let *h* be the hypothesis, and let *o* summarize the observed experimental results in question. Let *k* summarize all the facts and laws of nature, other than *o*, which are known at the time when the experiment is undertaken. We want to determine the probability of *h* relative to the conjunction of the observed results *o* with all the facts and laws of nature already known independently of the experiment and its outcome, i.e. we want to determine $P[h;(k\&o)]$. In order to do this, we have only to substitute *h* for *a*, *k* for *c*, and *o* for *b* in formula (I) above. We get

$$P[h;(k\&o)] = P[h;k] \times P[o;(k\&h)] \div P[o;k] \quad (1)$$

Now $P[h;(k\&o)]$ may be described as 'the probability of *h* *subsequent to* the observations *o*', and $P[h;k]$ may be described as 'the probability of *h* *antecedent to* the observations *o*'. So the formula may be put into words as follows: 'The probability of *h* *subsequent* to the observations *o* is equal to its probability *antecedent* to those observations, *multiplied by* the probability (relative to the facts and laws already known, *together* with the hypothesis *h*) that the results of the experiment would be as they have been observed to be, and *divided by* the probability (relative to the facts and laws already known, *without* the hypothesis *h*) that the results of the experiment would be as they have been observed to be.'

We can now proceed to transform equation (1) into a form in which it is convenient for expressing the odds against *h* rather than the probability of *h*. In order to do so, we make use of another axiom of the calculus of probability. Let *a* and *c* be any two propositions. Let *b* be any third proposition, and let us symbolize its contradictory, not-*b*, by $\bar{b}$. Then the axiom is

$$P[a;c] = P[(a\&b);c] + P[(a\&\bar{b});c] \tag{III}$$

Applying Axiom (I) to this, we get immediately

$$P[a;c] = P[b;c] \times P[a;(c\&b)] + P[\bar{b};c] \times P[a;(c\&\bar{b})] \tag{IV}$$

For our purpose we want to apply this to P[*o*;*k*], the denominator in the fraction on the right-hand side of (1). Accordingly, we substitute *o* for *a*, *k* for *c*, and *h* for *b*, in (IV). We get

$$P[o;k] = P[h;k] \times P[o;(k\&h)] + P(\bar{h};k) \times P[o;(k\&\bar{h})] \tag{2}$$

Substituting this value for P[*o*;*k*] in (1), we get a new expression for P[*h*;(*k*&*o*)], viz.

$$P[h;(k\&o)] = P[h;k] \times P[o;(k\&h)]$$
$$\div \{P[h;k] \times P[o;(k\&h)] + P[\bar{h};k] \times P[o;(k\&\bar{h})]\} \tag{3}$$

Now we have seen (Chapter I, p. 32) that, if *p* be the probability of a proposition relative to any datum, then the odds relative to the same datum against the proposition being true are $(1/p - 1)$ to 1. Applying this to the hypothesis *h*, we see that the odds against *h* being true, *subsequent to* the observed results of the experiments, are $\{1/P[h;(k\&o)] - 1\}$ to 1. And from formula (3) this works out to be

$$\{P[\bar{h};k]/P[h;k]\} \times \{P[o;(k\&\bar{h})]/P[o;(k\&h)]\} \text{ to } 1 \tag{4}$$

Now P[$\bar{h}$;*k*]/P[*h*;*k*] is the odds to one against *h* being true, relative to all that was known *antecedently to* the experiments being done and the results summarized in *o* being observed. It may therefore be called 'the odds to one against *h* being true *antecedently to* the observed results of the experiments'. So formula (4) may be put into words as follows: 'The odds to one against the hypothesis *h* *subsequent* to the experimental observations *o*, are equal to the odds to one against it *antecedent to* those observations, *multiplied by* the probability that the results would have been such as they have been found to be on the assumption that *h* is *false*, and *divided by* the probability that the results would have been such as they have been found to be on the assumption that *h* is *true*.'

The reasoning so far has been completely general. It applies equally to any hypothesis and any experimental results whatsoever. We have now to apply it to the particular hypothesis and the particular experimental results with which we are concerned in these guessing experiments.

The hypothesis h is here of a rather peculiar and purely negative kind. It is that the nature of the patient's response on any occasion, and the nature of the object focused by the agent on that or a closely adjacent occasion, are *completely contingent* to each other. From the point of view of the calculus of probability, what this means can be expressed as follows. The probability (in relation to any datum) of the *conjunctive* proposition that the agent will focus a certain one of the five possible objects on a certain occasion *and* that the patient will make a certain one of the five possible responses on that occasion, is simply the product of the probabilities (in relation to the same datum) of each of the two propositions taken severally. Mutual contingency, in this sense, would of course be incompatible with there being any *causal influence*, direct or indirect, between the agent's focusing a certain one of the possible targets and the patient's responding in a certain one of the possible ways open to him. But it is a wider notion than that of absence of all mutual causal influence, direct or indirect. Suppose, e.g., that the order in which the agent successively focuses the targets is not strictly random, in the sense in which that term is understood in the calculus of probability, but exhibits some kind of pattern. And suppose it should happen that the patient has a habit of making his successive guesses in an order which exhibits a somewhat similar pattern. Then, notwithstanding the absence of causal influence in either direction, the agent's focusings and the patient's guessings would not be contingent to each other in the present sense. All that needs to be said under that heading here is this. The argument under consideration presupposes that the knowledge k, which exists before the results of the experiment are known, includes knowledge (i) that the experiment is so designed as to exclude the possibility of causal influence, whether normal or abnormal (though not, of course, to exclude the possibility of *paranormal* causal influence), and (ii) that the order in which the agent focuses the targets is random, in the sense in which that term is understood in the calculus of probability. Whether those presuppositions are justified or not is an *empirical* question, and not one of pure logic or pure theory of probability.

Since the hypothesis h is that there is *neither* causal influence of any kind between the focusings and the responses, *nor* a non-causal likeness of pattern between the focusing-sequence and the patient's habitual guessing-sequence, its contradictory $\bar{h}$ is that there is *either* some kind of causal influence, *or* some non-causal likeness of pattern. It is evident, then, that h is extremely vague, since it covers every kind of unspecified possible causal influence and every kind of unspecified possible likeness of pattern.

We are now in a position to state clearly and to answer the purely logical question with which we are at present concerned. The question is this. Does the fact that the observed results of the experiments are such as would be extremely improbable on the hypothesis of chance-coincidence *suffice* to prove that the odds against that hypothesis, in relation to the observed experimental results, are extremely high? The answer is: No, it does *not* suffice. And the reason is obvious on looking at the formula (4) above.

That formula gives the odds to one against the hypothesis (h) of chance-contingency, subsequent to the experimental results, in terms (*inter alia*) of the probability, on that hypothesis, of the experimental results being such as they have been observed to be. Now the formula is the product of two ratios, and the probability in question, viz. $P[o;(k\&h)]$, enters into it as the *denominator of the second of these ratios*. The fact that the denominator is very small *tends* (other things being equal) to make this ratio great. But, in order to be sure that it is in fact great, we should have to know that its *numerator*, viz. $P[o;(k\&\bar{h})]$ is not itself of the same order of smallness or even smaller. Nor would it be enough, even if this were known for certain. For in formula (4) we cannot confine our attention to the second of the two ratios. We must consider also the magnitude of the first, by which the second is multiplied. Suppose that the first ratio were very small. Then, even if the second were very great, the product of the two (which gives the odds in question) might be quite small.

The above argument shows us that, granted the exceeding smallness of $P[o;(k\&h)]$, there are still two questions to be considered before we can draw any conclusion as to the magnitude of the odds against the hypothesis of chance-coincidence subsequent to the experimental observations. (i) May not $P[o;(k\&\bar{h})]$ be as small as or smaller than $P[o;(k\&h)]$? And (ii) may not the ratio $P[\bar{h};k]/P[h;k]$ be itself small in comparison with the ratio $P[o;(k\&h)]/P[o;(k\&\bar{h})]$? Let us now see whether there is anything to be said in answer to these questions.

(i) $P[o;(k\&\bar{h})]$ is the probability that the experiments would turn out as they were in fact found to do, given (*a*) all the knowledge of facts and laws which existed up to the time when the experiment began, and (*b*) the supposition that there is *either* some causal influence or other (normal, abnormal, or paranormal) between the agent's focusings and the patient's responses, *or* that there is some *de facto* likeness between a pattern in the agent's focusing-sequence and the patient's guessing-habits. It is plain that we have no hope of assigning any precise numerical value to this probability. One would hardly venture to say, with regard to any proposed fraction, say one in a million, that it is obviously greater or obviously less than that. I cannot see any positive reason for putting the value of this probability particularly high. The supposition (h) that the responses and the focusings are *not* completely contingent to each other covers the possibility of innumerable different kinds and degrees of unspecified causal connexion between them, and the possibility of innumerable different kinds and degrees of unspecified likeness between the patterns of the two sequences. Is it in the least obvious that, on such a vague supposition, the probability of the actual proportion of hits diverging (in one direction or the other) from the proportion most probable on the hypothesis of chance-coincidence, by an amount at least as great as that which is actually observed, is appreciably large? It is certainly not obvious to me.

(ii) Let us now turn to the other factor in the product in formula (4), viz. the ratio of P[h;k] to P[h;k]. This is the ratio of the probability (relative to all that is known *antecedently* to the experiment) that the focusings and the responses are *not* completely contingent to each other, to the probability (in relation to the same knowledge) that they *are* completely contingent to each other. Here, again, we are dealing with probabilities to which no precise numerical values can possibly be assigned. But I should have thought that one could reasonably venture on the following judgement as to the relative magnitudes of the two. Surely the hypothesis of complete *mutual contingency* between focusings and responses is much *more* probable, antecedently to the knowledge of the actual outcome of the experiments, than the hypothesis that there is either some kind of causal relation between them or else some kind of similarity of pattern in the two sequences. If that be so, this ratio is certainly less than unity, and it might reasonably be thought to be very much less.

Let me now summarize the results of my argument. The fact that the probability, on the hypothesis of chance-coincidence, of getting deviations in the actual proportion of hits at least as great as those actually observed in the experiments, is very small, is *not* by itself a sufficient reason for concluding that the odds against the hypothesis of chance-coincidence are very small in view of the experimental results. It would need to be supplemented by two additional premisses: (i) That the probability of getting such deviations *is not about equally small* on the *contrary* hypothesis also. (ii) Even if this condition were known to be fulfilled, so that the second factor in the expression in formula (4) were undoubtedly great, that would not suffice. For the first factor in that expression might be so small that the product of it and the second would not be great. Now this first factor is, in effect, the *odds*, antecedent to knowledge of the results of the experiment, *against* the hypothesis of complete mutual contingency between the focusings and the responses. So the second condition is that those odds shall be *fairly great*. Now I have tried to show (*a*) that we have no positive reason to think that the first condition is fulfilled, and (*b*) that there is some reason to think that the second condition is not fulfilled.

I would remark, finally, that our two conditions are interconnected in the following way. Each could be fulfilled to a greater or a less degree; and, if either condition were fulfilled to a *very high degree*, then it would suffice that the other should be fulfilled to a *moderate degree*. A competent mathematician could formulate all this much more accurately and more elegantly than I have done. But I think that the essential points have been brought out clearly enough, and a technical mathematical formulation of them would be intelligible only to a minority of suitably trained readers.

(2) *The argument considered from the Empirical Standpoint.* The calculus of probability is a branch of *pure* mathematics, in which terms are defined, postulates laid down, and theorems deduced. There is no doubt as to its formal correctness and internal consistency. Much, if not all, of it can in fact be reduced to, or exemplified by, the branch of algebra called 'Permutations and Combinations'. But the concepts used and defined in it are called by names, e.g. 'probability', 'randomness', 'chance-coincidence', etc., which were already used by ordinary men in the affairs of daily life long before the calculus was invented, and are still used by such persons in such contexts. Now, the moment one attempts to *apply* the calculus to any situation in the actual world, the question arises: How far does that situation answer to the concepts defined in the calculus and the postulates laid down in it? That is a question which essentially involves *empirical* considerations.

In reference to the experiments under discussion the question takes the following special form. Can we be sure that the order in which the agent focuses the five possible targets is *strictly random*, in the sense contemplated by the calculus of probability? Provided that it is so, it does not matter in the least what habits the patient may have in responding to the five possible targets. Now the calculations assume that it is strictly random, in the following sense. It is assumed that the probability (in the sense defined in the calculus) of the agent focusing any one of the possible targets on the r-th occasion in a sequence of such focusings is precisely equal to the probability of his focusing any other one of them on that occasion, quite regardless of (i) the *relative frequency* with which the various possible targets have been focused on the previous $(r - 1)$ occasions, and of (ii) the particular *order* in which the focusings of the various possible targets have been distributed throughout the previous $(r - 1)$ occasions. Now that condition is supposed to be secured by making a list of the numbers 1 to 5 from a so-called 'table of random numbers', and prescribing that the agent shall do his focusing in the order of the numbers in such a list. The same result was supposed to be secured in some of Dr Soal's experiments by drawing a counter on each occasion from a bag containing equal numbers of counters of five different colours. In those of Tyrrell's experiments where an explicit attempt was made to secure randomness in focusing, this was supposed to be secured by use of the mechanical selector.

Tables of random numbers have been constructed, so far as I am aware, by two different methods. One is by use of some kind of machine, of which Tyrrell's mechanical selector would be of a somewhat elementary instance. The other is by taking a table of logarithms of numbers, calculated to a large number of places of decimals, and extracting the last digit from each of a sequence of successive logarithms. It is obviously an empirical question whether a machine, made and operated to a certain specification, does or does not produce a sequence of the digits from 0 to 9 which is random, in the sense assumed in the calculus of probability. It is, presumably, also an empirical question whether the last digits of the logarithms of the successive entries in a logarithm-table do or do not form such a sequence. At any rate, I know of no proof that they *must* do so.

But, although the question is empirical, in the sense that, if it can be answered at all, the answer must be based on the results of observing certain features in the actual sequences in question, it is by no means obvious what observable properties one is to look for. The entries in a table are a *finite* collection of terms; and, indeed, it is only finite collections and their properties that can possibly be observed. Thus, the questions that can be answered empirically are all of the following kind. What are the relative frequencies with which 0's, 1's, ... 9's occur in the table? What are the frequencies with which doublets, such as (not-5, 5, 5, not-5), occur in it? What are the frequencies with which patterns of the form {not-(1 or 2), 1, 2, 1, not-(1 or 2)} occur in it? And so on.

Now, no answer to any one such question, and no accumulation of answers to any finite number of them, constitutes a *direct* answer to the question: Is the sequence of digits in the table strictly random, in the sense understood in the calculus of probability? What the calculus will tell us is something of the following kind. Let the table consist of N entries, each of which is one or another of the ten digits from 0 to 9 inclusive. Suppose that it had been constructed by making a truly random selection of N such digits from an enormous collection of equal numbers of each of the ten kinds. Then the *most probable* proportion of sub-sequences of such and such a kind in it would be such and such. And the *probability* of the actual proportion of sub-sequences of a given kind deviating from the most probable proportion by as much as or more than a given amount is such and such.

The utmost that can be done, then, in testing a table for randomness, is this. One can consider sub-sequences of various kinds, and count the number of instances of each such kind in the table. One can then note whether the proportion in each case differs from that which would have been most probable on the hypothesis stated in the immediately previous paragraph. And, if the actual proportion should differ (as it nearly always will to some extent) from the proportion most probable on that hypothesis, one can then proceed to note whether the difference is greater than would be *highly probable* on that hypothesis. If that difference, in the case of *any* of the sub-sequences under consideration, should be so great that the probability of such a divergence, on the hypothesis, would be pretty small, the table must be viewed with some suspicion. And, if that should happen for *several* of the sub-sequences under consideration, the suspicion will be greatly strengthened. If, on the other hand, the divergences are in no case under consideration so large as to be at all highly improbable on the hypothesis, the table will be regarded as satisfactorily 'random'.

It is evident that what we may call 'empirical' or 'practical' randomness is an essentially inexact and relative notion. The number of different kinds of sub-sequence which might be taken into account in testing any table is enormous. No good reason can be given for ignoring any of these, but no one is ever likely to make use of more than a small number of the most obvious of them in testing a table. In practice a table counts as satisfactorily 'random' if and only if (*a*) the relative frequencies with which each of the ten digits occur do not differ by more than would be quite highly probable in a strictly random selection, of the size of the actual table, from an enormously large universe consisting of equal numbers of each of the ten digits; and (*b*) if it passes the above-mentioned tests pretty well in respect of every one of three or four fairly obvious kinds of sub-sequence.

It should be remarked that those who compile such tables tell us that the sequence of digits, as it comes from the machine or the table of logarithms, does *not* as a rule answer very well in all its parts to the tests to which they subject it. Such crude sequences have to be 'doctored' before publication, in accordance with certain standard procedures, in order to improve their empirical randomness. There is, of course, nothing sinister or dishonest in this. Such tables are intended for certain kinds of use, and it is only common sense to employ any means available to adapt them as well as may be to the purposes which they are meant to serve.

All that has been said so far is perfectly general, and applies equally to *any* use that may be made of random-number tables. Let us now consider what bearing, if any, it has on the conclusions to be drawn from the results of such experiments in psychical research as those of Tyrrell and Dr Soal.

The fundamental fact is that a table, which is practically random (in the sense that it passes all the tests commonly applied) may yet not give a sequence of focusings which is random in the theoretical sense assumed in the calculus of probability. It may contain a most improbably high proportion of some rather out-of-the-way kind of sub-sequences, in respect of which it has never been tested. Now it seems to me that this might have two different bearings on the conclusions to be drawn from the results of the experiments. They are the following:

(i) The first thing which may be affected is the estimate of the odds, on the hypothesis of chance-coincidence, against obtaining so large a deviation as has actually been found, from the number of hits which would be most probable on that hypothesis. In making this estimate it is taken for granted that the most probable number of hits in n trials is $n/5$, that the standard deviation is $\frac{2}{5}\sqrt{n}$, and that the odds in question can be found by taking the ratio of the actual to the standard deviation and looking up in a table of the Error Function the entry corresponding to that ratio. Now all this presupposes that the order in which the agent focuses the five alternative possible targets is random, in the sense understood in the calculus of probability. If that assumption should be far from the truth, an estimate of the odds reached in this way may be quite unreliable. This difficulty is partly, but only partly, met (at the cost of considerable extra trouble in the calculations) by using Stevens's method for calculating the most probable number of hits and the standard deviation, on the hypothesis of chance-coincidence. That method obviates difficulties due to the various alternative kinds of target not all being focused *equally often* in a comparatively short run of trials. For it bases the calculation on the actual number of times that each kind of target was focused by the agent and the actual number of times that each kind occurred in the responses of the patient. But the calculations assume that, whatever may have been the *numbers*

83

focused of each kind of target, they are as likely to have been focused in any one as in any other of the various *orders* in which that could have happened.

(ii) The second, and more serious, possible effect of imperfect randomness in the order of focusing is this. There might be some unsuspected pattern of sequence in the order of focusing, and this might be correlated (either by similarity or by counter-similarity) with a pattern in the patient's habits of response. If there were similarity, an excess of hits would be scored, and, if there were counter-similarity, a defect of hits, of such a magnitude as to be highly improbable on the hypothesis of chance-coincidence. And this, which would have a perfectly normal explanation, would be claimed as evidence for paranormal influence.

Now it is quite useless just to make this suggestion in its general form, and then to throw up one's cap as if one had exploded in a hand's turn all the conclusions drawn by Tyrrell and Dr Soal. What needs to be answered by empirical investigation is such questions as the following. Was there a specific kind of pattern, which can be indicated, in the order in which the targets were focused? Was there a similar or counter-similar pattern in the order in which the patient would habitually respond to the possible targets when there was certainly no influence on him by the agent, e.g. when the agent was not in fact focusing anything, but the patient believed him to be doing so? If both those questions can be answered in the affirmative, was the similarity or counter-similarity of pattern sufficient to account for the kind and the degree of divergence between actual and most probable number of hits observed in the course of the experiments? To attempt to answer these questions would demand an immense amount of extremely boring work, for which one could expect no monetary recompense, and from which one would derive very little professional credit, no matter what the result might be.

What has been done in detail in this matter will be found summarized in two papers in the S.P.R. *Journal*, viz. A. T. Oram, 'An Experiment with Random Numbers' (Vol. XXXVII, No. 682), and J. Fraser Nicol, 'Randomness: The Background and some new Investigations' (Vol. XXXVIII, No. 684). Mr Oram worked with the tables of *Kendall and Babington Smith*, which, I understand, were based on sequences produced by a machine, and were tested and in certain respects 'doctored' by the authors before publication. Mr Fraser Nicol reviewed and in certain respects extended this work, and he himself investigated the tables of *Fisher and Yates*. These are stated to have been constructed from A. J. Thompson's tables of 20-figure logarithms, and tested and 'doctored' before publication.

The table with which Mr Oram and his collaborators worked consists of 100,000 entries of the digits from 0 to 9, printed in 2,000 pairs of parallel columns, each with 25 entries in a column. They made two kinds of comparison, viz. (*a*) of entries in the *same* row of parallel columns, and (*b*) of the entry in each row of a left-hand column with the entry in the row immediately below it in the parallel right-hand column. If the two entries in (*a*) happen to be the same, that may be compared to a *direct* hit in a card-guessing experiment. If the two entries in (*b*) happen to be the same, that may be compared to a $+1$ fore-hit in such an experiment. Evidently, there are $2,000 \times 25$, i.e. 50,000 *direct* comparisons possible, and there are $2,000 \times 24$, i.e. 48,000 comparisons of the (*b*) kind possible.

The upshot of the investigation may, I think, be fairly summed up in the following propositions. (i) In neither the (*a*) nor the (*b*) comparisons did the total number of 'hits' differ significantly from the number most probable on the hypothesis of randomness. (ii) In neither kind of comparison did the number of sets of 25 in which there were 0 hits, the number in which there were exactly 1 hit, the number in which there were exactly 2 hits . . . and so on up to the number in which there were 10 or more hits, differ significantly from the respective numbers which would have been most probable on the hypothesis of randomness. (iii) In case (*a*) the 50,000 pairs of digits were subdivided into 20 successive sub-groups, each of 500 successive pairs, followed by 40 successive sub-groups, each of 1,000 successive pairs; and the accumulated number of hits at each of these 60 points was noted. In case (*b*) the same plan was followed, the difference being that the 48,000 pairs of digits here were subdivided into 20 groups, each of 480 pairs, succeeded by 40 groups, each of 960 pairs. In neither case did the accumulated number of hits at any of these 60 points diverge significantly from the most probable number on the hypothesis of randomness.

So far the table of Kendall and Babington-Smith comes well out of the tests which Mr Oram applied to it. It does so, in spite of the fact (which is pointed out by Mr Fraser Nicol in his paper) that Mr Oram compared entries in the same row (or in immediately successive rows) of *adjacent columns*, whilst the authors of the table give a warning that they have tested the randomness of the entries *only* when taken in *rows*, and not when taken in columns. Suppose that the entries in the left-hand one of a pair of adjacent columns really had represented a sequence of responses by the patient in an experiment such as Tyrrell's or Dr Soal's. And suppose that the corresponding entries in the same row (or in the row immediately below, as the case may be) in the right-hand column of the pair really had represented the focusing of such and such a target by the agent immediately before (or immediately after, as the case may be) each such response. Then no one, using the statistical criteria which Tyrrell and Dr Soal did in fact use, would have had the slightest ground to question the hypothesis of chance-coincidence.

So far, so good. But there remains an interesting and curious anomaly, which was pointed out (with not unnatural delight) by Mr Spencer Brown (to whose mill it came as very welcome grist) in a letter which appears in Vol. XXXVIII, No. 683 of the S.P.R. *Journal*. It is more fully investigated by Mr Fraser Nicol in the paper already mentioned in the same volume of the *Journal*.

In order to explain the point, it will be necessary to go into a certain amount of detail, which is not very explicitly brought out in the writings in question, but is implicit in them and can be extracted from them.

On each half-page of the tables of Kendall and Babington-Smith there are 20 *double* columns, each consisting of 25 rows, i.e. 1,000 entries. Since there are 100,000 entries in all, there are 100 such half-pages. Now each of Mr Oram's scorers was instructed to take the 20 double columns on any page of the table supplied to him for annotation in groups of 5 from left to right of that page, and to enter the number of hits in any one of the 4 groups of 5 double columns into the corresponding one of the 4 columns on his scoring-sheet. Each of these 4 columns had 25 lines, corresponding to the 25 rows in each column of the table. The scorer entered any hit in the appropriate line of the appropriate column.

From the aggregate of all the scoring-sheets, after revision and correction for mistakes, Mr Oram compiled the following two contingency-tables:

NUMBER OF HITS

(a) *Direct*

Order of sets of 5 rows in columns of table of random numbers	Order of sets of 5 double columns from left to right in table of random numbers			
	1–5	*6–10*	*11–15*	*16–20*
1–5	259	246	271	265
6–10	269	251	261	224
11–15	257	263	257	243
16–20	231	264	251	226
21–25	251	251	246	243

(b) +1 *fore-hits*

1–5	251	283	225	249
6–10	246	247	249	229
11–15	226	219	237	220
16–20	242	262	203	218
21–25	253	233	222	230

Now it has been claimed that, in certain actual experiments in guessing or dice-throwing which have been recorded in this way, the following statistical fact has emerged. The number of hits in the *top-left-hand corner* of such a table tends to exceed the number of hits in the *bottom-right-hand* corner by an amount which is highly improbable on the hypothesis of chance-contingency between response made and target focused. This has been adduced as evidence for paranormality in the experiments in question, and has been ascribed to a systematic decline in paranormal achievement in the course of each set of trials. (It may be remarked that no such 'decline-effect' was noted, or made the premiss of an argument for paranormality, in the case of Tyrrell's or Dr Soal's experiments. It has figured mainly in the arguments for the existence of paranormal influence by certain subjects on the fall of dice.)

The question therefore arises whether, if we were to treat Mr Oram's two contingency-tables as if they were the records of actual experiments, we should find a similar statistical pattern exhibited. That question has been answered by Mr Fraser Nicol in his article. Suppose that, in each of Mr Oram's tables, we take (i) the sum of the entries in the first two rows of the first two columns, and (ii) the sum of the entries in the last two rows of the last two columns. We can then make up a contingency-table corresponding to each of Mr Oram's tables, and can see whether in either of them the difference between these two sums is so great as to be highly improbable on the hypothesis of randomness in the original table of random numbers. (I have ringed the relevant parts of each of Mr Oram's tables.) In (*a*) these two sums are 1,025 and 966 respectively; in (*b*) they are 1,027 and 873 respectively. The two contingency-tables are given below.

(*a*)

	Left-hand top section	Right-hand bottom section
Hits	1,025	966
Misses	8,975	9,034

(*b*)

	Left-hand top section	Right-hand bottom section
Hits	1,027	873
Misses	8,573	8,727

(It will be noted that the sum of hits and misses in each section of (*a*) is 10,000, whilst in each section of (*b*) it is only 9,600. The latter total must have been reached in the following way. In any double column the maximum number of +1 fore-hits is 24, since there is nothing in the right-hand single column for the 25th entry in the

87

left-hand single column to be a $+1$ fore-hit upon. Therefore, in the 10 double columns under the headings *1–5* and *6–10* on any page of the table of random numbers there are 240 possible $+1$ fore-hits. Now the two rows *1–5* and *6–10* together constitute 10/25 of the column. Therefore the number of possible $+1$ fore-hits in the top left-hand corner of Mr Oram's table (*b*) is 240 × 0·4, i.e. 96, per page of the table of random numbers. There are 100 pages in the latter, so that the total number of possible $+1$ fore-hits in this section of Table (*b*) is 96 × 100, i.e. 9,600. Precisely similar reasoning applies to the bottom right-hand corner.)

Now at last we can return to the question at issue, and to Mr Fraser Nicol's answer to it. In both his Table (*a*) and his Table (*b*) the number of hits recorded in the left-hand top section of Mr Oram's corresponding table exceeds the number recorded in the right-hand bottom section. Is that excess, in either case, so great as to be highly improbable on the hypothesis that the table of Kendall and Babington-Smith is really random when taken by columns? In order to test this it is only necessary to calculate the value of the function known as χ^2 for each of Mr Fraser Nicol's tables, and then to look up, in a table of that function, the probability that so high a value of χ^2 would occur by chance-coincidence in a four-cell contingency-table, such as these are.

The answer is this. For Table (*a*) $\chi^2 = 1·94$, and P = 0·16. So the difference in the case of direct hits is quite consistent with the hypothesis of randomness. But it is a very different story with Table (*b*). Here $\chi^2 = 13·85$, and P = 0·0002; i.e. the odds against getting so high a value of χ^2, on the hypothesis of randomness, are 5,000 to 1. Had anyone found such a significantly high decline-effect in an actual experiment he would have been much disposed to adduce it as evidence for the presence of something other than chance-coincidence.

What conclusions are we to draw from this? (i) The table of Kendall and Babington-Smith, even when taken by columns (where the authors do not guarantee its complete randomness), answers very well to all the tests for randomness which are parallel to the criteria used by Tyrrell and by Dr Soal for judging whether the results of their experiments can reasonably be ascribed to chance-coincidence between the responses of the patient and the focusings (assumed to have been made in a random order) of the agent. (ii) As regards the test of presence or absence of a significant 'decline-effect' of a certain specific kind, explained above, the table answers very well to the test for randomness, if entries *in the same row* of the left and the right columns in a double column are compared with each other. But it answers very badly to the test, if the entry in one row of the left column be compared with the entry in the *row immediately below* in the right column of a double column. (iii) Such decline-effects, whether in respect of direct hits or of $+1$ fore-hits, were *not* adduced by Tyrrell or by Dr Soal as part of their argument to show that the results of their experiments could not reasonably be regarded as a matter of chance-coincidence. It would appear, therefore, that the imperfect randomness of the table, in respect of this particular test, has no direct bearing on the validity of that argument.

The plain fact is that the contention that Dr Soal's results are *not* merely a matter of chance-coincidence rests *statistically* on one quite simple premiss. This is the enormous odds, on the hypothesis of chance-coincidence, against getting anything like so great a deviation as actually occurs from the number of hits most probable on that hypothesis; it being assumed that the use of a reputable table of 'random numbers' ensures that the targets are focused in something approaching pretty closely to an ideally random order. Mr Oram's investigations, notwithstanding the oddity of the significant decline-effect for $+1$ fore-hits in the pseudo-experiment, pointed out by Mr Fraser Nicol, seem to me to show that that assumption is justified, for the purpose in hand, in the case of the table of Kendall and Babington-Smith. It may be added that Mr Fraser Nicol, in the article quoted, reports the results of elaborate tests which he has made on another well-known table, viz. that of Fisher and Yates. This comes with flying colours through all the tests which he applied. On the other hand, he found that the last digits of successive entries in a logarithm-table, which have often been used for randomization, stood up to his tests very imperfectly.

So the cautious quotitative psychical researcher may be advised (a) to cast aside his table of 20-figure logarithms; (b) to use his *Kendall and Babington-Smith* with confidence, when he is basing his argument on *large primary* statistical effects, but with considerable caution when he is relying wholly on *secondary* statistical features, such as decline-effects; and (c) to be in a position to say, in (approximately) the words of Gibbon: 'When I took my walks abroad, a copy of *Fisher and Yates* was often in my hand, always in my pocket.'

In conclusion I would say this. The suggestion which we have been asked to consider is that the highly significant excess of direct hits or of $+1$ fore-hits, scored by certain subjects, may be due to a purely contingent combination of (a) some subtle pattern in the order in which the digits occur in the table used for randomizing the agent's focusings, and (b) a causally independent, but correlated, pattern in the order in which those subjects habitually write down the names of the five symbols, or open the five boxes, when set in the experimental situation. Now, in order to refute this, it is not *necessary*, though it is interesting and useful, to examine the tables of random numbers for signs of unexpected patterns, as Mr Oram and Mr Fraser Nicol have so thoroughly done. It is sufficient to point out certain features, reported by Tyrrell or by Dr Soal, which are either inconsistent with or strongly counter-indicative of this suggestion. The following are some of them.

(1) In Tyrrell's experiments Miss Johnson's rate of scoring repeatedly sank to chance level when any new condition was introduced, and then gradually returned to the usual significantly high level. We should have to suppose that Miss Johnson started with a habit of opening boxes in an order which happened to coincide with the order in which Tyrrell habitually depressed keys, and then gradually developed (without any causal influence from either Tyrrell or his randomizing machine) a habit of opening them which happened to coincide with a pattern in the sequence of numbers turned out by that machine. Or else we should have to suppose that the order in which Tyrrell habitually depressed keys happened to coincide with a pattern in the sequence of numbers turned out by the machine, and that Miss Johnson gradually resumed her old habit after a period of confusion caused by the disturbance of knowing that a new condition had been introduced.

(2) Mr Shackleton succeeded repeatedly with a certain few agents, and failed to reach anything above chance level with all the others who were tried. The relevant pattern, if there was one, in the order of numbers taken from the table must have been the same in all cases. Are we to suppose that his habit of writing down the initials of the names of the five symbols in an order which happened to coincide with that pattern was in operation only when those few persons acted as agents, and was in suspense when all the others did so? And, if we are to suppose this, can we do so without inferring that there must have been some causal influence from the successful agents, and from them only, which activated the habit just when they were focusing the cards?

(3) Mr Shackleton was about equally successful when the randomizing was done by means of numbers taken beforehand from a table and when it was done contemporaneously by drawing counters from a bag. If there is a pattern in the order of the entries in the table, and a pattern in the order in which a particular individual draws counters of various colours from a bag, why should those two patterns be so much alike that a habit which happens to fit in with one happens also to fit in with the other?

90

(4) When runs done under conditions which would exclude the possibility of telepathy were interspersed, without Mr Shackleton's normal knowledge, among runs done under conditions which would permit of telepathy, the scores fell to chance level in the former case and were at the usual significantly high level in the latter. Now, any pattern present in the order of the numbers used for randomization must have been present throughout. Is it credible that Mr Shackleton's habitual pattern of response should have been switched on and off in the course of a single experiment in exact coincidence with recurrent changes of conditions, of which he had no normal knowledge?

(5) The last point which I will make is this. (i) In those of Tyrrell's experiments in which the commutator was used, the order in which the lamps were lighted differed from the order in which the keys were depressed. Moreover, with any one order of depressing the keys the order in which the lamps were lighted would be different for each different setting of the commutator. (ii) In all Dr Soal's experiments with Mr Shackleton the order in which the various *symbols* was focused depended, not only on the order in which the agent focused the five *cards*, but also on the order in which the cards were laid out. And the latter order was changed by shuffling between each set of 50 guesses. The obvious consequence is the same in both cases. A *de facto* correlation between Miss Johnson's habitual order of opening boxes and Tyrrell's habitual order of depressing keys, or between Mr Shackleton's habitual order of writing down the initials of the names of the five symbols and some pattern in the entries in the table of random numbers, would have been completely irrelevant or positively detrimental to success. For the order in which the lamps were lighted, in the one case, and the order in which the symbols were focused, in the other, had been repeatedly 'scrambled' out of all recognition by the commutator or by shuffling, respectively.

It is time to cease labouring the obvious. To speak plainly, the suggestion, which has been seriously put forward and which I have tried to treat with becoming seriousness, seems to me completely ridiculous in reference to such results as are reported by Tyrrell and by Dr Soal. Those results, or the fact that they were reported, *may* conceivably be susceptible of some causal explanation in normal or abnormal terms. But the idea that they can be accepted, and then explained by a non-causal coincidence between the patient's habit of making his responses and some pattern in the allegedly random order of the agent's focusings, is just moonshine illuminating a mare's nest.

Note to Chapter III

A SUGGESTED EXPLANATION OF THE RESULTS OF DR SOAL'S
EXPERIMENTS WITH MR SHACKLETON BY THE HYPOTHESIS
OF COLLUSION

In S.P.R. *Proceedings*, Vol. LIII, there is a paper by Mr C. E. M. Hansel, in which he elaborates a suggestion, which he had already made in correspondence with Dr Soal (see Soal and Bateman: *Modern Experiments in Telepathy*, pp. 192–5). The suggestion is that the significant degree of success obtained by Shackleton with certain agents might be explained by supposing fraudulent collusion of a certain kind between him and each of those agents, viz. the two women, R. E. and G. A., and the man J. Al.

In attempting to convey a rough idea of the hypothesis, as I understand it, I shall confine myself to the case of +1 fore-hits, and shall assume that the intention is to get by fraudulent means a significant excess of such hits. The method would apply equally well to getting a significant excess of hits in any pre-assigned position. That being understood, the hypothesis may be stated as follows:

(1) Shackleton chooses *beforehand* certain rows, e.g. the 2nd, 4th, 6th, 10th, and 14th, in one of the two columns of 25 rows in his scoring sheet, and decides *beforehand* which one of the initial letters of the five symbols on the cards he will write down in each of these pre-selected places. We will suppose, e.g., that he decides to write E in row 2, G in row 4, L in row 6, P in row 10, and Z in row 14, of column I on his scoring-sheet. He informs the agent (A) of this before the experiment begins.

(2) We must now remind ourselves of the experimental arrangements. (i) The agent has, lying face downwards on the table before him, in a row from left to right, five picture-cards, on the face of each of which is depicted a different one of a certain five animals, whose names begin with the letters E, G, L, P, and Z. The order in which they have been laid out is unknown to him or to anyone else at the beginning of the experiment. But, as the calling goes on, A turns up now one and now another of these cards, according to the numbers (1, 2, 3, 4, and 5) presented to him on successive occasions in a random order at the window of the screen facing him; looks at it; and is supposed then to replace it face downward in its old position. It may be assumed, therefore, that after a few calls A will acquire and retain a pretty fair knowledge of what kind of card is located at each of the five

92

positions in the row of cards in front of him. (ii) Since the original order of these cards is *not* known to the experimenter, the latter will not know, when he turns them up at the end of the second of the two runs of 25 calls, whether the agent has or has not surreptitiously shifted them during the course of those two runs. (iii) What is essential to determine whether any entry in the percipient's scoring sheet shall count as a $+1$ fore-hit or not is simply the order in which the five picture-cards are lying *when the experimenter turns them over* at the end of the second of the two runs of 25 calls.

Suppose, e.g., that Shackleton wishes to secure a $+1$ fore-hit for each of his pre-arranged entries of E in row 2, G in row 4, L in row 6, P in row 10, and Z in row 14 in the first column of his sheet. And suppose that the numbers presented to the agent at the window at the 3rd, the 5th, the 7th, the *11*th, and the *15*th call, respectively, were 1, 5, 2, 4, and 3. Let us denote the positions of the cards from left to right on the table by I, II, III, IV, and V. Then it is necessary and sufficient for success that, at the end of the experiment, the cards should be so arranged that the one at I is an E, the one at V is a G, the one at II is an L, the one at IV is a P, and the one at III is a Z. This, then, is the state of affairs which A, knowing beforehand Shackleton's intentions and assumed to be in fraudulent collusion with him, has to try to bring about by the end of the second run of 25 calls.

(3) In order to do this, A may be supposed to proceed on the following lines. Let us take, for example, the 11th call, and suppose, as above, that the number 4 is presented on that occasion at the window to A. A then knows that there needs to be a P-card in place IV in the row before him, since he knows that Shackleton has written a P in the 10th row of his first guess-column, and that he wants to secure a $+1$ fore-hit with it. If A knows that the card in place IV is in fact the P-card, he has only to turn it up honestly, look at the face, and then replace it face downwards in its present position. But suppose he knows that the P-card is, e.g., in position II in the row before him. Then he must surreptitiously interchange the two cards, so as to get the P-card into position IV, and to shift the card which is in fact there into position II. A must act in the same way *mutatis mutandis* on each of the other occasions which he knows to be critical, viz. the 3rd, the 5th, the 7th, and the 15th call.

The above example should suffice to give a general idea of this hypothetical method of collusion. In practice there would have to be a number of complications. In the first place, it would not do for the conspirators to choose *the same* set of positions for this kind of cheating in a large number of successive runs of 50 guesses. For it might soon become obvious to the experimenter that $+1$ fore-hits were repeatedly recurring at the same group of places in one run of guesses after another, Again, it would be inevitable that successes by this method would tend to be scored in the *later* part of a run (when A would have got a pretty shrewd idea of the actual nature of the card in each position in the row before him), rather than in the earlier part. This might cause the experimenter to 'smell a rat', though it might equally well cause him to imagine some process of gradual 'warming up' of paranormal capacity in each run.

There is a further important qualification to be made to the simple example given above. This is pointed out (*inter alia*) by Dr Soal in a paper, also in S.P.R. *Proceedings*, Vol. LIII, in which he examines critically Mr Hansel's article. The point is this. In my example above I assumed that the numbers shown in the window to A on the successive relevant occasions were *all different*, viz. 1, 5, 2, 4, and 3. But, since the numbers are presented at the window in random order, there is no reason why that should always be the case. Now it is only if all are different that the maximum number of +1 fore-hits will be scored by this method.

Suppose, e.g., that two of these numbers had been the same; e.g. that the number 4 had been presented, not only at the 11th call, but also (instead of the number 1, as in the example above) at the 3rd call. If a +1 fore-hit is to be made by the entry in the 2nd row of the percipient's score-sheet (which is, and is known by A to be, an E), the card in position IV must already be, or have been made by A to be, the *E-card*. Similarly, if a +1 fore-hit is to be made by the entry in the 10th row of the percipient's score-sheet (which is, and is known by A to be, a P), the card in that same position IV must already be, or have been made by A to be, a *P-card*. But it is already occupied (as A knows) by the E-card. Therefore, A can secure that the 10th entry in the percipient's score-sheet shall be a +1 fore-hit only by *shifting the E-card* from position IV and replacing it by the P-card. And by so doing he *ipso facto* converts the 2nd entry from being a +1 hit to being a +1 *miss*.

It is plain, then, that when two of the five numbers presented at random on the relevant occasions are *the same*, and the remaining three are different, the maximum number of +1 hits that can be scored by this method is *four*, and not five. It is possible to work out the maximum possible score securable by this method for each of the other possibilities (e.g. with two numbers alike of one kind, two alike of another kind, and the remaining one different, the maximum possible score is 3).

Plainly, there are two questions to be raised, one practical and the other statistical. (1) Would it be possible for persons who were neither skilled conjurors nor gifted with exceptional memories for figures to carry out the operations supposed? And, if so, could the agent perform the necessary substitutions without being detected by the experimenter who was supposed to be watching him all the time? (2) Granted that all this were possible, would the most probable number of +1 fore-hits to be secured by this means differ significantly from the actual number secured by Shackleton in the sumtotal of those trials in which he was scoring at such a rate as to make it plain that something beyond chance-coincidence was involved?

(1) For a discussion of the first question, in the light of experiments deliberately carried out in order to answer it, the reader is referred to a paper by Mr Christopher Scott, entitled 'Notes on Some Criticisms of the Soal-Goldney Experiments', in the S.P.R. *Journal*, Vol. XL, No. 704, June 1960.

Mr Scott, in his then capacity of Supervisor of Experimental Research for the S.P.R., instituted a series of experiments in July 1958 at the Society's rooms, in which he acted as 'percipient', Mr Hansel as 'agent', and Mrs Goldney and Dr West (both of whom were familiar with the conditions which had prevailed at the experiments with Shackleton) acted as observers. The card-substitution technique was then tested under conditions which were intended to duplicate, in the main essentials, the *physical* (as distinct from the psychological) conditions prevailing in *most* of the original experiments.

The reader should study carefully the eight paragraphs of Mr Scott's summary of the results. I will content myself here with quoting §8, in which he states his own conclusion: 'My general conclusion from these demonstrations was that Hansel's method of cheating almost certainly could have been carried out under the conditions which probably existed in most of the original experiments.' To this he very properly adds: 'The conclusion that card substitution was *possible* is only one among many pieces of evidence bearing on the question whether card substitution *actually took place*' (my italics—C.D.B.).

(2) The statistical question is discussed very thoroughly in principle by Dr Soal in the paper already mentioned. But it is discussed on the assumption that, if the Hansel method of collusion is used at all, it is used *in exactly 5 places in the 50 on each scoring sheet*. I must confess that I see no reason why it should not be used more often than this, if it is used at all.

On that assumption the main points that emerge are these. (i) The average number of +1 fore-hits per sheet that would be produced in this way is 3·36, and the corresponding variance is 0·51. (ii) On each sheet there would remain $2 \times (25 - 1) - 5 = 43$ places, each of which could contain, by pure chance, a $+1$ fore-hit. So the average number of purely chance $+1$ fore-hits per sheet would be $43/5 = 8·6$, with a variance of 6·88. (iii) So, on the assumption in question, the average total number of such hits, produced by collusion and by chance, per sheet would be $3·36 + 8·6 = 11·96$. And the total variance per sheet would be $0·51 + 6·88 = 7·39$.

Now, if we consider all the trials with Shackleton which (a) occurred in experiments where the number of $+1$ fore-hits was *significantly above chance expectation* (so that the hypothesis of collusion is *applicable*), and (b) were such that they *could* have resulted in $+1$ fore-hits, we find that the total number is 6,759. The actual number of $+1$ fore-hits among these was 1,958. Now compare this with the results of the hypothesis that the Hansel method of collusion was applied in exactly 5 places on each sheet. Since only 48 places on any sheet could possibly contain a $+1$ fore-hit (for the *last* in each column of 25 obviously cannot do so), the number of sheets corresponding to the total number 6,759 of trials is the latter number divided by 48, i.e. approximately 141. Since the average number of $+1$ fore-hits per sheet, on the hypothesis and the assumption under discussion, is 11·96, the expected number in 6,759 trials is $11·96 \times 141 = 1,686$ approximately. Since the variance per sheet, on the same hypothesis and assumption, is 7·39, the total variance for the 6,759 trials is $7·39 \times 141 = 1,042$. The standard deviation is the square root of this, which is approximately 32·3.

So the actual number of $+1$ fore-hits (1,958) exceeds the number most probable on the hypothesis of collusion and the assumption that this takes place exactly 5 times on each sheet (1,686) by 272. This is approximately 8·4 times the standard deviation (32·3). The odds against getting a deviation (in one direction or the other) as great as or greater than this by chance are $3·6 \times 10^{14}$ to 1. We may therefore safely reject the proposition that the results are due to collusion *taking place as frequently as 5 times in each sheet of 50*. It is not clear to me that we can pass from that to rejecting as almost infinitely improbable the proposition that the results are due to collusion *on a much more extensive scale* on the Hansel lines.

Here I must bid a regretful farewell to *Hansel and Gretel*. Those who wish to pursue their adventures further may be recommended to study the papers referred to above, from which I have been endeavouring to abstract.

SECTION B

Veridical and *Prima Facie* Paranormal Cases of Hallucinatory *Quasi*-Perception

> *Me patris Anchisae, quotiens humentibus umbris*
> *nox operit terras, quotiens astra ignea surgunt,*
> *admonet in somnis et turbida terret imago . . .*
>
> *Nunc etiam interpres divum, Iove missus ab ipso,*
> *(Testor utrumque caput) celeres mandata per auras*
> *detulit. Ipse deum manifesto in lumine vidi*
> *intrantem muros, vocemque his auribus hausi . .*
>
> VIRGIL, *Aeneid*, Bk. IV, ll. 351 *et seq.*

IV

THE S.P.R.'S 'CENSUS OF HALLUCINATIONS'

IN Section A I have described and discussed some outstanding examples of experimental work in psychical research. In view of the statistical treatment of the findings of these experiments in guessing, such investigations are often described as 'quantitative'. They would be more accurately described as 'quotitative'. Quantitative work, in the usual sense of that phrase, is concerned with measurable variables and their correlation with each other. It seeks to discover and formulate laws of co-variation between the determinate values of correlated determinable magnitudes. Psychical research, so far as I am aware, has nowhere reached the level of quantitative experimental work in that sense.

In the present section I shall be concerned with a branch of psychical research which is observational rather than experimental. It is concerned with the reports of certain kinds of sporadic cases. They fall into various groups, indicated by such names as 'phantasms of the living', 'phantasms of the dead', 'out-of-the-body experiences', etc. These groups overlap and merge into each other to some degree. They have the following feature common and peculiar to them. Someone reports having had a *quasi*-perceptual experience, e.g. a dream or waking vision, of an outstanding kind. It is claimed that the content of this corresponds in its details with certain outstanding circumstances concerning a certain individual, alive or dead, to a degree which it is unreasonable to ascribe to chance-coincidence and impossible to account for plausibly by any explanation that falls within the field marked out by the accepted basic limiting principles.

It will be convenient to begin with cases which do not *prima facie* raise any question of *post mortem* existence and activity. The transition to these sporadic cases from the quotitative work which we have been discussing may conveniently be made by way of the S.P.R.'s

99

'Census of Hallucinations', since that involved a good deal of statistical reasoning of a simple and non-technical kind.

In 1886 Gurney, Myers, and Podmore published their classical collection of sporadic cases, *not* apparently involving posthumous activity, under the title *Phantasms of the Living*. The researches on which that book is based were followed up, extended, and confirmed by a committee of the S.P.R., consisting of Professor Henry Sidgwick, Mrs Sidgwick, F. W. H. Myers, his brother Dr A. T. Myers, Frank Podmore, and Miss Alice Johnson. They collected their evidence between the spring of 1889 and that of 1892. (Gurney, who would certainly have played a leading part in this work, had died suddenly, at the height of his powers, about half-way through 1888.) In 1894 this committee issued a masterly report, written mainly by Mrs Sidgwick and Miss Alice Johnson, in close consultation with Sidgwick. It is entitled *Report of the Census of Hallucinations*, and it occupies 400 pages of Vol. X of the S.P.R. *Proceedings*.

Before proceeding to consider the findings of this Report, I will say a word about the qualifications of the two ladies who wrote it. It is needless for me to dilate here on the personality and the achievements of Henry Sidgwick, one of the most acute and balanced critical thinkers of his day. Any reader, to whom these matters are not already well known, may be referred to two essays of mine, viz. 'Henry Sidgwick' in my book *Ethics and the History of Philosophy* (pp. 49–69), and 'Henry Sidgwick and Psychical Research' in my *Religion, Philosophy, and Psychical Research* (pp. 86–115).

Mrs Sidgwick (b. 1845, d. 1936) was the eldest of that remarkable family of three daughters and five sons, born to James Maitland Balfour of Whittingehame and Lady Blanche Cecil, daughter of the second Marquess of Salisbury and sister to the third Marquess, who was thrice prime minister. Among her brothers were Francis Maitland Balfour, a biologist of outstanding originality, who was killed in a mountain-climbing accident as a comparatively young man; Arthur Balfour, statesman and philosopher, who held the offices of prime minister and of foreign secretary; and Gerald Balfour, classical scholar, philosopher, and psychical researcher, who succeeded Arthur as second Earl of Balfour. Eleanor Mildred Balfour (for that was Mrs Sidgwick's maiden name) had a special interest in, and aptitude for, mathematics. One of her sisters was married to the third Baron Rayleigh, one of the most distinguished mathematical physicists of the nineteenth century. While Lord Rayleigh was Cavendish Professor of Experimental Physics at Cambridge, Eleanor Mildred Balfour collaborated with him in his classical researches on the silver voltameter and the Latimer Clark cell, which definitely established the electrical units of resistance, of current, and of electromotive force. They published three papers jointly in the *Philosophical Transactions* of the Royal Society. In 1892 Mrs Sidgwick became Principal of Newnham College on the death of the first holder of that office, Miss Clough. She had been Vice-Principal from 1880 to 1882, and was Treasurer from 1876 to 1919. She played a most important part in the administration of the S.P.R., from its foundation to the end of her long life. She took an active part in many important pieces of research, and contributed a number of articles and reviews to the *Proceedings* and the *Journal*. All these are models of calm critical thinking and clear exposition. I did not meet her until she was an old lady, and I never had the privilege of knowing her personally, but I could not but be immensely impressed with her. I have no hesitation in expressing the opinion, for what it may be worth, that there was no abler *woman*, and few if any abler *persons*, in the England of her time, than Mrs Sidgwick.

Miss Alice Johnson (who was not related to Miss G. M. Johnson, the percipient in Tyrrell's experiments) was born in 1860 and died in 1940. She entered Newnham College as a student in 1878. She was a member of a well known and greatly beloved and respected Cambridge family. One of her brothers was the eminent philosopher and logician, W. E. Johnson, Fellow of King's College, Cambridge. Miss Johnson studied natural science, and was placed in the equivalent of the First Class in the Natural Sciences Tripos in 1881. (At that time, and for long afterwards, women at Cambridge were not admitted to take degrees.) She was appointed Demonstrator in Animal Morphology at the Balfour Laboratory in 1884, and held that office until 1890. In the latter year she became private secretary to Mrs Sidgwick. She became Organizing Secretary to the S.P.R. in 1903, and held the post of Research Officer from 1908 to 1916. She had been trained for her work by Mrs Sidgwick, was brought up in the extremely high standards of intellectual and moral integrity so characteristic of the Sidgwicks, and was herself distinguished for the meticulous care and the critical acumen with which she collected and appraised evidence. She contributed important papers to the S.P.R. *Proceedings*, particularly in reference to 'cross-correspondences', a phenomenon which she was the first to detect and to lay stress upon.

I have now said enough about the writers of the Report to show that they can hardly be classified as 'softies'. The Report must, of course, in the end be judged on the merits or defects of its arguments, and not on the authority of those who set them forth. But a reference to the qualifications of the writers is in place as a warning against lighthearted *general* criticism without careful attention to *specific* details. It really is not very likely that the kind of objections which would arise in the mind of any assistant in a psychological laboratory while shaving would have escaped the notice of Sidgwick, of Mrs Sidgwick, and of Miss Alice Johnson. Those who indulge in that kind of criticism of the Report will almost certainly find themselves in the embarrassing company of those who undertake to teach their grandmothers to suck eggs. The Report is not light reading, and I can give only a rough summary of the argument, leaving out most of the refinements, which are of course an essential part of it. But I hope to be able to persuade the reader that it deserves very careful study, even after a lapse of more than sixty-five years.

The first and fundamental task of the committee was not directly concerned with paranormal experiences as such. It was to find out how frequently those experiences which we may call 'waking hallucinations' happen among persons who are commonly regarded as sane and normal members of the population of this country. For that purpose they conducted a census, in which people were asked to answer 'Yes' or 'No' to the following question: 'Have you ever, when believing yourself to be completely awake, had a vivid impression of seeing or being touched by a living being or an inanimate object or of hearing a voice; which impression, so far as you could discover, was not due to any external physical cause?'

It will be noted that the question was framed so as to exclude *dreams*, and all *sounds other than voices*. The census was made by 410 collectors, and answers were received from about 17,000 persons. The crude result was 2,272 affirmative and 14,278 negative answers. On further discussion a certain number of the affirmative answers had to be transferred to the negative group. The corrected result was 1,684 affirmatives, i.e. 9·9 per cent of those who returned an answer, positive or negative.

If the group investigated was a fair sample of the population, we may say about one English citizen in ten, living in the late eighties and early nineties of last century, could ostensibly remember having had at least one waking hallucination of the kind in question in the course of his or her life. Now some of the persons who answered 'Yes' ostensibly remembered having had more than one such experience, and a few ostensibly remembered having had a good many. So the total number of waking hallucinations which the members of the group ostensibly remembered having was considerably greater than the number of affirmative answers. How far does it enable us to form a satisfactory estimate of the frequency with which such experiences *actually happened* among the persons questioned?

The committee discussed very elaborately causes which would be likely to make the frequency of ostensibly remembered waking hallucinations a misleading guide, if not corrected. They came to the conclusion that much the most important factor is a tendency to *forget*

102

such an experience, if no striking external event, such as a death or an accident, happens to correspond to it. We may take as typical their discussion, from this point of view, of the particular class of *visual* waking hallucinations.

Of these 1,112 were ostensibly remembered and reported. Of them 87 were said to have happened in the last year, 57 in the last but one, 47 in the last but two, and so on. The numbers reported for eight, nine, or ten years back were each less than half the number reported for the last year. Moreover, of the 87 reported for the last year, 50 per cent referred to the latest quarter in it, 22 per cent to the latest month, and 14 per cent to the latest fortnight. Assuming, as seems reasonable, that in fact about as many such experiences would occur in any one year as in any other, and in any one period as in any other equal period in the same year, it appears from these figures that there is a strong tendency to forget them fairly quickly, unless there be some special circumstance connected with them which impresses them on the memory. How are we to allow for this?

We must remember that we are concerned, in this whole census, only with fairly impressive *waking* hallucinations; and that, in the part of it which we are now discussing, we are concerned only with waking *visual* hallucinations. These are certainly more impressive and startling than most others. It seems not unreasonable to suppose that a person who had had such an experience would on the average remember for at least a month that he had done so. Now the number of such experiences reported as having happened within a month from the date of the question was 19. If we assume that no such experiences have been forgotten in so short a time, and that they occur with about equal frequency in every month among a large group of people, we can estimate the annual frequency of waking visual hallucinations among the group of persons who answered the original enquiry as about 12×19, i.e. 228.

Now the average age of the group was 40 years, and the total number of waking visual hallucinations reported by them was 1,112. But of these about 90 were reported as having happened before the age of 10. The committee rightly held that these should be regarded with suspicion. They decided to discard them altogether, and to consider only the remaining 1,022 which were reported to have happened in the mean period of 30 years between the age of 10 and the mean age of 40. If such experiences had occurred throughout that period at the estimated rate, viz. 228 *per annum*, and if they had all been remembered by those who had had them at the time when the question was put, the estimated total number would have been 228×30, i.e. 6,840. The actual number reported was, as we have seen, 1,022, after discarding those alleged to have been experienced before the age of

103

10. So the committee concluded that the number of waking visual hallucinations reported as ostensibly remembered should probably be multiplied by about 6·5 to reach a satisfactory estimate of the number which actually happened.

The committee went rather elaborately into the details of the 42 cases reported as occurring in the latest quarter, the 19 reported as occurring in the latest month, and the 12 reported as occurring in the latest fortnight. They came to the conclusion that 140, rather than 228, is probably the best estimate of the annual number of genuine and unmistakable waking visual hallucinations in a group of 17,000 persons over 10 years old and of the average age of 40. That would make the factor, by which the reported number should be multiplied in order to give a fair estimate of the actual number that happened, to be 4 instead of 6·5. The committee concluded that it is fairly safe to put it somewhere between these two limits.

So far the investigation is not directly concerned with the paranormal, but only with the slightly abnormal. It is a psychological-statistical enquiry, and (so far as I know) the only one that has ever been made on anything like so large a scale, into the frequency with which a certain odd, but by no means extravagantly rare, kind of experience occurs among contemporary English citizens. I think it is most desirable that such a census should be repeated at the present day, with the greatly improved techniques which have been developed in recent years, both for getting a representative sample of the population and for working up the crude data statistically.

The following comments strike one *prima facie* as relevant. In considering the answers to a question of this rather peculiar kind, one ought to notice and try to allow for two factors, one of which would tend to swell the number of affirmative answers, and the other to diminish it.

(i) A certain proportion of the affirmative answers might be expected to be plain lies. These might be told with the object of 'pulling the leg' of the enquirer, or in order to minister to the answerer's desire to seem important and interesting, or simply out of a kindly wish to give to the enquirer what one thinks he would like. Of those affirmative answers which are given in good faith, a certain proportion would probably represent ostensible recollections which are *delusive*. Both these kinds of affirmative answer would tend to cause an *over*-estimate of the frequency of waking hallucinations. (ii) On the other hand, a certain proportion of those questioned might be expected to decline to answer, or to answer in the negative, for the following reasons. By confessing to have had a waking hallucination one admits to something which is, or is very commonly thought to be, typical of the mentally unstable or the positively insane. A person who had had such an experience might, for that reason, soon cease to be able to remember it. Or, if he could remember it, he might be unwilling to admit this to others. This factor would tend to cause an *under*-estimate of the frequency of waking hallucinations. I should think that it would be hard to come to any reasonable view as to the relative strength of these two opposite tendencies.

We can now turn to the bearing on psychical research of the results of the census. The question which the committee put to themselves was this. Everyone has heard stories of hallucinatory waking impressions coinciding in time and in detail in a marked way with certain events, such as deaths, accidents, etc., which the hallucinated person had no normal means of knowing about or suspecting at the time. What proportion of such stories are true? And is anything more than chance-coincidence needed to account for the correspondence in the residuum of true stories of this kind? The first question is one that can be answered only by careful enquiry, of the kind which is undertaken by lawyers, magistrates, historians, etc., e.g. consulting diaries, noting the dates of letters, interrogating narrators and witnesses, and so on. The second is one that can be answered only by adequate and relevant statistics. Apart from that factual basis, arguments *pro* and *con* are little better than vague gas, emanating from the desires, emotions, and habitual ways of thinking of those who put them forward.

For the purpose of this enquiry the committee thought it best to confine their attention to *deaths*, because death is a perfectly definite event, which happens once and only once to every individual and is officially ascertained and recorded. We begin, then, by noting their definition of a 'death-coincidence'. This is defined as a case which fulfils the following three conditions. (i) A certain person, A, had a waking hallucination which he *recognized at the time* as an appearance as of a certain other person, B. (ii) Within a period between 12 hours before and 12 hours after this experience of A's, B did *in fact die*. (iii) At the time A did not know of B's death by normal means, and had no normal reason to expect it.

In the census returns there were 80 first-hand reports of death-coincidences, as defined above. The investigators began by discarding all those alleged to have happened when the experient was less than 10 years old, and all those which happened to experients who had had more than one waking hallucination of the appearance of a living person. This procedure was no doubt wise, in order to be on the safe side; but it may well have excluded some quite genuine cases. It reduced the original 80 reported death-coincidences to 65.

Next, the investigators considered whether a disproportionately large number of death-coincidences might not have happened to get reported simply because the collectors might have been looking for that particular kind of answer. It is true that they had all been carefully and explicitly warned beforehand against that kind of biased selection. But most of us are specially interested in death-coincidences, and they tend to be talked about. Is there not a danger that a collector, who happened to know that a certain person had experienced a waking hallucination which was a death-coincidence, would for that reason tend to include him or her in the list of persons to whom he asked the census-questions? If so, the proportion of death-coincidences among the waking hallucinations reported would be unduly raised.

The investigators tried to deal with this difficulty as follows. Of the 65 reported death-coincidences left for consideration, 19 were *certainly known* to be such by the collector *before* he asked the question; 26 were *certainly not known* to be such beforehand; and with regard to the remaining 20 it was *uncertain* whether the collector did or did not know beforehand that they were death-coincidences. Now, of the 19 which were certainly known beforehand to be death-coincidences, there were 3 in which that knowledge *certainly influenced* the collector in putting his question; 5 in which such knowledge *certainly did not* influence him; and 11 in regard to which it is *uncertain* whether it influenced him or not. The 3 cases in the first sub-group must be *rejected* altogether for the present purpose, though they may be quite good cases in themselves. The 5 cases in the second sub-group can be accepted without further objection under the present head, and added to the 26 which were *certainly not* known beforehand to the collector to be death-coincidences. We thus get a nucleus of 31 cases to which this objection certainly does not apply.

Consider now the 20 cases with regard to which it was *uncertain* whether the collector did or did not know beforehand that they were death-coincidences. It is reasonable to estimate that they would *in fact* be divided into 'known beforehand' and 'not-known beforehand' in about the ratio which those *certainly* known beforehand to be death-coincidences bears to those *certainly not* known beforehand to be such. That ratio was 19 : 26. So we may estimate that of these 20 cases nineteen forty-fifths, i.e. about 9, *were* known beforehand to the collector to be death-coincidences, and twenty-six forty-fifths, i.e. about 11, were *not* known beforehand to be such. So we can add the estimated number of 11 not known beforehand to the nucleus of 31 cases in which the present objection does not apply. We thus get an estimated number of 42 cases immune to that objection.

There still remain to be considered the 11 cases, with regard to which it is *certain* that the collector knew beforehand that they were death-coincidences, but where it is *uncertain* whether that knowledge influenced him in putting his question to the individual concerned. To these must be added the 9 cases estimated above to have been known beforehand as death-coincidences. This gives us an estimated total of 20 cases still to be considered from the point of view of the present objection. Now the collectors were explicitly and strongly warned against allowing such knowledge to influence them in choosing the persons to whom they would put their questions. So it would not seem extravagant to suppose that they obeyed these instructions in at least 50 per cent of the cases in which they knew them to be applicable. If so, we can estimate that at least 10 of the residue of 20 cases now under discussion were not subject to the present objection. That would give us in all a conservative estimate of 52 cases (i.e. 42 + 10) of reported death-coincidences which were certainly or almost certainly not affected by unfair selection of the persons questioned, due to previous knowledge by the collector that those persons had had waking hallucinations which were death-coincidences.

Since the above argument is rather complex, I give below a table to illustrate and summarize it:

Death-coincidences Reported (65)

	Rejected	Kept
Certainly not known beforehand		26
Certainly known beforehand (19)		
(i) *Collector certainly uninfluenced*		5
(ii) *Collector certainly influenced*	3	
(iii) *Uncertain whether influenced or not* (11)		
(a) *Collector probably uninfluenced*		5·5
(b) *Collector probably influenced*	5·5	
Uncertain whether known beforehand or not (20)		
(i) *Probably not known*		11
(ii) *Probably known* (9)		
(a) *Collector probably uninfluenced*		4·5
(b) *Collector probably influenced*	4·5	
	13	52

So far we have been considering, and trying to allow for, a certain kind of *systematic* error, which would be liable to swell unfairly the proportion of reported death-coincidences in the returns of a census of waking hallucinations. Apart altogether from this, of course, each individual case in which a death-coincidence is reported must be scrutinized in detail with the utmost care, and the reporter and witnesses must, if possible, be interviewed and cross-examined, in order to see whether the report is trustworthy. When all these corrections had been made, and all these precautions had been taken, the investigators considered that there remained at least 32 undoubtedly genuine death-coincidences out of the 80 originally reported.

Now the total number of reported cases of a waking visual hallucination, in which the appearance of a certain person was ostensibly seen and recognized at the time, was 381. In order to compare this with the number of death-coincidences we must treat it in the same way, i.e. we must eliminate reported hallucinations experienced by persons under 10 years of age, and those experienced by persons who state that they have had several such hallucinations. That reduces the number of reported cases to 322.

We must now correct that figure for lapse of memory. It will be remembered that the investigators decided that the extreme factor by which the number of ostensibly remembered cases must be multiplied, in order to give a probable estimate of the number of actual cases in a population of the size of the census-group, is 6·5. That would give 2,093 as an outside estimate of the number of such hallucinations actually experienced by members of such a group after the age of 10. Now it has been concluded that at least 32 of these were undoubtedly genuine death-coincidences. So it emerges that 32 in 2,093, i.e. about *one in sixty-three*, of the waking hallucinations, in which the experient ostensibly sees a certain person whom he recognizes at the time, is preceded or followed, within a period of 12 hours, by the death of the person ostensibly seen.

Is this ratio of one in sixty-three compatible with the view that death-coincidences, in the sense defined above, are purely fortuitous? Let us compare it with a kind of death-coincidence which presumably would be so. Suppose I were to write on separate slips of paper the names of all the persons whom I could recognize by sight who were alive 12 hours ago. Suppose that I then were to mix up those slips in a hat, and to draw out one at random. Suppose that the person, whose name is written on the slip that I have drawn, should turn out either to have died within the 12 hours up to the time of the drawing or to die within 12 hours after it. Then the coincidence between my drawing his name at that moment, and his dying within the 24 hours of which that moment is the mid-point, is presumably completely fortuitous. The chance of the person, whose name I happen to have drawn then, dying within that period of 24 hours, is in no way different from the chance that *any* Englishman of his age who was alive 12 hours before, will be dead within 24 hours from then. Similarly, if the coincidence between the occurrence of an hallucinatory waking visual experience as of a certain recognized person and that person's death be purely fortuitous, the chance of such a coincidence will be in no way different from the chance of *any* Englishman of his age, who was alive 12 hours before the hallucination occurred, being dead within the 24 hours from then.

Now the annual death-rate for the population of England as a whole, during the period in which the various reported death-co-incidences fell, was about 19 per 1,000. Of course, it would vary greatly for different age-groups within the population. It would, e.g., be very much higher for persons under 1 year old and for persons over 80 years old; and it would be considerably lower, e.g., for those between 30 and 40 years of age. That would have been highly relevant to the statistical argument, if the reported death-coincidences had predominantly concerned the deaths of very old people or of infants. But in fact they did not. So far as could be ascertained, the age-distribution of the persons whose deaths were involved was very similar to the age-distribution in the population as a whole. It would, therefore, seem legitimate to take the general annual death-rate of 19 *per* 1,000 in calculating the frequency with which death-coinci-dences might be expected to occur, if the occurrence of a visual hallucination concerning a recognized person and the concurrence with it of that person's death were completely contingent to each other.

Since the chance of a person, chosen at random from the popula-tion, who was alive at a given date in the period under consideration, being dead within 365 days was 19 in 1,000, it is plain that the chance of his being dead within 24 hours of a given date is 19 in 365,000. That is roughly 1 in 19,000. So, if death-coincidences be purely fortuitous concurrences of two events, it is reasonable to conjecture that about *1 in 19,000* of such hallucinations as we have been con-sidering would be associated within 24 hours with the death of the person to whom the hallucination refers. But, as we have seen, the actual ratio was about *1 in 63*. It will be remembered, moreover, that this latter ratio was reached after severely *scaling down* the num-ber of reported death-coincidences, and generously *boosting up* the number of visual hallucinations concerning persons recognized at the time. For, in estimating the latter, the investigators multiplied the number of such hallucinations reported by the maximum factor of $6\frac{1}{2}$ in allowing for lapse of memory.

I think it is plain from these figures that there very probably is *some* connexion, direct or indirect, normal or paranormal, between the occurrence of a waking hallucination of this particular kind and the occurrence, within a short period around that moment, of the death of the person referred to in the hallucination. That conclu-sion may be reinforced by the following consideration. Let us make, for the sake of argument, the false and fantastic supposition that all the persons referred to in such hallucinations were between 80 and

90 years old. We are thus making things extravagantly easy for any hostile critic. Now the annual death-rate in that age-group was about 335 *per* 1,000. Therefore, even on this fantastic supposition, if death-coincidences be purely fortuitous, one would expect only about 335 of such hallucinations in 365,000 to be death-coincidences. This ratio is about 1 in 1,100, as against the actual ratio of 1 in 63.

Granted, then, that it is reasonable to think that there is *some* kind of causal connexion between the two concurrent events which together constitute a death-coincidence, can we think of any *normal* causal connexion which would account for the facts? Suppose, e.g., that in all the death-coincidences the hallucinated subject already knew that the person referred to was seriously ill, and that he was already feeling great anxiety about that person. Then that state of knowledge and emotion might tend to produce in the subject an hallucination referring to the sick person. And the fact known, viz. that he or she is seriously ill, is a state of affairs tending to bring about that person's death within a short period. That would explain, in normal terms, the relative frequency of death-coincidences among waking hallucinations of the kind in question. It is, therefore, important to examine the cases from the point of view of this possibility.

Of the 62 reported death-coincidences,[1] with which the statistical argument started, there were 19 in which it was positively stated that the fact of illness was *unknown* to the subject at the time when the hallucination happened to him. In 18 further cases, though it was known to the subject that the person in question was ill at the time, the illness was not regarded as serious and *no anxiety was consciously felt*. To these 37 cases we may add two more, in one of which the death was due to suicide, and in the other to an accident at sea. So there are 39 cases out of the 62 to which the proposed normal explanation certainly does not apply. In the remaining 23 cases there *was* either knowledge of serious illness, accompanied sometimes by considerable conscious anxiety, or the subject of the hallucination was emotionally preoccupied in some other way with the person referred to.

In considering whether the proposed kind of normal explanation is adequate to account for these remaining 23 cases, where it is at least a possible cause, it is necessary to bear the following facts in mind. In several of these cases the knowledge that the person was seriously ill, and the feeling of anxiety connected therewith, had existed in the subject *for some considerable time*. On the other hand,

---

[1] i.e. the original 65, less the 3 which were rejected, because the collector certainly knew of the coincidence before putting his question, and was certainly influenced by that knowledge.

no case is counted as a death-coincidence if the occurrence of the relevant hallucination is separated by more than 12 hours (in one direction or the other) from that of the death. In many cases the coincidence in time was much closer than that. Now, in all such cases it seems highly doubtful whether the *long-continued* state of knowledge and consequent anxiety will suffice to account for the occurrence of an hallucinatory appearance of the sick person to the subject just *within a very short period round about the death*. In such cases it seems quite reasonable to suppose that the prolonged state of knowledge and anxiety is a favourable background condition. But it still seems necessary to suppose that some other factor, operative only just about the time of the death, has to co-operate with the persistent state of knowledge and anxiety, in order to evoke the relevant waking hallucination in such close temporal proximity to the death.

It should be added that the purely quotitative argument, which we have been considering above, inevitably fails to make full use of the evidence available. For it leaves out of account those small and significant details, in which, in some of the cases, the content of the hallucination corresponded with the circumstances of the death. Knowledge by A that B is ill, and anxiety for him on that ground, cannot suffice to account for A's having an hallucination, at about the time of B's death, in which A ostensibly sees B as presenting an appearance which A has no reason to suspect, and which corresponds to B's actual state or circumstances at the time of his death.

I have now given in outline the statistical argument which led the committee, who were considering the matter in the late eighties and early nineties of last century, to the conclusion that there are sporadic cases of the paranormal action of one individual on another at the time of the death of one of the two. Anyone who wishes to challenge the argument may legitimately try to do so on either or both of the following grounds. On the one hand, he may try to point out defects in the way in which the data were collected, in the subsequent statistical handling of them, or in the arguments based on the data after such manipulation. On the other hand, he may try to indicate defects in the testimony for some or all of the alleged death-coincidences. Both these kinds of objection might consistently be combined, though few critics could be equally expert in both fields.

As to the first line of criticism, I have already said that it would be idle and impertinent, in view of the very high qualifications of the persons responsible for the Report, to undertake it lightheartedly and without a careful study of the details. I would remark that one line of criticism, which rather naturally suggests itself, is not directly relevant. It is an old and very true observation that an hallucination, which is found to correspond in a marked way with a certain roughly

111

contemporary event or state of affairs of an outstanding kind, tends to be talked about, to be written down, and perhaps to get into print; whilst one which is accompanied by no such known correlate tends not to be mentioned, and still less to be recorded. If, then, one merely collected already recorded instances of waking hallucinations, one might reasonably expect that a considerable proportion of them would be ones which had corresponded in a marked way to some outstanding and roughly contemporary event or state of affairs.

But that is not the situation represented by the census of hallucinations. The collectors were not collecting stories which had *already* been put on record. They were putting a definite question to a supposedly random selection of their contemporaries; and asking each of them, on the basis of his or her present recollection (as stimulated by being asked the question), whether they had or had not ever had a waking experience of a certain specified kind. The doubts that can properly be raised are: (1) May not the group questioned have been selected in some way which gave a bias in favour of a certain kind of answer? (2) May not the answers given have been, for one reason or another, a misleading guide to the actual number of such experiences had by the persons questioned? Now, as is evident from what has been said above, both those questions were explicitly before the minds of the committee, and they tried to deal with them in the ways which have been described. It is for the critic to point out, if he can, either (i) that there are other relevant questions which escaped the notice of the committee, or (ii) that their attempts to deal with the two questions which they did raise are faulty in certain specific ways.

For my part, I think it most desirable that such a census should be repeated at the present time; with all the refinements which recent experience in taking Gallup polls would suggest; and with due regard to the special causes which might lead persons, to whom this very peculiar kind of question is addressed, to lying (whether affirmative or negative), to concealment, to forgetting, or to delusive ostensible recollection. I should hope that, in any such repetition of the census, a much larger fraction of the population would be questioned, and that much more elaborate efforts would be made to ensure that those questioned constituted a fair sample. As to the last point mentioned, I should think it essential that it should not be left in any way to the collectors to decide what persons they should or should not question, but that the group to be questioned should be delimited beforehand on explicit principles which should be prescribed to the collectors.

V

SOME EXAMPLES OF WELL ATTESTED SPORADIC CASES *PRIMA FACIE* PARANORMAL

IN this chapter I shall give some examples of cases of the sort which the authors of the Census of Hallucinations used as the basis of their positive conclusion concerning a non-chance coincidence between (*a*) the occurrence of an hallucination in B concerning A, and (*b*) the occurrence at about the same time of some 'crisis' in A's life, such as accident, serious illness, or death.

Before doing so, I will make some general remarks on the questions which an investigator needs to raise and to try to answer, when he receives a report of such a case.

In considering whether a reported dream or waking *quasi*-perception is or is not an instance of an experience paranormally acquired or influenced, we need to raise the following five questions: (1) What in detail was the *content* of the experience? What precisely did the experient ostensibly see, ostensibly hear, and so on? (2) What in detail was the nature of the *corresponding state of affairs*, i.e. that state of affairs, existing elsewhere at about the time when the experience occurred, which is alleged to correspond so closely to the content of the latter as to make it reasonable to hold that it must have played an essential part in determining the occurrence of that experience in that person at that time? (3) What precisely was the *time-relation* between the two? (4) Were the relevant spatial and other relations at the time such that it would be quite unreasonable to suppose that the correspondence was due to *normal* processes of physical and psychological causation, combined perhaps with abnormal acuteness of the senses, abnormal powers of reviving the traces of information acquired normally, though perhaps unwittingly, in the remote past, abnormal powers of inference or of associative *quasi*-inference, and so on? (5) If so, is it unreasonable to regard the

113

correspondence in content and the approximate simultaneity of occurrence as just one of those strange coincidences which, we all know, do happen from time to time?

Of these five questions the first four are purely factual. As regards the first three of them we can add that they are largely non-technical. We should all agree as to the *kind* of evidence that is relevant, though different people might differ as to whether the evidence available suffices to give a certain answer in a particular case. Moreover, that evidence can be collected and evaluated by any responsible person of practical experience and good sense, though the special experience of a county-court judge or a barrister practising in the ordinary courts would be particularly useful. The fourth question is more technical. In some cases, at any rate, it is a matter where a layman should bow to experts in the physiology of the senses, in certain branches of abnormal psychology, and in certain departments of physics. Nevertheless, there are plenty of cases where there could be no serious difference of opinion between such experts and an intelligent and educated layman.

The fifth question is of a wholly different kind. What one person will find it impossible to believe to be a mere coincidence, another will have no difficulty in regarding as such. Moreover, if all the other conditions are satisfied, we are here faced with this very special alternative: *either* this is a mere coincidence, *or* it involves a breach of this, that, or the other accepted basic limiting principle. Any sensible person will be prepared to stretch the long arm of coincidence much further in such a case than he would elsewhere. And some quite sensible people will prefer to stretch it indefinitely, rather than to admit that a certain basic limiting principle has been broken. At that point there is little further room for rational argument; but the following reflexions may not be out of place:

(1) It would be a mistake to think that one's final attitude towards the results of quotitative experimental work, like Tyrrell's and Dr Soal's, is free from this element of subjectivity. As a result of such an experiment one may be able to say such things as this: 'The odds against getting as least as great a deviation as was actually found, from the number of hits most probable on the hypothesis of chance-coincidence, are, on that hypothesis and on the assumption that the method used for randomization worked satisfactorily, ten million to one.' But there is no rational ground for deciding whether or not to reject the hypothesis of chance-coincidence when the odds reach that (or any other) order of magnitude. Nor does it help much to point out that practically everyone in his senses would reject that hypothesis, even when the odds against it were much lower, in, e.g., such a ques-

tion as whether a die was or was not loaded, whether a pack of cards in an ordinary game was or was not properly shuffled and dealt, and so on. For in psychical research it is a question of choosing between accepting the result as an instance of chance-coincidence and rejecting one or more of the basic limiting principles.

(2) In the sporadic cases the odds against chance-coincidence cannot be stated numerically. One can judge only that, in some cases, they are very great; that they are very much greater in this case than in that; and so on. Nevertheless, the ordinary rules of probability hold. In judging the evidence for paranormal agency or for paranormal cognition, we must not, e.g., confine ourselves to this, that, or the other case, taken *severally*. What we have in the end to consider is the probability that *at least one* (no matter which) of all the numerous well attested sporadic cases really *did* happen as reported, was *not* a chance-coincidence, and *was* an exception to one or more of the basic limiting principles. That probability obviously tends to be greater than the probability, in regard to any particular case, that *it* happened as reported, that *it* was not a chance-coincidence, and that *it* was an exception to one of the basic limiting principles.

It is not unusual to discuss this matter in terms of metaphors, such as the strength of a chain being no greater than that of its weakest link, or the strength of a net being much greater than that of any single strand in it. It is much safer to avoid metaphors and to confront the logic of the situation directly. In regard to any particular reported case there are evidently two questions. (1) Did the events happen exactly as reported? Was nothing added, nothing relevant omitted, and nothing distorted? (2) If so, was it perhaps merely a chance-coincidence? We can be quite sure beforehand that the evidence in no single case will be absolutely watertight, and beyond the reach of all scepticism, however far-fetched. To expect that would be to demand something which is never fulfilled in the case of alleged crimes for which a person is convicted after a fair trial in a court of law, in the case of alleged historical events which competent historians all agree to have happened, and so on. The best that we can hope for is to get as numerous a collection as possible of cases which are as well attested as possible. The size of the collection of such cases plays two parts. (i) With a large and varied collection we may hope to find that, whilst the evidence in some cases is open to *this* objection, the evidence in others is open to *that* objection, and the evidence in every case is open to *some objection or other*, yet there are few if any objections which apply to *all* the cases. (ii) Whilst there is, for every case taken severally, some probability that it may be a chance-coincidence, the probability that every one of a large collection of such cases is a chance-coincidence is evidently much smaller. Moreover, a detailed comparative study of the various cases in such a collection may reveal features common and peculiar to them; or to certain sub-classes of them, which would be unlikely to be present in a collection of mere chance-coincidences.

(3) It would not be reasonable to confine one's background to the totality of well attested *sporadic* cases. One ought surely to include in it also the results of any reliable experiments which seem *prima facie* to conflict with the same basic limiting principles as would have to be rejected if the sporadic cases be not mere chance-coincidences.

Reverting now to the four questions which I have called 'purely factual', I would make this remark. It is useful to imagine an ideal case, a kind of psychical researcher's Christmas dream, and to state briefly what would be its characteristic features. No actual case is likely to fulfil completely all these conditions, though a few come fairly near to doing so. But any actual case can be compared with the ideal one, and we can then judge in what respects and to what extent it falls short.

The following would seem to be the main desiderata. (i) The experient should have written down a reasonably full account of the content of his experience, as he ostensibly remembers it, as soon as possible after having had it, and he should give the date and time and should sign his statement. (ii) He should have shown this as soon as possible to one or more responsible persons. These should have read it carefully, and then have attested independently that they had done so, and have given the date and time at which it was first presented to them. (iii) All this should have happened *before* the experient, or anyone with whom he could have conversed on the subject, had had any opportunity to acquire by normal means information about the corresponding remote state of affairs. (iv) There should be clear, certain, and independent evidence as to the occurrence, the date and time, and the details of that remote state of affairs. (This is generally fairly easy to acquire, if the event should be a death or a sudden accident or illness, happening in peacetime in a civilized country, and requiring medical certification or at least medical attention.) (v) The corresponding state of affairs should be one which the experient had no normal cause whatever to anticipate at the time when he had his experience.

In the cases which we are about to consider, A's experience nearly always refers to a certain other individual, B, who is already known to A, and to whom A at the time takes the experience as referring. I propose to call this other individual, B, the 'referent to' A's experience.

That is intended to be a quite neutral term. It would be unwise to call B the 'agent', unless one had a great deal of further information of a particular kind. For, even if it should be held that A's experience was correlated in content with B's more or less simultaneous state and situation, to a degree far beyond chance-coincidence, it would not follow that B was the only or the main agent in evoking A's experience. The important causal factor might, e.g., have been C's awareness of B's state and situation.

Now the referent in many of these experiences was certainly alive at the time when the experience happened, in others of them he had certainly been dead for some considerable time, and in a great many he had died shortly before or shortly after the occurrence of the experience. If A has an hallucinatory experience as of perceiving B, we may describe A's hallucinatory *quasi*-percept as a 'phantasm of B'. If B was certainly alive at the time, this would count as a 'phantasm of the *living*'; if B had been dead for a day or more, it would count as a 'phantasm of the *dead*'. Obviously there are marginal cases. The authors of *Phantasms of the Living* thought it desirable to extend that phrase to include cases in which A's experience takes place *within a few hours after* B's death. This is because there is some evidence that a telepathically initiated stimulus may not give rise to a conscious experience until some time after the event which initiated it. It is therefore possible that A's *quasi*-perception of a phantasm of B may be due to telepathic influence originating at or shortly before the moment of B's death, although its effects in A's consciousness did not emerge until some hours after that moment. Of course, no hard-and-fast line can be drawn, but in practice they did not count any hallucination as a phantasm of the dead unless the referent has been dead for at least 24 hours before the experience begins. I shall now consider in turn some examples of phantasms of the living, some marginal cases, and some examples of phantasms of the dead.

PHANTASMS OF THE LIVING

I will begin with the following general remark. A phantasm of the living is *prima facie* veridical, if A's experience happens at roughly the same time as a certain highly unusual event in B's life, e.g. accident, sudden illness, or death; if the detailed content of the experience corresponds in a high degree, either by literal resemblance or by perfectly obvious and unmistakable symbolization, with the detailed character of B's contemporary state and situation; and if we can rule out normal information, expectation, and inference (conscious or unconscious) on A's part concerning B's state and situation.

We may now detail some particular cases. They are all taken from an admirably critical paper by Mrs Sidgwick, entitled 'Phantasms of the Living', which occupies 407 pages in Vol. XXXIII of the S.P.R. *Proceedings*. This appeared in October 1922. It covers all cases reported to, and investigated by, the S.P.R. from June 1886 to the end of 1920. It excludes 54 cases, which were already available to the general reader through previous publication in books or in articles in the *Proceedings*. Mrs Sidgwick further excluded all cases in which more than five years had elapsed between the alleged experience and the first record of it, and a few cases where the evidence seemed too defective to be worth discussing. The exclusion of the 54 already published cases somewhat lowers the average value of the collection, since they were naturally selected for publication because of their special interest and evidential strength. Nevertheless, the 200 or so cases which are dealt with in the paper are a fair field from which to choose examples. It should be understood that, whenever I refer in the sequel to letters or written statements, they have been either written to, or put in the hands of, the persons investigating the case on behalf of the S.P.R. In giving references I shall mention the relevant pages in Mrs Sidgwick's paper.

(1) *Mr Powles and Mr Sharpe* (pp. 50 *et seq.*). The first case is a very trivial and unexciting one. It was related by Mr L. C. Powles, a member of the S.P.R.

On the afternoon of August 4th, 1913, Mr Powles, of Highlands, Rye, Sussex, went by invitation to tea at the house of a Miss B., a friend of the family living a few miles away, to meet Mr James W. Sharpe (Fellow of Gonville and Caius College, Cambridge), who was then on a visit there. Mrs Powles had been unwell, and so stayed at home and rested. At tea at Miss B.'s conversation turned on 'psychical' subjects, and Mr Powles asked Mr Sharpe whether he claimed to see 'auras' round people, and, if so, to report on Mr Powles' 'aura'. At first Mr Sharpe could see nothing, but after a while he claimed to see two things behind Mr Powles. One of them he described as 'a dark . . . half-human creature with knotted arms placed on [Mr Powles'] shoulder'. He described the other as 'a faint slight figure of a young woman with an oval face. . . .' Mr Sharpe considered that the animal figure symbolized 'illness near at hand . . .', and that the human figure 'tried to avert illness'.

Mr Powles got back to his house at about 6 p.m. His wife at once told him that she had been very anxious at his being out in the extremely cold wind then prevailing. (He had only lately recovered from pneumonia.) She told him also that she had been obsessed by a horrid story which she had been reading that afternoon, about a

118

man dressed up as a *gorilla*, who comes up *behind* the master of the house and *strangles him with his hands.*

Mr Powles claims to have made *on the same evening* a verbatim note of the words used by Mr Sharpe in describing his vision. He certainly did write *next day* (August 5th, 1913) to Miss B. a letter regarding Mr Sharpe's vision of the day before. For Miss B. happened to have kept that letter, and she submitted it to the S.P.R. It agrees in all essentials with the above statement, which was not written to the S.P.R. until July 2nd, 1916, i.e. about 3 years after the alleged events. It agrees also with a statement which Mrs Powles wrote, and sent to the S.P.R. on July 2nd, 1916, along with her husband's letter of the same date. She claimed to remember clearly her husband going to tea with Miss B. on August 4th, 1913. While he was away she had read, in the *Strand Magazine*, a very horrid story of a man disguised as a gorilla. She had had from childhood a horror of gorillas, and the story upset her very much, and she was longing for Mr Powles to return. Immediately he did so, she had told him of the story and of the state of nervousness into which it had thrown her. He had then told her something of Mr Sharpe's vision; but, lest he should frighten her, he had omitted certain details, and, in particular, the fact that Mr Sharpe had regarded it as foreboding an approaching illness.

Moreover, Miss B., in answer to a letter of enquiry in July 1916 from Mr Powles, wrote, stating that she clearly remembered Mr Sharpe saying that he saw a non-human creature standing behind Mr Powles, with knotted hands on the latter's shoulders; and that Mr Sharpe had also claimed to see a young oval-faced woman, trying to avert the monster's evil intentions.

The suggestion, then, is that Mrs Powles' reading of the story, and the state of fear into which it had thrown her that afternoon, were essential factors in determining the content of the vision, had at about the same time by the distant Mr Sharpe, in presence of and in reference to her husband. It should be added that Mr Sharpe's interpretation of the vision, as betokening illness or other trouble awaiting Mr Powles, had remained completely unfulfilled up to the date when the report was sent to the S.P.R. But it may not be irrelevant to recall, in this connexion, that Mr Powles had been seriously ill, and that his wife was anxious at the time lest his going out in the cold wind then prevailing should lead to a recurrence of his illness.

(2) *Mrs H. and the accident to the goods-train* (pp. 45 *et seq.*). This case was investigated by Rev. A. H. E. Lee of Leeds, and reported by him to the S.P.R., of which he was an associate member.

Mrs H. of Leeds, wife of a goods-inspector on the old London and North-Western Railway, went to bed on the night of April 16th,

1902, feeling depressed on account of the illness from which her child was then suffering and of her husband's absence from home on duty at the time. As was her wont, she put a glass of water on the table, in case the child should ask for a drink during the night. Mr H. was on night-duty on the line. The gas was left burning low, and, because of the child's illness, there was a bright fire in the grate throughout the night. So the room was illuminated, though somewhat feebly.

Mrs H. awoke with a start at about 3 a.m., feeling thirsty, and she reached out for the glass of water. When about to drink she was surprised to see, in the glass, a moving picture as of goods-wagons with a guard's van in the rear. As she looked, they seemed to smash into each other, and she noted that the van was the most damaged. She lifted the clock off the mantelpiece, noted the time, and put it on the table. She naturally thought of her husband, and wondered if he were safe. At about 9 a.m. on the morning of April 17th Mr H. returned safe and well. She at once informed him of her vision, and he thereupon told her that he had passed the scene of such an accident and that the guard of that train was seriously injured. (All this information is taken from a letter written by Mrs H. on May 26th, 1902, i.e. about 6 weeks later, and from a supplementary letter of June 30th, written in answer to certain specific questions.)

Along with Mrs H.'s first letter came one of the same date from Mr H. The gist of this, supplemented by a second letter of August 13th in answer to certain specific questions, is as follows. The accident happened at about 10 p.m. on April 16th to an express goods-train from Leeds to London, near Staley and Millbank station. Mr H. was travelling that night in a goods-train to Manchester. He passed the scene of the accident twice. The first time was at 3.10 a.m. on the 17th. He then saw the breakdown gang working on the line, with great fires burning and numerous lanterns, but could not distinguish any details. The second occasion was at 7.50 a.m. He then saw the brake-van and one or two wagons which had been in collision. On his reaching home, his wife had told him at once of the vision she had seen in the glass of water.

It would appear that Mrs H.'s experience must have been practically contemporary with Mr H.'s first, and rather sketchy, view of the scene of the accident. But it seems to have embodied certain details which corresponded with what Mr H. first saw clearly only on the *second* occasion, i.e. some five hours *after* Mrs H.'s experience was over. Possibly these details were due to the associations which would be naturally aroused in the wife of a railway-guard on being apprised paranormally, while her husband was away on duty, of an accident to a goods-train.

(3) *Prince Victor Duleep Singh and his father's death* (pp. 203 *et seq.*). On November 8th, 1894, the experient, Prince Victor Duleep Singh, wrote a letter describing an experience which he claimed to have had on October 21st, 1893, i.e. a little more than 12 months earlier. At the same time Lord Carnarvon wrote to confirm that Prince Victor had told him of his experience on the morning of October 22nd, 1893.

Prince Victor's account runs as follows. On October 21st, 1893, he was staying in Berlin in company with Lord Carnarvon, and the two went to a theatre in the evening. They returned before midnight to their hotel, and Prince Victor went to bed. As was his custom, he left the light on in his bedroom. As he lay in bed, still awake, he found himself looking at an oleograph which hung on the wall opposite to the head of his bed. He saw distinctly the face of his father, the Maharajah Duleep Singh, as it were framed in the picture-frame. He describes it as *not* like a portrait, but like the real head about filling the frame. He continued looking, and his father appeared to return his gaze with an intent expression. He was not at all alarmed, but was so puzzled that he got out of bed to see what the actual picture might be. It was a commonplace oleograph of a girl leaning out of a balcony holding a rose, with an arch forming the background. The girl's face was quite small, whilst the appearance of his father's head had been of life-size.

Next morning Prince Victor related the incident to Lord Carnarvon. That evening, on his returning late to the hotel, Lord Carnarvon handed two telegrams to him. They announced the death of the Maharajah. He had had an apoplectic stroke at about 9 p.m. on the 21st, had never recovered consciousness, and had died early in the afternoon of the 22nd. Prince Victor had known for some years past that his father was in poor health, but neither he nor Lord Carnarvon had any special cause for anxiety about him at the time, nor had he had any such experience before. Lord Carnarvon, in his letter, confirms that the telegram, notifying the illness and death of the Maharajah, arrived at about midnight on October 22nd, 1893, and that neither of them had any previous notification of those facts.

If Prince Victor's experience happened at about midnight of October 21st in Berlin, that would correspond to about 4.30 a.m. on October 22nd, in Central India, i.e. about $7\frac{1}{2}$ hours after the Maharajah had had his stroke and about $9\frac{1}{2}$ hours before he died.

(4) *Mrs Leir-Carlton and the death of Mrs Hoptroff* (pp. 131 *et seq.*). Mrs Leir-Carlton, of Graywell Hall, Winchfield, Hants, had a maid Matilda Hoptroff, whose mother, Mrs Hoptroff, underwent an operation on August 20th, 1898, in the Victoria Hospital, Bournemouth.

121

Matilda remained there with her mother until August 23rd. Mrs Hoptroff was then considered to be progressing satisfactorily, and she insisted on her daughter going back to her duties at Graywell Hall.

On August 26th, at about 9 a.m., Mrs Leir-Carlton was sitting at her dressing-table, brushing her hair and playing with her cat. Suddenly (as she puts it) she 'became aware of this assertion: "Mrs Hoptroff will pass to-day." ' Mrs Leir-Carlton says that there was no *sound*, but those five words were clearly and forcibly impressed on her mind. She also remarks that the word 'pass' is not one that she herself would normally use in reference to death. She was so much impressed that she sprang to her feet and wrote down the sentence on a bit of paper, dated it, and put it away.

Shortly afterwards two older servants, Mrs Tilley and Mrs Bolton, entered the room in the ordinary course of their duties, and Mrs Leir-Carlton asked them: 'What news of Mrs Hoptroff?' They answered that she was much better, that the sickness had left her, and that the doctor had ordered fish for her dinner. Mrs Leir-Carlton did not mention her experience to them, but merely said: '. . . I did not expect such good news . . . I had a feeling that she might die after all, and perhaps to-day.'

On the same evening (August 26th) shortly after 8 p.m., while at dinner, Mrs Leir-Carlton was handed a telegram, which Matilda Hoptroff had just received from the hospital at Bournemouth. It announced a 'change for the worse' in Mrs Hoptroff's condition. Mrs Leir-Carlton thereupon mentioned her experience to those present, and sent her son to fetch the memorandum which she had made that morning. He did so, and it was read to all present. On August 28th it was learnt that Mrs Hoptroff had in fact died on the evening of the 26th.

The above account was written by Mrs Leir-Carlton to the S.P.R. at some date before May 1899, and therefore not more than 8 months after the events reported. Her son sent a signed statement, dated August 28th, 1898, confirming the assertion that he had fetched his mother's memorandum during dinner on August 26th. Several of the guests present at the dinner also sent signed statements to the same effect. Finally, it should be mentioned that Mrs Tilley, one of the two older servants to whom Mrs Leir-Carlton spoke shortly after the experience, repeated her mistress's remark to Lucy Day, the housemaid, a few minutes later. Lucy embodied what she had been told by Mrs Tilley in a letter, which was signed by herself, and testified as correct by the signatures of Mrs Tilley and of Mrs Bolton (the other older servant who had been present). This letter confirms Mrs Leir-Carlton's account of what she had said on that occasion.

(5) *Mr Rider Haggard and the dog Bob* (pp. 219 *et seq.*). The novelist, Rider Haggard, settled down in later life as a country gentleman in Norfolk. On July 16th, 1904, he wrote a letter to *The Times*, which was published, with various annexed confirmatory documents submitted by him, in the issue of July 21st, 1904. The essential points are as follows:

Mr Haggard went to bed at about 12.30 on the night of July 9th, 1904. He had a nightmare, from which he was awakened by his wife calling from her bed at the other side of the room. Mrs Haggard confirms and amplifies this in a letter of July 15th. She states that she had been awakened during the night of July 9th by most distressing sounds proceeding from her husband. She describes these as 'resembling the moans of an animal—no distinct words'. After listening for a few moments, she awakened him.

To return to Rider Haggard's own account; he says that the nightmare itself, which he remembered as being long and varied, quickly faded. All that he could recollect was a sense of awful oppression and of desperate and terrified struggling for life. But, between the time when he heard his wife's voice and the time when he responded to it, he had another dream-like experience, which he could quite clearly recollect. In this he dreamed that Bob, a black retriever dog belonging to his eldest daughter, was lying on its side among rough undergrowth beside water. He felt as if he himself were in some way issuing from the dog's body, so that his hand was against its head, which was lifted up at an unnatural angle. The dog seemed to be trying to speak to him, and, failing in that, to convey in some non-verbal way that it was dying. At that point the vision ceased, and Mr Haggard definitely awoke to normal consciousness, hearing his wife asking why he was making such fearful noises. He states, and Mrs Haggard confirms, that he then told her that he had had a nightmare, in which he had been in some fearful struggle connected with Bob, and that Bob had been trying to talk and to explain that he needed help. It was still quite dark at the time. Mrs Haggard reckoned that it would have been about 2 a.m. on July 10th.

At breakfast on July 10th both Mr and Mrs Haggard repeated the story. This is confirmed by their daughter Angela, in a letter dated July 14th. She states that they all laughed at the story at the time. She had herself seen Bob at 8 p.m. on July 9th, and they had no reason to believe that anything was amiss with him. Further confirmation is provided in letters, dated respectively July 14th and 15th, from a relative, Miss Hildyard, and from Mr Haggard's secretary, both of whom had been present at breakfast on the 10th.

It was not until the evening of July 10th that Mr Haggard learned, from a young daughter who was wont to feed Bob, that the dog was missing. And it was not until the morning of July 14th that Mr Haggard and his groom, Charles Bedingfield, found Bob's body floating in the river Waveney against a weir at Falcon Bridge, Bungay. This is confirmed in a statement signed by Bedingfield and dated July 14th.

Mr Haggard then had the remains examined by a veterinary surgeon, Mr Mullane. The latter reported, in a letter of July 14th, that the body was in a very decomposed state, blown out with gas. The skull had been fractured in three places and smashed almost to pulp. He concluded that the body must have been in the water over three days, and that the dog was probably killed on the night of July 9th. Since both fore-legs were fractured below the knee, Mr Mullane suggested that Bob might have caught his foot in a large trap, probably an otter-trap; that he had then gone down to the river to drink, dragging the trap with him; and that some person had afterwards found the body and thrown it into the river.

That theory, however, proved to be mistaken. On July 15th Mr Haggard went in to Bungay, with the intention of offering a reward for the discovery of the persons whom he assumed to have killed the dog. On his way thither he was hailed by two platelayers, George Arterton and Harry Alger. They informed him that the dog had been killed by a train; took him on a trolley down to an open-work bridge on the line between Ditchingham and Bungay; and there showed him the evidences of the accident and death.

Alger gave a verbal account, which was written down and then signed by him as correct. He states that he was on duty on the line between Bungay and Ditchingham at 7 a.m. on July 11th. He had found the broken collar of a dog lying there, and had had to scrape off dried blood and some bits of flesh from the line. From the way in which the flesh had been carried he concluded that the dog must have been stricken by a train going towards Bungay. There were marks of blood on the piles of the bridge, where the dog had fallen from it into the reeds, which grow there in deepish water. Alger had looked, but had not seen the body in the river. It was first seen in the water by his mate Arterton, on the afternoon of July 11th, after it had risen to the surface.

Mr Haggard identified the collar as Bob's, and he himself found on the line portions of the black hair of a dog. It seems certain that Bob was killed on *July 9th* by an excursion-train which left Ditchingham at *10.25 p.m.* in the direction of Bungay. The following day was a Sunday, and there were no Sunday trains on that line. At the time when Alger found the traces of the accident, in the early morning of Monday, July 11th, one train had passed, viz. at 6.30 a.m. But its driver did not report having run over a dog; and two men, who had been working near the bridge, denied, when questioned by Alger, that they had seen or heard any dog there. Moreover, the state of the body, when found, presupposed a longer period since death. It therefore seems pretty certain that it was at some time after 10.25 p.m. on the night of *July 9th* that Bob was stricken and fatally injured on the line; that his body, dead or moribund, fell from the bridge among the reeds in the river; and that it later on rose to the surface and floated down to the weir, where Mr Haggard and his groom found it on the morning of July 14th. Thus, the accident and the death happened a few hours *before* Mr Haggard had his nightmare and his subsequent dream-like experience as of being in and rising from Bob's body and receiving a message from the dying animal. This is one of the most curious, and also one of the best documented, of the reported sporadic cases.

(6) *Miss Patterson and her brother's stroke and death* (pp. 243 *et seq.*). The following case was first reported to the S.P.R. by Sir George Beilby, who investigated it and collected the testimony. In June 1915 Miss Mary M. Patterson, of Sale in Cheshire, related orally to Sir George an experience which she claimed to have had on April 4th, 1913. On October 4th, 1916, she wrote out an account of it, in response to a request by him. The gist of this is as follows:

On the evening of April 4th, 1913, Miss Patterson had been attending a committee meeting in support of the candidature of Rev. Joseph Johnson in the election to the Knutsford Board of Guardians, which was to take place next day. (The date of the election, and therefore of this meeting, is confirmed in a letter of October 28th, 1916, from Mr Johnson to Miss Patterson, in answer to a question from her on that point.) After an animated session, and thinking only of what had been happening at the meeting, she left before the end, and went out alone into School Road, Sale, which was at the time brightly lighted and full of people. After walking a few paces, she was startled to see, as in a cinema-show, the following scene, as it were staged in the air before her. There was a clear-cut picture of her brother in Australia, lying with all the appearance of a man who had just fallen dead or in a swoon. She noted his clothes and his thick curling hair. She felt that something awful must have happened to her brother, and she began to pray for him. The picture faded, and she turned from the brightly lighted and crowded School Road into the quiet and dimly lighted Washway Road. When she was half-way along it the picture again appeared to her, this time against the dark background of the sky. As before, it soon faded away. The time was between 8 and 9.30 p.m.

Miss Patterson's sister, Mrs Emily Francis, was living in the same house with her. She had not been very well, and was in bed at the time. On reaching home, Mary ran up to Emily's room, told the whole story to her, and said that she was sure that something dreadful had happened to their brother Edgar. Emily tried to comfort and reassure her, but she remained uneasy. On April 7th they were relieved at receiving a cheerful letter from Edgar, written from Hobart, where he had been staying with some cousins. The letter was dated March 4th. But on April 10th Emily received an official letter from the firm of Messrs Huie and Ramage, chartered accountants in Edinburgh, enclosing a cablegram which they had received from Melbourne, announcing the sudden death of Edgar Patterson on *April 7th.*

Details of his last illness and death were supplied later in letters from his widow to the Patterson sisters. From these three letters, dated April 15th, May 14th, and June 24th, 1913, the following facts emerge. Edgar was taken ill quite suddenly on board ship, when on his way to Melbourne, some time between 10 and 11 a.m. (Victoria local time) on Friday, April 4th, 1913. (This corresponds to between midnight on April 3rd and 1 a.m. on April 4th G.M.T.) He was fully dressed at the time of his seizure. On the arrival of the ship at Melbourne on April 5th, he was taken, still unconscious, to hospital, and died there on April 7th. It would appear, then, that Miss Patterson's two visions happened about 20 hours after her brother's stroke, and during the period of unconsciousness which lasted until his death. (One may compare this with the Duleep Singh case, where the son's vision happened whilst the father lay in a state of unconsciousness which ended in death.)

(7) *Mr and Miss Lawson's dream of Mr Stephen's illness* (pp. 268 *et seq.*). This case was sent to the S.P.R. by Mr Tyrrell, the experimenter and agent with Miss G. M. Johnson, and afterwards President of the Society. The names 'Lawson' and 'Stephen' are pseudonyms. Mr Tyrrell was personally acquainted with the father and daughter who were the experients in the case.

In a letter of November 21st, 1916, to the S.P.R., Mr Tyrrell enclosed a written statement which he had received from Mr Lawson. The latter was unfortunately unable to remember the date on which he had written it. The essential points in this statement were as follows:

Mr Lawson and his daughter were staying in Somersetshire in July 1916. On the night of July 3rd Mr Lawson had the following vivid dream. He dreamed that he was in a bedroom and saw his brother-in-law, Mr Stephen, lying unconscious on the floor. With some difficulty he lifted the body on to the bed, but it showed no trace of life. He then sprinkled some water over the face. This had no effect, so he ran to the door and called for help. As no one came, he ran out into the road, where he saw two men and a woman. He told them of the illness, and asked them to go to the nearest public house for some brandy. The men declined, but the woman said that she would try to get some. Mr Lawson, in his dream, gave her a shilling, and she went away, but never returned. He then, in his dream, went back into the bedroom and found Mr Stephen's body still lying there. In a great state of distress he hunted all over the house, but could find no one. Just as he was giving up hope, he awoke, and was relieved to find that it was only a dream.

Next morning at breakfast he told his daughter of this dream. She remarked, with great surprise, that she had had a very similar one. In a note, written by her and sent to Mr Tyrrell, she confirms her father's statement that he had told her of the dream at breakfast next morning, and gives the following account of what *she* had dreamed on the night of July 3rd, 1916. She dreamed that her uncle, Mr Stephen, had come running up to her, looking very ill. He handed her a book, and asked her to take it into the town. She asked what was the matter, and he said that he was very ill, and then left the room. The next thing that she remembers of the dream is that he was lying unconscious, and no one seemed able to go to his help.

Two days later, i.e. on July 5th, Mr and Miss Lawson returned to their home. Mr Lawson relates that he called on Mr Stephen the same evening, found him looking very ill, and was told the following story by him. On the night of July 3rd he had found himself lying on the floor of his room, feeling very unwell. He must have been unconscious for some time, and could neither move nor call for help. Early in the morning he did manage to call the cook. He then remembered nothing until 7 *a.m.*, when he sent for the doctor. Miss Lawson states that Mr Stephen called at their house on July 6th, still looking very ill, and with a nasty cut on his nose, due to the fall.

The doctor, after looking up his diary, wrote, on November 26th, 1916, that he had been called at *3.45 a.m.* on July 4th, 1916, to Mr Stephen's house. Mr Stephen had by then recovered consciousness, after having been unconscious for a considerable time. He was suffering from the effects of a rather severe haemorrhage due to a wound caused by a fall.

Further details are given in a statement, written and signed by Mr Stephen's cook for Mr Tyrrell. She says that she was awakened at 1 a.m. on July 4th, 1916, by hearing a thud, which seemed to come from Mr Stephen's room. She sat up and listened, but, hearing nothing further, went to sleep again. At 3.45 a.m. she was awakened by Mr Stephen knocking at her door and saying: 'Come quickly, I am very ill.' She aroused the housemaid, went with her to his room, and found him lying unconscious on the floor. The housemaid fetched some whisky and they poured a little into his mouth, and then lifted him with difficulty on to the bed. He revived a little, and said: 'I am feeling very ill. I think I am dying.'

There is a curious difference in testimony as to the time when the doctor was first summoned. As I have mentioned, he himself recorded it in his diary as *3.45* a.m., whilst Mr Stephen said that it was not until 7 a.m. In this the cook's testimony agrees with her master's. She says that she had *wanted* to send for the doctor as soon as they had got Mr Stephen on to the bed, but that he did not consent to this until she revisited him at 7 a.m.

The exact time at which the doctor was summoned is not directly relevant for our special purpose. The relevant facts are (i) that Mr Stephen had a seizure at about 1 a.m. on July 4th, 1916, fell and cut his face, and then lay unconscious on the floor for a long time, and was eventually given whisky and with difficulty lifted on to his bed by the two servants; and (ii) that on that night both his brother-in-law and his niece, who were then in a house in another part of England, and who state that they had no reason whatever to expect him to fall ill, dreamed of him as undergoing something very like what was in fact happening to him at the time.

(8) *Miss Steele and Mr Burgess* (pp. 398 *et seq.*). This case was reported by Mr W. W. Baggally, an experienced and active member of the S.P.R., who was in Brighton when it happened, and investigated the details at once.

Mr Burgess, an invalid suffering from partial paralysis, had been staying for some months at the private hotel of Miss Steele, at 16 and 17 Sillwood Place, Brighton. On February 15th, 1912, he left there and took up residence at 10, Belgrave Place, Kemp Town, Brighton. Miss Steele had not seen Mr Burgess, and had had no occasion to think specially about him, from the time when he left her hotel until the night of March 5th, 1912, when she had the following experience, which she described in a letter to Mr Baggally, dated March 13th, 1912.

On the night of March 5th, 1912, Miss Steele went to bed at her usual time. She awoke in the night to find herself standing in the middle of her bedroom, answering: 'All right, I'm coming' to Mr Burgess, who, as it seemed to her, had called three times: 'Miss Steele! Miss Steele! Miss Steele!' She put on her dressing-gown, lighted the gas, and then realized that Mr Burgess was no longer a guest in her hotel. She looked at the clock, and noted that the time was exactly 3 a.m. On coming down next morning (March 6th), she told her cook of the dream, and expressed the hope that nothing was amiss with Mr Burgess. The last point is corroborated in a statement made orally on March 13th by the cook to Mr Baggally, recorded by him, and signed by her as correct.

Miss Steele's letter of March 13th continues as follows. In the afternoon of March 6th (i.e. the day following the night of her dream) a man called and left a note from Mr Burgess. The note, which she enclosed for Mr Baggally's inspection, ran as follows: 'I had a funny dream about you last night. I dreamed that you appeared at about 3 a.m. Just a glimpse of you. It's funny, isn't it?'

We turn now to Mr Burgess's account of *his* experience. On March 13th, 1912, he dictated and signed a statement to the following effect. He had awoken with a start at about 3 a.m. on March 6th. He then saw, as it seemed, Miss Steele, standing at the door of his bedroom. As he had shut the door when he went to bed, he took it that she must have opened it. She was in ordinary dress. The apparition lasted about five seconds. He was not frightened, and soon afterwards fell asleep again. Next morning (March 6th) at about 11 a.m. he wrote a note to Miss Steele, telling her of his experience. He handed this to his landlord, Mr Watkins, and asked him to send it to Miss Steele.

In answer to questions, Mr Burgess said that his room was quite dark. Nevertheless, Miss Steele appeared to him as in a bright light, not as self-luminous or phosphorescent; in fact just as she would have appeared if standing in the room in daylight. He also explained that he called his experience a 'dream' merely for want of a better word; he had recently awoken when he saw the apparition.

Enquiries made by Mr Baggally of Mr Watkins, and at the Church Army Labour Home in Brighton, confirmed that Mr Burgess had handed a note to Mr Watkins for conveyance to Miss Steele; and that, at Mr Watkins' request, a man in the employ of the Labour Home had delivered the note at Miss Steele's house in the afternoon of March 6th.

It may be remarked that the first report of Miss Steele's experience was given orally by her as early as the evening of March 6th, i.e. a few hours after she had received Mr Burgess's note. It happened that Mrs Baggally was in the drawing-room of Miss Steele's sister that evening on a visit, and Miss Steele arrived there in great excitement with the note and told her story. Mrs Baggally related it to her husband that night on his return to Brighton, and he was in touch with the case from the very beginning.

SOME MARGINAL CASES

Under this heading I shall give the reports of three cases. The first of them falls neither under the head of a phantasm of the living nor under that of a phantasm of the dead, for the hallucinatory figure ostensibly seen was not identified by either of the percipients. The other two would count as phantasms of the *living* according to the convention mentioned above. But, if posthumous telepathic agency be allowed to be possible, it might be thought to have been involved in these two cases.

(1) *Lady B.'s and Miss B.'s collective hallucination* (pp. 363 *et seq.*). This experience was reported orally by the two ladies concerned, about eighteen months after its alleged occurrence, to Mr Barkworth of the S.P.R. He took down what they said, and they signed his account as correct. As will be seen, there was, from the nature of the case, no possibility of independent corroboration. The case is, therefore, evidentially weak; but it has certain points of interest which lead me to mention it, for what it may be worth.

The experience took place at night in the bedroom of a house in a London square. There was no source of light in the room at the time; thick blinds were drawn over the windows, and the only external source of light in the neighbourhood was a gas-lamp in the street, opposite to the house.

The story is as follows. Lady B. and Miss B. were sleeping in their respective beds in this room. In the middle of a certain night both of them awoke suddenly and simultaneously, without any apparent cause, and saw a female figure, dressed in a white garment which might have been a nightdress, with dark curly hair hanging down her back. It was standing in front of the fireplace, above which was a mirror. The position was such that the face appeared *directly* in quarter-profile to Lady B. from her bed. Miss B. could see directly from *her* bed only the back of the figure, with its long, dark hair, but not the face. She could, however, see quite plainly the *reflexion* of the face in the mirror. Both ladies exclaimed, and sprang out of bed to the doors, taking the figure to be an intruder. They found the doors shut and locked. When they turned round again, the figure had vanished. From the nature of the circumstances, there can have been only the feeblest natural illumination in the room at the time, but it seemed to both of them to be lighted up.

The interest of the case lies in its combination of a certain positive and a certain negative feature. On the one hand, the two simultaneous hallucinatory *quasi*-perceptions were correlated with each other in the kind of way in which the normal visual perceptions of the two ladies would have been, if they had both been seeing in daylight, from their respective points of view, a real person standing in front of the mirror over the fireplace. On the other hand, so far as could be ascertained, there was nothing, either in the physical world or in the simultaneous dream or waking hallucination of any third person, to correspond to those two correlated *quasi*-perceptions.

(2) *Captain Eldred Bowyer-Bower* (pp. 167 *et seq.*). Captain Eldred Bowyer-Bower, of the Royal Flying Corps, went out in his plane at dawn on March 19th, 1917, to reconnoitre over the German lines. After being out for about an hour, he was pounced upon by a number of enemy planes, shot down, and killed. The news was received by his Colonel from a cavalry patrol between 10 and 11 a.m. on the same day. This information comes from the *Court Journal* of June 1st, 1917, and from a letter to the dead officer's mother from his Colonel. This death is alleged to have been the origin, both in time and in space, of a number of curious hallucinatory experiences. I shall here describe only the one which is best attested.

Shortly after the Captain's death, his *fiancée*, Miss Highett, had a sitting with the professional medium, Mrs Brittain. At this various statements, which appeared to be correct and outside the medium's normal knowledge, were made about Captain Bowyer-Bower. In particular, Mrs Brittain stated (correctly) that he had a sister, not in this country, who had a little daughter called *Joan*. And she correctly stated that the sister's name was *Dorothy*.

Miss Highett reported these communications to Captain Bowyer-Bower's mother. Shortly afterwards the latter wrote to her step-daughter, Mrs *Dorothy* Spearman, the mother of *Joan* and half-sister to Captain Bowyer-Bower. She referred in her letter to Miss Highett's sitting with Mrs Brittain.

Mrs Spearman answered from Calcutta on January 2nd, 1918. The essential points in her letter are these. In the latter part of the morning of *March 19th, 1917*, she was sitting in her room in a hotel in Calcutta talking to her baby son. Her little daughter Joan was in the room with them. Suddenly Mrs Spearman had a feeling that she must turn round. She did so, and there (as it seemed) was her half-brother Eldred, standing in the room. He looked perfectly natural, and she took for granted that he had been posted to India and had come to call on her at the first possible opportunity. She said: 'Fancy coming out here', and told him that she would just put the baby into a safer place and that then they could have a talk. During this period she had turned away from him and towards the baby. On turning round again, intending to go up and embrace her half-brother, she found that he had vanished. He did not appear again, and the little girl Joan showed no signs of having seen anything. Mrs Spearman naturally had a great shock, and she claims to have felt the presence of Eldred in the church that afternoon, when her baby was being christened.

131

The case was reported to the S.P.R. and investigated for them by Mr Hubert Wales, a member who has conducted some interesting experiments in telepathy (see *Proceedings*, Vol. XXXI, pp. 124 to 216). In a letter to him the Captain's mother states that this baby was christened on the day on which her son Eldred was killed, and that Eldred was to have been godfather to the child. Mrs Spearman also states, in a later letter to Mr Wales, that the christening took place at 2 o'clock that afternoon.

It will be noted that the *first* report which Mrs Spearman made to anyone of her experience was some nine months later, in a letter to her stepmother of January 2nd, 1918. In that letter she opens the subject by saying that she had not hitherto mentioned the matter to her correspondent, lest she should be misunderstood and perhaps thought to be hysterical. In a letter of August 3rd, 1918, to Mr Wales, Mrs Spearman says that she did not tell her husband at the time, because she knew that he would regard the experience as a mere illusion; as, indeed, she herself had been inclined to do until the death-coincidence became known to her. The fact that no report was made of the experience at the time is obviously a serious evidential weakness. But, if we accept Mrs Spearman's ostensible memory of it as adequate evidence that it happened, there can hardly be any doubt that it did so on the morning of the day on which the baby was christened. And there is no doubt that that was March 19th, 1917. Since Captain Bowyer-Bower was shot down in *Flanders* in the early morning of that day, and since Mrs Spearman had her hallucinatory *quasi*-perception of him in *Calcutta* in the latter part of that morning, the two events must have very nearly coincided in time.

(3) *Lieut. McConnel and Lieut. Larkin* (pp. 152 *et seq.*). The experient in this case was Lieut. J. J. Larkin and the referent was Lieut. David McConnel, both officers in the R.A.F. McConnel was killed in an air-crash, and, at about the same time, Larkin would appear to have had a waking visual and auditory hallucination of him as having returned safe and well from the flight which had, in fact, proved fatal.

The case was first reported in a letter from Mr D. R. McConnel, Lieut. McConnel's father, in a letter to Sir Oliver Lodge, dated January 16th, 1919. The writer was not personally acquainted with Lodge, but addressed him *sua sponte* as an eminent scientist known to be interested in such matters. Enclosed in Mr McConnel's letter to Lodge was a letter, dated December 22nd, 1918, which he had received from Lieut. Larkin, describing his experience. This was accompanied by corroborative statements, signed by two of his fellow-officers, Lieut. Hillman and Lieut. Garner-Smith.

The essential facts about Lieut. McConnel and his death are these.

He was an extremely able and promising young airman in his 19th year. He and the other officers concerned were stationed at Scampton airfield, near Lincoln. On the morning of December 7th, 1918, at about 11 a.m., he went to the hangars at Scampton intending to take a machine out to the 'Aerial Range' for machine-gun practice. As he was on his way, he was asked by his O.C. to take one of two 'Camel' planes to Tadcaster airfield, some 60 miles from Scampton. He therefore returned to the room, in which he had left Lieut. Larkin shortly before, at about 11.30 a.m., and told the latter of the change in plans. He said: 'I expect to get back in time for tea.' He thereupon walked out, but about half a minute later knocked at the window and asked for his map, which he had forgotten, and which Larkin handed to him.

McConnel then set off in his Camel to Tadcaster. He was accompanied thither by another officer in an 'Avro' plane, in which he was to return to Scampton after leaving the Camel at Tadcaster. At Doncaster the two planes ran into fog, and made a landing. McConnel telephoned to his Flight Commander, asking for instructions, and was told to use his own judgement. The two pilots decided to continue their journey. Between Doncaster and Tadcaster the fog became very thick. The pilot in the Avro successfully made a forced landing. McConnel in his Camel circled round until he knew that the other pilot was safe, and then proceeded on his journey. Camels were difficult planes to fly, imposing a great strain on the arms; and McConnel, who had been to a dance the night before, had got up late and had missed his breakfast. He was therefore probably both tired and hungry. The fog had become very dense, and he did not approach Tadcaster until nearly 3.30 p.m., by which time he had been in the air from three to three and a half hours. The plane was seen first to side-slip, then to right itself and fly on steadily for a short while, and then to nose-dive and crash, with the engine full on. McConnel was thrown violently forward against the gun in front of him and was killed instantaneously. His watch was found to have stopped at 3.25 p.m. His mother, who saw the body at midday on December 9th, observed that his hands were tightly clenched and that the forearms were swollen.

We come now to Lieut. Larkin's experience. After handing the map to McConnel at 11.30 a.m. on December 7th he had lunch and then spent the afternoon reading and writing letters, sitting in front of the fire. At some time between 3.15 and 3.30 p.m., while he was thus seated, reading and smoking, with his back to the door about eight feet away, he heard someone walking up the passage. He heard the door open with the usual clatter that McConnel was wont to make, and he heard McConnel's voice crying: 'Hello, boy!' Larkin

133

turned half round in his chair, and saw as it were McConnel standing in the doorway, half in and half out of the room, holding the door-knob in his hand. He was dressed in his full flying clothes, but wearing his *naval* cap, and there was nothing unusual in his appearance. Larkin remarked: 'Hello! Back already?' The figure replied: 'Yes. Got there all right. . .', and added some such words as: '. . . Had a good trip' or '. . . a fine trip'. Larkin was looking full at him during all this. The figure then said: 'Well, cheerio!' shut the door with a bang, and went away.

Larkin went on reading, and thought that McConnel had either gone to see some friends in other rooms, or to the hangars about some of his flying gear. At 3.45 p.m. Lieut. Garner-Smith came into the room, and remarked that he hoped that McConnel would get back early, as they were going in to Lincoln that evening. Larkin replied that McConnel was already back, and had been in the room a few minutes ago, and that he had probably not yet had his tea, but was in one of the adjacent rooms. Garner-Smith thereupon went out to look for McConnel.

Larkin then went into the mess and had his tea, and afterwards changed and went to Lincoln. In the smoking-room of the Albion Hotel there he overheard a group of officers talking of a crash and mentioning the names 'Tadcaster' and 'McConnel'. He could not believe that McConnel had crashed on his flight to Tadcaster, and assumed at first that he must have gone up again and met with an accident. But later in the evening he learned the facts. He was, naturally, dumbfounded. Next morning he and Garner-Smith had a long discussion on the matter. Garner-Smith tried, and failed, to persuade him that he must have been mistaken in thinking that he had seen and spoken with McConnel at 3.30 p.m. on the previous day, i.e. almost exactly the time (3.25 p.m.) when McConnel had been killed at Tadcaster. It is plain from Larkin's letter to Mr McConnel that he was profoundly perplexed by the incident, but remained absolutely convinced that he had been fully awake at the time.

Both Garner-Smith and Hillman read through the statement which Larkin wrote out on December 22nd, 1918, for Mr McConnel. The former testifies that it agrees almost word for word with what Larkin said to him at 3.45 p.m. on December 7th, i.e. some hours before either of them knew of the crash. The latter testifies that Larkin had told him on the morning of December 8th exactly the same story as he had since written down. Both these fellow-officers, who knew Larkin well, express complete confidence in the truth of his story.

The only possible normal explanation would seem to be in terms of mistaken identity. There is not the least positive evidence for this, and there are at least two circumstances which make against it. One is that Larkin recognized the voice, the manner, and the noisy entrance and exit, as typical of McConnel. The other is that the figure was seen as wearing a *naval* cap. McConnel had begun his flying career in the R.N.A.S., had retained his naval flying uniform, and was wont to wear it when about the aerodrome. Only two other men at Scampton were in a position to wear such uniform. Mr McConnel was personally acquainted with both of them, and stated explicitly that neither 'could either in height, or build, or manner, or voice, have been mistaken for my son'. It should be added that the investigator on behalf of the S.P.R. wrote to Lieut. Larkin to enquire specifically about the state of lighting in the room at the time of his experience. In a letter of June 27th, 1919, he states that the electric light was on, that a good fire was burning in an open stove, and that there were no shadows or half-shadows in the room.

It is impossible to say whether Larkin's experience happened immediately before or immediately after McConnel's death. It will be noted that the hallucinatory *quasi*-perception represented McConnel, not as he actually was at the time, but as he would have appeared if he had just returned safely. That might suggest that the details of the *quasi*-percept were supplied mainly by the percipient, from his memories of McConnel, and not from the referent. But it is also possible that McConnel may have swooned just before the end, from exhaustion and hunger, and that Larkin's hallucinatory *quasi*-percept corresponded to McConnel's own emotionally toned dream-image of himself as safely back at Scampton in time for tea. Finally, if we admit the possibility of a person's consciousness persisting after his bodily death, we cannot rule out the possibility that Larkin's *quasi*-percept might correspond to a delusion in McConnel's mind about himself immediately after his sudden and violent separation from his physical body.

PHANTASMS OF THE DEAD

Cases in which B has already been dead for some considerable time before the occurrence in A of an hallucinatory *quasi*-perception obviously referring to him, differ in one important practical way from cases in which B was alive at the time and lived for some considerable time afterwards. In the latter cases, i.e. phantasms of the *living*, we can find out, by direct enquiry or otherwise, whether, at about the time when A had his hallucination concerning B, B was or was not in the peculiar state and situation in which he appeared to A to be. But, even if in some sense or other the spirits of the dead survive, we cannot interrogate them.

A phantasm referring to an identifiable deceased person B is of significance from the point of view of psychical research, if any one of the following conditions be fulfilled; and it becomes of course much more significant if several of them be fulfilled:

(i) If two or more persons, without normal communication with each other, should have very similar hallucinations, all referring to a certain dead person, at very much the same time, that would *suggest* a common cause independent of all the percipients. That, however, would not be conclusive. For it is possible that one of these persons, say A_1, may have had an hallucination of purely intra-subjective origin, and that this may have telepathically induced similar hallucinations in the other persons, A_2, A_3, etc.

(ii) Suppose that the hallucination should convey to A information about the deceased B, which A could not have got at the time by any normal means. Suppose, e.g., that B dies at a certain moment. Some time later A, who neither knows of this nor has the least reason to expect it, has an hallucination, obviously referring to B, in which he is either 'told' or shown by unmistakable symbolism that B is dead. Suppose that the hallucination corresponds very closely in detail to the circumstances of B's death, and that those circumstances were very peculiar. And suppose, finally, that B would have a very strong motive for wishing to communicate the facts about his death to A, and that such anxiety on his part is apparent in the details of the hallucination. Then it would certainly look *prima facie* as if B, or some part of him, had survived the death of his body and were fulfilling certain persistent desires and intentions by appropriate telepathic action upon A.

(iii) Suppose that a number of persons, who were on different occasions in the same limited region of space (e.g. a certain room) and were never in normal communication with each other, were to have hallucinatory *quasi*-perceptions which are obviously so much alike that it is natural to regard them as successive appearances of the same individual. And suppose that all those appearances could plausibly be referred to a certain identifiable person, who had lived and died in that house and had been specially concerned with the room in question. Then that would certainly suggest the persistence of *something or other*, specially connected with a certain deceased person, which is in some way localized in its sphere of action, and is capable of generating markedly similar hallucinations in different percipients on a sequence of disconnected occasions over a longish period. The evidence in *most* cases of alleged 'haunting' turns out on examination to be not very impressive. And, even when there is good evidence for the occurrence of a sequence of reiterated localized hallucinations, of somewhat similar content, the claim to refer all these appearances to a certain deceased former inhabitant of the house is seldom found to be well attested. When one studies the details of the best cases of 'haunting' they do not, I think, on the whole suggest the presence of any persistent desire or intention. They suggest, rather, an aimless mechanical repetition of the dreams or waking fantasies of a person brooding over certain incidents and scenes in his past life.

I do not wish to suggest that the fulfilment of any one, or of all three, of the above-mentioned conditions would *force* a reasonable enquirer to conclude that *post mortem* agency was an essential factor in producing such phenomena. But I would assert that, when any of those conditions are fulfilled, the alternative explanations have to invoke *paranormal* cognition and *paranormal* agency on the part of the *living*. Such cases are therefore of importance to psychical research in general, even though they cannot be adduced as conclusive proof of the persistence and continued activity of some part of a human individual after the death of his physical body.

I proceed now to give some examples:

(1) *The Chaffin Will Case* (S.P.R. *Proceedings*, Vol. XXXVI, pp. 517 *et seq.*). This case was brought to the notice of the S.P.R. by a Canadian member, whose attention was first called to it by a newspaper report. The incidents took place in North Carolina, and the Canadian member instructed Mr J. McN. Johnson, a lawyer of Aberdeen, N.C., to investigate on the spot. Mr Johnson did so very thoroughly, and he submitted to the S.P.R. a full report, including (i) the original newspaper article, (ii) the official records of proceedings in the Superior Court of Davie County, N.C., and (iii) a statement, sworn by Mr Johnson, as to interviews which he had had with some of the principal persons concerned, together with sworn statements from two of them.

The essential background of the case is as follows. James L. Chaffin was a farmer in Davie County, N.C. He had a wife living and four sons, John A., James Pinkney, Marshall A., and Abner C., in that order of age. On November 16th, 1905, James L. Chaffin made a will, which was duly attested by two witnesses. In this will he left his farm to his third son, Marshall, and appointed him executor. He left nothing to his wife or to the other three sons.

On January 10th, 1919 (as afterwards appeared), he made a new will, moved thereto (as he states in the preamble) by reading Genesis xxvii (which contains the story of that disreputable patriarch Jacob deceiving his blind father Isaac and fraudulently securing the latter's blessing intended for the first-born Esau). In this will he divided his property equally among his four children, and confided their mother to their care. This will was *not* attested, nor, so far as

137

can be ascertained, did Chaffin ever divulge its existence to anyone in his lifetime. Instead, he placed it (as was afterwards discovered) between two pages of a family Bible, formerly belonging to his father, Rev. Nathan S. Chaffin. These pages were the ones containing Genesis xxvii. He folded them so as to form a kind of envelope, in which he secretly put the will. Though he never mentioned the existence of this second will to anyone, he secretly stitched a roll of paper (which was afterwards found) in the inside pocket of an old overcoat of his, on which he wrote the words: 'Read the 27th chapter of Genesis in my daddie's old Bible'.

Old Chaffin died, as the result of a fall, on September 7th, 1921. His third son Marshall, executor and sole heir under the first will, obtained probate of it on September 24th, 1921. His mother and his three brothers did not contest the will, since they knew of no valid reason for doing so. It was not until the middle of 1925, i.e. between three and four years after old Chaffin's death, that anything relevant happened. The following account of the events that then occurred is taken from a sworn statement, obtained on April 21st, 1927, by Mr Johnson from the second son, James Pinkney Chaffin. The gist of this is as follows.

Early in June 1925, James Pinkney Chaffin began having very vivid dreams as of his father appearing at his bedside but saying nothing. Some time later the father again appeared, wearing an old black overcoat, with which the son was familiar. This time the dream-figure spoke. It pulled back its overcoat, said, 'You will find my will in my overcoat pocket', and then vanished. Next morning James P. went to his mother's to look for the coat, but found that she had given it to his brother John, who was living some twenty miles away. On or about July 6th James P. went to his brother John's home and found the coat there. On examining it, he discovered that the lining of the inside pocket had been sewn up. On cutting the stitches, he found a little roll of paper, tied with a string; and on this was written, in his father's hand, the words: 'Read the 27th chapter of Genesis in my daddie's old Bible'.

At this stage James P. very wisely decided to have witnesses with him before going further. He therefore called on a neighbour, Mr Thomas A. Blackwelder; related the story to him; and asked him to accompany him to his mother's house in search of the Bible. All this is confirmed by a sworn statement from Mr Blackwelder. Arrived at the mother's house, they found the Bible, after a longish search, in the top drawer of the bureau in an upper room. There were present at the time, besides Mr Blackwelder and James P. Chaffin, the latter's mother, wife, and 15-year-old daughter. The book was very dilapidated, and fell apart into three bits. James P. took two of these, and Blackwelder the remaining one. It happened that it was this that contained the book of Genesis, and it was Blackwelder who found the will folded into the pages of Chapter xxvii.

As already stated, this will had not been witnessed. But, under the laws of North Carolina, it would be valid, provided that the courts were satisfied that it was in the alleged testator's handwriting. Marshall Chaffin, the sole heir under the old will, had died within a year of his father; but he had left a widow and a young son, R. M. Chaffin. This boy was made defendant in a suit to prove the second will, being represented by his mother as guardian.

The case came on for hearing before a judge and jury in the Superior Court of Davie County, N.C., in December 1925. When it began, Marshall's widow and son were prepared to contest the new will. During the luncheon interval, however, they had an opportunity of inspecting it, and they at once admitted that it was in old Chaffin's handwriting. Had they not done so, there were ten witnesses prepared to testify to this. So the case was settled amicably, and the first will cancelled.

Mr Johnson states that he interviewed and cross-examined James P. Chaffin, his mother, wife, and daughter on April 1927, with a special view to the possibility of there having been subconscious normal knowledge of the existence of the paper in the overcoat pocket, or of the will in the old Bible. He states (and his testimony is important, as coming from a lawyer resident and practising in that part of the country) that he was 'much impressed with the evident sincerity of these people, who had the appearance of honest, honourable country people, in well-to-do circumstances'. To all his attempts to make them admit the possibility that one or other of them might have had normal but subconscious prior knowledge of the relevant facts they answered: 'Such an explanation is impossible. We never heard of the existence of the will till the visitation from my father's spirit.' What is not certain is whether James P. Chaffin's experiences took the form of vivid dreams or waking hallucinations. Mr Johnson came to the conclusion that the experient himself was uncertain on that point.

(2) *Mr and Mrs P. and Mr P.'s deceased father* (S.P.R. *Proceedings*, Vol. VI, pp. 26 *et seq.*). On June 9th, 1885, a lady, who wished to be known by the pseudonym of 'Mrs P.', wrote to Gurney a letter to the following effect:

In the year 1867 she and her husband moved to a new house in the town of S. Towards the end of 1869 Mr P., who had been of a cheerful disposition, began, for reasons which his wife sought in vain to discover from him, to be dejected and moody. Mr and Mrs P. and their baby daughter were invited to spend the whole of Christmas Day 1869 with an aunt and uncle, who lived in the neighbourhood. On Christmas Eve they retired early to their bedroom, after carefully seeing (as was their wont) that the doors of the house were securely locked and bolted. The arrangement of the room is shown in the diagram below.

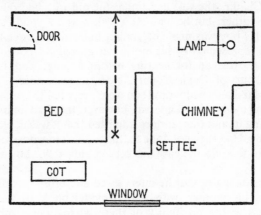

The baby was asleep in the cot, and the only light in the room came from the lamp in the position indicated on the chest of drawers. By about 9.30 p.m. Mr P. was lying in bed, still awake, on the left-hand side, with his face towards the left. Mrs P. was sitting up in bed on the right-hand side, expecting the baby to awake shortly and intending to give it some warm milk when it should do so. The only light was from a lamp on the chest of drawers to the left of the chimney, as indicated in the plan.

At that moment Mrs P. saw, as it were, standing at the foot of the bed, a man dressed as a naval officer, with a cap on his head having a projecting peak. He was leaning on his arms, which were resting on the foot-rail of the bed. Mrs P., in astonishment, touched her husband's shoulder, and said: 'Willie, who is this?' Mr P. turned, lay for a second or two gazing in astonishment at the figure, and then raised himself and shouted: 'What on earth are you doing here, Sir?' The figure drew itself up, and said in a reproachful voice: 'Willie! Willie!' Mr P. in great agitation sprang out of bed, as though to attack the intruder, but stood petrified by the bedside. Meanwhile the figure moved slowly in the direction of the dotted arrow in the plan, and disappeared into the wall.

It is of interest to remark that Mrs P. noted that the light-and-shade of the figure were such as would have been displayed by an ordinary physical object under the conditions of illumination then prevailing in the room. Thus, when the figure first appeared standing at the foot of the bed, the face was in shadow to Mrs P. And, again, as it passed the lamp, on its way to disappearing into the wall, the room was thrown into shadow by it.

Mr P., in a great state of agitation, now caught up the lamp and announced his intention of searching all over the house. This appeared to Mrs P. to be futile; but she wisely said nothing, while Mr P. *unlocked* the door, and set out on his errand, leaving her in the dark, quite literally 'holding the baby'. She had not recognized the figure, and now, in view of its naval dress, began to wonder whether the experience might forebode some disaster to her brother Arthur, who was in the navy and on a voyage to India at the time.

Mr P. soon returned, very much shaken, having found nothing to explain the occurrence. He sat down on the bed and said: 'Do you know what we have seen?' She answered: 'Yes, it was a spirit. I am afraid it was Arthur, but I could not see his face.' 'Oh! no,' exclaimed Mr P., 'it was my father.' The father had been dead for fourteen years. He had been a naval officer in early life, but had retired, through ill health, before Mr P. was born. Mr P. had seen him only once or twice in uniform, and Mrs P. had never seen him at all. The couple related their experience to their uncle and aunt next morning, and Mr P. remained very depressed and agitated.

A few weeks later Mr P. became very ill. In the course of his illness and convalescence, he confided to Mrs P. that he had been in great financial difficulties; and that, at the time of the experience, he had been intending to act upon the advice of a certain individual, which (as he now realized) would have led to financial ruin and perhaps criminal action. Mr P., who had hitherto been an avowed disbeliever in the possibility of *post mortem* appearances and influence, was convinced for the rest of his life that his father had saved him on that occasion, by intervening with an impressive warning which he could not ignore.

Two friends of the P.'s, a Dr and Mrs C., wrote on June 16th, 1885, stating that the narrative written by Mrs P. agreed with what she had related orally to them some years earlier. And, in a letter of June 17th, 1885, Mr P. confirms that the details in his wife's letter are quite correct, and the occurrence took place as described by her.

There is an interesting feature in this case, besides the one already noted, of the figure behaving *optically* like a normal physical object. It is that the figure appeared first to *Mrs P.*, who had never met her father-in-law or thought of him as a naval officer, and was not directly concerned. It was only a moment later, on being called to by Mrs P., that Mr P., the person primarily concerned, saw the apparition. In this connexion it may be relevant to add that Mrs. P, as a young woman, had had one previous externalized visual hallucination, as of her father, shortly after his death (see S.P.R. *Proceedings*, Vol. VI, pp. 25–6). There is nothing to suggest that this experience was not of purely *intra*-subjective origin. But it may well be that the capacity, thus indicated, to 'see things', may have made Mrs P. more directly susceptible than her husband to an influence which (whatever its origin may have been) was pretty certainly *trans*-subjective.

(3) *Recurrent appearances in Dr H.'s house* (S.P.R. *Proceedings*, Vol. VI, pp. 270 *et seq.*). The accounts of the following case were collected by Mr More Adey of Wotton-under-Edge, who had seen the persons concerned. The written documents are undated, but appear to have been sent to him in the latter part of 1883. The main document is written by Mrs H., the wife of Dr H., but the latter had seen what she had written and had testified to its correctness. We may divide the experiences into (A) those of persons residing in Dr H.'s house, and (B) those of a cousin, while on a visit to it.

(A) The experiences of those living in the house were had (i) by Dr H., and (ii) at a considerably later date by two of his daughters at about the same time on the same day.

(i) Dr H.'s experience, as described by Mrs H., was as follows. She says that it happened some time between January 1863 and January 1865, i.e. about twenty years before she wrote her account of it. Dr H. returned to the house one evening at about 9 p.m., after visiting patients. He and his wife were expecting some friends that evening for music, and he was somewhat late. He ran upstairs to his dressing-room in order to change. As he was going up the stairs, he saw on the landing a few steps above him a little child, which ran before him into Mrs H.'s room. His little son B. was at that time sleeping in that room, and so Dr H. at first took the child to be he, though he thought it looked larger. On entering the room, however, Dr H. found that B. was fast asleep in his cot. He informed Mrs H. later that evening, and on the following morning she made enquiries which satisfied them both that the figure seen could not have been any of the other children. The H.'s never referred to the matter again in presence of the children or of strangers.

(ii) Some years afterwards (according to Mrs H., in January 1877) two of the daughters, Miss G. H. and her eldest sister, Miss H. (afterwards Mrs A.), had the following experiences. There are written accounts by both of them. The longer is by Miss G. H., and it appears to have been written about five years after the events described.

These two sisters slept in adjoining bedrooms with a door from one to the other which was always left open. Miss G. H. mentions that the door into her room from the landing was locked at the time, so that her room could be entered only through that of her elder sister, Miss H.

They had agreed to get up early one winter's morning in order to read. They did so at some time between 5 and 6 a.m., i.e. at about daybreak. Miss G. H. began to go downstairs, in the half light. On passing the room at the head of the stairs where her youngest sister, M. H., slept, she noticed that the door was open. She took hold of the handle, in order to pull the door towards her to shut it, when she noticed a child standing in a corner formed by a wardrobe placed against the wall about 18 inches from the door. Taking this to be M. H., she exclaimed: 'Oh, M! you shouldn't startle me so!' and closed the door. But immediately afterwards she opened it again, feeling that it could not possibly be M. H. whom she had seen. She then found that M. was in fact fast asleep, and that there was nothing in the corner in which she had ostensibly seen the child. G. H. describes the figure as having dark complexion, hair, and eyes, and a thin oval face, with a mournful look, full of premature care and trouble. (It strikes one that this is a good deal to 'see' during a momentary glance in the half light of a winter's dawn.)

We come now to Miss H.'s experience. She states that G. H. had left the room that morning about three minutes when she (Miss H.) happened to look towards her (G. H.'s) room through the open communicating door. She saw a small figure in white, standing near a table. She did not clearly see its face, but attributed this to her own short-sightedness. For a moment, she thought it was G. H. Then, realizing that it could not be, she was overcome with fear and fled from the room. During the morning she told G. H. of her experience, and the latter then told her of her own experience at much the same time in M.'s room.

(B) So much for the experiences of Dr H. and of two of his daughters. In *Notes and Queries* for March 20th, 1880, there appears a communication from Mr H. C. Coote, who had received it from a Miss J. A. She was in fact a cousin of the H.'s, and had been on a visit to them in the July of 1879. She had also been there for a few days in the previous summer, but had had no unusual experiences and had heard no stories.

On the second visit she arrived early in the afternoon; went out boating with some members of the family; and, after a cheerful evening, went to bed tired but not in the least nervous. She slept soundly until just about daybreak, and then awoke. After a short while she seemed to hear the door of her bedroom open and shut again. Thinking it might be one of the servants, she called out: 'Come in!' Shortly afterwards the door seemed to open again. No

143

one visible came in, but the curtains of a hanging wardrobe beside her bed began rustling. This sound continued, and Miss J. A. began to have an uncomfortable feeling that she was not alone. This continued for some minutes, and then she saw, as it were, at the foot of her bed, a child of about 7 to 9 years old. The child seemed as if it were *on* the bed, and it came gliding towards Miss J. A. It bore the appearance of a little girl, with dark hair and a very white face, in her nightdress. She seemed in great trouble; her hands were clasped, and her eyes turned up with a look of entreaty. Slowly unclasping her hands, she touched Miss J. A. on the shoulder, and the touch felt very cold. She had tried to summon up courage to speak to the apparition, but it now vanished.

By the time she came down to breakfast next morning she had almost persuaded herself that the whole experience had been an unusually vivid dream. The family noticed that she was looking pale; and, in answer to their questions, she said that she had had a nasty nightmare, and that, if she had believed in ghosts, she would say that she had seen one. No comment was made except by Dr H., who said, in his medical capacity, that she had better not sleep *alone* in that room again.

So, on the following night one of her cousins slept in that room with her. As neither of them experienced anything uncanny, Miss J. A. decided that her first experience had been mere fancy, and insisted (against the wishes of the family) on sleeping alone in the room next night. As she was kneeling by her bed to say her prayers, the wardrobe curtains again began their rustling and she again had the experience of not being alone. Fortunately, one of her cousins came in to fetch something that she had left in the room; and, seeing how scared Miss J. A. looked, asked her if she had seen anything. She described her feelings, and decided to leave the room with her cousin. Mrs H. was informed at once, and she took the line that the 'nightmare' had made such an impression on Miss J. A. that it would be unwise for her to sleep in that room again. Accordingly, she was transferred to another bedroom for the rest of her visit, and had no further troubles.

During all that period, and during a further fortnight which she spent, together with her eldest H. cousin, at the house of another uncle, the incident was never referred to except as a 'nightmare'. But, at the end of that fortnight, her cousin revealed to her that the little girl had been seen by three members of the family on three previous occasions. As, however, nothing had been seen or heard of her for at least ten years, the H. family had almost ceased to think of these incidents, until reminded by Miss J. A.'s recent experience. (In fact only two years had elapsed since the latest of them, in January 1877.)

144

This account by Miss J. A. of her experience was shown to Mrs H., and she wrote a letter, dated November 21st, 1882, certifying that it agreed exactly with what Miss J. A. had told the family next morning.

Mrs H. herself was inclined to connect all these appearances with an actual little girl, J. M., who had died in what was then an adjoining house but was later united with its next-door neighbour to form the larger house in which the H.'s were living at the time when the various experiences took place. This girl died on January 21st, 1854, at the age of 10, a few years after her mother, and soon after the H.'s first came to the adjoining house. The appearance to Miss H. (afterwards Mrs A.) was in the room in which the girl died. The other appearances, viz. to Dr H., to Miss G. H., and to Miss J. A., were all in what would have been the adjoining house at the time of the death. Mrs H. had seen the child the day before she died, and remembered her as having fine dark eyes, black hair, an oval face, and a pale olive complexion. This would answer pretty well to Miss J. A.'s description of what she saw. But, obviously, no great weight can be attached to such identifications, in default of other supporting evidence.

(4) *Mr F. G.'s vision of his dead sister* (S.P.R. *Proceedings*, Vol. VI, pp. 17–20). On January 11th, 1888, a Mr F. G., of Boston, Mass., wrote to the American S.P.R. a letter, in which he reported the following experience, which, he said, had befallen him in 1876, i.e. twelve years earlier. The case was investigated by Richard Hodgson, one of the ablest of the early members of the English S.P.R., who spent the later part of his life in U.S.A. The family were known to him and also to Professor Royce of Harvard, the distinguished American philosopher and logician. The original letter was supplemented in a further letter to Hodgson, in answer to certain specific questions. It was also confirmed by letters from Mr F. G.'s father and brother. The essential points are as follows.

The G. family lived at the time of the incident in St Louis, Missouri. In 1867 Mr F. G.'s only sister, Annie, died there at the age of 18 of cholera. In course of time Mr F. G. became a commercial traveller. He had the experience in question in 1876 in the city of St Joseph, Missouri, which he had been visiting to solicit orders for his firm. He had had a very successful trip, and was in his room at his hotel in a cheerful state of mind forwarding to his employers the many orders which he had received. It was noon, the sun was shining brightly, and he was sitting at the table, writing his business letters and smoking a cigar. He had not been thinking of his sister, who had been dead for some nine years.

Suddenly he became aware of someone sitting on his left, with one arm resting on the table. He turned, and as it were saw his sister and looked straight in her face. The figure looked perfectly natural, and was dressed in clothing which she had worn in her lifetime. From his position at the table he could see the figure only from the waist upwards. He had time to notice the collar and a little breast-pin and a comb in her hair. She looked, in fact, precisely as he had known her when alive and well, except for one thing which he noted, viz. a *bright red line or scratch* on the right-hand side of her face. Mr F. G. sprang up to touch the figure; and, as he did so, it vanished.

So impressed was he by his experience that he interrupted the business trip, which would otherwise have lasted for a month, and took the next train back to his parents' home in St Louis. Arrived there, he related to his father and mother and others what he had seen. When he came to the matter of the scratch on the right cheek, his mother was deeply affected and nearly fainted. On recovering, she related that this was a fact of which no one living but herself could have had normal knowledge. It was she who had accidentally made the scratch on the face of the corpse. She had been deeply distressed at what she had done, had tried to obliterate all trace of it with powder, and had never mentioned the incident to anyone before. So impressed was the mother with this feature in her son's experience that, after retiring for the night, she got up and dressed again and came to tell him that *she* at least felt certain that he had seen the spirit of his dead sister.

On January 20th, 1888, Mr F. G.'s father wrote to him, in answer to an enquiry as to whether he remembered the incident. He confirmed all the details in his son's report which fell within his knowledge; and he enclosed a letter from another son, stating that he was present when F. G. first came home and related his experience, and confirming F. G.'s report of what had happened then and there. F. G.'s mother died a few weeks after the incident.

I have now submitted four fairly well attested cases of 'phantasms of the dead', which seem *prima facie* not to be mere chance-coincidences and not to be wholly explicable within the framework of accepted basic limiting principles. Anyone who wishes to pursue this topic further would be well advised to read carefully the following important papers in the early S.P.R. *Proceedings*, viz. Mrs. Sidgwick: 'Notes on the Evidence, collected by the Society, for Phantasms of the Dead' (Vol. III, pp. 69–150); Myers: 'On Recognized Apparitions occurring More than a Year after Death' (Vol. VI, pp. 13–65); and Podmore: 'Phantasms of the Dead from Another Point of View' (Vol. VI, pp. 229–313).

It must be confessed that 'a watched ghost never walks'; and that anyone whose house may be troubled by one could hardly take a more effectual means of securing at least temporary relief than by inviting the S.P.R. to send one or more of its members to sleep in the allegedly haunted room. That is, perhaps, what might be expected on almost any view of the phenomena.

Each reader must form his own conclusions on this whole perplexing topic. To indicate my own position I cannot do better than quote the following typical sentence from Mrs Sidgwick's paper:

. . . I can only say that, having made every effort . . . to exercise reasonable scepticism, I yet do not feel equal to the degree of unbelief in human testimony necessary to avoid at least provisionally the conclusion that there are, in a sense, haunted houses, i.e. that there are houses in which similar *quasi*-human apparitions have occurred at different times to different inhabitants, under circumstances which exclude the hypothesis of suggestion or expectation.

For my own part, I would extend this, *mutatis mutandis*, to cover such other forms of 'phantasms of the dead' as I have exemplified above.

EXPERIMENTAL CASES

It would plainly be of very great interest and importance if a person A could deliberately and repeatedly produce in another person B, who was at the time out of the range of normal communication with A and had no reason to believe that A was making an experiment, an hallucinatory *quasi*-perception as of A being present to him. It would add enormously to the weight to be attached to well attested sporadic cases of phantasms of the living, and it might well throw light on the mechanism of their causation. There have never been many well authenticated reports of such cases. None had been received by the S.P.R., at the time when Mrs Sidgwick wrote her paper 'Phantasms of the Living' in 1923, since the late eighties and early nineties of the last century. Nor, so far as I am aware, have any been received since then. I must therefore content myself with quoting two old, though quite well attested, cases. It is very much to be desired that such experiments should be repeated; though they are laborious for the agent, and, if successful, somewhat upsetting for the patient.

(1) *Mr Kirk and Miss G.* (S.P.R. *Proceedings*, Vol. X, pp. 270–273). On July 7th, 1890, Mr Kirk, an employee in the administration of Woolwich Arsenal living at Plumstead, wrote to the S.P.R., describing the following experiments which he had undertaken from June 10th to 20th of that year. In these he had tried to make his friend, Miss G., have a visual *quasi*-perception of him as present in her room.

It should be noted that Mr Kirk had, during the previous four years, tried on four occasions to produce a *general* impression of his presence on Miss G., as distinct from a specifically *visual quasi-*perception. In this he claimed to have had some success. Miss G. was aware that these previous experiments had taken place; but she had no normal knowledge that Mr Kirk was doing any experiments during the period from June 10th to 20th, 1890. Still less had she any idea that he was then trying to produce in her a *visual quasi-*perception of himself as present. In all the experiments during the period in question, with one exception, Mr Kirk was in his own house, and the time was between 11 p.m. and 1 a.m. The one exception was on June 11th, which was a Wednesday. This experiment was made in his office at Woolwich Arsenal, and the time was between 3.30 and 4 p.m.

During the period Mr Kirk met Miss G. from time to time. She complained to him of sleeplessness and restlessness, and spoke of an uneasy feeling which she could neither describe nor account for. One night, she said, that feeling had been so strong that she had got up, dressed, and done some needlework, and had not returned to bed until 2 a.m. Mr Kirk made no comments and dropped no hints, but he naturally suspected that his experiments were having *some* effect, though rather an unpleasant one and not the one that he was trying to bring about.

In point of fact the one experiment done in the afternoon in the office on June 11th was successful, and it was the only one of the series which was so. In a letter, written on Saturday, June 28th, Miss G. described what had happened to her on the afternoon of the previous Wednesday week. Her account is as follows.

She had taken a long walk in the morning and was tired. In the afternoon, while sitting in an easy chair near the window of her room, she fell asleep. Suddenly she found herself wide awake, ostensibly seeing Mr Kirk standing near her chair. The figure was dressed in a dark suit, which was quite familiar to her. He was standing with his back to the window, and he passed across the room from it to the door, which was opposite to the window and at about 15 feet from it. The door was shut. When the figure got to within about 4 feet of it, it vanished.

Remembering that Mr Kirk had tried to impress her telepathically on certain occasions in the past four years, the thought crossed her mind that this hallucination might have been produced telepathically by him. But she at once dismissed the idea, because she knew that he would be busy at his office at that time on a week-day. She concluded that her experience had been purely fortuitous, and resolved not to mention it to Mr Kirk. That resolution she kept until June 23rd, when she almost inadvertently told him all about the experience. He had been much pleased, and had thereupon asked her to write out her account of what had happened. Miss G. insisted that she was fully awake at the time of the hallucination.

So much for Miss G.'s account; now for Mr Kirk's. He, in his letter to the S.P.R. of July 7th, from which I have already abstracted, adds the following details. He had made this particular trial on the spur of the moment. He had been doing some auditing work, which had tired him; had laid down his pencil; and, while stretching himself in his chair, had had the impulse to try to appear to Miss G. He did not know where she would be at the time. But, either by luck or possibly through some telepathic influence from her, he had thought of her as in her bedroom and had tried to project himself thither. Another stroke of luck was that she was at the time dozing in her chair, which may have made her specially receptive. When Miss G. mentioned her experience to Mr Kirk on June 23rd, he had asked her to describe how he was dressed. Without any prompting, she had asserted that he had appeared as wearing his *dark* suit, and that she had distinctly noted the *small check pattern* on it. Mr Kirk states that he had in fact been wearing that suit on the occasion in question, because the light coat, which he generally wore in the office, happened to be away at the tailor's for some repairs.

(2) *Mr Godfrey and Mrs H.* (*Phantasms of the Living*, Vol. I, pp. lxxxi to lxxxiv). The Rev. C. Godfrey of Eastbourne had read, in Vol. I of *Phantasms of the Living*, the account on pp. 104 to 110 of some successful experiments in which a Mr S. H. B. had voluntarily appeared to certain friends, the Misses V., in their house, at some miles distant from his own. He wrote on November 17th, 1886 (wrongly dating his letter November 16th), to Podmore, one of the three joint-authors of *Phantasms of the Living*, to describe a successful experiment of the same kind which he had been led to make. The essential points are as follows.

On the night of November 15th, 1886, he determined to try to appear to his friend, Mrs H. He did not mention or hint at this resolution to her. He went to bed at 10.45 p.m., and endeavoured with all his might to picture himself as in her bedroom, standing at the foot of the bed, and trying to attract her attention. After carrying on this mental effort for about eight minutes he fell asleep. He then dreamed that he met Mrs H. next morning and asked her if she had seen him last night, and that she answered that she had done so. He then awoke, and found that it was 3.40 a.m. on the morning of November 16th. He immediately made a brief written note.

On November 17th Mr Godfrey went to call on someone else who was living at the same house as Mrs H. As he was leaving, Mrs H. called to him from a window that she had something special to tell him. Later on the same day she came to his house, and, without any prompting from him, gave the following account of her experience on the previous night.

At about 3.30 a.m. on November 16th she had awoken with a start, under the impression that there was someone in the room. She ostensibly heard a curious sound, but took it to be due to the birds in the ivy outside. She felt so restless that she lit a candle and went downstairs for some soda-water. As she was returning, and had reached the bottom of the stairs, she ostensibly saw Mr Godfrey on the landing about eleven steps up. The appearance was quite lifelike at first, and he was dressed in his usual style of dress by day. The figure stood still, and she held up the candle and gazed at it for three or four seconds. Then, as she went up the stairs, it grew more and more shadowy and finally faded away altogether. She judged that the time would have been 3.45 a.m.

Mr Godfrey, on hearing this account from Mrs H., asked her to go home at once and write it down. She did so, and he enclosed her written account in his letter of November 17th to Podmore. Podmore suggested to Mr Godfrey that he should repeat the experiment, of course without letting Mrs H. know or guess that he was doing so. He made one trial almost immediately after getting Podmore's suggestion. This was unsuccessful. He did not try again until the night of December 7th, i.e. almost exactly three weeks after the first successful experiment. This time he succeeded again. He wrote an account of the experiment to Podmore on December 8th, and enclosed a statement written on the same date by Mrs H. The essential points which emerge from these two accounts are the following.

Mr Godfrey, while undressing on the night of December 7th, concentrated his thoughts on Mrs H. After getting into bed, he spent some ten minutes in an intense effort to imagine himself transported to her room and making his presence felt both by voice and by putting his hand on her head. He then fell asleep. As on the former occasion, he dreamed that he met her next day; that he asked her if she had seen him; and that she told him that she had done so, though only indistinctly.

Next morning Mrs H. came to see Mr Godfrey, and her first words to him were: 'Well, I saw you last night, anyway!' According to the account which she wrote out, at his request, her experiences had been as follows.

She had gone to bed at 10.30 p.m. on December 7th and had fallen asleep. Suddenly she had heard a voice saying: 'Wake!', and had felt as it were a hand resting on the side of her head which was not in

150

contact with the pillow. She became wide awake in a very short time and ostensibly saw a figure leaning over her. The only physical light in the room came from a lamp outside in the street. This made a long line of light on the wall above the wash-stand, and she noticed that the phantasmal figure *obscured* a part of this, as it would have done had it been a physical object. She turned round in bed, and the hand seemed to slip from her head to the pillow beside her. The figure seemed to be stooping over her. She felt as if it were leaning up against the bed, and all the time she ostensibly saw the arm resting on the pillow. The face seemed to her to be obscured, as by a kind of mist; but she claims to have recognized the figure as that of Mr Godfrey by the appearance of the shoulders and the shape of the face. At the beginning of these experiences she had ostensibly heard a curious sound, which she describes as something like that made by a Jews' harp; and throughout the experience she ostensibly felt a draught of cold air streaming through the room, though the door and the window were in fact shut. At the time of the experience it seemed to her that the apparition had slightly pulled back the curtain of the bed; but in the morning she found it in its usual position. She estimated the time at about 12.30.

The above two cases seem to be as well attested as such things can reasonably be expected to be. One's only ground for suspicion (and that not a very cogent one logically) is that no reports of similar cases have been received by the S.P.R. in the last seventy years. But 'what man has done, man can do'. Readers (if any) of this book could hardly be more innocently occupied than in trying such experiments for themselves, and, if successful, carefully recording the facts and reporting them to the S.P.R. Their narratives would be treated as strictly confidential, if they should wish to avoid all imputation of 'spookiness' on the part of their friends, relatives, and professional colleagues or business connexions, and the unwelcome attentions of the popular press.

It would be very rash to base any generalizations on such a small amount of empirical data. It is of interest to note that the apparition in the second experiment with Mrs H., like that in the case of Lady B. and Miss B. quoted above, behaved *optically* as a physical object would have done. It is also of interest to note that Mrs H. had, not only a visual hallucination, but also correlated hallucinations of touch, of hearing, and of temperature. It may possibly be significant that the experient in each of the experimental cases was asleep or dozing at the time when the experiment was made; that she awoke suddenly; and that the hallucination occurred very shortly after awaking. It may also be worth noting that, in the Godfrey case, the agent made his effort just before going to sleep; that the effect on the patient manifested itself at a later hour, when the agent was himself asleep; and that he had a dream on each occasion concerning the outcome of the experiment. In the case of Mr Kirk's successful experiment, though he was not asleep at the time when he made the relevant effort, he was in a temporary state of relaxation after having just completed an exacting task in the office, which had tired him considerably.

VI

DREAMS AND 'OUT-OF-THE-BODY' EXPERIENCES

THERE is one kind of hallucinatory *quasi*-perception with which nearly all of us are quite familiar, viz. an ordinary dream had by a sane person in good health during normal sleep. I think that it will be useful, for that reason, to begin with some account of ordinary dreams, as familiar instances of what we might call '*normal* hallucinatory *quasi*-perceptions'. From them I shall pass to accounts of a certain rather peculiar kind of dreams, which are certainly *abnormal*, even if there be no need to suppose that there is anything *paranormal* about them. These will form a convenient stepping-stone to a very interesting and important class of experiences, which a few persons have had repeatedly, and which a fair number of persons have had once or twice in their lives under very special conditions of stress or crisis. These are called 'Out-of-the-Body' Experiences.

ORDINARY DREAMS

Most human beings, on first awaking from sleep, occasionally have ostensible memories as of certain highly specific and detailed dream-experiences. Speaking for myself, I very often do, and have done so for as long as I can remember anything. Such ostensible memory-experiences generally fade very quickly after awaking and cease to be revivable at will, unless one pays particular attention to them and rehearses them before one's mind's eye at once. But occasionally a vivid ostensible memory of a dream recurs involuntarily, or can be voluntarily revived, over a considerable period. Again, it sometimes happens that some event in waking life, or some waking train of thought, will evoke a vivid ostensible memory as of a certain incident in a long-forgotten dream. Still commoner is the experience of ostensibly remembering *that* one has been dreaming, although

153

one has little or no ostensible recollection of *what* one has been dreaming.

It would, no doubt, be logically possible to take an extremely sceptical view about all such ostensible memory-experiences. They cannot be checked in any of the numerous ways in which one can often test one's own or another person's ostensible memories of earlier *waking* experiences. It would, therefore, be logically possible to hold that all ostensible memories of dreams are delusive, either in principle or in detail. The extreme sceptic might say that we have no good reason to believe that anyone ever has *any* experiences while asleep. (It may be remarked that this can easily degenerate into a truism; for one may tacitly assume or explicitly lay down such a criterion for 'being asleep' as would make the sentence 'X had experiences while asleep' self-contradictory.) The more moderate sceptic might say that, although people probably do sometimes have experiences while asleep, there is no good reason to believe that the experiences which a person has had while asleep resemble at all closely what he ostensibly remembers them to have been when he first awakes. Such scepticism cannot be refuted, and it is part of the stock-in-trade of certain professional philosophers. But I do not see any good reason to accept it. I think it is reasonable to take *any* ostensible memory as probably in the main veridical, unless *either* it can be shown in detail to be delusive *or* it has features which are known to be positively correlated with delusiveness. Acting on this principle, I shall assume that the occurrence of ostensible memories of dreams is a good reason for believing that people do dream. And I shall assume that the fact that a person on awaking ostensibly remembers such and such a dream is a good reason for believing that he has recently had a dream more or less of that kind.

Before leaving this question of the evidential value of ostensible memories of dreams, I will add the following two remarks. (1) In view of the very rapid fading in detail of such ostensible memories, I think it not unreasonable to suppose that a dream may often have been considerably more detailed, and perhaps more coherent, than it is ostensibly remembered as being by the dreamer even on his first awaking. (2) I am inclined to think that the ostensible memories of dreams, which a person has on awaking, refer generally, if not invariably, to dreams had *immediately before* that awaking. There seems to be little *direct* evidence for the occurrence of dreams during the interval between falling asleep on one occasion and just before awaking on the next occasion. Of course, it might be argued on grounds of continuity that, since dreams occur at the end of a period of sleep, they probably occur also earlier in such a period. But that would be a precarious argument. For, presumably, when one is just about to

154

awake, one's internal state or one's external conditions or both must differ in a characteristic way from what they were in the course of a period of continuous sleep. And it might well be that just those factors which are about to cause awakening are necessary conditions of dreaming.

A better ground for arguing that dreams occur at other times besides just before waking is this. A sleeper may give external signs, such as talking in his sleep, striking out with his fists, etc., which in waking life are expressive of his having certain simultaneous experiences. That, so far as it goes, is presumptive evidence for the occurrence of dreams in the midst of periods of at any rate *restless* sleep. But I do not know of any satisfactory evidence for the occurrence of dreams in the midst of periods of *peaceful* sleep, and I think it would be somewhat rash to argue from the former to the latter.

Likenesses and Unlikenesses between Dreams and normal waking Sense-perceptions. Dreams are in certain respects very like, and in certain respects very unlike, normal waking sense-perceptions. I will now consider the main similarities and dissimilarities. Each of them can be considered under three heads, viz. likenesses and unlikenesses in (1) *content*, (2) *interconnexion*, and (3) *causal conditions*. I will now say something under each of these heads in turn.

(1) *Content.* The *quasi*-sensory content of dreams is exactly the same as the sensory content of ordinary waking perceptions. One's dreams are certainly experiences of colour, sound, tactual qualities, temperature, and kinaesthetic and somatic feelings, just as our waking perceptions are.

But the resemblance goes much deeper than that. In a vivid dream one does not experience just isolated patches of colour, isolated sounds, etc. Nor does one experience just undifferentiated coloured fields, auditory fields, etc. On the contrary, exactly as in waking life, the colour-experiences, the touch-experiences, the sound-experiences, and the kinaesthetic and somatic experiences, are of such kinds and are so interconnected with each other that one ostensibly sees, touches, hears, and interacts with certain external things and persons. Sometimes those ostensibly perceived things and persons seem to the dreamer to be identical with certain things and persons familiar to him in daily life. He may, e.g., have a dream as of being in his room talking to persons whom he knows well and habitually meets. Often, however, the scenery and the persons in a dream seem to the dreamer to be quite unfamiliar, as if he had travelled or had been transported to new surroundings and were there meeting strangers.

Again, in many dreams, as in waking life, the dreamer appears to

155

himself, not as a mere passive spectator, but as an active participant. It is for him as if he were doing and suffering, talking and listening, asking questions and receiving answers. These ostensible interactions with ostensibly perceived things and persons are often accompanied by feelings and emotions of the same kinds as are felt in waking life. These are often as intense as any that we feel when awake, and are sometimes more so. In my own case, at any rate, a dream is often accompanied too by the same kind of *sotto voce* running commentary and reflexive appraisal as commonly accompany my waking perceptions and actions. I consider, e.g., what another person, to whom I take myself to be talking in the dream, will think of me, and how he will react, if I should say so-and-so to him or should behave towards him in a certain way. Just as in waking life, I may find his reaction answer to my expectations, or be surprising or embarrassing, and so on.

It will be appropriate at this point to consider the occurrence, within dreams, of higher intellectual processes, such as reasoning. Speaking for myself, I often reason in my dreams. And the reasoning, as I ostensibly remember it on waking, is often at least as coherent as any that I perform in waking life. Sometimes in the course of a dream I have been led to consider whether I am (as one generally takes for granted in dreams) awake and perceiving normally with my senses, or am asleep and dreaming. Arguing in the dream from certain features of it, I have sometimes concluded that I am awake, and sometimes that I must be asleep and dreaming. Even when the conclusion has been false (viz. that I am awake), the argument that I have used seems to me, when I awake and review it in memory, to have often been quite valid in principle.

Often the dream-reasoning is concerned, not with the question whether one is awake or asleep, but with something that falls altogether within the dream. Not long ago I had a vivid dream, in which I was, as it were, present at a magical ceremony, conducted by two adepts of some occult order. After undergoing certain treatment by them, I seemed to myself to be levitated and to be flying round and round the room at a height of about eight feet. In doing so I repeatedly passed a high shelf over a fireplace, and I noted that a pair of heavy glass vases were standing one at each end of this. The experience was interesting and mildly pleasant, but I was in that critical mood which becomes a member of the S.P.R. I said to myself: 'This may well be just a result of hypnotic suggestion, and not genuine levitation.' In order to test this, I decided to catch hold of one of these vases as I passed them in my flight, and to bring it to the floor. I argued that, if it were still there afterwards, the levitation would have been genuine. Soon after I had done this my two adepts decided that I had had as much levitation for one day as was good for a beginner, and they brought me gently to the floor. I was delighted to find that one of the two heavy vases was lying where I had set it down in the course of my flight. So I concluded that I had been genuinely levitated, and not just the victim of an hallucination. My conclusion was, indeed, mistaken; for I had neither been levitated nor hypnotized, but had merely been asleep and dreaming. But the critical attitude which I adopted, and the argument which I used in my dream, would surely have done no discredit to the late Mr Podmore or his present-day representatives on the S.P.R.

So much for the main *likenesses* in content. It is plain that they are very far-reaching. Let us now consider the main *unlikenesses* in this respect.

In many dreams the scenes and the persons ostensibly perceived are not identifiable with any that the dreamer has perceived or heard tell of in his waking life. They do, indeed, fall under the same general categories, e.g. inorganic material things, plants, animals, men, etc., but in detail they may be very different from anything that the dreamer has ever heard of or met with while awake. Again, even if he identifies the things and persons that he is ostensibly perceiving with certain things and persons familiar to him in waking life, there are often strange differences; and these may strike him forcibly while he is still dreaming. One may find oneself in a dream taking for granted without hesitation that a certain dream-person, with whom one is ostensibly talking, is so-and-so, whom one knows well. And yet at that very moment it may strike one that he does not look or talk in the least like so-and-so. I have quite often had this experience, and I can well remember puzzling over it in the dream. In a similar way, what one takes to be a certain familiar scene or room often seems to one at the time to look strangely unlike itself.

Another curious difference between dream-experience and normal waking experience, which I have sometimes noticed, is this. In normal waking life one perceives things and other persons from one and only one point of view at any one moment, and that is always located within one's own body. One is aware of oneself and of one's own doings and sufferings, and of no one else's, from *within*; and of other men and their doings from *without*, as an external spectator. Now it does seem to me that sometimes in dreams I am aware of what I then take to be my body and of its doings and sufferings, *both* in the ordinary way from within it, and also simultaneously from without it as an external spectator. (I would be inclined to describe the experience as that of being at once actor and spectator. Of course, it may be that one very rapidly oscillates between the two attitudes, and never really has both of them at precisely the same moment. My memory is not accurate enough to enable me to decide with any confidence.)

Moreover, I am inclined to believe (though with rather less conviction) that I sometimes have in my dreams an experience which might be described as complementary to this. I seem to remember, on subsequent reflexion when awake, that in my dream I was ostensibly perceiving another person's body and its behaviour in the ordinary way from my own point of view outside it; and yet that I was at the same time ostensibly aware of his doings and sufferings from *within* his body, as if I were literally 'in his skin'.

This curious experience, of being at once a self-conscious actor and an external spectator of the agent and his doings and sufferings, is frequent in my dreams. I do not think that I have ever had anything like it in my normal waking life; and ordinary language is, from the nature of the case, ill-adapted to express it. Unless I am peculiar in this respect, it is an important dissimilarity between waking experiences and some quite common dreams.

(2) *Interconnexion.* I pass now to likenesses and unlikenesses of interconnexion, in the case of dreams on the one hand and waking experiences on the other. Under this head we may first consider the connexions between various phases of what the dreamer takes to be a single dream; then those between what he takes to be different dreams during a single spell of sleep; and lastly those between his dreams during different spells of sleep with a waking interval between them.

Within a single dream the connexions between successive phases are often quite like those within a short stretch of normal waking perception. But they are often very unlike. In particular, transitions often take place without the intermediate links which would exist in a course of events perceived during a continuous stretch of waking life. In a dream it often happens, e.g., that one seems to be inside a certain room for a while and then to be elsewhere, without any consciousness of moving or having been moved from the one place to the other and of observing a set of objects which spatially separate and interconnect the two places.

It is little more than a platitude to say that the discontinuity between different dreams within a single spell of sleep is even more complete. For, presumably, such profound discontinuity is part of our criterion for speaking of two successive dreams rather than two successive phases in a single dream.

It is more important to notice the contrast between (i) the *inter*connexions of what a person perceives just before going to sleep and just after waking again, and (ii) the *dis*connexion of (say) his last dream on one night and his first dream on the next night. In general one's body is not moved relatively to its immediate surroundings during sleep, and those surroundings do not greatly change. So what one perceives on awaking is usually easy to identify with what one perceived just before going to sleep. There may be, and indeed generally are, certain differences in detail; e.g. ashes in the grate instead of a fire burning there, the sun shining instead of the moon, and so on. But these fit in with the assumption that certain changes have been going on while one was asleep in the ways in which one has often perceived them to do while awake. Similar remarks apply to minor changes of detail in one's bodily feelings; as, e.g., when one goes to sleep feeling replete and wakes up feeling hungry.

Now it is extremely rare for any such connexions to be noted, either at the time or on subsequent waking reflexion, between the last dream of one night and the first dream of the next night. Scarcely ever does one dream on Tuesday night of a scene and of persons that seem to be the same in outline as those which one dreamed of on Monday night; with only such variations in detail as might reasonably be expected, on the supposition that the changes which one ostensibly perceived to be taking place in the former dream had continued in the normal way during the interval of waking life between it and the latter dream.

To this should be added the well known fact that the duration of a dream, as measured by objective physical tests, may be very short; although the dreamer himself has ostensibly been perceiving a train of events which seemed to him to take a long time, and which would in fact have done so if they had happened in the world which we perceive in normal waking life. It may happen, e.g., that one wakes up and looks at one's watch and then dozes off, and is awakened in a few minutes or even seconds by someone knocking at the door or pulling up the blinds. During those few minutes or seconds one may have dreamed of a sequence of events which would have taken hours, if undergone or perceived in waking life. And one may seem to oneself to have been occupied for hours. I think that this fact tends to reinforce my earlier contention that it would be rash to assume that one's memories of dream-experiences on first awaking are good evidence for the occurrence of dreams *long before* awaking.

So far I have been speaking of connexions and disconnexions between *successive* waking experiences, and between *successive* dream-experiences, of the *same person*. We must now consider *simultaneous* experiences of *different persons*.

If two waking persons are near together in space, and are not separated by opaque screens, etc., their visual and auditory experiences at any moment are generally very much alike, and the differences in detail between them are correlated in a familiar way with the differences in position and orientation of their bodies. We may say that both perceive substantially the same set of material things and physical events from slightly different points of view. But, if two persons sleep in the same room, and both dream simultaneously, there is in general no such correlation between the contents of their respective dreams. Nor is there any such correlation between the dreams of either of them and the simultaneous sense-perceptions of a third person who is awake in the room in which they are asleep.

(3) *Causal Conditions*. This brings us to the likenesses and unlikenesses between the causal conditions of dreams and those of waking sense-perceptions.

If a waking person is to have a normal visual perception, it is necessary that the objects around him shall be either emitting or reflecting light to his eyes; that his eyes shall be open to receive that light; and that his retina, optic nerve, and brain shall be intact and functioning normally. But a sleeping person has vivid experiences of ostensible seeing in his dreams, when his eyes are shut and the room in which he is sleeping is quite dark. Indeed, those negative conditions, which exclude normal waking vision, are almost necessary conditions for dreaming.

The objects seen by a waking person at any moment are those and only those from which his eyes are then receiving light. If we exclude very distant objects, such as the heavenly bodies, we may say that the things which a waking person sees at any moment are confined to those which were still in being just before then. (These may, of course, have existed for long before, and they may continue to exist for long afterwards.) Again, at any moment he sees those objects in the states in which they were just before then. (Such states may, of course, be transitory or of long duration.) But in a dream one often ostensibly sees persons who have long been dead, and things which have long ceased to exist; and one often ostensibly sees persons and things, which do still exist, in states in which they have long ago ceased to be.

Dreams are determined by a person's past experiences, and the traces left by them, in a way and to a degree in which waking sense-perceptions are not. What a waking person sees at any moment is, no doubt, greatly dependent on the *general* fact that he has been having perceptual experiences of various kinds since childhood, that these have occurred in certain oft-repeated patterns of co-existence and sequence, and that traces have been left and have become interwoven into complex dispositions. But this determines mainly the *general principles* in accordance with which a waking grown person interprets his present sensations in terms of physical things and

160

events. Again, it is no doubt true that the *details* of what a waking person sees at any moment are in part determined, not only by habitual associations, but also by such expectations, desires, and emotions as happen to be prevalent in him at the time. These may lead him to ignore certain details within his field of vision, to concentrate attention on certain others, and perhaps even ostensibly to see certain details which are not really present. But, granting all this, it remains true to say that what a waking person sees at any moment is largely independent of any *particular* past experience, and of his desires and emotions at the time.

Now contrast this with the case of dreams. It is obvious that, in many if not in all dreams, the *quasi*-sensory raw materials are reproductions of the contents of many waking experiences. These are dissociated from their original contexts, and then re-synthesized in a particular pattern for the occasion. In the case of many dreams it is obvious, too, that the synthesis takes place around the memory of some fairly recent waking experience, and under the influence of a certain desire or emotion. It is reasonable to suppose that this is often so, even when it is not apparent to the dreamer himself on subsequent reflexion.

I think that it is important, however, to note at this point the following contrasts between dreaming and the occurrence in normal waking life of visual, auditory, and other kinds of *imagery*, originating in past sense-perception. In the first place, the images which arise sporadically or are called up deliberately in waking life are, in most persons and at most times, feeble in intensity and vividness and definition, as compared with actual sensations. Moreover, they usually occur in relative isolation, and are very vaguely located in a kind of private 'image-space', which one takes to be 'inside one's head', 'at the back of one's eyes', and so on. In these respects they are utterly unlike the elaborately organized and highly differentiated contents of the visual fields of ordinary waking perception. Now the *quasi*-sensory contents of dreams resemble waking sensations, and are quite unlike ordinary waking imagery, in their vividness, their elaborate *quasi*-spatial arrangement, and their complete independence of one's conscious volitions. The dreamer is, as it were, faced with scenes and actors, and himself takes part in transactions, which are as vivid, and seem as much thrust on him from without, as anything that he perceives and interacts with in his waking life. He appears to himself, and they appear to him, as having a place and date in the public space of nature and the public time of history. If, in some sense, all this be due to oneself, one can only marvel on subsequent reflexion at the dramatic and plastic powers of what Tyrrell called the 'producer' and the 'stage-carpenter' within one, whose designs

161

and whose methods of staging them are utterly hidden both from one's waking and one's dreaming self.

SO-CALLED 'LUCID DREAMS'

I pass now from quite ordinary dreams, such as most of us have had on many occasions, to dreams of a rather peculiar kind, which seem to be intermediate between ordinary dreams and full-blown 'out-of-the-body' experiences. I shall here summarize the observations made on his own dreams by a Dutch physician, Dr van Eeden.

Van Eeden began to study his own dreams in 1896, making a record in his diary of the most interesting of them. Two years later he began to keep a special record of a certain kind of dream, which seemed to him to be of special interest. These he called 'lucid dreams'. He read a paper to the S.P.R. on April 22nd, 1913, and this was published in *Proceedings*, Vol. XXVI, under the title 'A Study of Dreams'. By that time he had recorded in all 500 dreams, of which about 70 per cent were of the lucid kind.

Van Eeden was familiar with two well known theories of dreams, viz. those of Freud and of Havelock Ellis. Freud's view is, very roughly, that most dreams are symbolical expressions of a subconscious wish, which is generally erotic. Havelock Ellis's view may be briefly summarized as follows. When a person is asleep his brain continues to receive stimuli from the various internal organs, from the involuntary muscles, the beating heart, the breathing lungs, and so on. Even when asleep a person is always engaged in correlating his sensations on the same general plan as he habitually follows when awake. This causes the sleeper to generate hallucinatory *quasi*-perceptions as of persons, things, situations, and transactions, which he takes to be related to his dream-sensations as real persons, things, etc., are related to his waking sensations. Now van Eeden did not find that either theory fitted the kind of dream which most interested him, viz. what he called 'lucid dreams'.

We will now consider his description of such dreams. The essential peculiarity of them is this. In an ordinary dream the dreamer does not raise the question whether he is awake or asleep, any more than one does in normal waking life. He takes for granted (in the sense in which we may be said to do so when in fact awake and in a normal state) that he is *awake*, and he takes for granted that his ordinary physical body is located within the scenery of the dream and is interacting in the ordinary way with the things and persons ostensibly perceived in the dream. But there are dreams in which the dreamer clearly remembers his waking life, contrasts it with his present state, and is fully aware that he is asleep. He experiences no outstanding bodily sensations, whether due to internal or peripheral stimulation, at such times. But he can direct his attention at will within the scenes which he ostensibly perceives in his dream, and can freely attempt various experiments upon this or that object, just as he might do with the objects of normal waking sense-perception. It is such dreams that van Eeden describes as 'lucid'. In a lucid dream, as in an ordinary one, the experience of having a body, and of perceiving with its sense-organs, speaking with its speech-organs, and acting with its limbs, is perfectly distinct. But, in a lucid dream, the dreamer is at the same time perfectly well aware that his physical body is asleep and quiescent, and quite differently located and oriented from the body which he is ostensibly animating in his dream. On awaking he remembers with equal distinctness both the actions of his dream-body and the simultaneous quiescence and passivity of his physical body. Van Eeden noted that in such cases his sleep was deep, that his physical body was quite at rest, and that he awoke feeling refreshed.

Between January 1st, 1898, and December 26th, 1912, van Eeden had recorded 352 lucid dreams which he had had. Before giving examples, I will mention a dream which bore an interesting partial resemblance to one described by the eminent philosophical physicist Ernst Mach.

One night in June 1897 van Eeden dreamed that he was floating through a landscape with trees bare of leaves. He took for granted in the dream that the month was April. He noted, whilst dreaming, that the perspective of the branches and twigs changed as he moved about, in much the way in which it would have done in waking life under similar circumstances. This struck him, on reflexion, as strange, on the hypothesis that the scenery was just a set of images generated by some stratum of himself. Some ten years later he read a passage in Mach's *Analysis of Sensations* (English translation, p. 115, note), in which the author records an experience of his own, which partly resembles and partly differs from this of van Eeden's. Mach too had dreamed that he was moving about in a landscape with trees, and had noted in his dream that there were changes in perspective as he did so. But, while still dreaming, Mach had observed certain discrepancies between these changes and those which would have taken place under similar circumstances in waking life. He had inferred from this, *in his dream*, that he must be dreaming. But he had also noted that, as soon as he became aware of these defects in the dream-perspective, they were *automatically corrected*.

So much for Mach; we will now give some examples of van Eeden's lucid dreams:

(1) On the night of January 19/20, 1898, van Eeden dreamed that he

was lying face downwards in his garden outside the window of his study, and that through the glass he saw his dog in the room. Meanwhile he knew quite well that he was in fact asleep and lying on his back in his bedroom. He resolved to try to wake up slowly and carefully, and to try to note the transition from the dream-experience as of lying on his chest to the waking experience of lying on his back. He describes the transition as 'like the feeling of slipping from one body into another'. He remarks that such experiences lead almost inevitably to the notion of having two bodies, viz. one's ordinary physical body and what may be called a 'dream-body'.

(2) On September 9th, 1904, he had a lucid dream as of standing by a table in front of a window. On the table were several objects, including a small tablet of glass and some thin claret-glasses. He was perfectly well aware at the time that he was dreaming. In his dream he tried the following experiments. He took the glass tablet, laid it on two stones, and beat it with a third stone. He could not break it. He then took one of the claret-glasses and gave it a hard kick, realizing at the time that this would be a dangerous thing to do in the world of real life. At the time the glass remained unbroken. But, soon afterwards, when he looked at it again, he found that it was in fragments. (He compares this with Mach's observation of the automatic correction of the faulty perspective of the twigs and branches in his dream, shortly after he had noticed it.) Van Eeden compares Mach's case and his own case of the claret-glass to the behaviour of an actor who has missed his cue, and then picks it up a moment later. While still immersed in this dream, van Eeden made the reflexion that the dream-world is a kind of *fake*-world; a very clever imitation of the physical world, but betraying itself to a careful observer within it by small defects. At that point in his dream he threw the fragments of the glass out of the window, in order to discover whether they would tinkle. They did so; and he saw in his dream two dogs running away. Then he noticed in his dream a decanter of claret. He tasted the contents, and remarked to himself: 'This has quite the taste of wine, so we can have . . . impressions of taste and smell in the dream-world.'

(3) In some of his lucid dreams van Eeden seemed to himself to be conversing with certain persons whom he knew at the time to be dead. The following two dreams, had on Christmas Day, 1911, are of interest in this connexion.

(i) After a very pleasant experience, as of floating in the air over vast brightly lighted landscapes, he saw his brother, who had died five years before, seated. He went up to him and said: 'Now we are both dreaming!' The brother answered: 'No, *I* am not!' Van Eeden then remembered that his brother had long been dead. The two had an animated conversation about the conditions of life after death, but the brother could or would give very little information in answer to any specific question that van Eeden put to him.

(ii) After an interval, occupied by an ordinary non-lucid dream, van Eeden had a second lucid dream. In this he saw the eminent Dutch physical chemist, van't Hoff, whose lectures he had attended as a student, standing in an academical room, surrounded by many learned persons. Van Eeden was well aware in his dream that van't Hoff was dead. He went up to him and asked him questions about conditions after death. In particular, he asked van't Hoff how one could be at all certain, in the *post mortem* state, that a person, with whom one was ostensibly talking, was a real person and not just a subjective hallucination. Van't Hoff answered: 'Just as in ordinary life, viz. by one's general impression.' This did not satisfy van Eeden, who remarked that, in ordinary life, we have various kinds of mutually confirmatory evidence which we lack in dreams. Van't Hoff replied that, after death, one has the same kind of evidence, and that the feeling of certainty in these matters is the same as in ordinary life. During this dream-discussion van Eeden had a strong impression that it really was van't Hoff who was conversing with him. He put to van't Hoff the same detailed questions about life after death as he had put to his brother in the earlier of the two lucid dreams; and, as before, he got only hesitating and dubious answers.

(4) In some of his lucid dreams van Eeden tried the experiment of calling for some specific person. Sometimes a figure would appear, answering to the appearance of the person called. He gives numerous examples; but concludes by saying that, on later reflexion, he feels no conviction of the genuineness of these dream figures, though in the dream he felt no doubts. He adds the interesting remark that the feeling of certainty that the dream figure is So-and-so may be *completely absent* even when it looks *exactly like* So-and-so. (I have already remarked on the converse of this, in some of my own dreams. One may feel no doubt that a certain dream-figure *is* So-and-so, though one notices in the dream that he does *not* look or speak in the least as So-and-so habitually does.)

Passing from particular instances of lucid dreams to features common to all or most of them, we may note the following points which van Eeden makes. (i) There is a high positive association between lucid dreams and dreams of flying or floating in the air. In the first place, a lucid dream often begins, or is accompanied, with a pleasant experience as of swift continuous flying or of peacefully floating over wide and beautiful landscapes under a clear, sunny sky.

Moreover, though experiences as of flying or floating aloft *may* occur in dreams of a *non*-lucid kind, a sequence of such dreams on two or three successive nights was generally followed, in van Eeden's experience, by the occurrence of a lucid dream. (ii) Van Eeden did not generally wake up *directly* from a lucid dream, unless he had deliberately resolved to do so. Generally such a dream would give place to one of a non-lucid kind, and it was from the latter that he would wake up. Very often he would *dream* that he had awakened from a lucid dream, and that he was relating it to someone; and it would be from that dream that he *really* awoke.

What van Eeden calls 'false-awakening dreams' were fairly common with him, and I suppose that most of us are quite familiar with them. He notes that Mach, in his *Analysis of Sensations* (English translation, pp. 87–8, footnote), described such an experience, which he had often had. Van Eeden's own account of such dreams may be summarized as follows. The general nature of a false-awakening dream is this. The dreamer seems to himself to wake up in his bedroom. Then he begins to realize that there is something odd in or about the room. Then he realizes that he is still asleep and dreaming. That experience is generally unpleasantly disturbing. The sleeper *wants* to wake up really, and gets frightened. When he really does wake up, he often finds himself with palpitating heart, sweating, and so on. (All these remarks fit very well such false-awakening dreams as I can remember.)

An interesting point which van Eeden makes is this. His general bodily health throughout the whole period had been excellent, and he had been able to detect very little correlation between the nature of his dreams and the contemporary state of his bodily health. On one occasion he went to bed suffering from violent toothache. Eventually he managed to fall asleep. He had disturbed and unpleasant dreams. But, in them, he had a perfect recollection of his actual bodily state. He *knew* intellectually that he was lying in bed asleep and that his tooth was aching. But he did not *feel* toothache, and in fact slept all night without experience of pain. On awaking next morning the tooth was aching as before, and he had it extracted.

Before leaving van Eeden it may be of interest to note his description of a certain type of non-lucid dream which he often had. He called these 'Demon Dreams'. In such dreams he was, as it were, located in scenes, and observed or took part in actions, which were horrible or obscene; and he ostensibly perceived and conversed with the beings who were responsible for those scenes and actions. These creatures were themselves obscene and lascivious. They had no constant sex, were continually changing their bodily form, and they used to mock at the dreamer and try to draw him into their doings. Van

Eeden remarks that the medieval painters of devils have got a very fair picture of the beings who appear in such dreams. It is interesting to speculate on how far seeing such pictures may have contributed to these dreams of van Eeden's; and how far such dreams, on the part of medieval monks, may have been the source of these pictures. In these 'demon dreams' van Eeden often had the experience as of struggling vigorously with the demons. He remarks that he was generally in good bodily health when he had such dreams, and that he would awake from his struggles with the demons feeling fresh and cheerful. It may be worth while to give one typical example of such a dream.

Immediately after a succession of very beautiful lucid dreams a demon dream began. Van Eeden found himself as it were surrounded by a number of these creatures. They started singing, like a mob of half-savage beings. In the dream he began to lose self-control, and, as it seemed, started throwing his bed-clothes and pillows about. At that point he noticed one of the demons, who looked less vicious than the rest. This one said to him: 'You are going wrong!' Van Eeden answered: 'Yes, but what shall I do?' The demon (evidently a stranger to modern enlightenment in regard to delinquency) answered: 'Give them the whip on their naked backs!' Thereupon van Eeden, thinking of a relevant passage in Dante, proceeded to 'materialize' a whip of leathern thongs with leaden balls at the ends of them. He threatened the demons with this, and shook it at them, whereupon they slunk away.

'OUT-OF-THE-BODY' EXPERIENCES

The essential feature of these experiences is this. The experient has what appear to him at the time to be ordinary sense-perceptions of actual things and persons (including very often his own physical body), from a point of view located in the ordinary space of nature outside the position occupied by his physical body at the time. Generally he appears to himself to be provided with a kind of secondary body, resembling his physical body more or less closely in shape, size, and outward appearance, but much more plastic and less ponderable. This is believed by some of the experients to be normally located within (or, perhaps more properly, to be infused throughout) the physical body; but to be capable on occasion of issuing from the latter, of reorienting itself, and of travelling to considerable distances whilst retaining some kind of extended *quasi*-material link with the physical body. On such occasions the main consciousness of the individual in question is often (but not always) felt by him to be 'centred in' this secondary body, in the sense in which it is felt to be 'centred in' one's ordinary physical body in one's normal waking life.

We may subdivide the cases to be considered into the following classes. (A) Those in which consciousness is centred as in a secondary body outside the physical body, and the physical body is ostensibly perceived as one external object among others. (B) Those in which consciousness remains centred in the physical body, but the experient ostensibly perceives from that point of view a secondary body, which he may or may not be able to control by his volitions. (C) Experimental cases, in which X manages, by deliberate volition, to cause another person Y, who is at a distance, to have an ostensible perception as of X being present in Y's immediate neighbourhood. In these cases X may or may not at the time have an experience as of being present in a secondary body in Y's neighbourhood. (D) Cases that do not fall very clearly under any of the previous headings.

I shall begin by considering, under each of these heads, some *sporadic* cases. Thereafter I shall say something of accounts which have been given by certain persons who have claimed to have had 'out-of-the-body' experiences, of one kind or another, fairly regularly.

Sporadic Cases. These seem most often to be associated with a serious accident, the crisis of an illness, the taking of an anaesthetic, or some such outstanding event in the life of the experient; but sometimes they occur without any obvious occasioning cause.

(A) *Consciousness centred as in a Secondary Body*

(1) *The Case of Miss Hendry* (Muldoon and Carrington: *The Phenomena of Astral Projection*, pp. 194–6). This case was reported to Mr Muldoon by Miss M. Hendry, of Cleveland, Ohio, U.S.A., in January 1938. He cross-examined her on certain points in her narrative. The experience which she described had happened some nine years earlier, when she was 35 years old. She says that she disliked the experience, which scared her considerably. But it led her to look into the case for Spiritualism, and at the time when she wrote to Mr Muldoon she had for some while been a Spiritualist.

The essential points are these. Miss Hendry was, at the time when she had her experience, a graduate nurse. In that capacity she was one day assisting a doctor who was performing an operation in a small country hospital. Suddenly she seemed to herself to be located at the doctor's side of the table, behind his back, and looking over his shoulder at her physical body facing her from the other side of the table and performing there the various operations required of an assistant. She had had no consciousness of the separation taking place, but simply found that it had done so without warning. At the

168

end of the operation she seemed to herself to float up over the table, to alight by the side of her physical body, and then very suddenly to be merged in it.

In answer to certain questions by Mr Muldoon, Miss Hendry made the following statements. She definitely appeared to herself to be *embodied in another body*, when seeing her physical body as from behind the doctor and over his shoulder. During the experience she had *no* simultaneous awareness of herself as being also embodied in her physical body; she simply saw it from outside as one might see another person's body. She had every reason to believe that the doctor noticed nothing odd in her behaviour. She was in good health at the time, and had been feeling perfectly normal up to the moment at which the experience began.

(2) *The Case of Dr 'X'* (S.P.R. *Journal*, Vol. XXXIX, No. 692). This case was contributed by the late Professor F. J. M. Stratton, of Gonville and Caius College, Cambridge, to the *Journal*. The experient, Dr X, was a friend of long standing. He was an M.D. and F.R.C.P., and a retired consulting physician. His name, and all the relevant details, are in possession of the S.P.R. The main defect of the case is the great lapse of time between the occurrence of the experience (April 21st, 1916) and the writing of the account of it by Dr X for Professor Stratton (summer of 1956).

At the time when the incident happened X was medical officer to the Second Brigade of the R.F.C. His headquarters were at Clair Marais aerodrome. From there he was suddenly summoned one day to Abeele aerodrome, to treat a pilot who had been shot down and had landed there. It was decided that X should be flown to Abeele; and Major Malcolm, the officer in command at Clair Marais, determined at the last moment to act as pilot of the plane.

Malcolm was a notoriously bad pilot, and the Clair Marais aerodrome was very ill-sited. On taking off, the pilot did a steep climbing turn too early, and the plane crashed with X in it.

X remembers that, during the brief period when it was evident that a crash was inevitable, he felt uninterested in his fate, and speculated idly on whether the upper or the lower of the two wings of the machine would strike the ground first. He became certain that it would be the upper one. He notes that there was *no* experience as of 'going over the whole of one's past life in a flash'. He remembers nothing of the actual impact. What in fact happened was that the pilot escaped unhurt, whilst X was thrown out of the cockpit well clear of the wreckage, landed on his back, and sustained injuries which caused extensive paralysis. His body lay there showing no signs of consciousness.

Before describing the next experiences which X ostensibly remembers, it will be well to state what was in fact happening. It should be premised that the landing and taking-off ground at Clair Marais lay in a grassy hollow near a farm. All the Squadron buildings (including the medical unit) were near to the farm almost at the top of a small rise. Any plane on the landing ground or the take-off ground would be invisible (even as regards its upper wing) by anyone standing at the hangars. A sentry was stationed at the time on the crest. Observing a steeply banked plane first rising above the ridge and then diving out of sight, he gave a signal for the standard routine in case of accidents to be put into action. This was that the Crossley tender (which was fitted up as an ambulance, and was always standing in readiness, but had no self-starter) should at once move to the scene with medical help.

We can now detail X's ostensibly remembered experiences. The first was that he was as it were looking down on his physical body, as it lay on the ground, from a point of view about 200 feet vertically above it. As from that position he ostensibly saw the following things. (i) The Brigadier, the Lieut.-Colonel, and the pilot running towards his body. X wondered why they were interested in it, and wished that they would let it alone. (ii) The following sequence of events: (*a*) The Crossley starting out of the hangar in which it was garaged, and almost immediately stalling; and then the chauffeur jumping out, pulling the starting-handle, running back to his seat, and starting to drive to the scene of the crash. (*b*) X's medical orderly meanwhile rushing out of X's medical hut near by, and jumping into the back of the Crossley. (*c*) The Crossley stopping again, the medical orderly getting out, running back into the hut to fetch something, and then jumping into the Crossley, which now resumed its journey. (None of these things, of course, would have been visible from the place where X's body was lying, even if he had been normally conscious, which he was not.)

X ostensibly remembers observing all this, and wondering why they were making such a fuss. He then had the experience of travelling, in his secondary body, from the original position vertically above the scene of the accident. It seemed to him as if he were going in the direction of Hazebrouck, and not in that of Abeele; but it seemed evident that he was to go far beyond Hazebrouck. At that stage he states that a 'rather subtle change took place'. He seemed to be moving westwards, first over Cornwall and then out over the Atlantic. He was content to let things take their course. Then he seemed to lose speed in that direction. Next he had the experience as of being pulled back, definitely without turning, until he was once more hovering for a while over his physical body.

170

Suddenly he resumed normal consciousness in his physical body, aware of the medical orderly pouring *sal volatile* down his throat. X told him to stop; and, realizing that he was extensively paralysed, gave orders that he should be left undisturbed until a qualified medical officer should arrive to deal with his case. X was in fact paralysed in all four limbs, the diaphragm, and the lower six ribs. He was transferred to hospital with great skill by a Dr Abrahams of the R.A.M.C. The latter was still living in 1956, and kindly wrote to the S.P.R., confirming the details of the accident and of his medical treatment of X on the aerodrome. Dr Abrahams states that X, on arrival at hospital, was put under the care of Capt. (later Col.) C. S. Jones of the R.A.M.C. Attempts made by Professor Stratton to contact Col. Jones had been unsuccessful up to the time when the report was published in the *Journal*.

X states that he soon recovered completely his normal mental state. He realized immediately on reflexion that it would have been physically impossible for him to have *seen* all the events which he ostensibly remembered seeing, since he was lying on his back in a hollow on the ground when they took place. He was impressed by this, and mentioned his experience to the C.O. of the Clair Marais aerodrome, when the latter visited him in hospital. X states that the C.O. (i.e. the Major Malcolm who had acted as pilot) took down at his dictation a full account of X's experiences as he then remembered them. Major Malcolm was, however, killed in a flying accident some weeks later; and this statement, so far as is known, does not survive. X says that the story was later recounted to Sir D. Henderson (then head of the R.F.C.), and that some time afterwards he himself related the story orally to Lady Henderson at her husband's request. Still later he repeated the story, by request, to Father Dolling, to Sir Oliver Lodge, and to A. J. Balfour.

X remarks that this experience has removed from him all fear of death. He also notes that his main feeling at the time might be expressed by the words: 'Why are they bothering about my body. I am entirely content where I am.' (It may be remarked that that appears to be the usual attitude, towards the fate of their physical body, of those who are having such experiences at times of accident or the crisis of an illness.)

I think that the minimum which must be accepted is that Dr X almost certainly had, very soon after recovering normal consciousness, very vivid and detailed ostensible memories as of having had, whilst his physical body was lying prone and showing no signs of consciousness, such experiences as have been detailed above. If an extreme sceptic should say that those ostensible memories may (for all that we can know) have been completely delusive, and that Dr X

171

may in fact have had no experiences at all during that period, there is no means of refuting him. But, for my own part, I regard such extreme scepticism as idle, except perhaps as a philosophic exercise. On the other hand, it seems to me that we do not now have any satisfactory evidence that Dr X's experiences, if he did in fact have them, were *veridical* (to a degree that surpasses normal explanation) in regard to those details in respect of which they could have been tested at the time.

(B) *Quasi-perception, as of a Secondary Body, from the Physical Body*

(1) *The Case of Mr Simons* (S.P.R. *Journal*, Vol. VI, pp. 267–8). The report of this case is contained in a letter, dated December 29th, 1891, from Mr C. E. G. Simons, then a young medical man. The essential points are as follows. Early in January 1890 Simons was in Aberdeen, reading for his second professional examination in medicine. One afternoon he was in his room, half-lying on the sofa, reading notes on surgery. He was thinking over the reading to be done next day, and of how he would arrange to fit it in with his lecture hours. In the room were two student friends of his, H. T. H. and R. N. de B. Of these H. was writing at the table and de B. was playing the piano. De B. left the room and went out of the house.

Shortly after this Simons began to feel, as one sometimes does in a nightmare, as if bound hand and foot. But he could move his eyes in any direction and open and shut his eyelids. He was fully aware of everything in the room, and noted the time, which was 3.49 p.m. He looked at the book lying open on the table in front of H., and saw that H. was transcribing notes on *materia medica*. Simons reflected whether, in spite of all this, he could possibly be asleep. This condition lasted for three minutes by the clock. During all that time he had a feeling as of an *external force* inhibiting his movements. This seemed to act from, and to be concentrated at, a point at the level of his shoulders, slightly behind him, and at about a yard away.

Suddenly he seemed to himself to be *divided*, by means of this force, into two distinct beings. One of them (which we will call No. 1) remained motionless on the sofa. The other (No. 2) could move to a little distance, and could face No. 1. Between the two was what felt like an elastic tension, holding them together. Simons (located at No. 1's position) could at will make No. 2 lie on the floor, or move to some distance about the room. As the distance increased, the elastic tension between the two grew greater, and at a limit of about two yards he could effect no further separation.

During this period Simons remained fully conscious of all that was going on in the room. He saw and heard de B. re-enter and start to play the piano again, and he saw H. making wry faces at the music. With a great effort, Simons managed to call out H.'s name. H. looked round, but went on writing and made no answer. (H. said afterwards that this was because he thought that Simons was trying to fool him.)

The dual condition lasted for about five minutes more. Then fusion began to set in. At first Simons resisted this, and found that he could do so with some success. Then he let it go on, and thereafter No. 2 and No. 1 united rapidly. Then he tried, and this time failed, to get into the dual condition again. This attempt at separation seemed to be prevented by the same force as had previously inhibited bodily movement.

Simons then began trying to think of some possible explanation; and, while he was doing so, the inhibiting force grew weaker and gradually disappeared. There was no experience as of *awaking* from sleep; there was simply a slow cessation of the previous abnormal condition.

He claims to have found that all the observations that he had made of the events in the room had been minutely accurate. After 'coming-to' he deliberately remained for some time in the same position on the sofa, in order to see whether anything further of interest would happen. Nothing did. Shortly afterwards he got up and related his experience to his two friends. They were amused, and thought that he was just making it up.

(2) *The Case of Mrs Hall* (*Phantasms of the Living*, Vol. II, pp. 217–18). Mrs S. J. Hall, of Gretton, near Kettering, wrote to Gurney in December 1883 an account of the following incident, which she stated had happened to her in the autumn of 1863. There is, unfortunately, no independent corroborative evidence, as Mrs Hall stated that the three relatives concerned had all died within some six years after the event. The essential points are as follows.

Mrs Hall was living, at the time in question, with her husband and a baby of eight months old, at a lonely house, 'Sibberton', near Wansford, Northants. During the winter a married cousin and her husband came on a visit. As the visitors and Mr and Mrs Hall were sitting at the dining-table having supper, *all four of them* saw, at the end of the sideboard, an apparition of Mrs Hall dressed in a spotted light muslin dress. It was Mr Hall who first had the experience, and he attracted the attention of the others by exclaiming: 'It is Susan!' None of them felt any fear, for it all seemed so natural. Mrs Hall says that it seemed as remote from herself and her own feelings as a picture or a statue. The dress was *not* like any that Mrs Hall had at the time, but she wore one like it some two years later.

If Mrs Hall's testimony can be accepted, this case is interesting as being *collective*. We could describe it either (*a*) as a *phantasm of the living*, which was ostensibly seen, not only by others, but also by the referent herself; or (*b*) as an *out-of-the-body case*, in which the secondary body was ostensibly seen, not only by the owner of the corresponding physical body, but also by others in her neighbourhood.

(C) *Experimental Cases*

Well authenticated cases of experimentally induced out-of-the-body experiences are extremely rare. The writings of the earlier mesmerists contain a number of such stories, but I should hesitate to put much trust in any of them. I believe that no well attested case has been reported to the S.P.R. since the time when Gurney was collecting the materials for *Phantasms of the Living*, which first appeared in 1886.

It should be mentioned that one of the most entertaining and *prima facie* well attested of the cases adduced by Gurney under this head must regretfully be dropped. This is the case of young Mr Cleave, under hypnosis by his room-mate Mr Sparks, paying an astral visit to his girl-friend Miss A. in presence of her small brother, and subsequently returning to his physical body and correctly reporting what he had seen (*Phantasms of the Living*, Vol. II, pp. 671–5).

This case was first brought to Gurney's notice in January 1886 by Mr Sparks, the hypnotizer of Mr Cleave. Gurney investigated it with his usual care, as will be seen by anyone who reads his account. Nevertheless, there appeared in Vol. XIV, p. 114, of the S.P.R. *Proceedings* (1898–9) the following *Note* on this case: '. . . by the wish of the two surviving part-authors of *Phantasms of the Living*, and considering the close connexion between that book and the S.P.R. . . . we think it right to mention here that one of the cases in the "Additional Chapter", Vol. II, p. 671, must now be withdrawn. There is no reason to doubt the *bona fides* of Mr Sparks, the principal informant; but Mr Cleave, then 18 years of age, whose evidence is essential to the case, has admitted that the alleged apparition of himself, when entranced, to a young lady in London, was a hoax.'

That being so, I can only refer the reader back to the two experimental cases detailed in the concluding section of Chapter V above (pp. 147–51), viz. that of Mr Kirk of Woolwich Arsenal and that of the Rev. C. Godfrey of Eastbourne; in the hope that the responsible office of the former, the sacred calling of the latter, and the mature age of both, made them immune to the temptation to 'pull the leg' of psychical researchers, to which that teenage butterfly, Mr Cleave, so regrettably succumbed.

(D) *Cases not readily classifiable under any one of the previous Headings*

Under this head I propose to describe one old and famous case, which combines a remarkable variety of paranormal features.

The Wilmot Case (S.P.R. *Proceedings*, Vol. VII, pp. 41–7). This case is given, and very fully discussed, by Mrs Sidgwick in her paper 'On the Evidence for Clairvoyance' in the volume of *Proceedings* referred to above.

On February 21st, 1890, Mr W. B. H. of Bridgeport, Connecticut, sent to Richard Hodgson of the S.P.R. a manuscript for his inspection. W. B. H. stated that he had written this down about five years earlier from memory, to put on record a story which had been related to him orally by Mr S. R. Wilmot, a manufacturer of Bridgeport, concerning certain experiences had by himself, by his wife, and by a Mr W. J. Tait in 1863. Mr W. B. H. stated that he had submitted the manuscript to Mr and Mrs Wilmot at the time, in order to ensure its correctness; and that Mr Wilmot had made corrections and marginal notes in pencil, and, subject to these, had signed the manuscript as a correct record of the events as he remembered them.

Both Mr and Mrs Wilmot were still alive at the time when Hodgson received the manuscript, and they were very willing to answer questions. Hodgson both called on Mr Wilmot and corresponded with him and with Mrs Wilmot. He received also certain confirmatory evidence from a sister of Mr Wilmot's.

The essential points of the story are as follows:

As can be verified by public record, the steamship *City of Limerick* (Capt. Jones) left Liverpool on October 3rd, 1863, and Queenstown on October 5th, for New York, where she arrived safely, after a very stormy voyage, in the morning of October 22nd. Another steamer, the *Africa*, left Queenstown for Boston on October 4th, and struck on rocks at Cape Race in a dense fog in the night of October 12th. She was reported in the U.S.A. papers as lost; but in fact got away safely, though with considerable damage to ship and cargo, and put into St John's, Newfoundland.

Mr Wilmot sailed from Liverpool in the *City of Limerick*. On the evening of the second day out a severe storm began and lasted for nine days, doing very considerable damage to the ship and its tackle. It was not until the night following the eighth day of the storm, i.e. the night of Tuesday 13th, to Wednesday 14th, of October, that Mr Wilmot was able to enjoy a fair night's sleep. Towards morning he had the following dream. He dreamed that Mrs Wilmot, then at home in the U.S.A., came to the door of his state-room, clad in her night-dress. At the door she seemed to discover that there was another

175

occupant of the state-room beside her husband, and hesitated for a little. Then she advanced to Mr Wilmot's side, stooped down and kissed him, and after a few moments withdrew from the cabin.

The other occupant of the state-room was Mr Wm. J. Tait. He was an Englishman by birth, of about 50 years of age, who had for long been settled in Cleveland, Ohio, where he held the post of Librarian to the Associated Library. Mr Wilmot describes him as 'a sedate and very religious man, whose testimony upon any subject could be taken unhesitatingly'. Mr Tait was sleeping in a berth on a higher level than that of Mr Wilmot, but not directly above it. When Mr Wilmot awoke in the morning, he was startled to find Mr Tait sitting up and looking fixedly at him and eventually exclaiming: 'You're a pretty fellow, to have a lady come and visit you in that way.' After some pressing Mr Tait stated that, whilst lying wide awake in his berth, he had witnessed a scene corresponding exactly to what Mr Wilmot had dreamed. Wilmot cross-questioned Tait on three occasions before leaving the ship, but he stuck to this story.

On October 23rd, the day after landing at New York, Mr Wilmot travelled to Watertown, Connecticut, where his wife and children had been for some time on a visit to friends. Almost the first question which Mrs Wilmot put to him when they were alone together was the startling one: 'Did you receive a visit from me a week ago last Tuesday?' He pointed out the physical impossibility of this; but she replied that, nevertheless, it had seemed to her that she had made such a visit. He asked her, thereupon, to explain what made her think so. Her account of her own experiences was as follows. Knowing of the stormy weather in the Atlantic, and having heard reports of the wreck of the *Africa*, which had sailed from Liverpool at practically the same time as the *City of Limerick*, she had gone to bed, feeling very anxious for her husband's safety, on the night of Tuesday, October 13th. She had lain awake for a long time, thinking of him, and at about 4 a.m. it seemed to her that she 'went out to seek' him. It was as if she crossed a wide, stormy sea; came at length to a low, black steamer; somehow went up its side and descended into the cabin; and passed through it into the stern until she came to her husband's state-room. She seemed to see a man in the upper berth, looking right at her, and she was for a moment afraid to go in. Then she did so; went up to the side of Mr Wilmot's berth, bent down and kissed him, and then went away.

It should be added that, in the course of her story, Mrs Wilmot put the following question to her husband: '. . . Do they ever have state-rooms like the one I saw, where the upper berth extends further back than the under one . . .?' Mrs Wilmot had never seen the ship in her normal state, and, as will be remembered, the berths were in fact arranged in that rather unusual way in the state-room occupied by Mr Wilmot and Mr Tait.

Mr Tait had died some time before Mr W. H. B. wrote down Mr Wilmot's account of the experiences of the night in question, and therefore could not be interrogated by Hodgson. But Hodgson was able to obtain some secondhand confirmation of the account of Mr Tait's part in the drama. Mr Wilmot's sister, Miss Eliza E. Wilmot, had been a fellow-passenger with him on the *City of Limerick*. She was still living, and Hodgson got in touch with her. She wrote a letter to him, to the following effect.

It appears that Mr Wilmot had been too sea-sick to leave his berth for several days; but Miss Wilmot had been able to totter to the breakfast-table, with Mr Tait's help, on the morning after the incident. Mr Tait astonished her by asking whether she had been in to their state-room in the course of the previous night to see her brother. She had answered: '*No!* why?', and Mr Tait had then told her that he had seen *some* woman in white, who had gone up to Mr Wilmot's berth. Soon after this conversation Miss Wilmot did go in to visit her brother, and she remembered his saying that Mr Tait had wondered at her coming to see him during the previous night. Some three years later Miss Wilmot visited the Taits at their home in Cleveland, and she states that Mr Tait then 'spoke of the wonderful coincidence', which had evidently impressed him.

This is a very strange story. The only serious evidential weakness is that the first written report of it depends on the memories of Mr and Mrs Wilmot as they were some twenty years after the date of the events reported. For my own part, I do not think it reasonable to doubt that these ostensible memories, supported by those of Miss Wilmot, were in the main correct. But I wonder whether a possible explanation of an important part of the reported facts might not be that Miss Wilmot did in fact walk, *in her sleep*, into the state-room, and go up to her brother's berth and touch him, and then go out again. That would fully explain Mr Tait's waking experience, and it might possibly explain Mr Wilmot's dreaming at that moment of his wife as present and leaning over him. What would remain to be accounted for is the close coincidence in time between these events and Mrs Wilmot's dreamlike experience as of crossing the ocean, entering the ship, hesitating at the door of the state-room, and then going in and leaning over her husband's berth and touching him. That *might* be just a chance-coincidence. But it might be due to some kind of telepathic action between Mrs and Miss Wilmot, inducing the latter actually to do, *in her sleep*, what the former, in a state of great emotional tension, was then *dreaming of herself as doing*. There would still remain to be accounted for Mrs Wilmot's alleged

177

knowledge of the peculiar arrangement of the berths in that state-room. Now that arrangement would, of course, be quite familiar to Miss Wilmot, who had no doubt repeatedly visited her brother while he lay confined to his berth by sea-sickness. On the present hypo-thesis, we might suppose a kind of reciprocal telepathic action be-tween Miss and Mrs Wilmot, whereby the latter, whilst influencing the sleep-walking of the former, was in her turn influenced by the former's normal knowledge of the internal arrangements of the state-room.

I need hardly say that I attach no particular weight to the above very speculative suggestions. But they occurred to me while reading Miss Wilmot's letter to Hodgson, which plays only a minor part in the evidence presented; and I put them forward for what little they may be worth.

If we take the case at its face value, it is, as regards Mrs Wilmot, an *out-of-the-body* experience, in which the details ostensibly per-ceived by her from her transferred point of view corresponded with the actual scene to which her point of view had been shifted. As re-gards Mr Tait, it is a waking *quasi*-perception of a *phantasm of the living*, corresponding in its content to the *dream*, which was being simultaneously had by Mr Wilmot, and to the *out-of-the-body* experi-ence which Mrs Wilmot was then having.

Out-of-the-Body Experiences frequently occurring to the same Person

Certain persons claim to have had frequent experiences as of being out of the body, and some of them claim to have learned how to put themselves, more or less at will, into that state. The two most impor-tant writers in English who have made and elaborated such claims are, so far as I know, Mr Oliver Fox and Mr Sylvan Muldoon. I propose to give some account of their statements.

(1) *Mr Oliver Fox.* In the *Occult Review* for 1920 there appeared two articles by Mr Fox, entitled *The Pineal Doorway* and *Beyond the Pineal Doorway.* The gist of them is as follows:

In 1902 Mr Fox, then a student at a technical college, dreamed one night that he was standing in the street outside his house. Looking down, in his dream, he noticed a certain anomaly in the orientation of the paving-stones. The *long* sides of these appeared in the dream as *parallel* to the kerb, instead of being perpendicular to it, as he re-membered them to be. This persuaded him that he was dreaming, without awakening him. Thereupon he had a strong and very delight-ful feeling of clarity in himself and of beauty in the objects ostensibly seen, which were the ordinary surroundings of his home glorified. Shortly afterwards he woke up. He thought it would be interesting to try to repeat such experiences. His progress was slow and chequered, but he was able to make the following general observation. Whenever he noted in a dream some incongruity, which convinced him that he was dreaming but did not awaken him, he experienced the feeling of clarity in himself and of beauty in the dream-objects which he had had on the first occasion.

It is most interesting to compare Fox's experiences, at this stage, with those of Mach and of van Eeden. What Fox was having is recognizably what van Eeden called 'lucid dreams', and the conditions which Fox describes as conducive to getting such dreams are precisely those noted by Mach and by van Eeden. Van Eeden's paper in the S.P.R. *Proceedings* was not published until 1913, so Fox cannot have been influenced by suggestions from it. And Fox's paper was not published in the *Occult Review* until 1920, so van Eeden cannot have been influenced by it.

At this stage Fox found, just as van Eeden had done, that he could do little tricks in his dreams at will, e.g. levitate, pass through seemingly solid walls, 'materialize' objects, and so on. But he could get such dreams only at intervals of several weeks, and on each occasion only for a short time. He now noticed the following facts. (i) If he tried to prolong such a dream, he felt a pain in the part of his head which he took to be the region of the *pineal gland*, and this increased rapidly in intensity. (ii) In the latest moments of prolonging such a dream, and while the head-pain was intense, he would have an experience as of *bilocation*. He would feel himself as (*a*) outside his physical body, and yet (*b*) as lying in his bed in the ordinary way. He could sometimes, as it were, hover between the two states, emphasizing either of them at will. He did *not*, however, have the experience of, as it were, *seeing* his physical body on the bed from outside it.

At length an occasion came when he decided to disregard the head-pain and to try to remain outside his physical body. The first time he succeeded in this, he had the following experiences. A kind of 'click' was felt in his head, and the pain there vanished. At the same time the sense of bilocation ceased, and he felt as if he were shut out of his body and wholly located within the scenery of his dream. This appeared to be a kind of glorified counterpart of the sea-shore about a mile from his home. He had lost the ordinary sense of time; and he noticed that the dream-persons, who passed close to him in the dream-scenery, seemed completely unaware of his presence. He felt utterly lonely, began to wonder if he were dead, and finally became panic-stricken. He began willing to get back. This was at first without effect, but eventually he again felt the 'click' in his head, and thereupon found himself located in his ordinary physical body in his bed.

179

At first he could neither see nor move; but gradually, with a great effort he regained normal control of his physical body and normal consciousness. He jumped out of bed, and immediately collapsed on the floor, overcome with nausea. After a considerable interval he tried the same experiment again, with similar unpleasant results. He came to the conclusion that such experiments are dangerous, and resolved to try no more of them.

When he made no special effort to prolong one of these lucid dreams, but allowed it to come to a natural end without interference, he noted that he seldom awoke *directly* out of it. Most often it was immediately followed by a *dream* that he was awake in his bedroom; and then, a little later, he would really awake. Here again it is interesting to compare Dr van Eeden's precisely similar statement about his lucid dreams generally terminating in false-awakening dreams.

So far Fox's attempts at voluntary control had been confined to producing the following effects. (i) He had managed voluntarily to *prolong* for a while a lucid dream, once such a dream had begun. (ii) When such a voluntarily prolonged lucid dream was about to come to an end, he had managed to force a further continuance, and to give himself the impression of being totally separated from his physical body. (iii) He had managed voluntarily to bring himself back from that state to his normal state of consciousness. That transition had been mediated by a kind of trance-state, in which he felt himself to be located in his physical body, but was at first powerless to make those bodily movements which are normally under the direct control of the will. He had not so far attempted voluntarily to *initiate* an out-of-the-body experience. He now set himself to do this.

To that end he sought to put himself deliberately into a state of cataleptiform waking trance, like that which had mediated his return from an out-of-the-body experience to normal waking consciousness. It seemed not unreasonable to suppose that this might be an essential stage on the way out, as it had proved to be on the way back. Now it will be remembered that he had felt a characteristic kind of 'click' in his head, marking the transition from the out-of-the-body state to the state of cataleptiform waking trance. He had located this 'click' in the place where he believed his pineal gland to be situated. (In this connexion, it may be remarked that there has been a long tradition in occult circles, associating this part of the brain with paranormal experiences. Again, Descartes regarded the pineal gland as the one place at which the soul and the body directly interact. Fox would almost certainly have heard or read of these theories.)

Acting on this belief (which was probably as good as any other for the purpose in hand) Fox imaged the pineal gland as a kind of *door* in his brain, and thought of the 'click' as associated with the opening and shutting of this door. In order to induce the trance-state he would lie, with muscles relaxed, eyelids closed, and his eyes (as it seemed to him) rolled upwards and slightly squinting. He would try to exclude all other thoughts, and to concentrate his imagination on the pineal 'door' in his brain, while keeping his body wholly passive.

The first thing that he would notice would be a *quasi*-visual experience as of seeing the room, through his closed eyelids, as pervaded by a golden colour of varying intensity. At this stage it was not uncommon for him to have visual and auditory hallucinations, often of a very unpleasant nightmarish kind. Gradually his body would become numb, beginning at the feet and extending thence upwards.

In order to pass from this self-induced cataleptiform state into an out-of-the-body experience, he would imagine vividly the following transaction. He would think of himself as having an 'astral' body, contained within his physical body, and he would imagine this as hurling itself at the pineal 'trap-door' in his brain, and trying to force its way through. At that point the golden light would increase in intensity, so that the whole room would seem to him, with his eyes shut, to be in flames. Often several attempts were needed before he could get away. After an unsuccessful attempt he would feel as if his 'astral' body subsided, and the golden light would die down. These unsuccessful attempts were most unpleasant and frightening experiences. After a successful attempt he would hear the 'click' in his head (which he would interpret as the sound of the pineal 'door' shutting behind him), and he would then be in the out-of-the-body state, having lost all fear, and enjoying a much greater mental clarity then he ever experienced in normal waking life.

Generally there was a short interval of complete unconsciousness between a successful attempt to break through the 'pineal door' and the beginning of the out-of-the-body state of consciousness. But eventually Fox came to be able to pass in either direction without any interval of unconsciousness. He says that it took him fourteen years of pretty regular experiment and practice to attain this capacity. One has the impression that Fox is a sensible and balanced man. He is careful to warn his readers not to take too literally his talk about the 'pineal door'. That phraseology describes, in the best way that he can, the experience as it feels to him at the time when he has it. What anatomical or physiological facts may lie behind it is, as he realizes, another question, which he does not profess to answer.

For my own part, I should not have the patience or the courage to try to repeat Fox's experiments, and I would strongly dissuade the average reader from making such attempts. But I cannot help hoping that a few indomitable persons, of strong nerves and good mental balance, will take the undoubted risks; and that, if they get positive results, they will record them with as little delay as possible, and will submit their records to the S.P.R.

Unlike many of those who have had out-of-the-body experiences, Fox never ostensibly saw *his own* physical body from without, whilst in the out-of-the-body state. He asserts, on the other hand, that he repeatedly 'saw' *his wife's* physical body, when he was in that state and she was lying asleep in their bedroom. He says that the *scenery* of these experiences was in principle ordinary earthly scenery, though in detail it was generally quite unfamiliar to him. The *persons* in those scenes seemed to be ordinary human beings, engaged in their ordinary occupations. He appeared to be *invisible* to them. I take this to mean that they normally showed no signs of being aware of his presence, and that there was no conversation between him and them. That is, of course, in strong contrast to what happens in our ordinary dreams. Fox says that occasionally the persons whom he 'saw' as being in his immediate neighbourhood during an out-of-the-body experience behaved as if they sensed his presence without seeing him, and appeared to be frightened. On such occasions *their* fright produced an emotional shock in *him*, and this tended to draw him back into his normal waking state of consciousness.

Experiences as of moving at a height over extensive landscapes, spread out to view beneath, played a large part in Fox's out-of-the-body states, just as they did in van Eeden's lucid dreams. He distinguishes the following three kinds of locomotion, other than ordinary walking. (i) Skimming over the surface of the ground at a height of only a foot or so above it. (This is a very enjoyable experience which I have often had in dreams, and I suppose that it is not uncommon.) (ii) Rising gradually to a considerable height, as if one were immersed in a fluid of slightly greater specific gravity than that of one's body, and then progressing laterally by a process like swimming. (iii) Suddenly rocketing to a very great height, from which a very extensive view could be enjoyed.

(2) *Mr Sylvan Muldoon.* Mr Muldoon was born in 1902 and has lived most of his life in the Middle West. He had his first out-of-the-body experience at the age of 12. He was brought up in Spiritualistic circles, and had heard that there were people who could voluntarily induce that state. He tried to get in touch with such people and failed, and he then began experimenting for himself.

Some time in 1927 he read a book by the late Mr Hereward Carrington, in which there was a synopsis of work on this topic by a French writer, Charles Lancelin. Muldoon, then aged about 25, wrote to Carrington to say that, if this was all that Lancelin knew about the matter, he himself knew more and better. A correspondence followed, and Carrington urged Muldoon to write a book on the subject, promising to revise and edit the manuscript and to provide an introduction. Much of this book was written while Muldoon lay in bed seriously ill. It appeared in 1929, in the joint names of the two, under the title *The Projection of the Astral Body*. In 1936 Muldoon published singly a book entitled *The Case for Astral Projection*. In this he gave some additional data and published a number of cases reported by others. In 1951 he again collaborated with Hereward Carrington, publishing a book entitled *The Phenomena of Astral Projection*. Part II of this contains an interesting collection of reported cases of out-of-the-body experiences, classified under nine headings according to the circumstances under which they happened.

It will be of interest to describe fairly fully Muldoon's first out-of-the-body experience. This happened in 1914, when he was 12 years old, at Clinton, Iowa, where his mother and he were on a visit. He went to bed at about 10.30 p.m., soon fell asleep, and remained asleep for several hours. He then had a bewildering and unpleasant experience, which he compares with those often had on first awaking after an anaesthetic. The dominating thought was: 'Where am I?'

Gradually he became aware that he was lying *somewhere*, and soon after that that he was lying on a *bed*; but he felt bewildered as to his correct *orientation*. (This last is an experience which I can well remember having had on several occasions, particularly in a false-awakening dream, and once when I had a rather high temperature.) He tried to move, but at first felt as if he were *glued down* to that on which he was lying. That feeling was later replaced by one of *floating*; and at the same time his body seemed to him to be in rapid oscillation up and down as a rigid whole. While this was going on he had a feeling as of very strong *pressure at the back of his head*, coming in rhythmic waves, which seemed to pulsate through his whole body. He was still unable to move any of the parts of his body which are normally under direct voluntary control, but he now began hearing ordinary familiar sounds.

Next he began to have visual experiences. He ostensibly *saw* his bed a few feet *below* him, and *felt* his body as floating rigid and horizontal above it. Gradually he got a clearer and clearer sight of the room and its contents as from that point of view. He felt himself to be still moving upwards, horizontal and rigid, with the strong pressure at the back of his head, and the feeling of pulsation throughout his body. He states that so far he had taken for granted that it was his *ordinary physical body* that was concerned in all this. It would seem to follow that, although he had, as it were, seen *his bed* from above it, he had not as yet had any experience as of seeing *his body* lying on it.

When he took himself to be about six feet above the bed, he found himself *turned* from floating horizontally to standing upright on the floor, still in the cataleptiform state. Next he became free to move at will, and he turned round and faced the bed. He then, for the first time, ostensibly saw his physical body lying on the bed, and noted that he was viewing it and the other contents of the room from a point of view external to his physical body and located within another body, which I will call (without thereby committing myself to any view as to the objective facts at the back of these experiences) his 'secondary body'. He ostensibly saw a kind of *elastic cord*, extending about six feet from the region of the *medulla oblongata* of the secondary body to somewhere between the eyes of the physical body on the bed. (Presumably, the identification of the region with that of the *medulla oblongata* must be the result of reflexion at a much later date. It is hardly to be supposed that a boy of 12 would know the name, or locate anything in terms of the thing.)

All this time the secondary body, in which he felt himself as located, was swaying from side to side, and he was finding it hard to keep his balance. He made his way, against the pull of the cord, to the door of the room, in the hope of getting into the next room and waking others. He tried to open the door in the ordinary way by the handle; failed; and found himself, as it were, passing through the closed door. Then he had an experience as of wandering about the house, trying to attract the attention of others, and failing completely. All his senses, except that of *touch*, seemed to be working normally. He *heard*, e.g., a clock strike 2, and, looking at it, *saw* the hands registering 2 o'clock. But, when he attempted to touch things which he ostensibly saw, he could feel nothing.

He had these experiences for about 15 minutes, and became very frightened, deeming that he must have died. Then the tug of the cord grew stronger and stronger, pulling the secondary body back to the physical body. The secondary body again became cataleptic, and was turned from the perpendicular to the horizontal till it again floated above and parallel to the physical body on the bed. The pulsations began again, and the secondary body was slowly drawn downwards to the physical body. Finally, at the moment of coalescence, every muscle of the physical body jerked, he felt a pain as if he had been split open, and he resumed normal consciousness.

This first experience is fairly typical of the 'several hundred' which Muldoon says that he had had by the age of 27, when he and Carrington published their first book.

The 'cord', uniting the physical body to its secondary counterpart, is a feature which has fairly often been reported. It played no part in Fox's experiences, so far as I am aware. But, in the famous Wiltse case

(S.P.R. *Proceedings*, Vol. VIII, pp. 180–94), Dr Wiltse reported that he noted 'a small cord, like a spider's web' running from the shoulders of his secondary body to the front part of the neck of his physical body. It should be remarked that he said, in a letter to Hodgson, that he was already familiar with the doctrine of such a connecting cord, before he had his out-of-the-body experience, but had not previously accepted that doctrine. A similar feature seems to have been prominent in the case of the Rev. L. J. Bertrand (S.P.R. *Proceedings*, Vol. VIII, pp. 194–200), though it is not quite clear whether he ostensibly *saw* the cord, or only felt the pull of it and inferred its presence. While his physical body was sitting in a numbed condition at the edge of a ravine in the Alps, he seemed to himself to be like an air-balloon, floating in the air, but attached to his physical body (which he could see clearly from a considerable height above it) by *an elastic string*. He states that he longed to be able to *cut the cord*, by which he felt himself to be attached to his disgusting-looking physical body. And his return to normal consciousness was preceded by an experience as of being, to his intense regret, *pulled back* by this cord to his physical body.

Whatever may be the objective basis of such experiences, it is plain that they are a recognizable constituent in many, though by no means in all, well developed out-of-the-body cases. It is therefore of some interest to note what Muldoon has to say about *his* experiences of the cord.

When the two bodies are separated by only a few inches the cord is about $1\frac{3}{4}$ inches thick. As the separation increases, the thickness diminishes, through $\frac{3}{4}$ inch (when he describes it as 'looking like a garden-hose'), to a minimum (when it is about as thick as a bit of sewing-thread). If the separation should increase further, the thickness remains constant thereafter. With a subject in fairly good health, the critical extension is about 15 feet. While the separation lies within those limits, the cord has two kinds of movement. One is a regular pulsation, corresponding to each beat of the heart. The other is a slight rhythmic contraction and expansion, felt as an alternate pushing and pulling at the back of the head of the secondary body. This appears to be correlated with breathing.

So long as the separation does not exceed the limit, beyond which no further decrease in the thickness of the cord accompanies further separation, the pull-and-thrust is *greater* when the separation is *less*. It is unusual for the secondary body to get beyond this critical distance. But, if it should do so, it can thereafter move about without appreciable pressure or tension from the cord. Any strong emotion, experienced when in the out-of-the-body state, tends to pull the secondary body back into the physical body. (Cf. similar statements by Fox, above.) Muldoon describes an experience of being pulled back from an incipient projection by the shock occasioned by the sudden noise of someone rattling the doors of the furnace in his home. When coalescence takes place suddenly, a violent shock is felt in the physical body. This he calls 'repercussion'. Many of us are familiar with an experience of this kind, whether or not we accept Muldoon's account of the events underlying it.

Muldoon alleges that the secondary body is *itself* generally in a cataleptic state on separating from the physical body, and that it generally remains in that state so long as the separation is within the critical range. If, as occasionally happens, the secondary body should cease to be cataleptic while within that range, it tends to stagger about like the body of a drunken man, owing to the pushes and pulls of the cord. The experient tends to become giddy; that induces fear; and that emotion tends to make the secondary body cataleptic again, and to draw it back into the physical body.

When the secondary body was within fairly close range of the physical body, Muldoon has had *quasi*-visual experiences of the following kinds. (i) He has, as it were, seen his secondary body from the point of view of his physical body, although the physical eyes were shut and there was no light in the room. (ii) That experience has sometimes *alternated* with the complementary experience as of seeing the physical body from the point of view of the secondary body. (iii) He alleges that sometimes, though very rarely, these two kinds of visual experience have for a short period *co-existed* with each other. (iv) In any of these three alternative cases, if the secondary body should pass beyond the critical range of separation, vision from the point of view of the *physical* body immediately *ceases*, and there is only vision from the point of view of the secondary body.

It is of interest to compare and contrast these experiences with comparable features in those of Mr Fox and of Dr Wiltse. Fox, it will be remembered, never had any experience as of *seeing* his physical body from outside it. But, when deliberately prolonging a lucid dream, he often had an experience of bilocation, i.e. of *feeling* himself at one and the same time as outside his physical body and as lying on his bed. In the case of Dr Wiltse (*loc. cit.*) the experient reported the following odd observations. Shortly after the separation of his secondary body from his physical body, which was lying to all appearance moribund on his bed, he found to his astonishment that he could ostensibly *see* details on the *back* of his secondary body. This seemed to him highly paradoxical at the time; for, as he noted, the eyes of the secondary body were in the normal position, and not situated like those of an owl, which can see its own back by turning its head. Wiltse concluded that he must still be able to use the eyes of his physical body, although

186

he felt himself to be located in and seeing from his secondary body.

Since Muldoon was brought up in Spiritualistic circles, and had no doubt heard and read much about various 'astral planes' and their inhabitants, it is interesting to note that his out-of-the-body experiences, like Fox's, were quite mundane as regards scenery and persons encountered. He states that he always found himself somewhere on earth, and not in other planets or in any of the 'astral' planes or spheres described by many Spiritualists. Generally the places in which he found himself or to which he 'travelled' were already well known to him in normal waking life, though occasionally he would find himself in distant parts of his own country or in foreign lands. Usually he met no one. Occasionally he met persons familiar to him, whom he knew to be dead. (Cf. van Eeden's 'meetings', in his lucid dreams, with his brother and with van't Hoff.) Sometimes he met complete strangers, and some of these were friendly, whilst others were evil and hostile.

He feels certain that much that one ostensibly perceives, when in the out-of-the-body state, is constructed by some subconscious level of oneself. He often found that objects, which he was ostensibly seeing, would vanish when he approached them and tried to inspect them. He found too that he could not ostensibly *touch* the objects which he ostensibly *saw*. He says that one passes through them, or they pass through one, without there being any experience of contact. He has the good sense, however, to emphasize that different persons have different kinds of out-of-the-body experience, and that it would be dangerous to generalize from those of any one individual. We must remember, too, that most of those who have an out-of-the-body experience at all have such an experience only once or twice in their lives; that it generally lasts only for a short time; that they are often intellectually confused during it; and that they tend to be scared by it, and in a state of emotional tension. They are, therefore, not well situated for making accurate observations. We are, therefore, greatly indebted to the few persons, such as van Eeden, Fox, and Muldoon, who have had such experiences often enough to have learned to keep their heads, and have made and recorded generalizations based at any rate on a large amount of self-observation.

It has often been pointed out that apparitions nearly always are provided with some kind of *clothing*, and certain inferences have been drawn from that fact. It may, therefore, be worth while to summarize some statements on this topic made by Muldoon, and to compare them with some made by Dr Wiltse.

Muldoon says that, so far as concerns his own secondary body, it generally appeared to him as clothed in whatever way his physical body happened to be clad at the time. Sometimes, however, it appeared to him as clothed in a kind of white gauze-like material. It should be noted, in this connexion, that Muldoon takes seriously the traditional doctrine of the human 'aura', and that his views on the present topic presuppose it. So far as I can understand him, the theory is as follows. On separating from the physical body, the secondary body is, in any case, surrounded with its 'aura', which is an extended *quasi*-material substance. This is extremely plastic, and it tends to be moulded automatically by one's habitual subconscious thoughts. Since a normal grown-up person in the Western hemisphere and in northern latitudes habitually thinks of himself as clothed in one way or another, rather than as naked, his 'aura' tends to be moulded automatically into some kind of clothing for his secondary body, when that is separated from his physical body. The particular kind of clothing into which it would be moulded on a particular occasion would be likely to be determined by one's knowledge of what one's physical body was wearing at the time (e.g. a pair of blue-striped pyjamas), or by one's habitual thought of oneself as dressed in a certain way when awake and active (e.g. in a policeman's uniform, if one were a police-constable).

It is interesting to compare Dr Wiltse's observations (*loc. cit.*) with Muldoon's views on this point. At the beginning of his experience of existing in a fully separated secondary body, the latter appeared to him as translucent, bluish in colour, and *completely naked*. As there were two ladies in the room, watching beside what they took to be his death-bed, he felt somewhat embarrassed at his nudity, and he fled towards the partially open door of the sick-room. But, on reaching the door, he found himself *completely clothed*. At a somewhat later stage in his out-of-the-body experience he began wondering about his clothes, and how he had got them. They were no fig-leaves. He examined the fabric, and describes it as made of 'some kind of Scotch material . . . A good suit, though not handsome.' (It was shortly after this that he had the experience, described above, of looking at the back of his own secondary body. What he noticed there was the *seam of the coat*.)

It is obvious that the psychological causes, invoked by Muldoon to explain the 'moulding' of the 'aura', might be expected to produce similar experiential effects, if we rejected altogether the doctrines of the objective existence of a human aura and of a secondary body, and supposed instead that out-of-the-body experiences are primarily *dreams* of a peculiar kind, which may occasionally produce correlated experiences in others by a kind of telepathic infection. In all such matters it is most important to keep a firm hold of the distinction between (i) a purely phenomenological account of the reported

188

experiences, and (ii) this or that *theory* as to their epistemological status or their causal conditions.

In this chapter we have been describing certain experiences of a very odd kind, which nevertheless are and have always been frequent enough in perfectly sane persons to make them worthy of more attention than they have hitherto received from psychologists and anthropologists. It seems to me plain that they must have played an important part in the development of what may roughly be called an 'animistic' view of man and his environment, and that they have coloured the conceptions and beliefs of many religions. What is certain is that they occur fairly widely; that they follow a fairly definite ground-pattern, though with considerable variations in detail; and that they seem at the time, to those who are having them, to suggest very strongly the existence of a secondary counterpart to the physical body, which can separate temporarily during life from the latter, and become for a while the centre for a kind of perceptual consciousness very like that experienced by the subject in his normal waking life in his physical body.

Such experiences begin to be of special interest to psychical researchers, when any of the following conditions are fulfilled. (i) If the observations which the subject claims to have made, while in the secondary body, should accord, either (*a*) with details of the contemporary state and environment of his *physical body*, which he could not at the time have normally perceived or readily guessed, or (*b*) with details of the contemporary state and environment of *some remote individual*, whom he claims to have 'visited' in his secondary body. (ii) If the individual, whom he claims to have 'visited' in his secondary body, should at that time have had a *quasi*-perception *of him as present*; and, still more, if *several persons in company* should have had such a *quasi*-perception of him, at the time when he claims to have 'visited' the room in which they were collected.

Naturally, the interest for the psychical researcher would be at a maximum, if *all* the conditions (i) (*a*), (i) (*b*), and (ii) were to be fulfilled simultaneously. My impression is that there are extremely few well attested cases in which any of them are fulfilled, and hardly any in which all of them are so. But I cannot claim to have made an exhaustive critical study of the literature. Readers who may wish to pursue this topic further are recommended to read the paper entitled 'Six Theories about Apparitions', by Professor Hornell Hart and his collaborators, in S.P.R. *Proceedings*, Vol. L; and then to look up the reports of the cases referred to in it.

VII

SOME THEORETICAL POINTS ARISING FROM THE CASES ADDUCED: (I) THE NATURE AND CLASSIFICATION OF HALLUCINATIONS

I shall conclude Section B with three chapters in which I attempt to make more precise certain terms which I have used in the previous chapters of it. I shall deal in turn with (I) the Nature and Classification of Hallucinations, (II) The Notion of Telepathy in connexion with Sporadic Cases, and (III) Theories about Collective and Reciprocal Hallucinations.

The term 'Hallucination'. I will begin with the term 'hallucination', which has frequently been used. I think that this word is employed in common life, and in normal psychology and medicine, in such a way as to imply or at least very strongly suggest that an experience so denominated is *totally delusive*, and that the person who has it is at the time in a *pathological condition*. In psychical research that implication or strong suggestion must be explicitly rejected. For, on the one hand, the question at issue often is whether such an experience was or was not, in important respects, *veridical*. And, on the other hand, it is quite certain that many of the persons who have had such experiences were, by any of the usual criteria, perfectly sane and normal individuals, and were neither physically nor mentally perturbed at the time.

For the present purpose we may define the term 'hallucination' or 'hallucinatory *quasi*-perception' as follows. We shall say that a person was having such an experience on a given occasion, if and only if the following two conditions were fulfilled. (i) He was ostensibly seeing, hearing, touching, or otherwise sensibly perceiving a certain

190

thing or person or event or state of affairs, as external to his body. Whilst (ii) at that time his eyes, ears, fingers, or other receptor sense-organs were *not* being affected in the normal physical manner, either directly or by reflexion or refraction, by any such thing, person, event, or state of affairs as he was ostensibly perceiving, nor by any physical reproduction of it, such as a cinematograph film, a gramophone record, the pattern of disturbances in a television screen, and so on.

As remarked in Chapter VI, an ordinary dream, had by a sane person in good health during normal sleep, is a good example of a kind of hallucinatory *quasi*-perception which is perfectly familiar to most of us. It is therefore convenient to begin with this familiar example, and to classify other kinds of hallucinatory *quasi*-perception by comparison and contrast with it.

A person, while asleep and dreaming, generally takes his dream to be an ordinary waking perception. His eyes are shut; the room is generally dark; and often there are few or no physical sounds going on in it. So the background and the principal figures in an ordinary dream are all of a piece. The whole context is hallucinatory, though certain features in it may ultimately originate in specific sensory stimuli from within or without the dreamer's body. But, as we have seen, a sane person in good health may suddenly have an hallucinatory *quasi*-perception when he is wide awake. Here the principal figure, and possibly some of its immediate appurtenances, are hallucinatory; but the background is usually that of normal waking sense-perception. The experient's ingrained knowledge of the normal behaviour of physical objects will at once force on his attention the fact that his ostensible seeing of that human form, his ostensible hearing of that voice, etc., is *not* normal sense-perception. If he considers the question at all, he will realize that his experience is hallucinatory; and, since he is sane and awake, he can hardly fail to have the question thrust upon him. So we may first divide hallucinatory *quasi*-perceptions into (A) those which at the time are taken by the experient without question as normal waking sense-perceptions, and (B) those which he recognizes at the time to be hallucinatory.

Now there is one and only one respect in which *every* hallucination, as such, may be said to be to some extent delusive. It always masquerades as a normal sense-perception, which it is *not*. So there is always at least an initial tendency for the experient to take it uncritically as a normal waking sense-perception; and therefore a tendency for it to evoke in him by association such beliefs, expectations, bodily and mental adjustments, etc., as would be evoked by a normal sense-perception similar to it in content. In ordinary dreams this initial tendency is unchecked, partly because there is no background of normal perceptual content to put the experient on his guard, and partly, no doubt, because one is generally in a less critical and more acquiescent state when fast asleep than when fully awake. So this kind of delusiveness is here at its maximum. Even in the case of dreams, as we have seen, some incongruity may be noted at times by the sleeper, and that may lead him—sometimes with rather surprising consequences, as in the cases of van Eeden and of Fox—to realize, without awaking, that he is dreaming. In the case of an hallucination occurring to a sane waking person, in good health and not under the sway of any strong emotion or desire, the initial tendency is checked almost at once. The hallucinatory *quasi*-perception may, and often does, persist unchanged in content; but it is almost immediately recognized as hallucinatory. The kind of delusiveness, which we are here discussing, is in such cases evanescent. We may give the name 'tendency to be mistaken for normal' to this particular form of delusiveness (or, more properly, *misleadingness*), which is inherent in every hallucination as such.

I pass now to a kind of veridicality or delusiveness which is of much greater interest and importance for our purpose. This I shall call '*epistemological* veridicality or delusiveness'. We can understand what is meant by this, if we compare and contrast (i) a normal sense-perception, had by a sane waking person, with good sight, hearing, etc., in favourable circumstances, such as a good light, freedom from distorting media, etc.; and (ii) an ordinary dream. The former is a typical example of a perceptual experience which is completely, or almost completely, *veridical* in the epistemological sense. The latter is a typical example of a *quasi*-perceptual experience which is completely *delusive* in that sense.

When we say that a normal sense-perception, had by a sane waking person in good health and under favourable conditions, is wholly or almost wholly veridical, we mean something like the following. At the time when the experience was occurring, or at such an earlier time as would be required by the finite velocity of light, sound, etc., there existed, independently of the experient and his sensory and intellectual equipment, at a certain place outside his body, a certain thing, person, event, or state of affairs, so correlated in detail with the content of his experience that it could properly be said to be '*the* object presented, in certain of its parts and certain of its aspects, to him, by way of such and such of his senses, in and through that experience'.

In the case of normal waking sense-perception, epistemological veridicality is a matter of degree. We take for granted, unless there be some known positive reason to doubt it, that such an experience is *in the main* veridical. But we all know, and learn to allow for, the fact that such an experience may be to some extent delusive. Its content may in some respects, and to some degree, misrepresent the corresponding features in the presented object. That happens, e.g., when a straight stick, half in air and half in water, presents itself to sight as having a kink at the surface of separation between the two media.

Some such distortions are confined within fairly narrow limits, and vary systematically and simply with changes in the position and orientation of the percipient's body. These everyone learns in early youth to allow for automatically; indeed psychologists tell us that, within limits, the *visual appearances themselves* are automatically modified so as to approximate to what the percipient knows or takes to be the actual shape, size, and orientation of the object seen. Other distortions, such as occur in connexion with the straight stick half in air and half in water, are not thus automatically allowed for, and they might easily cause an unsophisticated or unwary percipient to make false judgements or to react inappropriately in regard to the object which he is seeing.

There is at least one systematic distortion which is recognized only by persons of scientific training, and some of the consequences of which can be worked out only by mathematical reasoning. This is the fact that, on the one hand, the content of a visual or an auditory perception corresponds to the state of the perceived object at the time when the light or sound, which evokes that perception, *was emitted from it*; whilst, on the other hand, the percipient automatically takes himself to be perceiving the object in the *state in which it is while the perception is going on*. Now, the state of perception begins *slightly* later than the moment at which the relevant stimulus begins to reach the percipient's eyes or ears, and that in turn is always *somewhat* (and sometimes *very much*) later than the moment of emission from the perceived object. It follows that the state and the place of the object may have changed greatly in the interval, or that the object may even have ceased altogether to exist, by the time when the perception begins. The error, which is entirely unsuspected by the plain man, and can be allowed for and corrected even by an instructed percipient only on subsequent reflexion and calculation, may be very considerable.

I have spoken above of the 'content' of a sense-perception, and I have defined the notion of epistemological veridicality in terms of the correlation of the content of such an experience with something external to the percipient's body and independent of him and his sensory and intellectual equipment. I must now indicate what I mean by 'content' in this connexion. Suppose that all perceptual or *quasi*-perceptual experiences had been completely veridical, or at any rate that we had never had any reason to recognize that some of them are not so. Then I doubt whether it would have occurred to anyone to distinguish in thought between the *content* of such an experience and the *object presented to the percipient* in and through it. But, when one recognizes such facts as I have been mentioning about the partial delusiveness even of normal perceptions which are predominantly veridical, and when one reflects on them, one can hardly fail to draw the distinction in question. When a person tries to describe, whether to himself or to another, as accurately as possible just how that which he is seeing *looks to him*, how that which he is hearing *sounds to him*, how that which he is touching *feels to him*, and so on, what he is trying to describe is what I call the 'content' of his visual, auditory, tactual, or other perception.

I do not think that the distinction between content of perception and object perceived is explicitly drawn except by fairly reflective persons, who deliberately consider the facts of perception and *quasi-perception*. And I do not think that it is explicitly present to the minds of any of us when we are about our daily business, and our perceptions are working normally in the service of our practical ends. It would, therefore, be incorrect to say that the plain man, or the reflective person in his practical daily life, *identifies* the content of his perceptions with the objects presented to him in and through them. For that would imply that the conceptual distinction between content and presented object had been recognized by him and was before his mind at the time. The former is not true of the plain man, and the latter is not true of the reflective person in his practical daily life. But a reflective person, who had recognized the distinction, and who had it before his mind at the time, might *proceed to argue* that the content of perception and the object presented in and through it *are* in certain favourable cases, or even in all cases, *one and the same* existent entity, regarded in different relationships or aspects. Such a person might properly be said to identify the two in those particular cases, or in all cases, respectively. Conversely, a reflective person, who had recognized the conceptual distinction and who had it before his mind at the time, might *proceed to argue* that the content of a perception and the object presented in and through it are always *two numerically different existents*, and even that they are always of *radically different kinds*. What I want to emphasize is that the former, just as much as the latter, is holding a *philosophical theory*, in regard to which there are various arguments *pro* and *con*. The fact is that the word 'identify' can be used in two senses, one purely negative, and the other positive. In its negative sense it means 'failing to distinguish conceptually'; in its positive sense it means 'distinguishing conceptually, but holding that the two concepts apply to one and the same existent particular'.

194

Now, if the distinction between content and presented object has to be recognized on reflexion even in the case of the most veridical of normal sense-perceptions, it simply hits one in the eye in the case of totally delusive *quasi*-perceptions, such as ordinary dreams. For the characteristic feature of such experiences is this. On the one hand, each particular one of them resembles a normal waking sense-perception so completely in its content and its internal organization that the experient unhesitatingly takes himself at the time to be presented through his senses with such and such independently existing things, persons, events, and states of affairs. But, on the other hand, if he himself on subsequent reflexion, or if other men for him, apply to any ordinary dream those tests for veridicality which are accepted alike by plain men, by scientists, and by philosophers of all schools, that *quasi*-perceptual experience has to be declared *totally delusive*. There is every reason to *deny* that there existed, at the time when the dream occurred, or at such earlier time as would be required by the finite velocity of light, sound, etc., *any* thing, person, event, or state of affairs, so correlated in detail with the content of the dream that it could properly be said to be '*the* object presented, in certain of its parts and certain of its aspects, by way of such and such of his senses, in and through that experience'.

We are now in a position to appreciate the paradoxical nature of those paradoxically named experiences, '*veridical* hallucinations' or '*veridical* hallucinatory *quasi*-perceptions', with which certain branches of psychical research are concerned. On the one hand, they are all *quasi*-perceptual experiences of a typically *delusive* character. That is why they are called 'hallucinations'. Some of them are, in fact, dreams. Others are waking experiences. But it is certain, by all the usual criteria, that there is at the time no object, in the place in which such and such a person is ostensibly seen or heard as engaged in such and such a way, correlated in detail with the content of the experience, and affecting the experient's eye by light emitted from it, his ear by sound emitted from it, and so on. On the other hand, they are *veridical* in the following special sense. There did exist, at about the time when such an hallucinatory *quasi*-perception occurred, at a certain one place in the world a certain person in a certain state and in certain surroundings, so peculiar and so closely correlated in detail with the content of the experience that it is difficult or impossible to believe that the coexistence in time and the correlation in detail can be purely contingent.

The problem raised by such facts is this. Assuming that the state and circumstances of the remote person are so peculiar, and that their correlation with the content of the hallucinatory *quasi*-perception is so detailed, that mere chance-coincidence is incredible, we are naturally inclined to look for some kind of *causal* connexion between the two. To be more specific; we are naturally inclined to suppose that either (*a*) the *actual* state and circumstances of the remote referent, or (*b*) his own or some other person's state of *awareness of them or belief about them*, must be an essential factor in causing the contemporary or nearly contemporary hallucination, whose content is so closely correlated in detail with them. We *know* that this is so in the case of the correlation between the content and the object of a *normal waking sense-perception*; and in that case physicists and anatomists and physiologists can tell us a great deal about the nature of the causal processes involved. Now a veridical hallucination closely resembles a normal waking sense-perception in the nature and internal organization of its content; whilst the correlation between the detail of its content and the state and circumstances of the remote referent is often very like the correlation between the content and the object of a normal waking sense-perception. So we are naturally inclined to look for some causal process, in the case of veridical hallucinatory *quasi*-perception, analogous to that which we know to play an essential part in the case of normal waking sense-perception.

But here we come up against a blank wall. Even if the hallucination occurs *simultaneously with or slightly later than* the correlated state and circumstances of the remote referent, the very facts which make us classify such an experience as *hallucinatory* exclude all the usual kinds of causal transaction between perceived object and percipient, which account satisfactorily for the correlation between content and object in the case of normal waking sense-perception. Suppose that the correlation *is* due here to some causal transaction between (*a*) the actual state and circumstances of the remote referent (or, alternatively, his own or some other person's state of *awareness of*, or *belief about*, his state and circumstances), and (*b*) the person who has the simultaneous or slightly later hallucination. Then the causation involved cannot, it would seem, be just an unfamiliar variant of a familiar type of causation. It must be of a wholly different and hitherto unrecognized kind of causation. That conclusion is reinforced, when we remember that sometimes the hallucinatory experience occurs in the subject *before* the remote referent has begun to be in the state and circumstances which correspond in detail to the content of the hallucination. For there are well attested cases of veridical hallucinations which are *pre*-presentative, and they do not seem to differ in any other respect from those which are not pre-presentative. Up to the present, so far as I am aware, no one has managed to offer an intelligible concept, still less an imaginable schema, of the *modus operandi* of veridical hallucination, which would enable a psychical researcher to infer what might be expected to happen in assignable circumstances and then to test his inferences by observation.

That being granted, it may still be useful to note the following point. It is commonly assumed that an immediate necessary condition for a person to have either a normal waking sense-perception or an ordinary totally delusive hallucinatory *quasi*-perception, such as an ordinary dream, is the occurrence, at the time, of a specific and correlated modification of *his brain*. There are, no doubt, strong, if not absolutely coercive, grounds for that assumption. Are we, or are we not, to make a similar assumption in the case of *veridical* hallucinatory *quasi*-perception?

Considerations of similarity in content and of continuity would suggest that it is reasonable to make that assumption here also, if it is reasonable to make it elsewhere. If so, the causal problem is this. How does the crisis in B's life (or B's own or some other person's awareness of, or belief about, that crisis) determine the nearly simultaneous occurrence of that state of A's *brain*, which is (on the present assumption) an immediate necessary condition of the occurrence of A's veridical hallucination concerning B? Essentially it would be a problem of the paranormal causation of a quite normal kind of *neural* event. There would be, so far as I can see, neither more nor less difficulty in the case of a veridical hallucination than in the case of an ordinary waking sense-perception or an ordinary dream, in understanding why or how the occurrence of such and such a state of A's brain should be immediately accompanied by and correlated with the occurrence in A of a *quasi*-perceptual experience having such and such content. The fact would be equally mysterious in one sense, and equally commonplace in another, in all three cases.

Suppose, on the other hand, that we were to abandon, in the case of *veridical* hallucinations, that assumption of psycho-cerebral parallelism which we commonly make in the case of normal waking sense-perceptions and of totally delusive *quasi*-perceptions, such as ordinary dreams. Then, I take it, the causal problem would be this. We should have to suppose that A's veridical hallucination is somehow caused *directly*, without the mediation of any physical or nervous transmissive process or of any consequent modification of A's brain, either by B's roughly simultaneous state and circumstances *themselves*, or else by B's or some other person's *awareness of*, or *belief about*, B's state and circumstances. This is an extremely difficult notion even to entertain, and still more to envisage and work out in detail. Both the alternatives just indicated are fraught with difficulty and obscurity. But I think that it would plainly be reasonable

197

to try to keep the assumption of psycho-cerebral parallelism and to start with the former alternative, and to resort to the latter only if all attempts to formulate a satisfactory causal theory on the former lines had failed.

Suppose, however, that one should be forced in the end to contemplate, in the case of veridical hallucinations, some kind of *direct*, *unmediated* causation of the relevant hallucinatory experience in A, either by the roughly contemporary state and circumstances of B, or else by B's or some other person's awareness of, or beliefs about them. Then, I think, we should have to re-examine seriously the assumption of psycho-cerebral parallelism in the cases of normal waking sense-perception and of completely delusive *quasi*-perceptions, such as ordinary dreams. For veridical hallucinations are so similar to normal waking perceptions and to ordinary dreams, in the nature and the internal organization of their content, that it seems unlikely that the connexion between the experience and the contemporary state of the experient's brain can be radically different in the one case from what it is in the others.

In this connexion it may be worth while to make the following remark. The doctrine of the one-sided dependence of every perceptual or *quasi*-perceptual experience upon a contemporary state of the experient's brain, and of the complete parallelism between the content of any such experience and the details of the brain-state on which it one-sidedly depends, is (so far as I am aware) little more than a working hypothesis which has hitherto proved useful in physiology and experimental psychology. It obviously starts from important and well established facts; but it goes far beyond them, and, from the nature of the case, its more detailed and sweeping claims have never been, and probably never could be, experimentally established. Therefore, while it is sensible, when speculating on the causation of veridical hallucinations, to begin by treating this working hypothesis with decent respect, it would be foolish to allow one's range of speculation to be permanently cramped by anything like a superstitious reverence for it.

Suppose that it should prove possible to retain the doctrine of psycho-cerebral parallelism both for veridical hallucinations and for ordinary wholly delusive ones, such as our everynight dreams. Then the *last link* in the causal chain which ends with a veridical hallucination would not be different in kind from the *last link* in the chain which ends with an ordinary dream or a totally delusive waking hallucination. If, on the other hand, we had to drop the doctrine of psycho-cerebral parallelism for *veridical* hallucinations, but were able to keep it for non-veridical ones, even the last link in the chain of causation would be different in kind in the two cases. What is certain

198

is that, on either alternative, the *remoter links* must be fundamentally different. That must be so, even if we confine our attention to veridical hallucinations corresponding to a *past or contemporary* state of a person who was *still alive* at the time when the hallucination occurred or else *died only very shortly afterwards*.

But we cannot confine ourselves within those limits. I have already remarked that the nature of the causal process becomes still more paradoxical when the veridical hallucination corresponds to a state of a living person which did not begin until *after* the hallucination had ceased. I would now add that we cannot confine ourselves to veridical hallucinations concerning those who were living at the time or who died very shortly afterwards. We must also include in our survey hallucinations concerning a person *long since dead*, which seem hard to explain except on the assumption of *post mortem* persistence of information not in the normal possession of anyone still living, and of *post mortem* deliberate action. (Cf., e.g., the Chaffin will case.) An essential factor in initiating a phantasm of the *living* might be the state of the referent's *brain*, which is the cerebral correlate of that experience of his, to which the subject's veridical hallucination corresponds. But no such suggestion could, from the nature of the case, apply to the causation of a veridical hallucination concerning a person long since dead. For his physical brain has ceased to function, or indeed to exist.

Now phantasms of the dead and post-presentative and pre-presentative phantasms of the living all resemble each other in their content and their internal organization as experiences. That essential resemblance needs to be explained somehow. One possible explanation would be that the *immediate* conditions of all of them are of the same nature, viz. states of the experient's brain, similar to those which are the immediate conditions of ordinary dreams. On that supposition, it would be open to us to assume, if we should find it helpful, that the *remoter* links in the causal chains, leading up to the three kinds of veridical hallucination, are of *fundamentally different* kinds. An alternative line of speculation would be the following. We might suppose that the essential similarity in content and internal organization of the three kinds of veridical hallucination is due, *not* to the essential likeness in their immediate cerebral correlates, but to all three of them being caused by a paranormal process of *the same kind*, which evokes the experience directly, and not through the intermediary of a specific cerebral state.

Classification of Hallucinations. I will now say something about the classification of the various kinds of waking hallucination with which psychical research is concerned. It will be useful to continue to bear in mind the comparison and contrast with ordinary dreams, on the one hand, and with normal waking perceptions on the other.

The vast majority of dreams are, so far as we know, *uncorrelated* experiences. By this I mean at least a combination of the following two things. (i) If a person ostensibly perceives certain persons, things, and events on a certain night in a dream, it is most uncommon for other persons, whether asleep or awake, to have other experiences at much the same time, which are so correlated with that dream that they seem to be perceptions of the same objects. (ii) It is also most uncommon for one and the same person to have a number of dreams on successive occasions, which are so correlated with each other that they seem to be perceptions of the same objects, either as unaltered, or as having undergone certain changes in the intervals.

Now *most* waking hallucinations are, so far as we know, uncorrelated experiences, as are the vast majority of ordinary dreams. But there are also *correlated* hallucinations, i.e. groups of hallucinations, occurring either in the same person at different times or in different persons at the same or at different times, which are so inter-related that they seem to refer to the same person, thing, event, or state of affairs. I shall call any such group of experiences a 'co-referential set' of hallucinations.

Such a set may take various forms, of which the following are perhaps the most important:

(i) Two or more persons, present together in the same small region of space, may simultaneously have hallucinatory *quasi*-perceptions, as of, e.g., a figure which seems to enter through a closed door, to cross the room, and to vanish into the opposite wall. On comparing notes, one or other of the following facts may emerge. (*a*) They may find that each ostensibly saw such different parts of the same figure as each would have seen from his own position if a real human figure had crossed the floor before his eyes in normal illumination. Or (*b*) one of them may, e.g., have had an hallucinatory *visual* experience as of seeing a figure in a silk dress crossing the room and opening her mouth as if shrieking, but he may *not* have ostensibly *heard* any corresponding sounds. The other of them may at the same time have had an hallucinatory *auditory* experience as of hearing the sound of footsteps, of the kind of rustling that a silk dress would make, and of a shriek; but he may *not* have ostensibly *seen* anything corresponding.

I should class these two alternatives together as instances of a '*collective* hallucinatory *quasi*-perception'. As examples we may refer to two cases described in Chapter V, viz. the experiences of Lady B. and Miss B., and those of Mr and Mrs P. in connexion with the phantasm of Mr P.'s deceased father. It may be noted that, in the B.

case, there is no evidence that the collective hallucination was *veridical*, since the phantasm did not present the appearance of any identifiable individual, whether living or dead. In the case of Mr and Mrs P. the collective hallucination had the kind of veridicality which can attach to a phantasm of the dead.

(ii) The following kind of case might be imagined. Suppose that, at much the same time and independently of normal communication, a number of persons in different places had hallucinations which all seemed obviously to refer to the death of the present Pope by poisoning. One man in London might have dreamed that he saw the Pope's corpse lying swollen and bloated with froth at the mouth. Another in New York might have ostensibly heard a voice crying: 'The Pope has been poisoned'. A third in Stockholm might have been shaving, and might have ostensibly seen his mirror cloud over and then exhibit the image of a newspaper with the Swedish equivalent of the headlines: 'Death of the Pope; Poison suspected'. And so on. These hallucinations would constitute a co-referential set; for they would all plainly refer to a single outstanding possible event, whether actual or not. But they would not have the very special kind of interrelations which would make them a collective hallucinatory *quasi*-perception. I will describe such cases as instances of a '*disseminated* co-referential hallucination'.

Even if sets of disseminated co-referential hallucinations were in fact fairly common, it is plain that most of them would fail to be noted and reported. It is also plain that those which were *veridical* would be much more likely to be noted and reported than those (if such there be) which are not so. If the Pope really had been poisoned at the time, there is at least a likelihood that some or all of the isolated experients would write about their experiences to the papers, or to the S.P.R. or some analogous society. But, if nothing had been amiss with the Pope at the time, they would probably have held their tongues and failed to take up their pens. The case, cited in Chapter V, of the dreams had by Mr Lawson and by Miss Lawson about the illness of Mr Stephen, is an instance of a disseminated co-referential hallucination. The two experients happened to be in the same house and were father and daughter, and their hallucinations were veridical. Otherwise, we should most probably never have heard of them.

This is perhaps the most appropriate place for the following remark. An uncorrelated hallucination or a set of co-referential hallucinations, whether veridical or not, may refer to a certain identifiable person, and to a certain possible state or situation of that person, in two very different ways. The reference may be either immediate and *quasi*-perceptual, or it may be more or less *symbolical*. On the former alternative it will be for the experient as if he were perceiving that person in that state or situation, though he may realize at the time that this cannot be normal waking sense-perception. Good examples are provided by the case of Mr and Mrs P. and the Bowyer-Bower case, described in Chapter V. On the latter alternative the experient does not ostensibly perceive a person or scene or incident. Instead, he is aware of something which he realizes to be of the nature of a *mental image*, visual, auditory, or of some other kind. He takes this to symbolize a certain person undergoing a certain crisis.

The symbolization may be *imitative*, and may be comparable to the part played by a vivid memory-image in recollecting a past scene or incident. Or it may be merely *associative*, as when an image of the Swedish flag calls up in me a thought of the royal palace at Stockholm. Numerous examples were quoted in Chapter V. Among them I may mention Mrs H.'s vision, in the glass of water, of an accident to a goods-train; Prince Victor Duleep Singh's image of his father's head as located in an actual picture-frame on the bedroom wall; and Miss Patterson's two successive externalized images, located in the clouds above her, of her brother's body lying unconscious. It is perhaps worth remarking that many people, on experiencing *any* vivid hallucination which obviously refers to a certain known individual, are inclined automatically to take it as probably betokening something *amiss* with the latter, e.g. accident, sudden illness, or death. This tendency evidently rests on a very ancient and widespread folk-belief, which may or may not have a sound basis in the experience of mankind.

From this digression I revert to the subdivision and classification of hallucinations. The next point to notice is this. A person might on various occasions have hallucinations, e.g. dreams, which were so correlated with each other that in all of them he ostensibly perceived the same persons and scenes, with such differences on successive occasions as might have taken place if they had persisted and changed independently in a normal way during the intervals. A celebrated case of this kind was investigated many years ago by Professor Flournoy and reported in his book *Des Indes au planète Mars*. I shall describe such experiences as '*reiterative* hallucinatory *quasi*-perceptions'.

We may consider next the well known and fairly well attested phenomenon of a 'haunted' room. This introduces further complications, which it is important to notice.

To say that a certain room is 'haunted' implies *at least* that, over a considerable period, a number of different persons, who have been in it on different occasions, have each had on at least one such occasion an hallucinatory experience. So 'haunting' combines at least the following features, viz. (*a*) that the hallucinations are *collocated* as opposed to disseminated, (*b*) that they are *reiterative* as opposed to confined to a single occasion, and (*c*) that they occur in *more than one individual*.

Sometimes, however, there are further correlations. One possibility is that the hallucinations experienced on different occasions, whether by the same person or by different persons, are so correlated that on all such occasions much the same figure was ostensibly perceived as performing much the same actions. That would be a case of *reiterative quasi*-perception, not necessarily confined to a single experient. A further possibility is that there might also be *collective quasi*-perception, i.e. that on some of the occasions several persons present at the same time may have had ostensible perceptions as of one and the same figure seen from their several points of view. The 'ideal haunt' would involve both reiterative and collective *quasi*-perception. It would also involve something further, viz. that the figure ostensibly perceived could be identified, as to its appearance, with a certain individual who had frequented that room or had died in it; and that the figure should be ostensibly perceived as in certain state, or as doing or suffering certain things, characteristic of that person in life or at the point of death.

A good example of a fairly well attested 'haunt', which approximates to the ideal, is the 'Morton ghost'. This was first reported, with pseudonyms for the names of the persons and the place concerned, in S.P.R. *Proceedings*, Vol. III, pp. 311 *et seq.* Later, when all need for concealment had ceased, it was reported more fully in a book by Abdy Collins entitled *The Cheltenham Ghost* (1948). Most of the well attested cases fall far short of the ideal. Often the most that can be accepted with certainty is this. Several persons, who had not been in communication with each other and had not previously been told any story of a certain room being haunted, have had hallucinatory experiences of one kind or another when occupying that room. There is seldom adequate evidence that their hallucinations were inter-related as they would be if they were actual perceptions of one and the same figure simultaneously from various points of view, or successively at the same or at different phases in its history. Still rarer is it that there is really satisfactory evidence to connect the figure, in respect of its appearance and its behaviour, with a certain former occupant of the room and with his or her doings or sufferings when living there. The case, described in Chapter V, of the recurrent appearances in Dr H.'s house, is a fair example of a 'haunt' which is considerably better attested than the run of such stories which are *prima facie* worth serious consideration.

203

I turn now to another interesting class of hallucinations. Most of the experiences which we have discussed may be described as 'unilateral'. A has an hallucinatory *quasi*-perception referring to B and his state and circumstances at the time, but B has no simultaneous and complementary hallucination referring to A. There are, however, certain cases of what may be called '*reciprocal* hallucinations'. One simple, but very well attested, example was quoted in Chapter V, viz. the case of Miss Steele and Mr Burgess. Here Miss Steele had an *auditory* hallucination as of being called by Mr Burgess; and at much the same time Mr Burgess, in a house in another part of Brighton, had a *visual* hallucination as of Miss Steele standing near the door inside his bedroom. A much more elaborate case, where both the reciprocal hallucinations were visual, is that of Mr and Mrs Wilmot and Mr Tait, which I have detailed at length in Chapter VI. The Wilmot case is outstanding, since it involves both reciprocal and collective hallucination. As regards Mr Wilmot and Mr Tait, who both ostensibly saw Mrs Wilmot enter their cabin, hesitate, and then go up to Mr Wilmot's berth and lean over him, it was *collective*. As regards Mrs Wilmot, on the one hand, and Mr Wilmot and Mr Tait, on the other, it was *reciprocal*. Mr Wilmot's dream and Mr Tait's simultaneous waking hallucination were so correlated with Mrs Wilmot's simultaneous dream-like experience that what *they* ostensibly saw was Mrs Wilmot, in the place where *she* then seemed to herself to be, and doing what *she* then seemed to herself to be doing.

Location in connexion with Hallucinations. Such cases (and there are quite a fair number of them) make it desirable at this point to consider in more detail the notion of *location*.

In the vast majority of cases of waking visual hallucination we need to consider only two positional features, viz. (i) the actual location of the experient's physical body, and (ii) the ostensible location in the physical space immediately around it of his hallucinatory *quasi*-percept. In such cases the hallucinated subject's physical body is, and is felt and seen by him to be, located (say) in a certain chair in a certain room. And the hallucinatory objects which he ostensibly sees are ostensibly seen by him as located near to him among the real objects in the room which he is actually seeing. His ostensible seeing of the hallucinatory objects, and his actual seeing of the real objects, take place for him as from one and the same point of view, and that can be identified with the actual location and orientation of his physical body.

No essential modification is introduced by those out-of-the-body cases where the hallucinatory object which the experient ostensibly sees happens to be a *simulacrum of his own physical body*, viewed from outside as it would appear from the position which his actual physical body is occupying, and is felt and seen by him to be occupying, at the time. (Cf. the cases of Mr Simons and of Mrs Hall, described in Chapter VI.) Such cases might be described as instances of '*autoscopic* visual hallucination'. The case of Mrs Hall happened also to be collective; but, so far as she herself was concerned, it was a pure instance of autoscopic visual hallucination. She no more *felt* herself to be identical with the figure which she ostensibly saw than one would do on seeing an image of oneself in a mirror. The case of Mr Simons involved a good deal more than mere autoscopy. For, while the experience lasted, he felt himself as *divided* between 'No. 1' (motionless on the sofa) and 'No. 2' (moving about and facing him at a little distance away). Yet I have the impression that he identified himself throughout primarily with 'No. 1', and felt as if 'No. 2''s movements were directly initiated and controlled by his volitions in his capacity of 'No. 1'.

The Simons case may perhaps be regarded as transitional to certain other kinds of out-of-the-body experience, which undoubtedly require further additions and modifications in respect of the notion of location. I allude to those cases in which a person, whose body is in fact lying motionless in a certain place, will have an experience as of seeing it from outside, as of moving from it to this or that place in ordinary physical space, as of entering real houses, rooms, etc., and seeing from near at hand the real persons and things in them. Here the most noteworthy features are the two following. (i) An experienced shifting of the subject's point of view from its normal location within his physical body to a position in physical space outside the latter. (ii) An experience as of seeing, from the transferred point of view, actual persons and things (including often the subject's own physical body), which *would* be visible normally to a person whose physical body was situated there, but would *not* normally be visible at all or would present very different appearances, from the position actually occupied by the subject's physical body.

A very simple example is the case of Miss Hendry, described in Chapter VI. This might be regarded as the complement to the case of Mrs Hall. Miss Hendry ostensibly saw, as from the doctor's side of the operating-table and from behind his back, her own physical body, as it in fact was, situated at the other side of the table facing the doctor, and assisting, as it in fact was doing, in the operation. Mrs Hall, from the position occupied by her physical body at the dining-table, ostensibly saw a *simulacrum* of her body standing by the sideboard facing her. This was also ostensibly seen, from their several points of view, by the three other persons at the table. The cases are alike in that Miss Hendry and Mrs Hall each felt herself to be simply a disinterested external observer, in the one case of her own physical body from the transferred point of view, and in the other case of the *simulacrum* of her body from the normal unshifted point of view. The case of Miss Hendry is singular, among out-of-the-body experiences, only in the fact that her physical body was at the time showing all the external signs of being awake and active, whilst in most such cases the physical body is either lying asleep (as in the experiences of Mr Fox and of Mr Muldoon) or lying immobile and without sign of consciousness as a result of accident or illness (as in the case of Dr X).

Before going further, it will be well to consider the case of ordinary everynight dreams. Here the dreamer unhesitatingly takes the objects which he is ostensibly seeing to be located in ordinary physical space; and he takes for granted that his ordinary physical body is located at a certain position among those objects, that it is oriented in a certain direction, and that he is seeing them from a point of view determined by that position, and in a direction determined by that orientation. The objects which the dreamer ostensibly sees around him may look quite familiar, and he may take himself to be in a particular place well known to him. Even when that is not so, he takes himself to be in his ordinary body in some part of the ordinary world and surrounded with ordinary physical objects, with which he just does not happen to be familiar. At most he may be surprised at finding himself now in one environment and now in a quite different one, without any clear recollection of moving or being moved from one to another. There is, however, every reason for us on reflexion to believe that, in an ordinary dream, neither the objects ostensibly seen nor the point of view from which the dreamer ostensibly sees them are located *anywhere* in physical space. The point of view from which the dreamer ostensibly views the objects which he ostensibly sees in his dream is certainly *not* located within his physical body, lying asleep on the bed. But, on the other hand, the dreamer does not (as does a person who is having an out-of-the-body experience) take it to be located somewhere in physical space *outside* his physical body.

We may now proceed to classify the theoretical possibilities in the following way. (1) We may consider first the various possibilities as to the *point of view* from which the subject appears to himself to be viewing the objects which he is ostensibly seeing. (2) We may then consider the various possibilities with regard to the nature and location of that which may *correspond in reality to the object ostensibly seen*. We can then combine each alternative under (1) with each alternative under (2), and thus get a complete list of all the possible combinations.

(1) The *point of view*, from which the experient seems to himself to be viewing the objects which he ostensibly sees, may (1,1) appear to him to be located at some point in physical space *outside* the region which he takes to be occupied by his physical body at the time. Or (1,2) there may *not* appear to him to be any such shift in his point of view. He may unquestioningly take himself to be viewing the objects which he ostensibly sees, from a position located in the normal way *within* the region of physical space which he takes his physical body to be occupying at the time. We may call experiences of the first kind 'excursive', and those of the second kind 'non-excursive'. Lucid dreams and other kinds of out-of-the-body experiences are *excursive*. Ordinary dreams and the vast majority of waking hallucinations are *non-excursive*. In excursive experiences, as we have seen, the subject very often has characteristic experiences which lead him to take for granted that his shifted point of view is centred in a peculiar kind of *non-physical* counterpart body, in the way in which his normal point of view is centred in his physical body. It is one thing to have an *out-of-the-body* experience, and another thing to have an experience as of animating a *non-physical secondary body*. But the former is very often accompanied by the latter; and I should suppose that the latter would not be very likely to occur except as an accompaniment or a sequel to the former.

(2) Before we can usefully enumerate the alternative possibilities with regard to the *location of something real corresponding to the object ostensibly seen*, it will be necessary to make two elucidatory remarks concerning the *temporal* aspects of the experiences in question.

(i) I am concerned here only with experiences of ostensible *seeing*. Now, in *actual* seeing, an experience of seeing a certain object as in a given place and state at a certain time can begin only when the light emitted from that object in that place and in that state shall have reached the percipient's eye. That is, it can begin only after an interval (varying directly with the distance between the place in question and that occupied by the percipient's body). Such intervals are, however, extremely small except in the case of seeing objects and events at an astronomical distance from one's body. I propose, in what immediately follows, to neglect them altogether. When I say, in the immediate sequel, that such an object as is ostensibly being seen by the subject 'is *now* physically occupying' a certain position in physical space, I am neglecting the very short interval which would have elapsed, in a case of actual vision, between the emission of the relevant light from that place and its reception by the percipient located elsewhere. And, when I say that such an

207

object as is being ostensibly seen by the subject '*has been* (but is no longer) physically occupying' a certain position in physical space, I am assuming a lapse of time *greater than* that very short interval.

(ii) It is necessary to introduce these tiresome complications about time, for the following reason. Some veridical hallucinations are *post*-presentative, i.e. what makes them veridical is the fact that there *has been* (but no longer is), in the relevant position in physical space, a certain object in a certain state, corresponding to the object which is now being ostensibly seen and to the state in which it is now ostensibly seen as being. Again, some veridical hallucinations are *pre*-presentative. What this means can be defined by substituting '*will be* (but is not yet)' for '*has been* (but no longer is)' in the above definition of *post*-presentative veridical hallucinations.

I have not given any examples of *post*-presentative or *pre*-presentative veridical hallucinations. There are in the literature plenty of accounts of experiences of each kind, which are more or less plausibly claimed to be veridical. The famous story of the experiences of Miss Moberly and Miss Jourdain at Versailles may be mentioned as a case in point. In the case of most of them it is hard to establish both the veridicality and the paranormality of the experience; but it would be absurd to ignore them in a theoretical discussion, such as we are now engaged upon.

Subject to the explanations given in (i) above, we can now proceed to formulate the alternative possibilities under (2). They are as follows.

The object ostensibly seen may be either (2,1) such an object as (*a*) is now, or (*b*) has been (but no longer is), or (*c*) will be (but is not yet), physically occupying *that position in physical space at which it is now ostensibly seen to be*; or (2,2) such an object as (*a*) is now, or (*b*) has been (but no longer is), or (*c*) will be (but is not yet) physically occupying a certain position in physical space *other than* that at which it is now ostensibly seen to be; or (2,3) such an object as there is no good reason to believe to be now occupying or to have occupied or to be going to occupy *any* position in physical space.

I have no intention of boring the reader by considering in detail each of the 14 possible alternatives which arise from combining each of the two possibilities under (1) with each of the seven ultimate possibilities under (2). I shall content myself with a few general remarks.

(i) Most well attested veridical visual hallucinations, of a *prima facie* paranormal kind, fall under the heading (1,2). They are *non-excursive*. The subject does *not* at the time seem to himself to be viewing things from a position outside his physical body. And most of these fall under the heading (2,2) (*a*). The subject ostensibly sees a certain familiar individual as present before his eyes *in his own immediate neighbourhood*, and as doing or suffering something unusual and unexpected. At *much the same time*, but at *some distant place*, the individual in question is in fact doing or suffering or looking correspondingly.

(ii) In most *non-excursive* cases the object which the experient ostensibly sees appears to him as located at some place which would fall within the *normal field of vision* of an observer situated where the experient is, oriented as he is, and surrounded with such physical objects as do in fact surround him. In practice, if he is at the time in a closed room, this means that the object which he ostensibly sees generally appears to him as located in the unobstructed region between him and the wall which he is facing.

But, while this is much the most usual state of affairs, there is no kind of necessity about it. There might be (and I believe that there are) cases where the experient, *without* appearing to himself to be outside his physical body, ostensibly sees an object as located in a place where it would be physically impossible for him to be actually seeing any object at the time. One possibility would be ostensibly seeing a certain object as located *behind one's back*. Another would be ostensibly seeing it as located inside *a closed box with opaque walls*. A third would be ostensibly seeing it as located at some distant place quite *out of range of normal vision*. We might describe the second of these possibilities as 'non-excursive ostensible *cryptaesthesia*'; and we might describe the third of them as 'non-excursive ostensible *telaesthesia*'.

Now suppose that there should *in fact* be, at the time when the experience happens and in the place at which the object ostensibly seen by the experient appears to him to be, something answering to the description of that object. Then the experience would fall under the heading (1,2) (2,1) (*a*). It would be an instance of *veridical* non-excursive simultaneous cryptaesthesia or telaesthesia, as the case might be.

(iii) Perhaps the more interesting cases of ostensible telaesthesia are, however, the *excursive* ones. Here the experient appears to himself to be away from the place where he knows his physical body to be located at the time; to be located somewhere within a certain remote region of physical space, e.g. a certain room in a house in a distant town; and to be seeing, as from that point of view, the persons and things occupying that region. Suppose that there should actually be, at that time and in that place, persons and things answering to the description of those which the experient ostensibly sees, from his transferred point of view, as surrounding him. Then the experience would fall under the heading (1,1) (2,1) (*a*). It would be an instance

209

of veridical excursive simultaneous telaesthesia. Mrs Wilmot's 'dream-like' experience is a case in point.

(iv) As we have already noted, the Wilmot case is also an instance of *reciprocal* and of *collective* hallucination. We will now consider such cases in rather more detail.

Suppose that X has an hallucination, in which he does *not* appear to himself to have changed his point of view, and in which the hallucinatory *quasi*-percept is as of a *human figure located in the room which he is actually occupying*. The situation will appear to him as an *invasion* of his room by a phantasm of that person. So we may describe an hallucination as 'ostensibly *invasive*', if (*a*) the experient's point of view continues to be located, in the normal way, *within* the region occupied by his physical body, and (*b*) his hallucinatory percept is as of a living being located in the *neighbourhood of his own physical body*. (The terms 'excursion' and 'invasion', in the present technical senses, are borrowed from F. W. H. Myers.)

The Wilmot case would be described as follows in this terminology. The hallucinations experienced by Mr Wilmot and by Mr Tait were ostensibly *invasive*, as regards the hallucinatory figure of Mrs Wilmot. For they ostensibly saw her as present in their cabin, where their physical bodies were actually located at the time. The hallucination experienced by Mrs Wilmot was ostensibly *excursive*. For it involved for her an ostensible displacement of her point of view, from the actual position of her physical body in bed on land to this cabin in a ship on the Atlantic; and she ostensibly saw Mr Wilmot and Mr Tait as located (as in fact they were) in the neighbourhood of her displaced point of view.

We can now give a general definition of the term '*reciprocal* hallucination'. It consists in the following concatenation of events. X has an hallucination, which is ostensibly *excursive*, as of seeing Y from a point of view *near to Y's body* and remote from the location of his own physical body. At the same time Y has an hallucination, which is ostensibly *invasive*, in which, without any displacement of his own point of view, he ostensibly sees X as in his own immediate neighbourhood.

There need be no further correlation than this between the two hallucinations. But there might be, and in the Wilmot case it is alleged that there was. The correlation might extend further in either of the two following ways. (*a*) The details of X's hallucination might correspond directly to Y's *actual* state, situation, surroundings, dress, etc. at the time. Or (*b*) they might correspond directly, *not* to those items themselves, but to the content of Y's perceptions or *quasi*-perceptions or beliefs, etc., concerning those items. On the latter alternative, the details of X's hallucination would correspond to X's *actual* state, situation, surroundings, dress, etc., only in so far as Y's perceptions or *quasi*-perceptions of those items happened to be *veridical*, or as his beliefs about them happened to be *true*, and so on.

I have mentioned these two alternative possibilities in connexion with *excursive* ostensible telaesthesia; but they would, of course, be equally relevant to the non-excursive variety, if such there be. In either case it is important to distinguish them, for the following reason. If *either* of these further conditions (*a*) or (*b*) were fulfilled, X's ostensible telaesthesia would in a sense be *veridical*. But it would be veridical in a different sense, according to which of them was fulfilled. Suppose that what corresponds *directly* to the details of X's hallucinatory *quasi*-perception is the contents of Y's perceptions or *quasi*-perceptions of himself, his state, situations, surroundings, etc., and is *not* the *actual* state, situation, etc., of Y, as such. Then we should have to say that X's ostensible telaesthesia is in principle only *inter*-subjectively veridical, and not *extra*-subjectively so. It would indeed correspond to something which is foreign to and independent of X; but that something is itself a mental state, or the content of a mental state, of Y. If it should happen to correspond to something altogether *extra*-subjective, that would be merely because Y's mental state, to which X's telaesthetic *quasi*-perception *directly* corresponds, happens to be one of *true* belief, of *correct* perception, and so on, concerning that extra-subjective state of affairs.

Suppose, on the other hand, that what corresponds to the details of X's hallucinatory *quasi*-perception should be details in the *actual* state, situation, surroundings, etc., of Y, which Y is either completely *unaware of* or *mis*perceives or holds *false* beliefs about at the time. Then we should have to say that X's ostensible telaesthesia is in principle *extra*-subjectively veridical, and not merely *inter*-subjectively so. For it would correspond to something which is not only foreign to and independent of X, but is also something *existing in the physical world*, either unsuspected by Y or contrary to Y's misperceptions and false beliefs concerning it.

Now I think that the word 'clairvoyance' has generally been intended to denote ostensible telaesthesia which is *extra*-subjectively, and not merely inter-subjectively, veridical. It may be doubted whether there are any well attested cases which are indubitably instances of clairvoyance in this sense, but it is advisable to have a theoretical niche available for them. Accordingly, we must subdivide ostensible telaesthesia into two possible varieties, which may be described as 'telepathic' and as 'clairvoyant' respectively. The conceptual distinction between the two is quite clear, though it may be difficult or impossible in any particular case to decide with confidence under which heading it falls.

211

VIII

THEORETICAL POINTS ARISING
(continued)
(II) THE NOTION OF TELEPATHY
IN CONNEXION WITH SPORADIC
CASES

I have discussed in Chapter III the use of the terms 'telepathy' and 'clairvoyance' in reference to such experiments as Dr Soal's and Mr Tyrrell's. I said there that I would defer any general discussion of those terms until after I had given examples of the kind of sporadic cases in connexion with which they were first introduced. It is now time to undertake that discussion.

Usage of the term 'Telepathy'. I think that the word 'telepathy' would not be felt to be appropriate unless *two or more conscious beings* are concerned. We should not talk of 'telepathy' *within* a single individual, except possibly on the assumption that one and the same living organism may simultaneously be the body of two or more persons. (Cf., e.g., certain cases of multiple personality, in which one of the persons claims to be *co-conscious* with another of them.) Even in such cases, and taking the claim at its face-value, the use of the word 'telepathy' would be felt to be slightly paradoxical and to stand in need of some explanation and defence. I propose, therefore, in the immediate sequel to assume that the two or more conscious beings concerned do *not* share a common living organism as their body. The most obvious case is where each has a distinct physical body, as with two contemporary human beings living on earth. But I prefer to put the matter in the more negative way which I have adopted, for the following reason. On the one hand, I do not want to exclude the very possibility of talking of 'telepathy' between two persons who may have survived bodily death, or between one such person and another still alive in the physical body. On the other hand, I do not wish to assume that, if a person should survive the death of his physical body, he must necessarily have a body of some kind or other.

I have spoken of '*two or more* conscious beings'; for more than two may be involved in a case of telepathy. On the one hand, several persons, A_1, A_2, A_3, etc., may simultaneously have hallucinatory *quasi*-perceptions which all seem to be relevant to the then state and circumstances of the distant B. And, on the other hand, one person, A, may have an experience which seems to be due to the joint influence of several distant persons, B_1, B_2, B_3, etc.

With these preliminary explanations, we may proceed as follows. It is a commonly accepted basic limiting principle that B can influence the thoughts, sensations, emotions, volitions, or actions of A only in the following roundabout way. (i) B must give overt bodily expression to some thought, perception, sensation, recollection, emotion, or volition of his own. He may do this either (*a*) *verbally*, by making a statement, issuing a command, expressing a wish, etc., either orally in some spoken language, or else in some system of symbolism, such as writing, dumb-show, flag-wagging, etc.; or (*b*) by interjections, grimaces, and so on. (ii) A must either (*a*) perceive *directly*, by sight, hearing, etc., these overt bodily manifestations of B's mental states; or (*b*) perceive them *indirectly*, e.g. by hearing a telephone message or a gramophone-record or a wireless-transmission of B's audible utterances, by reading what B has written or transcriptions of it, and so on; or (*c*) be informed in one or other of these ways of B's utterances by some third person C. (iii) A must (as the case may be) either (*a*) understand the language or other system of arbitrary symbolism in which B made his original statement, uttered his original command, etc.; or (*b*) understand the translation of it which is presented to his senses; or (*c*) be able to interpret correctly B's interjections, grimaces, etc., or the reproductions of them which are presented to his senses; or (*d*) understand the utterances by which C attempts to inform him of B's utterances.

Now I think that the widest application of the word 'telepathy' is to any case in which there seems *prima facie* to have been a breach of this basic limiting principle. We should have a *prima facie* case of telepathy, if and only if it appeared that a certain thought, perception, recollection, sensation, emotion, or volition, or action of A's *had* been evoked or influenced by a certain roughly contemporary thought, perception, sensation, emotion, or volition of B's, *although* one or other of the following negative conditions had prevailed at the time. Either (i) B had given *no* overt bodily expression to the allegedly relevant mental state of his, at the time when it had its

213

alleged influence on A; or (ii) A had had *no opportunity* to perceive, either directly or indirectly, or to have reported to him, any overt bodily expression which B may have given to this mental state of his; or (iii) A *could not have understood* such expressions, if he had perceived them, nor such transcriptions or translations of them as may have been brought to his notice, nor such reports of them as a third person C may have attempted to give him.

In practice it is the alternative (ii) which is the most important. It is often fairly easy to decide that A, on a given occasion, was *not* in a position to have perceived directly or indirectly, or to have had reported to him, any overt bodily expression which B may have given to his apparently relevant mental state. And, if that can be established, the other two alternative conditions cease to matter. On the other hand, it is never easy to be sure that B did *not* express his mental state by any kind of overt bodily change. So, if A was in a position where he *might* have been aware of such a change, if it had happened; and *might* have been able to interpret it correctly (though perhaps unwittingly), if he had been aware of it; it would hardly ever be safe to postulate telepathy.

Before going further I want to make two explanatory comments on what I have so far said. They are these:

(1) I have used the phrase 'mental state' simply as an abbreviation for such a phrase as 'thought or perception or recollection or sensation or emotion or volition or . . . ', i.e. for an *actual experience*, of one kind or another, beginning at a certain moment in a certain person's mental history, going on for so long, and then ceasing; or for an outstanding practically instantaneous phase in such a strand of experience. But a no less essential feature of any but the most elementary kind of conscious being is his possession of specific *powers and dispositions* to have such and such experiences, or to perform such and such operations, on certain kinds of occasion. No less characteristic is the specific way in which a number of such powers and dispositions are interconnected and organized in an individual. Examples are one's *power* to recollect a certain incident at times when one is not actually doing so; one's *tendency*, when presented with an instance of X, to think of Y, which has frequently been presented to one along with X in one's past experience; one's *knowledge* of the rules of Latin grammar, of how to solve quadratic equations; and so on. Such powers and dispositions are, as a rule, gradually acquired, indefinitely persistent when once acquired, and subject to gradual modification.

Now, to ascribe a power or a disposition to an individual is in itself merely to state a conditional proposition about him of the form: 'If such and such conditions were to be fulfilled in him at any time, he would be likely thereupon to have such and such an experience or to perform such and such an action.' But it is commonly taken for granted that any such conditional proposition, which is true of an individual, is based on some *actual specific persistent modification in his internal structure* or on some *specific recurrent process going on continually within him.* In describing a power or disposition as 'mental' I mean to imply *only* that it is a power or disposition to have certain *experiences,* or to perform certain operations in which *actual experiences* of one kind or another play an essential part. I do not mean to imply or to exclude any particular view as to the nature or location of that structural modification or that rhythmical process which is assumed to be the basis of that disposition or power. Provided only that a disposition is such as to issue in the having of certain experiences, or in the performing of certain operations in which specific experiences play an essential part, it will be called a *'mental* disposition', even if its basis should be (as most orthodox psychologists and physiologists would unhesitatingly assume) purely *material,* viz. a modification in the structure of a person's brain, or a rhythmic electrical or chemical process in his brain. It may be added, though this is not essential, that specific mental dispositions are generally initiated and modified in an individual by certain specific experiences and concatenations of experiences of his.

All this being understood, I propose to extend the phrase 'the mental state of an individual on a certain occasion' to cover, not only his actual experiences on that occasion, but also the then state of whatever it may be that constitutes the basis of the mental powers and dispositions which he possesses at that time. The former may be distinguished as his 'state of *consciousness*' at the time, and the latter as 'the state of his *mental dispositions*' at the time.

Now, if we allow that B's state of consciousness can influence the mental state of A *at all,* whether by normal means or telepathically, it is obvious that its primary influence might sometimes be on A's *mental dispositions,* and not on his state of consciousness. It might modify existing ones or set up new ones, without directly initiating any experience in A or directly modifying any experience which A may already be having. Again, if we look at the situation from the other side, it is plainly possible that the event or process in B, which influences A's mental state on any occasion, might be some change then taking place in B's *mental dispositions,* which was not represented by anything in B's *state of consciousness* at the time.

(2) I pass now to my second explanatory comment. In stating the

215

circumstances in which it would be felt to be appropriate to use the word 'telepathy' I have purposely employed the extremely vague expression 'influencing'. Some of the ambiguities which lurk in the word 'telepathy' can be most conveniently exhibited by distinguishing the different ways in which this 'influence' of the mental state of one person on that of another has been conceived. This I will now proceed to do.

There would be no particular reason to contemplate the possibility of telepathic influence of B on A on a given occasion unless the following conditions were fulfilled. (i) A must have had at the time a certain fairly *outstanding and singular* experience. (ii) So far as can be discovered or reasonably conjectured, there was nothing in A's experiences in the remoter past, and nothing in his external circumstances, or in his bodily or mental condition just beforehand, which might plausibly be held to account for his having just that experience just then. (iii) At about the time when A had this outstanding and not readily explicable experience, B was having an experience which was *correlated* in some particularly close way with A's experience. So far as can be ascertained that was not true of *anyone but* B.

Let us now concentrate our attention on the positive part of the third condition, viz. the particularly close *correlation* between A's outstanding experience and a certain roughly contemporary experience of B's. Such a correlation might take various forms, since experiences of a certain kind are capable of one kind of correlation, and those of certain other kinds are capable of certain others. I think that the most obvious forms of possible correlation may be classified under the following five heads, which do not necessarily exclude each other: (i) Likeness in *quality* between two experiences; (ii) Partial or complete identity in the *objects ostensibly presented* in the two; (iii) Partial or complete identity in the *propositional content* of the two; (iv) An obvious *symbolical relationship* between the emotions felt or the objects ostensibly presented in A's experience and the roughly contemporary state and situation of B, as B (correctly or mistakenly) takes these to be at the time; (v) The relation between (*a*) being a *desire* in B that A should have such and such an experience or perform such and such an action, and (*b*) A's actually having such an experience or actually performing, or dreaming that he is performing, such an action. I will now explain and illustrate each of these possible forms of correlation.

(i) Mere qualitative likeness is about the only form of correlation possible between such experiences as bodily feelings, emotions, and the simpler kinds of externally referred sensations, such as those of taste and of smell. A might have a sudden and unaccountable feeling of stomach-ache and of nausea just at the time when B had swallowed poison and was suffering agonies of colic and was vomiting. Or, again, A might experience an unaccountable emotion of terror, just at the time when B was being threatened with imminent death in a climbing accident. Again A might have a vivid image or *quasi-sensation* as of the taste of peppermint or the smell of ammonia, just when B was sucking a peppermint-drop or getting a whiff of some ammoniacal solution. This kind of correlation may occur also in the case of fairly simple experiences of sound or of sight, though here we are on the border of (ii). An agent in an experiment may concentrate his attention on a red triangular figure on a white card, and the patient may at that time have a visual image or a *quasi-sensation* as of a red triangle on a white background.

(ii) There are certain experiences, of which the most obvious examples are normal waking states of visual, tactual, or auditory perception, which have the following characteristic features. In having such an experience one unhesitatingly takes oneself to be being *directly presented with* or *confronted by* a certain physical thing or event or process or state of affairs, existing or occurring or going on outside one's body and independently of one's present awareness of it. It might be, e.g., a table, a flash of lightning, the sound of a waterfall, a game of football, and so on. Moreover, such a presented object always presents itself, in and through such an experience, as *qualified* in certain ways, as *related* in certain ways to other objects presented simultaneously with it, as containing such and such a *pattern of interrelated items*, and so on. Lastly, the experient takes for granted that the object which is being presented to him in this way is in principle capable of being presented in a similar way at the same time to other persons like himself; and that it would in fact be presented to any such person who might be appropriately situated and oriented at the time.

I have said that the most obvious examples of such experiences are normal waking sense-perceptions of sight, touch, and hearing. I must now add that there are other experiences, viz. many dreams and waking *quasi*-perceptual hallucinations, which have precisely the same *experiential* or *phenomenological* features. The only essential difference is this. An instructed outsider, or the experient himself (if he should reflect critically, on that or on a later occasion), would judge, on applying the accepted tests for veridicality or delusiveness of perceptual experiences, that the experient was *fundamentally mistaken* in what he unhesitatingly took for granted in having the experience.

We can, therefore, quite properly speak of *one and the same object* being *ostensibly presented* either (*a*) by two normal waking sense-perceptions; or (*b*) by two dreams or by two waking *quasi*-perceptual hallucinations, or by a dream and a *quasi*-perceptual waking hallucination; or (*c*) by a normal waking perception and by either a dream or *quasi*-perceptual waking hallucination. Now a very common kind of correlation in alleged sporadic cases of telepathy is (as we have seen) when B has a *normal waking perception* of some outstanding physical event in a certain context, and A has at much the same time a *dream* or a waking *quasi*-perceptual hallucination, in which he is ostensibly presented with an event of just that kind, happening in just that kind of context.

(iii) We can speak correctly and intelligibly of A and B as 'thinking of', 'contemplating', 'being occupied with', etc., a *certain one fact*, e.g. the fact that the angles at the base of an isosceles triangle are equal, on either the same or on different occasions. Again, we may say correctly and intelligibly such things as: 'A and B were considering last night whether Francis wrote *The Letters of Junius*. A was inclined to believe that he did, and B to disbelieve it.' I should describe both cases by saying that A and B had states of mind 'with *the same propositional content*'. In the second case I should add that they had '*different mental attitudes*' towards that common propositional content.

These expressions are intended merely as convenient ways of indicating a kind of situation which is perfectly familiar to all of us, and which can arise only in connexion with what may be called '*discursive cognitive states*', such as 'contemplating' facts, 'considering' alternative possible answers to questions, and so on. They are *not* intended to recommend any particular analysis of such situations, or to carry with them any ontological implications as to there being entities of a peculiar kind, called 'facts' or 'propositions'.

Suppose, e.g., that A, who had never been interested in the authorship of *The Letters of Junius* and had never heard tell of the theory that Sir Philip Francis was the author of them, suddenly began to contemplate the proposition that Francis wrote *The Letters of Junius*. And suppose that this happened to A at almost the very moment at which his colleague B had been actively engaged in considering the problem of the authorship of those letters, and the evidence for and against the proposition that Francis wrote them. That would constitute at least a remarkable coincidence in respect of the *identity of propositional content* of A's thought and B's contemporary thoughts. And, if there were a number of such coincidences, one might be inclined to consider seriously the hypothesis of a telepathic influence of B's thoughts upon A's.

(iv) A very common form of correlation is that of a symbol to something which it quite obviously symbolizes in a well known and unambiguous way. Suppose, e.g., that A has an unaccountable feeling of depression, accompanied or immediately followed by a visual image or an hallucinatory *quasi*-perception as of a hearse with a coffin in it standing outside the gate of B's house. And suppose that B at about that time either actually was or mistakenly believed himself to be dying. That would constitute a very notable correlation between A's experience and B's roughly contemporary state and situation, as B (correctly or mistakenly) takes it to be at the time.

(v) The kind of correlation which I have in mind under this heading may be introduced by the following analogy. It often happens in daily life that B wishes A to act in a certain way; that he expresses that wish by uttering a command or a request or an admonition to A; and that, in consequence of hearing and understanding that utterance of B's, A acts in accordance with B's wishes. Again, to take a more abnormal case, B might be a hypnotist, and A a subject whom he has hypnotized. B expresses his wish in the form of an hypnotic suggestion; and A, on hearing this utterance of B's, automatically acts as suggested.

Now it might happen that A's action on a certain occasion corresponded to B's wishes at the time, in the kind of way in which it *would* have done, *if* B had expressed those wishes in the form of a command, a request, an admonition, or an hypnotic suggestion to A, and *if* A had heard, understood, and acted accordingly. But it may be certain that B did *not* overtly express his wishes; or that A was *not* at the time in a position to perceive with his senses any such utterances as B might have made; or that A could *not* have understood such utterances, even if he had perceived them or had had them reported to him. In such a case the hypothesis of a telepathic influence of B's wishes on A's actions might have to be seriously considered.

I have now stated and illustrated some of the most important kinds of correlation between an experience or action of A's and a more or less simultaneous state of consciousness of B's, which would need to be present if the question of possible telepathic influence of B's state of consciousness on A's experience or action is to be seriously considered. I would add the following remark at this point. Suppose that good evidence for telepathic influence could be produced by considering cases which plainly fall under one or more of these headings. Then I should think it very likely that telepathic influence may operate much more widely and more continuously than can be established

by *direct* evidence. For, in the first place, A's state of consciousness at any moment might be influenced telepathically by contemporary changes in the state of consciousness of other persons *whom
we have no means of identifying*. Again, A's state of consciousness at
any moment might be influenced by contemporary changes in the
structural or rhythmic *basis of another person's mental dispositions*,
which are not accompanied by any introspectable change in that
person's state of consciousness. Lastly, the effect of telepathic influence on A might be to produce changes in the *basis of his mental
dispositions*, unaccompanied by any introspectable change in A's
state of consciousness. In none of these possible cases would there
be any specific direct evidence of telepathic influence upon A.

This brings me to another matter which is of some importance.
If telepathic influence is exerted at a certain moment by B *on* A, and
not on X or Y, and if it is exerted *by* B, and not by C or D, that must
presumably be due to some kind of special *pre-existing relationship*
(whether of long duration or merely occasional) holding between B
and A. We may refer to this by the vague and old-fashioned word
'*rapport*'. In some cases we can plausibly suggest what is the relationship which constitutes *rapport*. In a telepathic experiment it would at
least include the fact that A and B are taking part in the same experiment, in which they are both interested, and in which a single definite
task is vividly before the minds of both. In certain sporadic cases it
seems plausible to suppose that an essential factor in the *rapport* is
special ties of blood-relationship, of friendship or love, or of some
other kind of emotional engagement. But there are well attested
sporadic cases where telepathy took place in the absence of all such
relationships; and there are of course innumerable cases where it did
not take place, although one or more of them existed to a high degree.

Telepathic Influence and Telepathic Cognition. It is one thing to say
that a certain experience of A's was *evoked or modified* by a certain
roughly contemporary mental state of B's. It is quite another thing
to say that A's experience was a *cognition*, either of B's experience
itself (if that should have been a feeling or an emotion), or of the
object ostensibly presented to B by his experience (if that should have
been a perception or a *quasi*-perception), or of the propositional content of B's experience (if that should have been a discursive cognitive
state, such as considering or believing such and such a possibility).
We should be inclined to make the latter assertion, if and only if we
had reason to think that one or other of the special kinds of correlation, enumerated and illustrated above, held between A's experience
and B's roughly simultaneous mental state. When all that we feel
entitled to assert is that a certain experience of A's was evoked or

modified by a certain mental state of B's ,we should confine ourselves to saying that A's experience was *'telepathically influenced by'* that mental state of B's. If and only if we can establish one or another of these special kinds of correlation, we are entitled to go further. We can then say that A's experience was *'telegnostic of'* either (*a*) B's mental state, or (*b*) the object ostensibly presented to B by that mental state, or (*c*) the propositional content of that mental state; as the case may be.

It is probably reasonable to assume that any experience which was telegnostic would be telepathically influenced. But the converse certainly does not hold. An experience of A's might be telepathically evoked or modified by a certain mental state of B's; but the effect of the telepathic influence might simply be to set A's mind at work to construct, entirely out of the traces of his own past experiences, a dream or waking fantasy having no special reference to B and no special correspondence with the causally relevant mental state of B. But, although this is plainly a theoretical possibility, and one which may in fact be quite commonly realized, it must be added that it would be difficult in such a case to find *any evidence* for telepathic influence. From the nature of the case, evidence for telepathic influence is generally evidence for some kind of telegnosis.

Even when the telepathically induced experience in A is so correlated with the roughly contemporary mental state of B that we can properly speak of 'telegnosis', we must distinguish between the following two alternative possibilities. (i) The correlation may be merely *de facto*, and such as may be discovered afterwards by A himself or by some third person C. A's experience at the time may not involve for *him* any explicit conscious reference to B or to any particular experience of B's. (ii) On the other hand, an essential feature of A's experience may be that *he* takes it *at the time* to refer to B and to something that is happening to B. In that case A's experience is, not merely 'an experience *which in fact refers to B'*, but is 'an experience *of reference to B'*. We might distinguish these two alternative possibilities as *'unwitting* telegnosis' and *'explicitly referential* telegnosis'. It is plain that telegnosis which is explicitly referential is much more likely to be followed up and tested for veridicality than telegnosis which is merely unwitting. For in the former case we have, what we do not have in the latter, a clear indication where to look for possible verification.

The mystery of telepathy is at its minimum when A's telepathically induced experience has no explicit reference to B, and has no content which cannot be plausibly accounted for in terms of A's own past experiences and the traces left by them and his own powers of constructive fantasy. Here the only paranormal feature would be the

221

initiation, by some more or less contemporary state of mind of B, who is not in normal communication with A, of the stimulus which sets those powers to work at that moment on those materials. The mystery and the interest are immensely heightened when the contents of A's experience are correlated with features in B's contemporary awareness of, or beliefs about, his own present state and circumstances, which could not by any normal means have been known or suspected by A at the time. Even if there should be nothing in the *raw materials*, out of which the content of A's experience is constructed, which could not plausibly be ascribed to his own past experiences and the traces left by them, we could not leave it at that. We should have to suppose some characteristic *organizing* influence, emanating from B and guiding or supplementing A's own powers of constructive fantasy. This would be needed in order to account for those 'home-grown' materials being so selected and moulded that the content of A's experience is correlated in this very special way with the contents of B's contemporary state of perception, *quasi*-perception, or belief. Nor is it by any means clear that this would be enough in all cases. It might sometimes be necessary to assume that B's influence *supplies some of the raw materials*, and does not merely select and mould in appropriate ways materials which are exclusively 'home-grown'.

An additional factor enters when A's experience is one of *explicitly referential* telegnosis. Here A's experience is not only *in fact* evoked or modified by the telepathic influence of B; and it is not only *in fact* so correlated with B's contemporary mental state as to constitute a cognition of the latter, in respect of its quality or of its ostensibly presented object or of its propositional content. Beside all this it is an experience which involves for A an *explicit reference* to B and to B's state and situation at the time. The influence here somehow carries with it a recognizable mark of its origin.

We may usefully compare the distinction between explicitly referential and merely unwitting telegnosis to the following distinction, which is perfectly familiar to most of us in our normal waking life. It happens from time to time that a vivid visual image suddenly presents itself to one's 'mind's eye'. It is reasonable to suppose that such an image does in fact usually originate in a past perception of a certain person, or thing, or scene, or in a past dream; and that it does in fact more or less accurately resemble the content of that past perception or *quasi*-perception. Now *some* of these images do present themselves to one as *memory*-images of such and such a person or thing or scene, which one *recollects* having witnessed or dreamed of. These may be compared to experiences of *explicitly referential* telegnosis. But many of them, though probably no less originating in and re-

222

sembling something actually witnessed or dreamed of, carry with them no such explicit reference to their source. At most they may have about them a vague flavour of familiarity, without any specific reference; and often they lack even that. Such images may be compared to experiences which are only *unwittingly* telegnostic.

In the essay entitled 'Normal Cognition, Clairvoyance, and Telepathy' in my book *Religion, Philosophy, and Psychical Research* I have gone fairly fully into the theoretical aspects of Telepathy in general and of Telepathic Cognition in particular (see pp. 46–67). I have nothing to add to what I said there. Nor should I wish substantially to modify it, though I might re-word certain parts of it in view of changes in philosophical fashion. The terms 'mind' and 'sensum' or 'sense-datum', which were then quite decent, have for the moment become 'dirty' words. I should have no difficulty in restating all the essential points without shocking the delicacy of my younger readers by the use of them. But I do not think it would be worth while to take up my space and the reader's time by submitting a bowdlerized version here and now. So I refer any reader who may be interested to the original text with all its regrettable crudity.

IX

THEORETICAL POINTS ARISING
(*continued*)
(III) THEORIES ABOUT COLLECTIVE AND RECIPROCAL HALLUCINATIONS

CASES of collective and localized *quasi*-perception and cases of reciprocal hallucination raise very important questions of interpretation. Their implications were the subject of a controversy between Gurney and Myers in the early days of the S.P.R., and the contributions of both parties are still very well worth reading and reflecting upon. They will be found in Chapters XVII and XVIII of *Phantasms of the Living* and in the 'Note on a Suggested Mode of Psychical Interaction' (Vol. II, pp. 277–316) contributed by Myers to that work. The latest discussion of the whole subject is the paper contributed to Vol. L of S.P.R. *Proceedings* by Professor Hornell Hart and others, entitled 'Six Theories about Apparitions'.

The alternative theories fall under the following two heads, viz. *Inter-subjective* and *Extra-subjective*. According to the first type of theory, the collective character of the hallucination is entirely due to *telepathy*, and there is no question of there being any kind of extra-subjective entity localized in space, which is the common object of all the correlated *quasi*-perceptions. According to the second type, telepathy is inadequate to account for the facts, and it is necessary to postulate such an extra-subjective localized common perceptum. Each type of theory can be developed in many different specific forms.

Inter-subjective Theories. Gurney suggested two alternative theories to account for collective hallucinations. The first is that a certain distant person B, who is undergoing some crisis, exerts simultaneously and independently a telepathic influence on A_1, A_2, etc., who happen to be together at the time, and that they thereupon have hallucinations which more or less closely resemble each other in content. This might be called the theory of *Multiply Directed Telepathic Initiation*.

As regards this theory Gurney made the following comments. (i) It obviously applies only to collective hallucinations which are *veridical*, i.e. where there is an event in the mental history of a person outside the group of hallucinated percipients which corresponds to the contents of their hallucinatory *quasi*-perceptions. It would, therefore, commit us to the hypothesis of some kind of survival in the case of phantasms of the *dead*. (ii) In the case of hallucinations which are known to be initiated telepathically, there is good reason to believe that the details of the hallucination are largely due to the phantasmogenic powers of the *recipient*, working up materials derived from *his* past experiences. It therefore seems unlikely that the hallucinations of two or more persons, stimulated telepathically at the same time by the same incident in the history of a certain other individual, would in general *much resemble* each other. (iii) We have also some reason to believe that there is often a period of latency between the reception of a telepathic stimulus and the production of an hallucination. That period would hardly be likely to be the same for different persons who happened to be in the same room on the same occasion. Therefore we should not expect the hallucinations, which were telepathically initiated in A_1, A_2, etc., by the same event in B's history, to occur *simultaneously*. (iv) There is good reason to believe that an event in B's history will influence A telepathically only if there be some pre-existing *rapport*, e.g. blood-relationship, close friendship, love, etc., between the two. We should, therefore, *not* expect that hallucinations would be generated telepathically in anyone in the room who was a complete stranger to B. But in fact such persons are often included among those in the room who share the collective hallucination concerning B. On the other hand, we *should* expect that what I have called '*disseminated* hallucinations' would be at least as common as collective ones. Persons who are in close *rapport* with B, but are widely separated from each other in space, might be expected to have roughly simultaneous hallucinations corresponding to a crisis in B's life. Now there are a few well attested cases of disseminated hallucinations, but they are much less common than cases of collective hallucinatory *quasi*-perception.

As regards the last of these objections I would remark that cases of disseminated hallucination would, as I have already pointed out, be very likely to be overlooked, even if they were fairly frequent.

There is, however, an objection to be added. It is alleged that, in many cases of collective hallucination, the experiences of the various experients are not just so many simultaneous *quasi*-perceptions as of a person of roughly the same appearance in approximately the same place in the room which they are all occupying. It is alleged that they are so correlated that it is as if those present were all perceiving that person as he would appear from their several points of view if he were physically located in the room. There is nothing in the theory of Multiply Directed Telepathic Initiation to account for this alleged detailed correlation between the various hallucinations. Whilst I strongly suspect that the available evidence for such detailed correlation has been greatly overrated, I think that *some* weight must be attached to this objection.

We can now pass to Gurney's second theory. According to this, one of the persons in the room (say A_1) starts to have an hallucination. This may arise from purely intra-subjective causes, or it may be telepathically initiated. (Presumably, in veridical cases, we should have to take the latter alternative.) In either case, A_1 telepathically influences A_2, A_3, etc., who are in the same room with him at the time, and they have hallucinations which resemble his. This may be called the theory of *Telepathic Infection*.

As it stands, this theory seems to me to be open to several of the objections which Gurney himself brought against the first theory. Is it any easier to see why the hallucinations produced in A_2, A_3, etc., should *resemble* each other, or be *simultaneous with* each other, when the initiating telepathic agent is A_1, who is one of the persons present in the room, than when it is B, who is at a distance? On the other hand, it is perhaps easier to account, on this theory, for the hallucinations being so correlated that the various persons in the room ostensibly see B as he would appear to them from their several points of view if he were physically present. For, if A_1 is seen by A_2, A_3, etc., to be staring in a certain direction and to be following something with his eyes, and if A_2, A_3, etc., each at the same time through telepathic infection ostensibly sees a figure before him, there will be a strong suggestion that it is one and the same figure which all of them are seeing from their several points of view.

An objection, which Myers brought forward, and which Gurney discussed, is this. If the theory were true, we should expect to find numbers of cases in which an hallucination, arising in A_1 from purely intra-subjective causes, would spread by telepathic infection to other persons who are in his neighbourhood at the time. Myers alleged that there are no clear cases of this. Gurney had to admit that they are not at all numerous. He quotes in detail a few cases of collective hallucination, where there is no apparent reason to think that the crop of hallucinations was started telepathically by any *living* person outside the group of adjoined percipients, and where there is no special reference to any *dead* person or indeed to any *person* at all. But in the end he has to admit that telepathic initiation by someone *outside* the group of percipients, though not a *necessary* condition for collectivity, is at any rate a *highly favourable* condition. That is, of course, compatible with the theory that the spreading of the halluci-nation is by telepathic infection within the group.

Anyone who is inclined to accept the theory of Telepathic Infection has to face the following question, which Gurney himself raised about the rival theory of Multiply Directed Telepathic Initiation. Why should telepathic infection affect those and only those who happen to be together in the same small region of space at the time, and who may be in no special pre-existing *rapport* with the one in whom the hallucination starts?

Gurney suggests that contiguity in space may be only indirectly relevant. The experiences of several persons who have been together for some time, especially if they have been in conversation with each other or have been taking part in some common occupation, have for the time much in common. They form a kind of interconnected pattern. Gurney suggests that this may suffice to form the basis of a temporary *rapport* between them, even in the absence of any deep or long-standing emotional relationship.

I would remark that this suggestion does not help to explain, in terms of telepathic infection, the *reiterative* character of the halluci-nations in the case of a 'haunted' room. For such hallucinations may occur in persons who occupy the room at various times, who have never occupied it together or been in any kind of normal communica-tion with each other, and have no kind of emotional link with each other.

Gurney himself was not satisfied with the theory of Telepathic Infection in its pure form. He proposed the following modification, in which the theory is supplemented by a diluted form of the theory of Multiply Directed Telepathic Initiation. Suppose that an halluci-nation is initiated telepathically in A_1 by some crisis in the life of the distant B, and that this spreads by telepathic infection to A_2, who is together with A_1 at the time. Then there are the following two alterna-tive cases to be considered.

(i) Suppose that there is already a long-standing and intimate relationship between B and *both* A_1 and A_2. Then B may be able to affect both of them telepathically, but the nature of the effect may be different in the two cases. In A_1 the effect may be to generate an hallucination relevant to B's contemporary crisis. In A_2 the effect may be only to make him more susceptible to telepathic influence from A_1, so that he is readily affected telepathically by A_1 and has an hallucination similar to his. This effect might be called '*direct telepathic sensitization*'.

(ii) Suppose instead that, whilst there is a long-standing and intimate relationship between B and A_1, A_2 is a complete stranger to B. In that case the temporary community of interests and ideas between A_1 and A_2 may suffice to place B in *temporary rapport* with A_2. That may be insufficient to enable B to generate, by direct telepathic influence, any hallucination in A_2. But it may be enough to make A_2 specially sensitive to telepathic infection from hallucinations produced telepathically in A_1 by B. This effect might be called '*mediated telepathic sensitization*'.

In this connexion Gurney quotes a few cases in which two persons were together and the relevant hallucination occurred *only* in the complete stranger A_2, and *not* in A_1, who was closely related to B. Here it looks as if the combination of the pre-existing *rapport* between B and A_1 with the temporary *rapport* between A_1 and A_2, constituted a temporary *rapport* between B and A_2, and enabled B to produce a relevant hallucination in A_2 *directly* and not through telepathic infection from A_1. This might be called '*mediated telepathic initiation*'.

Lastly, Gurney very tentatively proposed a further modification of the pure theory of telepathic infection, in order to cover cases which are not only collective but also *reciprocal*. Suppose that B is undergoing some crisis, and that A_1 and A_2 are together in a room in a place remote from B. Suppose that there is some pre-existing link between B and A_1, but that A_2 is a complete stranger to B. The modified theory is as follows. The first thing that happens is that A_1, in virtue of the *rapport* which already exists between him and B, has a telepathically initiated hallucination corresponding to B's crisis. Suppose now that this happens to be *reciprocal*. That implies that B has an ostensibly excursive hallucination, initiated telepathically by A_1, and corresponding to A_1's state of knowledge and belief about himself and his surroundings at the time. Since A_1's state of mind would include a perception of the room with A_2 in it, B's excursive hallucination would thus refer indirectly to A_2 as part of the object of A_1's perceptions and thoughts at the time. Gurney suggests that this might suffice to form a temporary *rapport* between B and A_2, which would enable B to initiate telepathically in A_2 an hallucination as of his presence in the room.

Gurney takes a very cautious attitude towards this last suggestion. In the first place, it is plainly irrelevant to all cases of collective hallucination where there is no evidence for *reciprocal* telepathy between any member of the assembled group and the distant person whose phantasm they ostensibly perceive. But, even in those collective cases where there is evidence for reciprocal telepathy involving the distant B, it is doubtful whether we can dispense with the theory of telepathic infection. The argument may be put as follows.

A_2, by hypothesis, is a complete stranger to B and has not the least idea what he looks like. Granted that the reciprocal telepathy between B and his friend A_1 puts B in a position to exert *some* kind of telepathic influence on the complete stranger A_2, who is within A_1's field of consciousness and interest at the time, why should the effect take the very special form of an hallucinatory perception *of B as present*? We can understand why the effect of B's telepathic influence on A_1 should be to produce in *him* an hallucination as of B's physical presence; for, by hypothesis, he knows B well and therefore has within himself the necessary materials for constructing such a phantasm. But the complete stranger A_2 has no such materials within *him*self. Gurney argues from this that, even in those collective cases which are reciprocal, we must suppose that the hallucinatory *quasi*-perception as of the presence of the remote B starts in one of the group who is already familiar with his appearance, and then spreads by telepathic infection to those members who are complete strangers to B.

It seems to me that Gurney has failed to notice that a precisely similar difficulty remains even if we make this supposition. The fact that the stranger A_2 has not within himself the materials for constructing a phantasm of B remains, whether we suppose the telepathic stimulus to come to him from A_1, who knows well what B looks like, or from B himself.

I think that the only advantage that A_1 would enjoy over B, as the possible telepathic source of a phantasm of B in A_2, is the following. A man's friends have a much more detailed and accurate idea of what he looks like from various external points of view than he himself can possibly have. One cannot see the back of one's own body, or more than a part of the front of it (and that from a very odd point of view), except indirectly by means of mirrors. Moreover, one would hardly expect that a person undergoing a crisis would be likely to be thinking at the time of the visual appearance which he would present to outside observers. It therefore seems most unlikely that B would have before his mind at the time a vivid image of his own outward appearance from various points of view. But, by hypothesis, his friend A_1 has, under the telepathic influence of B's crisis, generated from his memories of B an image so lively as to amount to an hallucinatory *quasi*-perception as of B's bodily presence. Now, experiments in the telepathic reproduction of drawings, e.g., suggest that under such circumstances A_2, if telepathically affected by A_1, would be likely to have an image resembling that which is vividly before A's mind. This is, I think, an essential missing step in the argument for Gurney's contention that telepathic infection is an indispensable factor even in those collective cases where there is reciprocal telepathy between one member of the associated group and the distant person whose phantasm they all ostensibly perceive.

Extra-subjective Theories. It is plain that theories, which try to account for collective and reciprocal hallucination wholly in terms of telepathy, have to be made very complicated and to make many *ad hoc* assumptions if they are to fit all the known facts. Suppose that each one of a number of persons in the same room at the same time ostensibly sees one and the same extended object, located at a certain position in front of him and looking as an actual physical object would look from the position which he is occupying and in the direction in which he is facing. Then it is *prima facie* simpler and more plausible to hold that there actually is an extra-subjective existent something, of a peculiar kind, located there, and that they are all actually perceiving it in a peculiar way. Suppose further that the object ostensibly seen bears the appearance of the body of a certain person who was in fact at a distance at the time; that that person afterwards states that he seemed to himself to be present in the room; and that his reports of what he ostensibly saw there, as from his transposed point of view, agree with facts which could not normally have been known to him or guessed by him. Then that seems *prima facie* to reinforce, by the testimony of the distant person, the above straightforward and 'common-sensical' interpretation of the collective hallucination. And it seems to supplement this by the following further information. It suggests *prima facie* that that peculiar kind of extra-subjective localized object, which those in the room all perceived in that peculiar way, and which looked like the body of the distant person, was in fact related at the time to that person's consciousness in the characteristic and unique way in which a person's physical body is related to his consciousness during his normal waking life.

I think that the most useful way to look at the question is this. There are certain criteria, which are accepted alike by plain men, by scientists, and by philosophers of all schools, for testing whether there is or is not an extra-subjective entity answering to a given ostensible perception. Ordinary dreams and non-collective waking hallucinations (including those which may be 'veridical' in the special sense which interests psychical researchers) answer so badly to these criteria that we have little or no hesitation in counting them as wholly delusive. The ordinary waking perceptions of a person in good health, with no obvious defects in his sense-organs, in a good light, etc., and without special emotional or other distractions or perturbations, answer so well that we have no hesitation in counting them as wholly or predominantly veridical. Collective hallucinations in general, and those of them in particular which are also reciprocal, occupy an intermediate position. They answer quite well to some of these criteria, and fail in respect of others. If one concentrates one's attention on the considerable degree to which they answer the tests, one is inclined to count them as veridical perceptions (though of a peculiar kind, not mediated through the normal sensory channels) of extra-subjective entities, having some, but not all, the properties of ordinary physical objects. If one concentrates on their *failure* to answer certain of the criteria, and on the *analogies* between them and ordinary dreams or non-collective and non-reciprocal waking hallucinations, one is inclined to deny that they can be genuine perceptions of extra-subjective existents. As always happens when we have a situation of this kind, it is open to each party with a little ingenuity to explain, by more or less plausible supplementary hypotheses, the admitted aspects of the facts which are *prima facie* unfavourable to his view.

I will now develop the above general statements in rather greater detail. Let us begin with some of the most obvious of the accepted criteria for veridicality. We may divide these into (1) *Direct*, i.e. tests which could be carried out *immediately* by the persons concerned, and (2) *Indirect*, i.e. waiting for future spontaneous developments or making experiments and awaiting their results. The direct tests can be divided into (1,1) those which can be applied by each individual severally, and (1,2) those which require consultation and comparing of notes by a number of individuals collected together. Each of these sub-classes can again be subdivided into (*a*) tests which involve only a *single* sense, e.g. sight, and (*b*) those which involve a comparison between the deliveries of two or more senses, e.g. sight and touch. I will now give some examples under each of these ultimate headings.

(1,1) (*a*) An important *direct* test, which each individual can make for himself *without needing to consult others*, and confining himself to a *single sense*, viz. that of sight, is this. He can (i) shut his eyes or turn his head for a moment, and note whether his previous ostensible visual perception as of a certain object located in front of him does or does not cease. Supposing that it does, he can then open his eyes or turn his head back into its immediately previous orientation, and note whether he does or does not again have an ostensible visual perception as of the same object, unchanged and in the same place, or as having moved slightly or slightly changed. If the results should be positive, that will be *pro tanto* a mark of veridicality. (ii) He can proceed to move about, varying the direction in which he is looking

231

so that his lines of sight always converge on the same small region of space, and note whether he does or does not ostensibly see all the time as it were different parts of one and the same object or the same parts in different perspective. Here again, if the results should be positive, that will be *pro tanto* a mark of veridicality.

(1,1) (*b*) A person, who is having an ostensible visual perception as of a certain object in his neighbourhood, may proceed to make the appropriate bodily movements for walking up to and touching such an object as he ostensibly sees. He may note whether he does or does not thereupon get tactual sensations correlated in the normal way with the details of his ostensible visual perception. If he does, the veridicality of that ostensible perception will be *pro tanto* confirmed; if he does not, it will be *pro tanto* invalidated.

It should be noted that this test presupposes that one is concerned with a *solid* object of fairly definite outline, if one is concerned with a genuine physical object at all. It would not be satisfactory as applied to a mass of coloured gas or a mist, although these are perfectly good visible physical objects.

(1,2) (*a*) Suppose that several persons, together in a room at the same time, were all looking in such directions that their lines of sight intersected at a certain point in the room. And suppose that at least one of them claimed to see a certain object occupying a region surrounding that point. Then (i) the question could be raised whether *all*, or *some but not all*, or *none* of the rest of them were ostensibly seeing such an object at that place. If *all* did, that would *pro tanto* be a mark of veridicality; if *none* did, that would *pro tanto* be a mark of delusiveness; if *some did and others did not*, this test would have turned out ambiguously. (ii) Suppose that more than one of them did ostensibly see much the same object as occupying the place in question. Then they could compare notes and find out whether the contents of their several ostensible visual perceptions were so interrelated as they would be if each of them were *actually* seeing, from his own point of view, that part of the surface of a single physical object, located in the place in question, which would be visible from where he is situated. If such were found to be the case, that would be *pro tanto* a mark of veridicality. If it were found not to be the case, that would point in the opposite direction.

(1,2) (*b*) What has been said under (1,1) (*b*) above can be adapted *mutatis mutandis* to the present case of *several* persons comparing the deliveries of two or more of their senses. All that I need add is this. It might happen, e.g., that the contents of A_1's and A_2's ostensible *visual* perceptions were interrelated as they would be if each were actually seeing, from his own point of view, one and the same physical object. But it might happen that, when each of them tried

232

to *touch* the object ostensibly seen by both of them, A_1 *would*, and A_2 would *not*, get the appropriate tactual sensations. In that case the correlation of their ostensible visual perceptions would tend to confirm the hypothesis of veridicality; whilst A_1's tactual experiences would tend to confirm it still further, and A_2's failure to get such experiences would tend to weaken it.

Before passing on to heading (2) I would make the following comments on what has been said under the previous headings. (i) Suppose that one of the persons present failed to get visual experiences corresponding to those of the others. Then it would often be much more reasonable to allege that there was something amiss with his eyes than to doubt the veridicality of the visual experiences of the rest. For one would here be alleging a defect, which is well known in principle, and which could easily be confirmed or refuted in detail by making a few tests on his eyes. If nothing were found amiss with his sight, it might be alleged that he had been subjected to a negative hypnotic suggestion which prevents him from seeing what is in front of his open eyes. That, again, would be an appeal to a known possible cause; though the explanation would be impossible to test on the spot, and might be difficult to verify or refute even if one had time and opportunity to follow it up.

Suppose, now, that a person who is inclined to interpret collective hallucinations in terms of the non-sensory perception of extra-subjective entities of a peculiar kind, is faced with the fact that one or more of the occupants of the room *fail* to share in the hallucinatory *quasi*-perceptions of the rest. He can easily go through the motions of accounting for this, consistently with his theory, on lines which are *formally* analogous to postulating defective eyesight or negative hypnotic suggestion. He can allege that those persons happen to be defective in respect of the mental or cerebral equipment (whatever it may be) which is required for non-sensory perception. Or he can allege that there is some temporary or habitual psychological hindrance (e.g. a state of rooted pro-materialist prejudice) which inhibits the exercise of that equipment. But it is important to notice just where the analogy breaks down. Defective eyesight and negative hypnotic suggestion are possible conditions which are already known to operate in other cases. A fair amount is known already about their causes, their *modus operandi*, and their normal effects. And their presence or absence in a given case can be tested by accepted and fairly readily applicable methods. None of this is true of the formally analogous explanation put forward by upholders of the extra-subjective theory of collective hallucinations. That explanation remains up to the present, therefore, a purely *ad hoc* hypothesis, put forward, without any independent evidence for it, in order to reconcile the theory with certain facts which *prima facie* conflict with it.

(ii) It is important to remember, on the other hand, that there are certain perfectly familiar and respectable 'objects', e.g. ordinary mirror-images, which display anomalies somewhat like those which dispose one to reject the extra-subjective account of collective hallucinations. A mirror-image is an extended, coloured, shaped 'object', visually located at a certain position behind the mirror for *all* those, and *only* for those, who are situated in front of the mirror. If any of those who 'see' it go up and try to touch it, they get no *tactual* experiences corresponding to their visual experiences. Moreover, the mirror-image is not an *independent* existent. It originates in and depends upon a certain ordinary physical object, which resembles it in appearance, and which is physically occupying a region of space remote from that which the image is visually occupying. We accept all this without worrying about it, because it is so familiar and because we understand the laws and the conditions which govern such phenomena. It would, of course, be absurd to pretend that there is any *exact* analogy between the image of a physical object in a mirror and the phantasm of a distant person ostensibly seen at a certain place in a room by a number of individuals present in it. Nevertheless, it is useful both for supporters and for critics of the extra-subjective theory of collective hallucination to be reminded that extra-subjective entities might resemble mirror-images, rather than full-blown physical objects, in their existential status and in the way in which they are located in physical space.

(2) I pass finally to the tests for veridicality which are *indirect*. These all rest on the general principle that, if a region of space is really occupied by such a thing as visually appears to be there, then that thing will have characteristic *causal properties*. It will act and react and change or persist unaltered in characteristic ways, quite independently of whether it is or is not under observation. Some of the expected results of this are such as to be in principle observable, either at the time and place in question, or, after an appropriate interval, at that or at some more or less adjacent place.

It is worth remarking that there are certain physical existents which are *never directly* observable. The most obvious examples are colourless gases, such as oxygen and hydrogen, which are quite ordinary macroscopic material objects. There are others, of a more recondite and 'highbrow' kind, which are not only never directly observable, but which also occupy space in rather peculiar ways, viz. electromagnetic fields. One might say that such an entity is continuously present throughout an indefinitely large region of space, but that it is *more intensely* present in some parts of it than in others. I suspect that philosophers, who discuss physical objects and our perception of them, have been too much inclined to concentrate their attention upon finite coloured hard bodies with definite contours, and to forget about such extended physical objects as gases and electromagnetic fields, to say nothing of mirror-images, rainbows, parhelia, and other optical anomalies. Both supporters and critics of extra-subjective theories of collective hallucination will do well to bear in mind that the way in which a solid body occupies a region is by no means the only way in which an existent entity may be extended and localized in physical space.

I have spoken so far of criteria for veridicality which apply equally, whether the object ostensibly perceived bears the appearance of an inanimate thing or that of a living human body. In the latter case, however, there are additional tests, which are not applicable in the former. The observers may ostensibly see and hear the ostensibly seen human body speaking to them. They will naturally conclude that the human body which they ostensibly see is the organism of a certain human person, and that he can testify, from 'internal evidence' (so to speak), to the real independent existence of that body. Each of them knows from his own inner experience what it is to have a body, to feel aches and pains and stresses and ticklings within it, and to act and perceive by means of it and from it as centre.

Now it is evidence somewhat of this kind, though a very odd variety of it, which is available in out-of-the-body cases in general, and, in particular, in those collective hallucinations which are also *reciprocal.* In the latter cases the person, whose phantasm was ostensibly seen in a certain place in a certain room by those present in it on a certain occasion, states afterwards that he seemed to himself at that time to be present in that room, and to be perceiving its contents as from the position which his phantasm was ostensibly seen to be occupying. When there is nothing but his unsupported statement to that effect, this does not add appreciably to the evidence for the extra-subjective interpretation of the facts. But suppose that his statements as to what he ostensibly perceived in the room agree with the facts as to what actually would have been visible from the position which his phantasm was ostensibly seen as occupying. And suppose that, at the time, he had no normal knowledge of those facts, and no data on which to base guesses about them. Then it would seem *prima facie* plausible to think that the phantasm may have been an extra-subjective entity, located at the place at which it was ostensibly seen to be; and that it temporarily stood to that person in at least some of the relations in which a person's ordinary physical body normally stands to him.

The respects in which collective visual hallucinations commonly fail to pass the tests for veridicality are these. (1) It is very seldom indeed that a person, who is ostensibly seeing a phantasm of a distant individual as present before him, can get any corresponding *tactual* experiences, if he tries to go up and touch the object ostensibly seen. To this it may be answered that the same would happen if the object seen were of the nature of a mass of coloured gas, or a mist, or a mirror-image or a mirage. (2) It may happen that the visual hallucination, though collective in respect of *several* of those present, is *not* experienced by the rest of them. As I have remarked, attempts to account for this by analogies with defective sight or with the results of negative hypnotic suggestion are unconvincing because purely *ad hoc*. (3) There are hardly any (if, indeed, any) well attested cases in which the object ostensibly seen showed any of the *causal properties* normally possessed by things of that visual appearance. Often the phantasm seems to enter and to leave through closed doors, to vanish into the wall, and so on. To this a supporter of the extra-subjective theory might fairly answer that he never supposed that phantasms were ordinary physical objects, and that therefore his withers are unwrung when they fail to behave altogether as such. More positively he might reply that they behave very much as do 'optical objects', such as shadows, reflexions, etc., which are, nevertheless, admittedly extra-subjective entities.

The upshot of the discussion, so far, seems to be this. If the phantasms ostensibly seen in cases of collective hallucination are to be reckoned as extra-subjective entities, then their existential status is more like that of coloured wisps of gas, or of optical objects, such as rainbows and mirages, than that of ordinary solid bodies. It was precisely in those two ways that our animistic ancestors thought of them. The words πνεῦμα, ψῡχή, and *spiritus* embody the former analogy; and the words σκιά, *umbra*, and 'shade', the latter. Every schoolboy will remember the lines about the phantasm of Creüsa, and Aeneas's vain attempts to embrace it:

> *Ter frustra comprensa manus effugit imago,*
> *Par levibus ventis, volucrique simillima somno.*

A difficulty which has often been raised against the extra-subjective theory is this. A phantasm is practically always seen as *clothed* in one way or another; and it is very often seen as accompanied by some kind of *material appurtenances*, inanimate or animate, e.g. as carrying a stick, as wearing eye-glasses, as accompanied by a dog, and so on. If we are to postulate an extra-subjective shadowy replica of a living person's physical body, separable from the latter, shall we not also need to postulate separable replicas of his clothes, his stick, his eye-glasses, and his dog? And is that not asking rather too much of us?

Advocates of the telepathic theory might fairly claim to be in a position to deal fairly plausibly with such facts. Either the distant B himself, or his friend A_1, with whom he is in primary telepathic contact and who 'infects' A_2, etc., habitually thinks of and pictures B as dressed in a certain way and having certain appurtenances. So it is natural enough that the telepathically induced hallucinatory *quasi*-perceptions as of a phantasm of B should present him as so clothed and so accoutred.

Supporters of the extra-subjective type of theory are wont at this point to have recourse to the doctrine of 'thought-forms'. I have never seen any very clear formulation of this, and I am not at all sure that I rightly understand it. What I take it to be is somewhat as follows.

One's ordinary physical body, in its outward form and its inward constitution, is hardly at all affected, except cumulatively and very slowly, by one's habitual thoughts, emotions, and desires. Their only direct and immediate visible effects on it are variations of facial and other kinds of bodily expression, e.g., smiling, frowning, weeping, etc. One cannot, by taking thought, 'add a cubit to one's stature'; still less can one directly create or alter the clothing and material appurtenances of the physical body. But a person's secondary body (which, according to the extra-subjective theory, is what those concerned in a veridical collective hallucination are all perceiving in some non-sensory way) is very much more plastic and immediately responsive to his habitual thoughts, emotions, and desires. Its whole outward and visible form is moulded and clothed by, and in accordance with, his habitual mental picture of his physical body and its usual clothing and appurtenances. The secondary body as a whole, and its clothing, etc., automatically express that habitual mental picture of oneself, in somewhat the way in which a certain set cast of the countenance of the physical body may automatically express years of ill-temper or of bodily pain. And the whole outward form and clothing and accoutrements of one's secondary body might vary with temporary variations in one's mental picture of oneself, in somewhat the way in which the face of one's physical body might pass from smiles to frown or to tears with changes in one's emotional mood.

Such a theory does not seem to me to be unintelligible, whether or not one may deem it plausible. Taking it for what it may be worth, we may now ask ourselves how far it agrees with the telepathic theory, and just where the two differ. Both agree that the phantasms of the remote B which are ostensibly seen by A_1, A_2, etc., are *ultimately* derived, as to many of the details, from B's thoughts about and emotions towards his own physical body. On the telepathic theory the derivation is directly from B, by telepathic action, either on *each* member of the group severally or on *one* of them from whom it is 're-diffused' by telepathic infection to the rest. On the thought-form theory the *immediate* effect of B's habitual image of himself, as modified perhaps by his temporary state of mind and body, is *not* on the several members of the group composed of A_1, A_2, etc. Its immediate effect is to mould and clothe a certain pre-existing extra-subjective entity, viz. his secondary body, into the likeness of his physical body as he pictures it at the time. The correlation between the *quasi*-perceptions of A_1, A_2, etc., depends immediately on the fact that this extra-subjective entity is spatially adjacent to all of them, and is the *common object* which they all are perceiving in some non-sensory way.

If the telepathic theory can be made to cover the facts, without having to make too many supplementary assumptions about tele-pathic action, for which there is no kind of experimental evidence, it enjoys *one* clear advantage over the extra-subjective theory supple-mented by the theory of thought-forms. Provided it is confined to phantasms of the *living*, the telepathic theory needs to assume no kinds of existent entity other than those which are already admitted to exist and to be concerned, viz. the living individuals B, A_1, A_2, etc. It must be confessed, however, that the telepathic theory, when applied to *reciprocal* cases, is much less plausible as an account of the experiences of the *person whose apparition is ostensibly seen* than as an account of the experiences of *those who ostensibly see it*. The telepathic theory has to play down, or to interpret in a very strained way, the accounts of *excursive* experiences given by the quite num-erous persons who have had them and reported them. Finally, it seems difficult to give any plausible account of the phenomena of 'haunting' in terms of the telepathic theory. Those phenomena do suggest rather strongly the persistence of a localized extra-subjective entity, capable of being perceived on occasion as a shadowy human form, and animated by a fragment of a personality which might almost literally be said to be 'not all there'.

PHILOSOPHICAL POSTSCRIPT

I wish to avoid, so far as possible, throughout this book all contro-versial philosophic questions. But the discussion of rival theories about the nature of collective hallucinatory *quasi*-perception would obviously be incomplete, if it were not brought into relation to rival philosophic theories about normal sense-perception. Conversely, it would do professional philosophers who theorize on that subject no harm, if they were to pay more attention than they commonly do to the facts of collective and reciprocal hallucination. I will, therefore, end this chapter with a brief discussion on the philosophy of normal sense-perception in relation to the facts and theories considered above.

I will begin with three points as to which there is no difference of opinion between scientists, on the one hand, and plain men and philosophers of all schools, on the other, provided that the latter have (and bear in mind) an elementary knowledge of the accepted results of physics, of physiology, and of psychology. These agreed points may be summarized under the heads (1) *Physical and physiological conditions*, (2) *Phenomenological characteristics*, and (3) *Criteria for veridicality or delusiveness*. I shall take these in turn, and shall confine myself mainly to normal waking *visual* perception.

(1) *Physical and Physiological Conditions.* Suppose that at a certain moment of my waking life I am seeing a certain external body at a certain place and in a certain state. To simplify the discussion I will suppose that it is a self-luminous object, such as an electric-light bulb, which is glowing because a current is passing through it.

There is an enormous mass of interconnected evidence for the following propositions. I should not have been seeing that object at that moment and as in that state unless light, emitted from it a little earlier, had entered my eye; unless this had set up a disturbance of a characteristic kind in my optic nerve; unless this had travelled up the nerve to a certain part of my brain; and unless it had there and then set up a certain kind of disturbance. When I do see the object, I see it as being in the place which it occupied and in the state in which it was at the moment when the light-waves by which I am now seeing it *were emitted from it*. That position and that state may, of course, be different respectively from the place that it occupies and the state in which it is *now*, when the relevant light-waves are entering my eye and the disturbance is reaching the optic centre of my brain. Owing to the very great velocity of light, those differences will in general be very small unless the object seen be very remote. But they may be appreciably large when the object is a distant heavenly body. Certain astronomical phenomena, e.g. the apparent annual periodic motion of the fixed stars, can be explained, both qualitatively and quantitatively, in terms of this, and (so far as I am aware) in no other plausible way.

(2) *Phenomenological Characteristics.* Such an experience as, e.g. seeing a certain electric-light bulb as glowing, is an experience as of being directly presented with a certain particular existent, which

239

presents itself to one as having a certain colour, extension, shape, position, etc., and as standing in certain spatial relations to one's own body and to other such particular existents which are simultaneously being presented to one in the same kind of way. I shall express this fact by describing such an experience as *phenomenologically prehensive*. Moreover, any normal person, after an early age, takes for granted that *what* is being directly presented to him in such an experience is a part of the surface of a certain three-dimensional object, e.g. a certain electric-light bulb. He takes for granted that this has approximately the colour, shape, position, etc., which it presents itself to him as having. He takes for granted that it has parts, which he cannot see from his present position, and that these now exist, and have colour, shape, size, position, etc., in *precisely the same literal sense* as do the parts which he is now seeing. And he takes for granted that it existed before he began to see it, and that *caeteris paribus* it will continue to exist after he ceases to be so placed and oriented as to be able to see it, and that at such times it has colour, etc., in precisely the same literal sense as when he is seeing it.

We may summarize this as follows. While a person is having a normal waking visual perception he automatically takes it to be *prehensive of the physical object which he would be said to be seeing* (or, to speak more strictly, of the part of its surface which is facing him at the time); and of certain of its states, qualities, and relationships, which he would be said to be *seeing it as having*. He takes for granted, in fact, that the function of normal visual perception is to present him directly with *the surfaces of independently existing material objects*, and with certain of the qualities, states, and relationships which such things possess independently of him and of any processes in his body or his mind which may be essential to his perceiving them.

(3) *Criteria for Veridicality or Delusiveness.* We must begin by distinguishing between the *meaning* of 'veridicality', as applied to such experiences, and the *criteria* for deciding whether a given experience of the kind is veridical or delusive. I have already stated and discussed these criteria fairly fully, and I need not repeat here what I have said earlier in this chapter. They all boil down in the end to the presence or absence of certain systematic correlations among the simultaneous or successive perceptual experiences (of the same or of different senses), either of a single individual or of a number of different ones, under conditions which can themselves be specified in terms of actual or obtainable perceptual experiences.

In considering what is *meant* by calling a perceptual or *quasi*-perceptual experience 'veridical' we at once enter into the region of philosophical controversy. For there is one type of philosophical theory, viz. *Phenomenalism*, according to which 'to be veridical' simply *means* to answer to those conditions which have been described above as 'tests for veridicality'.

Other types of philosophical theory would agree among themselves in distinguishing between the *meaning* of 'being veridical' and the fulfilment of those conditions which are criteria for deciding whether an experience is or is not veridical. According to them, what is meant by calling a perceptual or *quasi*-perceptual experience 'veridical' is roughly the following. It means that there did in fact exist, at the appropriate time and place, a certain entity in a certain state, correlated in a certain unique way with that experience; and that that entity would have existed there and then, and would have been in that state at that time, whether or not there had happened to be a percipient, with appropriate sensory and intellectual equipment for having the experience in question, at the place where the percipient was at the time when he had the experience.

Philosophical theories on the present question may be divided into (1) *Phenomenalistic*, (2) *Non-phenomenalistic*. And the latter can be sub-divided into (2,1) the *Prehensive Theory*, and (2,2) the *Representative Theory*. I will now say something about each of these in turn.

(1) *Phenomenalistic Theories*. These were the last word in philosophical 'up-to-dateness' some thirty years ago. They have now, so far as I can understand, fallen out of fashion and may be described in Oscar Wilde's words as 'having a great future behind them'. All that I need say about them in the present context is this. Suppose that what is *meant* by calling a perceptual experience 'veridical' is simply that it answers to those conditions which are commonly described as 'tests for veridicality'. Then, since some such experiences answer more fully than others to the criteria, there would be two alternative courses open to the Phenomenalist. One would be to make 'veridicality' a matter of degree. On that alternative we could say that some collective *quasi*-perceptual experiences have a very high degree of veridicality, but that probably none of them have so high a degree of it as do normal waking sense-perceptions had under the most favourable conditions. The other alternative would be to give the title 'veridical' to all those experiences and only those which answer above a certain degree to the criteria. It would then depend on where this limit was fixed whether collective *quasi*-perceptions should or should not be called 'veridical'.

On either alternative the Phenomenalist avoids an embarrassment

241

which confronts any kind of Non-phenomenalist. It is this. In each particular case, according to the Non-phenomenalist, there either did or did not exist, at the appropriate time and place, a certain extra-subjective entity in a certain state, correlated in a certain unique way with the perceptual or *quasi*-perceptual experience in question. That, for him, is a question of *Yes* or *No*, and not one of *more* or *less*. Yet, on the other hand, the criteria for veridicality may, as we have seen, be fulfilled in various degrees in different cases. The embarrassment is to assign, on any defensible ground, a certain limiting point, *above* which it is to be held that there *is* an extra-subjective entity corresponding to the experience, and *below* which it is to be held that there is *not*. I think that this embarrassment is to some extent mitigated, if we bear in mind the different kinds of way in which (as I have pointed out) different kinds of extended extra-subjective entity may be localized in space.

(2,1) *The Prehensive Theory.* The essence of the Prehensive Theory is to accept as literally true those propositions which, as I said in my account of the phenomenological characteristics of normal waking sense-perception, are instinctively and uncritically taken for granted by everyone when engaged in perceiving and acting. The problem, then, is to reconcile those propositions with the established facts about the physical and physiological conditions for normal visual perception.

Any attempt to do this would, I think, have to hold that the function of those processes is somewhat as follows. We should have to argue that the brain-state, which is the final outcome in the percipient's body of the process of emission, transmission, and reception of light, and of the subsequent transmission of a nervous impulse from the retina through the optic nerve to the brain, has a purely *evocative* and *directive* function, and not in any way a generative or creative one. Its sole function must be to evoke and maintain in the percipient a state of prehension or acquaintance, whose *immediate* object is a *certain part of the surface of the remote body* which has emitted the light that is now entering his eye and setting up this disturbance in the optic centre of his brain. And that state of prehension must be a direct revelation to him of certain of the qualities and relationships of that remote body, *as they were at the time when the light in question was emitted from it.*

Let us now consider some of the logical implications of such a theory.

(i) Suppose that there were to occur at a certain moment, through purely *internal* causes, a disturbance in the optic centre of a person's brain, precisely similar to that which would normally be caused by a certain body in a certain state and in a certain place having emitted light to his eye. And suppose that there had in fact been *no* such body in that place at that time. (These suppositions are certainly *logically* possible, even if it be most unlikely that they would ever be fulfilled in practice.)

Then it seems to me that, on the present theory, we should have to hold that *no* experience as of seeing such an object in such a state would be had by that person. For, if the experience which would be evoked in the normal case is essentially one of direct acquaintance with the emitting body, in the state in which it was when it emitted the relevant light-waves, no such experience could conceivably occur *unless* there were such a body, at the appropriate time and place and in the appropriate state, to serve as the immediate object of it. Either *no* experience at all would occur in the case supposed, or it would be an experience *without any kind of object*, and therefore an experience *of a radically different kind*.

(ii) Suppose now, instead, that light *were* emitted at a certain moment from a certain body at a certain place and in a certain state. But suppose that for some reason it *failed* to reach a certain person's eye, or, having done so, *failed* to set up a corresponding disturbance in the optic centre of his brain. And suppose, finally, that at the moment when such a disturbance *would* have been set up in his brain, *if* the physical and physiological processes had proceeded normally, a precisely similar disturbance should happen to occur in it from *purely internal* causes. (These, again, are suppositions which are certainly *logically* possible, however unlikely it may be that they would ever be fulfilled in practice.) I would now raise the question: What ought a supporter of the Prehensive Theory to expect to happen, on these suppositions, in the way of experience? I think that he might take either of the two following alternative views.

(*a*) He might argue that the person in question *would* see that external body at the place and in the state in which it was at the time when it emitted the light which somehow failed to evoke the normal disturbance in the optic centre of his brain. For, it might be said, the brain-state necessary for evoking a suitably directed and selectively prehensive perceptual experience has in fact been set up, though from purely internal causes. And the external body appropriate to be its immediate object was in fact existing at the appropriate place and in the appropriate state at the appropriate time. What more, it might be asked, is needed, on the Prehensive Theory, to evoke an experience of seeing that body at that place and in that state?

(*b*) A supporter of the Prehensive Theory might, however, avoid that rather startling conclusion. He might allege that an experience of seeing the external body would arise *only* if the disturbance in the optic centre were produced in the *normal way*, viz. by light emitted from that body entering the percipient's eyes and initiating a process in his optic nerve which travels to his brain.

We may sum all this up as follows. On the view that normal waking visual perception is literally prehensive of the *external body seen*, and of it as in the state and place in which it was *at a time earlier by the interval needed for light to travel from it to the percipient's body*, there are certainly *two* conditions *severally necessary* in order that a person may at a certain moment have an experience as of seeing a certain body at a certain place and in a certain state. (i) There must actually have existed at that place a body of that kind in that state, at a moment preceding that at which the perception occurs by the period needed for light to travel from that place to the percipient's eyes and for the disturbance to travel thence up his optic nerve to his brain. (ii) There must be occurring in the optic centre of his brain, at the moment of perception, such a disturbance as would normally be caused by light from such a body in such a state entering his eye and initiating there a process of transmission in his optic nerve.

The difference between alternatives (*a*) and (*b*) above is as to whether these two conditions are *jointly sufficient* for the occurrence of such an experience, or whether a *further* condition needs to be fulfilled. According to (*a*) they *are* jointly sufficient. According to (*b*) they are *not*; for it is *also* a necessary condition that light should actually have been emitted from the external body and received by the percipient's eyes, and that the disturbance in his optic centre *should in fact have been caused in that way*.

(2,2) *The Representative Theory*. The Representative Theory may be stated as follows. The immediate effect, on the mental side, of the disturbance in the optic centre in the brain, *no matter how* that disturbance may have been produced, is to call forth an experience which we will call a 'visual sensation'. This has a subjective and an objective aspect. In respect of the former, it is an event or process, with a date, duration, and context in the mental history of the person concerned. In respect of the latter, it is a sensation *of* a colour-expanse of such and such a hue and extensity, sensible duration, and sensible depth. When a person, who has had many such experiences of various kinds, which have formed associations and left complex traces, now has a visual sensation, he automatically tends to take the colour-expanse, *of* which it is a sensation, to be a certain part of the surface of a certain independently existing external body. And he takes the colour to be quite literally present on the surface of that body, and to be presented directly to him in and through the experience. But that instinctive belief, or *quasi*-belief, or 'taking for granted', which is (as we have seen) *phenomenologically* an essential factor in the experience called 'seeing a body', is simply *mistaken*. At the very best, the external extra-subjective entity which he sees is the locus of one cause-factor in a rather remote causal ancestor of the visual sensation which is the other essential factor in the experience called 'seeing a body'. There is no good reason to believe that the external extra-subjective entity in question has the colour which is presented to the percipient in his sensation (or indeed any other colour), in the literal sense in which he instinctively takes it to do so. For there is no good reason to think that colour is anything but a characteristic feature of those experiences called 'visual sensations', in their objective aspect.

Comparison between the Prehensive and the Representative Types of Theory. Theories of the representative type and of the prehensive type can, no doubt, take many different specific forms. But an essential difference between any form of the one and any form of the other is this. Both agree that a *necessary* condition for the occurrence of a normal waking perception at any moment is that a certain kind of disturbance should then be occurring in a certain region of the percipient's brain, and that this should simultaneously excite a certain organized pattern of traces left in his brain by his past experiences and their associations with each other. But from that common starting-point their paths diverge. According to the Prehensive Theory, as we have seen, those conditions are *not sufficient*, even on the bodily side. For, on that theory, at least one independently necessary condition is that there should actually have existed, at the appropriately earlier moment, a body of the kind perceived and in the state in which it is perceived as being, in the place in which it is perceived as located. For, otherwise, there would be nothing for this allegedly prehensive experience to be prehensive of.

According to the Representative Theory, on the other hand, those conditions *are jointly sufficient*, at any rate on the bodily side. Given that these conditions in the subject's brain and nervous system are fulfilled (from no matter what cause) at any moment, he will then and there have an experience as of seeing such and such an external body in such and such a state and at such and such a place, quite regardless of whether there was or was not, at the appropriately earlier moment, any such body in any such state at that place.

This difference is perfectly clear and definite. It might conceivably, with possible improvements in experimental technique, form the basis of an experimental decision between the two types of theory. Suppose that it should become possible to produce, by stimulating a person's brain directly by electrodes imbedded in it, a disturbance exactly similar to that which would be produced by an electric bulb being lighted in front of his open eyes. Suppose that that were done when, according to all agreed tests for veridicality, there was no such object before his eyes. And suppose that he were, nevertheless, to have a *quasi*-perception as of seeing such an object. Then, it seems to me, the result would be as nearly as possible decisive against the Prehensive Theory.

As I have remarked, the criteria for veridicality or delusiveness are accepted by everyone, whether he holds either theory or no theory. A supporter of either theory can interpret the fulfilment of these criteria in the way appropriate to the view which he holds. An adherent of the Prehensive Theory will say that, when these criteria are fulfilled, the perceptual experience is an *actual prehension* of a certain external body and of certain of its states, qualities, and relationships. In particular, he will ascribe the detailed *correlations* between the visual experiences of a number of observers (which are an important test for veridicality, on any view) to their all *prehending one and the same prehensum* (or, more strictly, adjoining or overlapping parts of the surface of a common *prehensum*). An adherent of the Representative Theory will say, under the same circumstances, that the perceptual experiences are *causal descendants* of certain processes in independent existents; and that the various characteristic features in the sensations, considered in their objective aspect, are *systematically correlated with* various states, qualities, and relationships of these independent sources of emitted influence. He will ascribe the detailed correlations between the visual experiences of a number of observers to those experiences being all evoked by influences of the same kind *emanating from a common source*.

Unless and until such experiments as I have imagined above become possible, we must content ourselves with more or less probable arguments based on such relevant facts as are available to us. The essential fact seems to me to be the continuity in phenomenological character between ordinary dreams, collective waking hallucinations, and normal perceptions. The argument based on this fact would run somewhat as follows.

Dreams, at the one end, and normal perceptions, at the other, are extremely alike in their content. They are exactly alike in that the experient at the time takes himself to be prehending contemporary things and persons and events, which exist or occur independently of him; and that he takes himself to be prehending them as having qualities, relationships, and states which they would possess, in the same quite literal sense, whether he happened to be perceiving them or not. Now it seems incredible that experiences, which are so fundamentally alike from the phenomenological point of view, should

246

be radically different epistemologically. Either *both* are directly prehensive of independently existing things, persons, or events, and of certain of their qualities, relationships, and states, or *neither* are. But the absence, in the case of dreams, of all those correlations with other experiences (whether of the dreamer himself or of others in his neighbourhood) which are the accepted marks of veridicality, makes it certain that *they* are not prehensions of independently existing things, persons, or states of affairs. Therefore we may fairly conclude that normal waking perceptions are not so either.

Of course it follows equally, from the failure of dreams to fulfil the accepted tests for veridicality, that they are not related to such external objects as are ostensibly perceived by the dreamer, in the way in which normal waking perceptions are related, according to the Representative Theory, to the objects perceived in *them*. Dreams are *not* (as normal waking perceptions *are*, according to the Representative Theory) remote causal descendants, by way of transmissive processes in the ether and in the nerves, of events in independent external objects correlated with what the dreamer is ostensibly perceiving.

The view that normal waking perception is literally prehensive of the objects perceived is in fact plausible *only* as regards perceptual experiences which answer fully or approximately to all the tests for veridicality. As perceptual or *quasi*-perceptual experiences depart further and further from fulfilling those tests, it becomes harder and harder to fit them into the Prehensive Theory in any plausible way. Yet at no place in the scale from the most normal of waking perceptions, through collective hallucinations, to ordinary dreams, is there any difference in the *phenomenological* character of each such experience taken severally. All alike are phenomenologically prehensive.

Now the Representative Theory has no particular difficulty in dealing with *quasi*-perceptual experiences of any degree of delusiveness. According to it, the *immediate* necessary and sufficient condition, on the bodily side, for a person to have such an experience at a given moment, is of essentially the same kind, whether the experience be veridical or delusive. If and only if there should then occur a certain kind of disturbance in a certain part of his brain, and if this should simultaneously excite a certain organized pattern of traces left in him by his past perceptual experiences and their associations with each other, he will thereupon have a perceptual or *quasi*-perceptual experience, whose details are completely determined by that brain-disturbance and the associations which it excites. On this view, the question whether that experience will be veridical or delusive depends primarily on the way in which this disturbance in the brain has been generated, and secondarily on the traces which it excites. If it has arisen in the normal way, through physical influences from without acting on the appropriate receptor organs and setting up transmissive processes in the sensory nerves connecting these with the brain, and if it excites the normal associations, the experience will be wholly or mainly veridical. If it has been generated by causes which are wholly within the experient's body, or if it has excited an unusual selection of traces in him, it will in general be completely or predominantly delusive.

The Representative Theory thus offers a unitary account of all the experiences in the scale from the most normal and veridical to the most delusive. It explains the *likeness* between all of them by the fundamental similarity in their *immediate* necessary and sufficient bodily conditions. And it explains the *unlikeness*, in respect of veridicality, between those at opposite ends of the scale by differences in the *causal ancestry* of their immediate necessary and sufficient bodily conditions. On the other hand, the Prehensive Theory can, so far as I can see, offer no plausible account of *quasi*-perceptual experiences, such as dreams, at the *non-veridical* end of the scale.

The only ground, so far as I can make out, for preferring the Prehensive Theory, as regards normal waking perceptions, is that it accords with the phenomenological fact that the experient instinctively takes them to be prehensive of external things, persons, events, and states of affairs. But precisely the same kind of ostensible prehensiveness is characteristic of the *quasi*-perceptual experiences of dreaming and of waking hallucination. *There* it is almost certainly misleading; so its mere occurrence is *nowhere* a guarantee of its validity. One likes to do as much as one honestly can for poor dear Commonsense; but one should not allow charity to degenerate into imbecility.

I think it would be fair to say that the Representative Theory is held by almost all contemporary physiologists, and is rejected with scorn by most contemporary English philosophers. Most of the latter, if I understand them aright, would profess some form of the Prehensive Theory. On such a question I would naturally prefer to find myself in agreement with the majority of my professional colleagues. But the evidence against the Prehensive Theory seems to me to be as nearly conclusive as evidence in philosophical matters can be, and I am quite unmoved by the 'flouts and jeers' with which the Representative Theory is currently assailed.

It only remains to note that one's decision as between the two types of philosophic theory concerning normal waking sense-perception is relevant to the interpretation which one might reasonably put on cases of collective hallucination. Suppose it should be held that certain cases of collective hallucination warrant the conclusion that all the hallucinated subjects are perceiving, in some non-sensory way, a certain extra-subjective entity of a peculiar *quasi*-physical kind. Then one would naturally interpret this in whichever of the two alternative ways in which one would interpret the normal perception, by a number of individuals, of an ordinary physical thing. On the one alternative we should hold that the collective hallucination consists in one and the same *quasi*-physical extra-subjective entity being the *common prehensum* of all the various hallucinatory *quasi*-perceptions of the members of the group. On the other alternative we should hold that the collective hallucination consists in one and the same *quasi*-physical extra-subjective entity being the *common remote source* of some kind of influence, which calls forth in each of the several individuals a *quasi*-perceptual experience whose content is correlated with certain features in that source.

SECTION C

Studies in Trance-Mediumship

'And when Saul enquired of the Lord, the Lord answered him not, neither by dreams, nor by Urim, nor by prophets. Then said Saul unto his servants: "Seek me a woman that hath a familiar spirit, that I may go to her and enquire of her." And his servants said to him: "Behold, there is a woman that hath a familiar spirit at En-dor."'

I Samuel xxviii, 6, 7.

X

GENERAL ACCOUNT OF TRANCE-MEDIUMSHIP

I shall begin the present section by giving a brief and very general account of the usual phenomena of trance-mediumship. For the sake of verbal convenience I shall refer to the medium as 'she' and not as 'he or she'. There have been and are male trance-mediums, but I think it is true to say that the great majority of eminent trance-mediums in Western countries during the past 150 years have been women.

When a trance-medium is about to give a sitting to a client, she generally begins by shutting her eyes while resting quietly in her chair. Soon after this she begins to breathe deeply, to groan slightly and to struggle, and in general to behave like a person who is profoundly but restlessly asleep and is suffering from a rather distressing dream. In a few minutes, as a rule, she becomes calmer, and one often hears a kind of whispering going on, as if she were talking to herself. Shortly after this she will begin to talk audibly, often in a very different voice and manner and sometimes with a very different vocabulary, from those which are characteristic of her normal waking conversation. Ostensibly the medium's normal waking personality has ceased to control her vocal organs, and a new personality has gained control of them.

The new personality may carry on a conversation with the sitter for an hour or more. Eventually it says that it must leave, and it bids the sitter good-bye. The process with which the sitting began is then repeated in the reverse order. In a few minutes, after a certain amount of struggling, groaning, and whispering, the eyes are again opened, and the medium resumes her normal voice and manner. She is generally ignorant of what has been happening during the sitting; just as a person who has been talking in his sleep is ignorant of what he has been doing and saying, and rapidly forgets what he has been dreaming, when he awakes. On the other hand, the trance-personality often claims to be aware of what was being done and perceived and thought by the medium at times when the normal personality was in control of the body and the trance-personality was in abeyance. So far as such statements can be and have been tested, they are often found to be true.

Mediumistic 'Controls'. If the same medium goes into a trance on many different occasions, the trance-personality which appears to take control is usually the same on each occasion. It has the same voice, mannerisms, and vocabulary; it calls itself by the same fancy name; and in fact it shows as much sign of being one and the same person, in spite of gaps during which it is not in control of the body, as does the normal personality of the medium. Moreover, it has often a remarkably accurate memory of incidents which happened during previous sittings with the same sitter, even when long periods have elapsed, during which the medium was partly in her normal state and partly in trance giving sittings to other sitters.

A trance-personality of this recurrent and self-consistent kind, associated with a given medium and manifesting itself whenever that medium goes into trance, is commonly called a 'Control'. Controls very often claim to be children, and talk in a childish voice and in childish language. Others often claim to be Red Indians or Negroes or Arabs or Chinese, and in that capacity talk the kind of broken English which they imagine that such persons would talk. Often the two claims are combined, and the control purports to be, e.g., a Red Indian girl. Such controls are often guilty of extreme ethnological confusion. I have been asked for 'the key of my *wigwam*' by a control who professed to be an *African Negro* child: and I have heard an entranced medium suggest that the sitters should sing '*The Swanee River*' to encourage a control who claimed to be a *Red Indian* chief. Controls often spin a yarn about having lived on earth as human beings in the past, and having voluntarily connected themselves with the medium at some time in her present life for the good of humanity. They sometimes have a good deal of individuality, and are not unamusing to talk to; though the childish mannerisms or the broken English or the hieratic pretensions can be a terrible bore. They often have (like the rest of us) a strong sense of *meum*, and a less highly developed sense of *tuum*; and are very jealous of praise, which they hold to be due to *them*, being given to the normal personality of the medium.

Now the occurrence of a self-consistent secondary personality, which alternates with the primary personality in controlling a common bodily organism, is a well known phenomenon apart from all

254

claims to mediumship. Many such cases have been carefully studied by psychiatrists, particularly in France and in the U.S.A., during the latter part of the nineteenth and the earlier part of the twentieth centuries. One of the best known and the most entertaining of such cases is that of 'Miss Beauchamp', studied by Dr Morton Prince, and described in his book *The Dissociation of a Personality* (1st Edition 1905). There was a longish interval during which few, if any, such cases presented themselves. But lately a typical case has been elaborately described and discussed by Drs Thigpen and Cleckley (*The Three Faces of Eve*, 1957). In these abnormal, but not even ostensibly paranormal, cases it is generally found that one at least of the secondary personalities (if there should be, as there sometimes are, several) is childish, as compared with the primary personality. It is sometimes jealous of the primary personality and even strongly hostile to it. And it is often highly individualized and rather engaging, as compared with the primary personality. There is, thus, a strong *prima facie* case for thinking that mediumistic controls, whatever else they may be, are closely analogous to some of the secondary personalities studied by orthodox psychiatrists.

Even if we ignore this likeness between mediumistic controls and the secondary personalities of patients who can make no serious claims to paranormal powers, we find that trance-mediumship is no new or isolated phenomenon. Contemporary mediumship in Europe and the U.S.A. is plainly one specific form of a generic type of occurrence which has manifested itself in other forms throughout human history and all over the world.

The description in the Sixth Book of the *Aeneid* of the Cumaean Sibyl being gradually controlled by Apollo, and then speaking with a changed voice and countenance and delivering the god's orders to Aeneas, is evidently a poetically heightened account of the less spectacular process which I have described as happening at a sitting with a present-day trance-medium:

> Cui talia fanti
> Ante fores subito non vultus, non color, unus,
> Non comtae mansere comae, sed pectus anhelum
> Et rabie fera corda tument: majorque videri,
> Nec mortale sonans, adflata est numine quando
> Jam propriore deo . . . .
> . . . .
> Ea frena furenti
> Concutit, et stimulo sub pectore vertit Apollo.

At that time, and in those social and cultural conditions, the control would claim to be a certain god, associated with a certain sanctuary. Contemporary Western spiritualism originated and developed mainly in the early nineteenth century among ignorant lower-middle-class citizens of the U.S.A. Hence, perhaps, the preponderance of Red Indian chiefs and Negro children among contemporary controls. It became mixed up with Theosophy, and with traditions on the continent of Europe going back to Cagliostro, Mesmer, and the Rosicrucians. That may account for the considerable sprinkling of controls who claim to be Egyptian priests or Hindu yogis or Chinese sages, and talk the kind of elevated hieratic twaddle which is thought to be fitting to such persons. In the later days of paganism in the Roman Empire, when Neo-platonism was fashionable, controls generally claimed to be *daimones*, i.e. non-human spirits intermediate in rank between heroes and gods. (For a fascinating account of this the reader may be referred to Professor E. R. Dodds's learned paper 'Why I do not believe in Survival', in S.P.R. *Proceedings*, Vol. XLII.) When Christianity became predominant the controls were officially assumed to be devils, and they no doubt brought their minds to their circumstances, and talked and behaved as such to the best of their ability.

If we look in other directions, we find what must be essentially the same phenomenon recorded in the Old Testament in the very curious story of King Saul, who, after having forbidden mediums to practise, found it expedient himself to consult a woman at Endor, who 'had a familiar spirit', and to induce her to bring him into contact with the ghost of the lately deceased prophet Samuel (I Samuel xxviii).

I have no wish to reject out of hand the abstract possibility that some controls may have been gods or *daimones* or devils; for it takes all sorts to make a world. And I should be delighted to believe that the spirits of some of the Red Indians, whom the European colonists in America expropriated, infected, and defrauded, took some of their conquerors captive. But there is little or no good evidence for the statements which controls make as to their own identities. And the fact that controls of the same period and social tradition make similar claims about themselves, whilst those of different periods and different social traditions make correspondingly different claims about *them*selves, seems to me to cast serious suspicion on all such autobiographical statements on the part of controls.

Ostensible Communicators. We can now return from these historical parallels to the phenomena of contemporary trance-mediumship. Suppose that a person has a sitting with a medium, and that the latter goes into a trance, so that her normal personality is replaced by that of her control. After a few minutes of greeting and general talk, the control will usually claim to be in communication with the spirit of some dead person connected with the sitter. Messages, names, and references to living persons and to past incidents in the earthly life of the spirit in question will be given. The dramatic form of the process is therefore that the control ostensibly acts as an inter-mediary between the surviving spirits of certain deceased human beings and the sitter. They are supposed to be communicating in one way or another with the control, and the latter is supposed to be conveying to the sitter through the medium's lips or by automatic writing done by her hands, the messages received. That is all that happens at the vast majority of sittings with trance-mediums.

But with certain mediums and certain sitters there is a further and much more spectacular development. The childish or hieratic or broken-English voice of the control ceases, and the medium's vocal organs produce the sounds of a new voice, very different both from her normal waking utterance and from that of her control. The new voice claims to come *directly* from one or another of the sitter's dead friends or relatives, who have previously professed to be communicating only *indirectly* through the control. The change of voice, manner, and personality on such occasions can be extremely startling, as I know from experience. The process is alleged to be very tiring, especially at first, and the voice tends to begin as a laboured and gasping whisper. Even so, it is strange to hear what seems to be the voice of an elderly man, with, e.g., an elaborately clerical manner, issuing from the lips of a woman who has been speaking a moment before in the high falsetto tones of a little girl. In some cases the so-called 'direct voice' improves with practice, and long conversations may be carried on in this way with the sitter. This phenomenon may be called 'Ostensible Possession', for the medium behaves as if her body were temporarily *possessed* by the spirit of a certain dead person.

Whether the messages to the sitter be conveyed indirectly through the control or by the direct voice, we may call the personalities from whom they come 'Ostensible Communicators'. Whatever their real nature may be, they are *prima facie* very different from controls. An ostensible communicator is a personality associated with a particular sitter or a small group of closely interconnected sitters. It usually manifests itself only when that individual or one of that group is having a sitting, and it does so again and again at each successive sitting at which such a sitter is present. If that individual, or members of that group, should have sittings with several different mediums, it may turn up at each of them. Occasionally, however, there are what may be called 'intrusions'. At a sitting with a certain individual an ostensible communicator, having no connexion with

257

him, may, as it were, either wander in or thrust himself in. Such an 'intruder' may be one of the regular ostensible communicators at sittings of other sitters with the same medium, or he may be completely unidentifiable.

There is one further point of considerable interest to be noted. In some few cases either the control or some of the ostensible communicators or both have tried to describe in elaborate detail how the process of communication takes place from their point of view. They have done this partly by indirect communication through the control, and partly by the direct voice. The sitter has been able to put questions and to raise objections, and to get various points cleared up. One noteworthy instance of this occurred in sittings held from 1909 to 1912 by the second Earl of Balfour with a lady, 'Mrs Willett', who was a non-professional medium. Here the ostensible communicators gave themselves out to be the spirits of Edmund Gurney and F. W. H. Myers, two of the distinguished Cambridge scholars who had been among the founders of the S.P.R. and active workers in psychical research up to the dates of their respective deaths in 1888 and 1901. Another example is provided by certain sittings held by the late Mr Drayton Thomas with the professional medium Mrs Leonard. Here the ostensible communicators gave themselves out to be his father, John, and his sister Etta.

Whether or not we accept the claims of such ostensible communicators to be the surviving spirits of such and such deceased persons, their statements about the process of communication are of considerable interest. The fact that such statements are made at all, and the specific content of them, constitute, on any view, important data for the study of the psychology of trance-mediumship. The various factors which the ostensible communicators distinguish and lay stress upon, must presumably correspond (even if in a distorted way) with real factors in the psychological mechanism of mediumistic trance.

It should be added that there is sometimes a further development in the 'direct voice' phenomena. The same voice may appear to the sitter at times to emanate, *not* from the medium's lips, but from a position external to her body. This form of the direct voice phenomenon may be described as 'Ostensibly Independent Speech'.

What I have been describing so far is fairly typical of the course of proceedings at sittings with a large number of trance-mediums in Europe and the U.S.A. in fairly recent times. There are many minor variations, in the case of different mediums and at different stages of development of one and the same medium, on this basic theme. But it should also be noted that some mediums hardly go into trance at all; and that, in the case of some who do, important statements

258

may be made when the medium is in something very like her normal waking state, or when she is in an intermediate state between the end of the trance-condition and the beginning of full normal waking consciousness. The latter was true, e.g., of the famous American medium, Mrs Piper, who was studied intensively by Professor William James and Dr Richard Hodgson.

If there were nothing more in trance-mediumship than what I have been describing, it would be of interest primarily to the psychologist and the anthropologist. Even so, it would be deserving of much more attention on their part than they commonly give to it. For it exhibits, in an impressive and fairly accessible way, some extremely odd possibilities in human personality, which are liable to be overlooked nowadays, but must have contributed important elements to popular belief and practice. It would thus serve as a valuable corrective to over-simplified accounts of human nature and human society.

But in fact that is only half the story. The other half is this. Controls and ostensible communicators often display a knowledge of facts about the past lives of dead persons and about the present actions and thoughts and emotions of living ones, which is too extensive and detailed to be reasonably ascribed to chance-coincidence, and it is quite inexplicable by reference to any normal sources of information open to the medium. I do not think that this would be seriously questioned by anyone, with a reasonably open mind, who had made a careful study of the recorded facts and had had a certain amount of experience of his own in these matters: though it is often dogmatically denied by persons who lack those qualifications.

On the other hand, these gems of correct, detailed, and relevant information are nearly always imbedded in an immense matrix of twaddle, vagueness, irrelevance, ignorance, pretension, positive error, and occasional prevarication. If one confines one's attention to the gems, it is often hard to resist the conviction that the spirit of a certain dead person has survived and is communicating, directly or indirectly, through the medium. If, on the other hand, one concentrates on the matrix, and if one also considers the immense antecedent improbability of a human personality surviving bodily death, it is hard to believe anything of the kind. The result is that, although instructed opinion is almost unanimous in holding that trance-mediumship supplies data which require a paranormal explanation of *some* kind, there is no consensus of experts in favour of any one suggested paranormal explanation.

The interest of these phenomena to the psychical researcher depends, of course, primarily on their containing this nucleus of something *para*normal, as distinct from merely *ab*normal. But he would be most unwise to confine his attention to this, and to ignore the question of the psychological processes at the back of the phenomena of trance-mediumship in general. For any particular view that one may take as to the nature of those processes will inevitably be relevant, favourably or unfavourably, to any particular type of proposed explanation of the paranormal features which characterize some of these phenomena.

In the next two chapters I shall give a fairly detailed account of what may be called the 'phenomenology' of two distinguished mediums, of very different kinds, viz., Mrs Leonard and Mrs 'Willett', who have been carefully studied by highly competent observers over considerable periods. Any reader who may be interested in this topic will be very well advised to study the classical paper by Mrs Sidgwick on the phenomenology of another eminent trance-medium of a somewhat earlier date, viz. Mrs Piper. This is to be found in S.P.R. *Proceedings*, Vol. XXVIII, under the title 'Psychology of Mrs Piper's Trance'. There is nothing that I could add to the 657 pages of that monumental essay, and nothing that I should wish to criticize in it; so I feel excused from discussing Mrs Piper's mediumship in the sequel.

XI

THE PHENOMENOLOGY OF
MRS LEONARD'S MEDIUMSHIP

FOR information on the phenomenology of Mrs Leonard's mediumship we have two main sources. One is a paper by Una Lady
Troubridge, entitled 'The *Modus Operandi* in so-called Mediumistic
Trance'. This appeared in S.P.R. *Proceedings*, Vol. XXXII, and
there is a short sequel to it in Vol. XXXIV. The other is two papers
by Mr Drayton Thomas. The first, entitled 'The *Modus Operandi*
of Trance Communications' is in S.P.R. *Proceedings*, Vol. XXXVIII.
The second, entitled 'A New Hypothesis concerning Trance Communication', is in Vol. XLVIII. Another important source of information is a paper by Mrs Salter, entitled 'Some Incidents occurring
at Sittings with Mrs Leonard, which may throw Light on their
Modus Operandi'. This is to be found in *Proceedings*, Vol. XXXIX.
In addition we have Mrs Leonard's autobiographical book, *My
Life in Two Worlds*, published in 1931. Finally, reference must be
made to a series of papers by Mr Whately Carington, entitled
'Quantitative Studies of Trance Personalities'. In these he describes
his application of certain psychological tests to Mrs Leonard and
certain other mediums under various conditions, and his statistical
treatment of the results. These papers are in Vols. XLII, XLIII,
and XLIV of *Proceedings*. In the last of these volumes there is a
valuable summary and criticism of this work, by Dr Thouless.

Mrs Leonard's mediumship is of the classical type, with a single
regular Control, and a number of Ostensible Communicators associated with various sitters. Her regular control gives herself the name
'Feda'. I shall refer to her as 'the Feda-persona'. The main ostensible
communicator at the sittings with Una Lady Troubridge claimed to
be the spirit of a lady who had been a very intimate friend of the sitter.
Her initials were *A.V.B.* In the sittings with Drayton Thomas the
main ostensible communicators claimed to be the spirits of his

261

father, *John*, and his sister, *Etta*. I shall refer to these ostensible communicators as 'the *A.V.B.*-persona', 'the John-persona', and so on. In neither case had Mrs Leonard ever met the persons whose spirits the ostensible communicators claimed to be, nor had she even heard of them before the sittings began. Both Una Lady Troubridge and Mr Drayton Thomas had sittings at fairly frequent intervals with Mrs Leonard over a long period of years, and they made and kept elaborate contemporary records of all that was said or done by the medium or by the sitter at each sitting.

With both Una Lady Troubridge and Mr Drayton Thomas, after they had had a good many sittings in which the ostensible communications were made indirectly by way of the Feda-persona, the phenomenon of Ostensible Possession developed. The habitual control was thrust aside, and from the medium's vocal organs there issued a voice, which was neither that of the Feda-persona nor that of normal Mrs Leonard, but purported to be the voice of the ostensible communicator *in propria persona*. Ostensible possession took place occasionally with other sitters too. With Mrs Salter, e.g., the occasional ostensible possessor claimed to be her father, Dr A. W. Verrall.

So far I have mentioned nothing that seems paradoxical, considered from a purely *physical* standpoint, except perhaps the production of a male voice on certain occasions by female speech organs. But certainly in Mr Drayton Thomas's sittings, and possibly in some others, there was a further development which looks *prima facie* like a paranormal *physical* phenomenon. At times, when a certain ostensible communicator was *not* in ostensible possession of the medium's body, but was ostensibly communicating indirectly through the Feda-persona, the following events were observed. The sitter would hear a single word or a fragment of a sentence or even a whole sentence spoken in an audible whisper, which appeared to come, *not* from the medium's lips, but from a position in empty space some two or three feet in front of her. Such sentences or fragments stand in close relationship to what is being spoken at the same time or immediately afterwards through the medium's lips by the Feda-persona.

Of the occurrence of these whispers, and of their very close connexion in content with the remarks which the Feda-persona is making at very nearly the same time, there is no doubt. Nor is there any doubt that they seem to the sitter at the time to come from a position in empty space some distance in front of the medium. Some experiments were made, with negative results, by Messrs T. Besterman and G. Heard to try to locate, with appropriate physical instruments, the source of these sounds. They are reported in the

S.P.R. *Journal*, Vol. XXVIII, pp. 84–5. I do not know how easy it would have been, with the apparatus available some thirty years ago, to establish or to refute the hypothesis that the sounds were physically emanating from a certain point outside the medium's body. As to the various voices which came from Mrs Leonard's lips, when ostensibly possessed by this or that communicator, there exist or did exist gramophone records. I have both been present at a sitting with Mrs Leonard at which a certain ostensible communicator took possession, and have heard gramophone records on which the voices of normal Mrs Leonard, of the Feda-persona, and of the ostensible communicator who claimed to be the spirit of the Rev. John Drayton Thomas (Mr Drayton Thomas's father), had been recorded. Obviously in any future cases of a similar kind it would be easy and most desirable to obtain, with a tape-recording apparatus, a complete record of all the voices which were audible in the course of any sitting. It would also be useful to discover, by means of a microphone, whether the barely audible occasional whispers, which appear to come from outside the medium's body, are in fact fragments of continuous speech.

I propose to call the articulate sounds, which appear to emanate from a point outside the medium's body, 'Ostensibly Independent Speech'. If an ostensible communication comes *either* by ostensibly independent speech *or* through the medium's lips when she is ostensibly possessed by a communicator, I shall call it a '*Direct* Ostensible Communication'. We can then sub-divide these into (*a*) those which are *ostensibly independent* of the medium's vocal organs, and (*b*) those which are *dependent* on them. If an ostensible communication comes in the form of a report by the Feda-persona, I shall call it an '*Indirect* Ostensible Communication'.

The *A.V.B.*-persona has not, so far as I am aware, attempted to give any detailed account of the process of communication from her own point of view. But the John-persona and the Etta-persona have volunteered a number of statements both about direct and indirect communication, and they have elaborated these in answer to questions put to them by Mr Drayton Thomas. Moreover, the Feda-persona has made many statements to sitters about the way in which she receives messages and the way in which she transmits them. Thus our information about the *modus operandi* of ostensible communication may first be divided into (1) *Circumstantial*, and (2) *Narrative*. The former consists of observations made by sitters on the behaviour of the medium's body; on changes in voice, mannerisms, etc.; on the characteristic kinds of mistakes made in the ostensible communications; and so on. The latter consists of statements made, either through the lips of the medium when in trance or by ostensibly independent speech, which purport to express the views, either of the habitual control or of one or another of the ostensible communicators, on the *modus operandi* of communication. The views of an ostensible communicator may be expressed either (i) *directly*, when he or she is in ostensible possession of the medium, or (ii) *indirectly*, as reported by the Feda-persona. And, finally, statements made by the Feda-persona, on behalf of herself or of others, may be confirmed, corrected, or amplified by whispers in ostensibly independent speech purporting to come directly from one or another of the ostensible communicators.

THE REGULAR CONTROL

I will begin with an account of the regular control in Mrs Leonard's trances, i.e. the Feda-persona.

(1) *General Account.* 'Feda' has a childish, rather squeaky, female voice, and certain peculiarities of pronunciation. Like a Chinese, she has a difficulty in pronouncing the letter *r*, and always substitutes *l* for it. She never uses the first personal pronoun, but always uses the name *Feda* or the pronoun *she* in referring to herself. She often adopts and then clings to certain nicknames for sitters, or some childish perversion of the real name. She is also liable to make rather amusing distortions of long or technical words, just as a child or a foreigner might do. Though childish in manner, she is by no means unintelligent. She regards herself as having a kind of mission to co-operate in the work of psychical research, and she appears to strive conscientiously to convey to the sitter, without addition or distortion, what she receives from the ostensible communicators. When she knows that she has failed to understand something which an ostensible communicator is trying to convey, she says so honestly and seeks to clear the matter up. She does not wittingly indulge in guessing, fishing, or embroidery.

She claims to be the spirit of an ancestress of Mrs Leonard, a Hindu girl who was married to Mrs Leonard's maternal great-great-grandfather, William Hamilton. According to the story which Mrs Leonard, when young, had often heard from her own mother, this girl died in childbirth at an early age round about the year 1800.

The history of the first appearance of the Feda-personality in Mrs Leonard's life is as follows. Mrs Leonard had become interested in spiritualism, in consequence of some personal experiences, before her marriage. Her husband was an actor; and, though he had no personal knowledge of spiritualism, he was sympathetic to her ideas and beliefs on this topic. At a suburban theatre in London Mrs Leonard met two sisters who were interested in spiritualism, and the three had a number of sittings together for table-turning in their spare time at the theatre. After a large number of completely blank sittings they began to get movements and messages through the table. It was at one of these that Feda first claimed, by tilting the table in accordance with an agreed code, to be present and to be Mrs Leonard's Hindu ancestress. She stated that she had been watching over Mrs Leonard since the latter's birth, and that she could put her into a trance and give messages through her. Mrs Leonard disliked the idea, declined to co-operate, and asked Feda to proceed in some other way. In subsequent table-sittings an ostensible communicator, calling itself 'Feda', took charge of the proceedings. She continued to press to be allowed to control Mrs Leonard, and the latter continued to decline permission. These events happened during the years 1908 and 1909.

Finally, after a rather upsetting sitting in the winter of 1909, in which there were some unpleasant and alarming *physical* phenomena, Feda insisted that Mrs Leonard should put herself in training to be a professional medium, with Feda as her control; and Mrs Leonard at last consented. But a great many sittings were held in the ensuing months without any result, and in particular without Mrs Leonard going into trance. Feda ascribed this to a sub-conscious resistance on Mrs Leonard's part. Mrs Leonard disliked the idea of becoming a professional medium; whilst Feda argued, in the messages through the table which purported to come from her, that mediumship was a whole-time job. In the spring of 1914 Feda began insisting that Mrs Leonard should forthwith take rooms and begin practice as a professional medium. All her messages at that time ended with statements to the effect that something terrible was about to happen to the world, and that Feda would be able, through Mrs Leonard, to give help and comfort to many. By the winter of 1914 Mrs Leonard had followed this advice, and was giving regular sittings in an entranced state with the Feda-persona as her control.

In the autumn of 1915 Sir Oliver Lodge had an anonymous sitting with her, in which there were ostensible communications, impressive in their content, purporting to come from his son Raymond, who had lately fallen in the war. Thereafter she was for many years regularly in touch with sitters who have been members of the S.P.R., and she has always been ready to co-operate in every possible way with competent and serious investigators.

People who have had many sittings with Mrs Leonard generally end by liking the Feda-persona. She has a sense of humour and is rather engaging. On the emotional side she is friendly, but seems to be devoid of any deep feelings. With sitters who have recently been bereaved she adopts a decently sympathetic manner; but she discourages all outbursts of emotion on their part, and plainly has no fellow-feeling with their sorrow. (After all, if she is what she claims to be, and knows what she claims to know, mourners are making mountains out of molehills.)

The attitudes of the Feda-persona and normal Mrs Leonard towards each other are not particularly cordial. Once the Feda-persona is in control of the organism she is most reluctant to give place to normal Mrs Leonard. Her attitude towards Mrs Leonard is one of slight contempt and mild antagonism, tempered by a certain appreciation of the latter's good qualities and by the knowledge that she cannot speak or act (in this world, at any rate) except with Mrs Leonard's consent and through Mrs Leonard's body. Mrs Leonard's attitude towards the Feda-persona is mixed. It is through Feda that she has gained a great reputation, and earned a decent living, as a trance-medium. But she is often justifiably annoyed with the Feda-persona for the consequences of what the latter has said or done while in control. The Feda-persona, e.g., has a very strong sense of ownership about any object which has been given or promised to the medium when she is in control. But her respect for Mrs Leonard's property is not developed to the same degree, and she has sometimes been very lavish in giving or promising to sitters or others bits of jewellery, etc., belonging to, and valued by, Mrs Leonard.

The *cognitive* relations between the Feda-persona and normal Mrs Leonard are as follows. (i) Mrs Leonard, in her normal state, has no recollection of anything said or done or thought while the Feda-persona is in control. She knows of such matters, if at all, only at second-hand. The only exception to this is that occasionally, if Mrs Leonard sits quietly by herself after awaking from a trance, isolated words or impressions, which she cannot connect with anything in her normal waking life, well up in her consciousness. These names and impressions are in fact often reproductions of names mentioned, or incidents experienced or spoken of, while the Feda-persona was in control. (ii) The Feda-persona claims to have the power of becoming aware at will of all that Mrs Leonard perceives or thinks or feels when awake or when normally asleep and dreaming. She says that she usually does not choose to exercise this power. It is obviously impossible to test in detail a claim of this kind; but it is certain that the Feda-persona knows a great deal about what the normal personality perceives and thinks and feels.

(2) *Comparison with Cases of Multiple Personality.* It is of interest to

compare the characteristics of the Feda-persona, and her cognitive and other relations to normal Mrs Leonard, with what has been noted in certain well known cases of multiple personality, which have been described and treated by psychiatrists, such as Janet, Morton Prince, and Walter Franklin Prince. Here there was no question of mediumship, no ostensible communicators, and little if any evidence for the occurrence of any knowledge which could not be accounted for by ordinary sense-perception, memory, conscious or unconscious inference, association, etc.

In each of the three classical cases of multiple personality the most outstanding of the secondary personalities had the characteristics of a child or young girl, although the body and the normal personality were those of a mature woman. In Janet's case this personality called herself 'Léontine', in Morton Prince's case 'Sally', and in Walter Franklin Prince's case 'Margaret'. Sally and Margaret were entertaining and likeable, but devoid of any deep feeling. Sally positively disliked the normal personality, 'Miss Beauchamp', and went out of her way to annoy her both physically and mentally. Margaret had the same attitude, and was equally spiteful in practice, towards the normal personality 'Doris Fischer'. Neither of them had any respect for the property of the normal personality, whilst each had a strong sense of possession about what she regarded as *her* property. Margaret was wont to pronounce words in a childish way, and to refer to her friends and acquaintances by nicknames or perversions of their real names. Miss Beauchamp had no memory of what had happened when Sally was in control of her body, and Doris Fischer had none of what had happened when Margaret was in control of hers. On the other hand, both Sally and Margaret claimed to be continuously conscious of all that was perceived, thought, or felt by Miss Beauchamp or by Doris Fischer respectively, whether the latter were awake or were asleep and dreaming.

Thus the resemblances between the Feda-persona, on the one hand, and the secondary personalities Sally Beauchamp and Margaret Fischer, on the other, are fairly strong. The differences, in respect of the features which we have just been considering, are of degree rather than of kind. Sally was more independent of Miss Beauchamp, and Margaret of Doris Fischer, than the Feda-persona is of Mrs Leonard. Sally and Margaret came and went without or against the will of the normal personality, and they often actively thwarted and annoyed the latter. But the Feda-persona cannot as a rule oust the normal personality and get control of the organism without Mrs Leonard's knowledge and consent; though this has occasionally happened, with somewhat embarrassing consequences for Mrs Leonard. Sally and Margaret claimed to be actually and continuously aware of all that went on in the normal personality, whether awake or asleep; but the Feda-persona claims only that she often is, and always can be if she chooses.

The fundamental *prima facie* differences may be summarized as follows. In Mrs Leonard's case there is *one* regular control, viz. the Feda-persona, and *several* ostensible communicators, each associated with a certain sitter or sitters. In both the Beauchamp case and the Doris Fischer case there were *several* regularly alternating secondary personalities and *no* ostensible communicators. These other secondary personalities, besides Sally in the Beauchamp case and Margaret in the Doris Fischer case, which alternated with the normal personality and with Sally or Margaret respectively in taking control of the organism, bore no obvious resemblance to the ostensible communicators which communicate indirectly through the Feda-persona and occasionally take ostensible possession of Mrs Leonard's body and communicate directly through her lips. The alternating personalities in question were, fairly certainly, submerged layers or dissociated fragments of a complex whole, of which the normal personality, Miss Beauchamp or Doris Fischer as the case may be, was the upper layer or the predominant part. They presented no appearance of being the surviving spirit of this or that deceased person. It is only a regular control, like the Feda-persona, which bears much resemblance to any of the secondary personalities studied by psychiatrists. That, at any rate, is what ordinary observations made by sitters with Mrs Leonard would suggest.

(3) *Whately Carington's Experiments*. The question has, however, been studied experimentally by Mr Whately Carington, and he has reported his findings in the papers entitled 'Quantitative Studies of Trance Personalities', referred to at the beginning of this chapter. Before leaving the topic of Mrs Leonard's regular control, I will say a few words about Whately Carington's results as bearing upon the nature of the Feda-persona and its relationship to normal Mrs Leonard.

Whately Carington was a man full of original ideas and fertile in designing experiments for testing them. He showed immense energy in carrying out such experiments, and spared himself no drudgery in the statistical presentation and elaboration of his experimental findings. But his familiarity with statistical methods was that of an enthusiastic amateur in a limited field, and not that of an expert in statistical theory or of an experienced practitioner in its application on a wide front. It is extremely easy to commit fallacies in statistical arguments and to misinterpret numerical data. Dr Thouless, in his careful and by no means hostile or unsympathetic critical 'Review of Mr Whately Carington's Work on Trance Personalities' (S.P.R. *Proceedings*, Vol. XLIV), makes it abundantly plain that serious fallacies were committed. Very little can be confidently accepted of the conclusions which Whately Carington drew, as to the nature of the habitual control and of the occasional communicators and as to their psychological relations to each other and to the normal personality of the medium. Nevertheless, the ideas and the methods of Whately Carington's work on this topic are essentially sound; and it is greatly to be wished that someone, better equipped than he and warned of the pitfalls, should carry out somewhat similar experiments and assess their results by somewhat similar methods.

The essential feature of the experiments is to administer on a number of occasions to each of the personalities concerned a certain psychological test, to measure the reaction of each personality on each occasion, and then to compare and contrast the results. Of the three kinds of test which were employed, we need consider only one, viz., the Reaction-time Test. For, of the remaining two, one proved quite unreliable, and the other gives a kind of all-or-none result which is not susceptible of the form of statistical treatment used by Whately Carington. The R-T test consists in reading out to each subject on each occasion the same list of 100 words in the same order. The subject is told to respond to each word with the first word that comes into his head after hearing it uttered by the experimenter. A stop-watch measuring fifths of a second was used. It was started as the stimulus-word began to be uttered, stopped when the response began to be given, and the time which elapsed was recorded. If the stimulus-word or the response-word should be polysyllabic, the time-lapse was reckoned from or to the accented syllable in either case. Abnormally long reaction-times are supposed to be signs that the stimulus-word has touched on something that is emotionally significant for the subject.

The same set of words are presented to each personality on a large number of occasions, and, as might be expected, the reaction-time of the same personality to the same word varies very considerably from one occasion to another. So the first thing to do is to test each personality for *self-consistency* in respect to his responses to the words in the list. To say that P is *self-consistent* in his responses on the various occasions would amount to the following: (i) There is *a differentiated pattern* in his responses to the various words on each occasion. (ii) After allowing for the common effect on his responses to all the words, of factors which may vary from one occasion to another, we can reasonably regard his responses on *all* occasions as exhibiting *one and the same* differentiated pattern, except for minor random variations from occasion to occasion. There are generally

269

accepted statistical tests for self-consistency, in the above sense, which it is needless to elaborate here.

It is obviously idle to institute comparisons between the reaction-times of two personalities, P and P', to the same set of words, unless there is good reason to believe that each has a fairly high degree of self-consistency in his reactions to those words. If that condition be fulfilled, we may proceed to investigate the following question. Do the *differences* in the reaction-times of P and of P' to each word in the list exhibit *one and the same differentiated pattern*, except for minor random variations, on *all* occasions; after allowing for the common effect on the differences of response to all the words, of factors which may vary from one occasion to another? The statistical test for what we might call 'consistency in difference of response' is precisely similar, *mutatis mutandis*, to that for self-consistency in response.

Suppose that each of the personalities P and P' is fairly self-consistent, and suppose further that there is a fair degree of consistency in the differences of response of the two to the same set of words. Then, and only then, it is worth while to enquire into the degree and the kind of *correlation* between the *mean responses of the one and those of the other* to the various words in the list. I will now explain what this notion of 'correlation' signifies.

If the mean of P's reaction-times on all occasions to a certain word W_r should be considerably *above* the mean of his reaction-times on *all* the occasions to *all* the words in the list, we will say that P's reaction-time to W_r is 'abnormally high'. The statement that P's reaction-time to W_r is 'abnormally low' is defined by substituting 'below' for 'above' in the immediately preceding sentence. Suppose now that the selection of words to which P's mean reaction-time is abnormally high should *largely overlap* the selection of words to which the mean reaction-time of P' is abnormally high. And suppose that the same were true, *mutatis mutandis*, when 'low' is substituted for 'high' in the immediately preceding sentence. Then we should say that the responses of P and of P' are 'positively correlated'; and that, so far as can be judged from this test, P and P' have 'positive similarity'.

Suppose, on the other hand, that the selection of words to which P's mean reaction-time is abnormally *high* should largely overlap the selection of words to which the mean reaction-time of P' is abnormally *low*, and *vice versa*. Then we should say that the responses of P and of P' are 'negatively correlated'; and that, so far as can be judged by the test, P and P' are 'counter-similar'. Counter-similarity is something much more determinate than mere unlikeness. It is the kind of relation which, e.g., a casting bears to the mould in which it was cast. Positive similarity, on the other hand, is the kind

270

of relation which two castings from the same mould bear to each other.

In the above account I have constantly had to use such phrases as 'considerably' above or below, 'largely' overlapping, etc. These are necessary, and they should be sufficient to enable any reader to grasp the general ideas involved in a comparison of two personalities by means of the average times taken by them, on the same number of occasions, to react to the various words in a common list. But it is the business of the statistician to devise a formula which will provide a measure of the degree of correlation, positive or negative, between the two sets of mean reaction-times. The quantity in question is called a 'correlation-coefficient' and it may be symbolized by $r_{PP'}$. Positive values of it indicate positive similarity, and negative values of it counter-similarity. Its highest theoretical positive value is $+1$; and its lowest theoretical negative value is $-1/(k-1)$, where k is the number of words in the list.

Now it is of no particular interest merely to learn that the value, positive or negative, of $r_{PP'}$, as worked out from the experimental figures, is so-and-so. What we need to know also is whether that value differs *significantly* (in the statistical sense), either by excess or by defect, from zero. The question is: What are the odds against obtaining, with the number of test-words actually used, a value for $r_{PP'}$ which differs (in one direction or the other) from zero by at least as much as the value actually found, on the supposition that there is in fact *no* correlation, positive or negative, between the mean reaction-times of P and of P' to the various words in the list? If and only if those odds are substantial (say 1,000 to 1 against, at least), then the value found for $r_{PP'}$ is statistically significant. For reasons which I shall not attempt to explain here, it is more convenient to operate, not with $r_{PP'}$ itself, but with a certain mathematical function z of it, and to apply the test for statistical significance directly to z instead of to $r_{PP'}$.

It should be remarked that one might reasonably expect to find a certain degree of *positive* correlation between the mean reaction-times of *any* two persons of the same sex, nationality, social position, etc., confronted at much the same time with the same list of fairly ordinary words. Therefore a rather high degree of positive correlation would be needed before it would be reasonable to infer any *special* positive similarity between a particular pair of personalities. On the other hand, any significant degree of *negative* correlation between the mean reaction-times of two personalities would deserve considerable attention. For it would strongly suggest that there is a special relation of *counter-similarity* between those two.

Having explained the nature of the tests, and sketched the

271

statistical treatment of the results, I will now give a brief account of the main findings, so far as they concern the relationship between Feda and normal Mrs Leonard.

In all, three different series of experiments were done by Whately Carington. Two of these were conducted with Mr Drayton Thomas as sitter. In the third series the sitter was another member of the S.P.R., the Rev. W. S. Irving, who, like Drayton Thomas, had had numerous sittings with Mrs Leonard, and, like him, had frequently witnessed ostensible possession of the medium's body by the personality of the ostensible communicator.

We will begin with the question of the *self-consistency* of Mrs Leonard and of the Feda-persona. Mrs Leonard is wont, before giving a sitting, to sit quietly by herself in preparation for the meeting with the sitter. It was found that, in this prepared state, her reactions tend to be very different from those which she gives if tested on occasions when she is not about to go into trance. We must therefore distinguish 'Leonard Normal' and 'Leonard Prepared', and we may denote them respectively by L_n and L_p. L_n was tested for self-consistency only in the first series of Thomas Experiments and in the Irving Experiments. In both she showed a quite significant degree of self-consistency, and in the latter a very high degree indeed. L_p was tested for self-consistency in all three series, and was *not* significantly self-consistent in any of them. Since she represents an intermediate state, between L_n and Mrs Leonard in the fully entranced condition, this lack of self-consistency is not perhaps surprising. However that may be, it would be idle to draw conclusions from comparisons in which L_p is one of the personalities compared.

The Feda-persona was tested in all three series of experiments. In the first Thomas Series and in the Irving Series she was significantly self-consistent, and in the latter very highly so. But in the second Thomas Series her self-consistency was quite insignificant. No explanation has been suggested for this.

Suppose we overlook Feda's lapse in the second Thomas Series, and, on the basis of her performance in the other two series, regard her as sufficiently self-consistent to be profitably compared with the self-consistent L_n. Then the following results emerge. (i) In *both* the series of experiments in which the two were compared (viz. Thomas I and Irving), there is a significant degree of consistency in the *differences* between the reaction-times of the two personalities to the same word in the list. In the first Thomas Series the odds are about 66 to 1 against such results as were actually observed emerging on the hypothesis that there is no real persistent pattern of difference and that it is all a matter of chance. In the Irving Series those odds are of the order of a million to one. (ii) The *correlation* between the mean reaction-times of the Feda-persona and of L_n to the various words in the list is *faintly negative* in both these series. But it is quite insignificant statistically. It would therefore be illegitimate to infer *counter-similarity* between the two personalities. (iii) What is certainly curious, and may possibly be of significance, is the following fact. The mean reaction-times of the Feda-persona are, to a preponderant extent, correlated *negatively*, not only with those of L_n, but also with those of the three ostensible communicators (John and Etta Thomas and Mr Irving's deceased wife Dora), when these are in ostensible possession of Mrs Leonard's body. Now each of these personalities is very significantly *self-consistent*, so that each is a legitimate subject of comparison with the Feda-persona. The details are as follows. In the three series of experiments the Feda-persona is concerned in *two* comparisons with L_n, in *two* with the personality purporting to be the Rev. John Thomas, in *two* with that purporting to be Etta Thomas, and in *one* with that purporting to be Dora Irving, i.e. in *seven* altogether. In all these, with the one exception of John in the first Thomas Experiment, the correlation is *negative*. It is true that it is barely significant in any of these cases; but the proportion of six negative correlations out of seven, which might be either positive or negative, is certainly striking and may be significant. It should be remembered, however, that if two personalities A and B should be positively correlated, then any third personality C which is negatively correlated with *either*, will tend *ipso facto* to be negatively correlated with *both*. Now L_n *is* positively correlated with John and with Etta in the first Thomas Experiment, and with Dora in the Irving Experiment: and John and Etta *are* positively correlated in both the Thomas Experiments. So the negativity of the correlations of Feda's reaction-times with those of these various personalities may not be so many *mutually independent* facts; and therefore the great preponderance of negative correlations where Feda is concerned may be much less significant than it might seem at first sight.

On the whole I am doubtful whether *any* conclusions as to the nature and relationships of the Feda-persona, normal Mrs Leonard, and the various ostensible communicators which from time to time ostensibly possess the medium, can safely be drawn from the results of Whately Carington's experiments. The non-statistically minded reader of this sub-section may well complain that there has been 'much cry and little wool'. I sympathize with him. But I am convinced that the ideas at the back of this work of Whately Carington's are sound and important and should be better known; and I feel an obligation to do what in me lies to secure that *tantus labor non sit cassus*.

OSTENSIBLE POSSESSION BY COMMUNICATORS

I pass now to the phenomenon of ostensible possession by *personae* who claim to be the surviving spirits of certain deceased friends or relatives of particular sitters. As to this we have two sources of information. One of them is circumstantial, viz. the observations of the sitters themselves. The other is narrative, viz. statements made by those *personae* themselves. These may be made either directly, or indirectly through the Feda-persona.

(1) *From the Sitters' Point of View.* From the sitters' point of view what happens is this. In the course of a sitting, in which the Feda-persona has been in control and has been acting as intermediary between the sitter and some ostensible communicator, she will announce that she is about to give way to that communicator. There is then a short period of complete quiescence. Then comes a long and steady exhalation of breath, which Una Lady Troubridge compares to letting the air out of an air-cushion. Then the medium's body becomes limp, and has to be supported by the sitter. It lies in the chair like a log, or flops against the sitter's shoulder. Then a quite different voice issues from the medium's lips, and it is as if a certain deceased person, e.g. A.V.B. or John or Etta, were using the body to speak with.

It is alleged by the sitters that the intonations, verbal mannerisms, etc., of the ostensible communicator are often reproduced with startling exactness, although Mrs Leonard has never met the individual in life or heard any reproduction of his or her voice. It would have been hard in the past to get an objective test of these alleged resemblances, but it should be easier now with tape-recording. However that may be, it is certain that the most surprisingly different voices and modes of speaking are produced, and that they range, e.g., from the gruff male voice of an elderly Scotsman afflicted with bronchial asthma, through the cultivated and rather exaggeratedly clerical tones of the John-persona, to the piping childish treble of the Feda-persona.

The initial attempts at possession by any ostensible communicator are generally attended with great difficulties. The voice seldom rises at first above a hoarse whisper, and the medium is liable to show signs of choking. Each such early attempt seldom lasts more than a few minutes. But certain ostensible communicators learn by practice, and, as they grow more experienced, the difficulties gradually diminish. The voice becomes as strong as that of the regular control or of normal Mrs Leonard; the medium is able to sit up in her chair and breathe fairly normally; and the greater part of a long sitting may be taken up with direct ostensible communication.

In this connexion the following two incidents are of some interest. (i) At quite a late stage, when the A.V.B.-persona was well practised in taking possession, she expressed a wish to sit upright instead of flopping against the sitter's shoulder as heretofore. The attempt succeeded quite well for a time. But on several occasions the medium began to show signs of asphyxiation, and fell forward into the sitter's arms. On one such occasion the A.V.B.-persona remarked: 'I nearly choked the medium, because I forgot to breathe.' (ii) On the first occasion when the Etta-persona took possession the phenomenon began with the issuing of a hissing sound from the medium's lips. Then came a slow faint voice, which said: 'I can't manage her breath. I shall soon do it. I don't now make that whistling sound.'

An ostensible possession is often cut off suddenly in the midst of a sentence. Even when the A.V.B.-persona had become able to speak for an hour or more on end, her spell of possession would conclude with a kind of sudden collapse. There is nothing like this when the Feda-persona ceases to control and is replaced by normal Mrs Leonard.

After a *long* spell of possession by an ostensible communicator the medium always comes-to as *normal Mrs Leonard*, and not as the Feda-persona. After comparatively *short* spells of ostensible possession she will occasionally come-to as the *Feda-persona*, and not as normal Mrs Leonard. But any spell of possession by an ostensible communicator, whether it be long or short, is always *immediately preceded* by a phase of control by the *Feda-persona*.

Normal Mrs Leonard has no more knowledge of the experiences of an ostensible communicator, who is in temporary possession of her body, than she has of the experiences of the Feda-persona. And the Feda-persona seems to be in much the same state of ignorance. There is no reason to believe that she is aware, either simultaneously or afterwards, of anything that an ostensible communicator perceives, thinks, feels, or says while in possession of the medium's body. Her knowledge about the ostensible communicators seems to be confined to what they choose to communicate to her when she is in control or during intervals between sittings. It should be remembered, however, that the Feda-persona, like the ostensible communicators, claims to be a spirit with a life independent of Mrs Leonard's body. Both the Feda-persona and the communicators claim to meet from time to time in that independent state between sittings, and then to communicate with each other directly.

(2) *Possession as described by the Ostensible Communicators.* The ostensible communicators say that they often do not know accurately

when their control of the medium's organism has become effective. In taking possession of the medium they have, so they allege, to attend simultaneously to the following three things. (i) They must watch over the vital functions of the medium's organism, and in particular her *breathing*. (ii) They must notice which of those ideas that they want to convey can be got through at the time, and which of them cannot. (iii) They must remember what has already been spoken, in order to avoid starting a train of talk which might misrepresent their meaning.

They say that their own mental state, when in possession, is far from clear. They describe the situation in which they find themselves as follows. They allege that the division of one's mind into a conscious and a subconscious layer, which is characteristic of all of us in this life, ceases at death; but that something analogous to that division *recurs* whenever they take possession of the medium. That part of an ostensible communicator's mind which is in control of the medium's body, corresponds (they say) to the *conscious* part of a person's mind in this life. This remains in some kind of connexion with the rest of the ostensible communicator's mind, which may then be compared to the *subconscious* part of a person's mind in this life. But the connexion is tenuous and is always liable to be interrupted, so long as the ostensible communicator is possessing the medium's body. They say that, when in possession of the medium, they sometimes forget altogether the contents of the part of their mind which is not in control of her body. Even when that does not happen, it is (they say) harder for them to get in touch with the content of that part of their minds than it is for us to avail ourselves of the content of our own subconsciousness.

They ascribe this to the fact that, when they are in temporary possession of the medium's brain and nervous system, they have to some extent to *share* it with the medium's mind; whereas each of us in ordinary life has just *one* mind associated with his brain and nervous system. A consequence of this is that the part of a communicator's mind which is in temporary possession of the medium's organism bears to his mind as a whole a much smaller proportion than that which the part of a normal human mind which is fully conscious and in control of its body bears to such a mind as a whole. When in possession of the medium, a communicator is very liable to be unable to recall things which he can remember perfectly well at other times.

The Etta-persona distinguishes between perceiving *through the medium's sense-organs* and using *her own sense-organs*. She alleges that, when in possession of the medium's organism, she *hears* what the sitter says through the medium's ears, auditory nerves, etc. On the other hand, she says that she does *not* as a rule *see* anything by means of the medium's eyes, optic nerves, etc. She does occasionally see and occasionally hear *one of the other communicators*, e.g. her father John, by using *her own* sense-organs. Finally, she asserts that the communicators avoid, as far as possible, using their own sense-organs while in possession of the medium's body, because doing so tends to make them lose control of it.

The ostensible communicators allege that there are two main difficulties in trying to communicate directly by means of the medium's organism. One is their own failure, when in possession, to remember things which they can recall quite easily at other times. This is said to be due to the limitations imposed upon them by their temporary animation of a foreign organism with a mind of its own. The other difficulty is their imperfect control in detail over the brain and nervous system of the medium. This often prevents them from getting the medium to utter the words and sentences which would express to the sitter the ideas which they wish to convey.

Any special effort by a communicator, while in possession, to get the medium to express a particular thought of his, is liable (they say) to be unsuccessful at first. As they put it, 'the medium's brain seems to stick'. It is then best for the communicator to turn to some other topic. If he does so, the process which he set up in the medium's brain by his original attempt may eventually work out to a successful conclusion. The communicator must then be ready to pounce on it and revert to the original topic. These remarks remind one of the familiar experience of trying in vain to recall a certain name, which one has 'on the tip of one's tongue' and yet cannot recall and utter. Often, if one turns one's attention to other things, an auditory image of the name will suddenly arise, or one will find oneself articulating the word.

It should be noted that the ostensible communicators not only claim to have bodies of some kind and sense-organs of their own, but also use expressions which imply that they feel themselves, when in possession, to be in some sense located in various parts of the medium's brain. I will quote in this connexion, for what it may be worth, a curious remark of the John-persona: 'When I talk easily I find myself in the forehead of the medium; not in the brain, but just above the eyes in front. . . . When I lose the sense of being just there, I find it difficult to express myself . . . I . . . find myself drawn to different parts of the head.' It is not easy to see what interpretation to put on such statements. But it may be worth while to recall, in connexion with them, the very ancient and widespread belief that the pineal gland is an important centre in reference to certain kinds of paranormal experience.

Before leaving this part of the subject I would like to make the following remark. It seems to me that the ostensible communicators offer no explanation of the fact that, when any particular one of them is in possession, the medium speaks with the kind of voice which was characteristic of the person whose surviving spirit he or she claims to be. Surely, if this be a fact, it is a very odd one, on *any* view of the causes of the phenomenon. Suppose, on the one hand, that we *reject* the claim of the ostensible communicators to be surviving spirits, and insist on regarding them as temporary secondary personalities of the medium. Then we shall have to ascribe to telepathic or telekinetic action, unwittingly exercised by the sitter, the extraordinary *physical* effect of so modifying the medium's vocal organs that a voice, resembling that of the deceased friend or relative who is ostensibly in possession, and exhibiting that person's characteristic mannerisms and phraseology, issues from her lips. A pretty 'tall order'! Suppose, on the other hand, that we *accept* the claims of the ostensible communicators regarding their personal identity. Does the causation of this phenomenon of 'the direct voice' become any less mysterious? The voice characteristic of a person when alive in the flesh must surely depend on certain features in the vocal organs of his *ante mortem* body. That body, on any view, is dead and gone. Even if we assume, not only that the mind of that person has survived the death of his *ante mortem* body, but also that it now animates some kind of *post mortem quasi*-material counterpart of that body, the difficulty remains. The voice is certainly produced by the *medium*'s vocal organs. Suppose, as the ostensible communicators allege, that the medium's vocal organs are being actuated at the time by the direct operation of a certain communicator on the relevant part of the medium's brain. Surely the result that one would expect would be that the medium would express the *communicator*'s thoughts with *her* usual voice, though perhaps in the kind of *phraseology* which was characteristic of him when alive in the physical body. Why on earth should the *voice*, which now comes from the *medium*'s vocal organs, resemble that which used to come from those of the communicator's *ante mortem* body?

INDIRECT OSTENSIBLE COMMUNICATION

I pass now to *indirect* ostensible communication. The dramatic form of this is that a message is given in some way or other by a communicator to the Feda-persona and is then transmitted by her, in her own characteristic voice, manner, and verbiage, through the medium's vocal organs to the sitter. There are therefore the following four things to be considered, viz. (i) the account given by the ostensible communicators of the ways in which they give messages to the Feda-persona; (ii) the Feda-persona's account of the ways in which she receives messages from them; (iii) her account of how she transmits messages to the sitter by using the medium's organism; and (iv) the sitters' descriptions of the medium's behaviour and utterances when indirect ostensible communication is taking place. I will now say something on each of these topics in turn.

(1) *The Account given by the ostensible Communicators.* It should be noted that the ostensible communicators give their accounts partly by direct, and partly by indirect, ostensible communication.

They and the Feda-persona agree in saying that an essential condition for communication is the presence of a kind of *physical emanation*, which comes mainly from the medium, but perhaps also to a slight extent from the sitter (and from the note-taker, if one should be present in addition to the sitter). This flows from the medium during the sitting, fluctuating in amount or in intensity from time to time, reaching its maximum at about the middle of an average sitting, and gradually ceasing to be produced. The Feda-persona calls it 'the Power'. (I believe that this is the common expression for it among Spiritualists. Another name which is also sometimes used is 'the Light'. We must allow for the effects of suggestion from the beliefs current in the *milieu* in which Mrs Leonard was trained as a medium. But we must remember that such explanations are never ultimate; for we cannot but go on to ask ourselves how such beliefs originally arose in those circles.)

In order for an ostensible communicator to convey a message to the Feda-persona he must enter the cloud of emanation, which, it is alleged, extends for a few feet in all directions round the medium's body. The ostensible communicators say that they can *feel* the emanation, but can seldom see it. The Feda-persona says that it is rarely *self*-luminous, but renders any thing or person (incarnate or discarnate) that is within its range visible to her. Although entry into the emanation is a necessary condition for communication, it has a detrimental effect for the time being on the mental powers of the ostensible communicators. They say that they at once begin to feel confused and fogged, and that they often cannot recall things which they would at other times remember with perfect ease. Sometimes, by temporarily withdrawing from the emanation, a communicator may regain a memory which had ceased to be available from that cause. He may then return to the emanation, and seek to communicate the item to the Feda-persona.

The ostensible communicators distinguish two quite different ways in which they communicate with the Feda-persona, viz. (i) by actually speaking to her, and (ii) by telepathy. They also distinguish between several modes of telepathic communication. Suppose, e.g., that it was a question of conveying a message about a *horse*. They might speak the word 'horse' to the Feda-persona. Or they might produce telepathically in her mind either (*a*) an hallucinatory auditory *quasi*-sensation or an auditory image of the word, or (*b*) an imitative visual image of the *written word* H–O–R–S–E, or (*c*) an imitative visual image of such an animal, or (*d*) a *symbolic* visual image, e.g. an image of a jockey with a whip; or finally (*e*) they might convey telepathically the *thought* of a horse, without using words or visual images, whether imitative or symbolic.

They say that it is harder for them to produce *actual sensations* of sound in the Feda-persona than to convey telepathically an auditory or visual image of a word, or an imageless thought. They allege that the Feda-persona is very liable to say that she has *heard* a sentence, or to speak in terms which would imply this, when really she has only received telepathically an auditory image of the words, or an imitative or symbolic visual image of the thing referred to, or even an imageless thought of the thing. Similarly, when the Feda-persona uses expressions which imply that she *sees* the communicators, this is often (according to them) not literally true. She has put that interpretation on certain impressions which she has received telepathically. These impressions may not even have taken the form of *visual* images. The Feda-persona may receive telepathically an imageless thought and then unwittingly clothe it in appropriate visual imagery, and this may finally take for her the form of a visual hallucination, i.e. a *quasi*-perception.

It should be added, however, that the ostensible communicators also allege that the Feda-persona sometimes makes the opposite mistake, i.e. she sometimes thinks that she got an impression telepathically, when in fact the communicator was *literally speaking* to her. It is important to emphasize the fact, whatever may be the right interpretation of it, that the ostensible communicators firmly maintain that it is *sometimes* quite literally true that the Feda-persona sees them, that they speak to her, and that she hears their voices. For this involves a claim, on the communicators' part, that they have something analogous to *human bodies*, that the Feda-persona has such an organism of her own, and that these *quasi*-material organisms have and use something analogous to eyes, ears, vocal organs, etc. We may find this claim very hard to swallow; but we have no right to ignore it and to concentrate our attention on other claims which may be less shocking to our preconceived ideas. The mere fact that it is made, and is insisted upon, must presumably have *some* significance.

The John-persona draws a distinction between two different processes which might be lumped together under the name of 'telepathy'. One of them is the deliberate *projection*, by a communicator, of a certain idea or image into the mind of the Feda-persona. The other is the *reading*, by the Feda-persona, of the mind of the communicator, and her thus becoming aware, without his knowledge or consent, of certain thoughts which he is thinking at the time. (We shall find a similar distinction drawn by the Gurney-persona in the case of the ostensible communications with Mrs 'Willett'.) The mind-reading process may lead the Feda-persona to take up some quite unimportant thought in the ostensible communicator's mind, and then to develop it on her own account in ways which are surprising to the communicator and misleading to the sitter.

It will be remembered that the ostensible communicators allege that their minds temporarily split up into a conscious and a subconscious part when they take possession of the medium's organism, and that it is the *conscious* part which then controls her body. In the same way, they allege, it is the *conscious* part of Feda's mind which controls the medium when in trance, and its operations are limited by the medium's brain and nervous system, by her habits of thought and of speech, and so on.

Suppose now that an ostensible communicator wishes to give to the Feda-persona a message, in which all the details of time, place, and circumstance are fairly determinate. It might be, e.g., the proposition which we should express by saying: 'I have been in the garden at home lately.' They say that this message *may* get through to a certain part of Feda's mind at the first attempt, but it may *not* get through to that part which is conscious and in control of the medium's body. In that case the communicator proceeds to reiterate the information in a schematic form, and then to fill in the details in answer to mental questions put by the Feda-persona. If we put the process into words, it might be expressed in the following dialogue: 'I have been in x at y at t.' '*What* have you been in?' '*A garden.*' '*Where?*' '*At home.*' '*When?*' '*Lately.*'

Sometimes, however, the communicators have, so they say, to proceed from the start by a piecemeal method, and to trust to the Feda-persona to make a successful synthesis of the bits. Suppose, e.g., that a communicator wanted to make the Feda-persona think of a *shilling*. He might first produce a visual image of the Queen's head, then one of the date, then a feeling of coldness, and finally a feeling of hardness; accompanying these with a general indication that they all referred to one and the same object. He might not be able to produce them simultaneously and synthetically, so as to give the Feda-persona straight away a thought or an imitative visual image or an hallucinatory *quasi*-perception as of a shilling.

281

(2) *The Feda-persona's Account of her Reception of Messages.* I pass now to the account which the Feda-persona gives of how she receives messages from the ostensible communicators. According to her, these messages come in various forms. She may, e.g., seem to herself to hear words spoken; to have auditory images of words; to see written words or imitative or symbolic pictures; or to have feelings of coldness, roughness, etc., when the ostensible communicator wants to convey to her the 'feel' of a thing.

She agrees with the communicators in drawing a distinction between a communicator *literally* speaking and *only mentally* 'speaking' to her. I suppose that the minimal meaning that we can attach to this distinction is the following. In the former case her experiences present themselves to her as *actual sensations*, arising by ordinary physical transmission from a source outside the medium's body. In the latter case they present themselves to her only as *auditory images*, welling up in her field of consciousness in the unaccountable way in which images do. Each of us is familiar with the first case, not only in normal waking life, but also (it is important to remember) in any vivid dream in which he is ostensibly conversing with other persons, or ostensibly hearing non-human sounds, such as the crackling of a fire in a wood, and so on. And most of us are familiar with the second case in waking reveries.

The Feda-persona says that she often has an experience as of hearing a certain communicator's voice, without *seeing* him; though in such cases she does ostensibly see something like a light in a certain position near the sitter, and the voice seems to come from the position marked out by this light. She generally needs to have had several sittings with the same sitter before she comes to have an experience as of *seeing* the communicator, though she may have an experience as of *hearing him speak* from the first. It is only rarely, and only with *personae* who have often ostensibly communicated through her, that she has an experience as of hearing, seeing, and touching the ostensible communicator *at one and the same time*.

When ostensible communications come to her in the form of *auditory images*, the simultaneous occurrence of *normal auditory sensations* (e.g. hearing the sitter's voice) does not confuse her. But, when she has an experience as of the ostensible communicator *literally talking to her*, the simultaneous hearing of normal physical sounds tends to create confusion. She describes her experiences in such cases in the following terms. She says that she listens, from within the medium's body, both to the ordinary physical sounds and to the communicator's voice; that she 'hears' both of them in the *same* literal sense of the word; but that she uses two *different sets of instruments*, viz. the medium's ears, etc., for hearing the physical

282

sounds, and her own auditory sense-organs for hearing the voices of the communicators.

I have already remarked that the ostensible communicators claim that both they and Feda have something analogous to human bodies, and use something analogous to human sense-organs. We now see that the Feda-persona makes a similar claim about herself. I repeat that we have no right to ignore such claims, however hard we may find it to swallow them. The fact that they are made must presumably indicate *something* genuine and important, even if it be only in the psychology of the medium.

Very often the ostensible communications, or parts of them, come to the Feda-persona in the form of *symbolic visual images*, which she has to interpret as best she can. She says that it is often much easier for her to receive impressions in that form than in the form of words and sentences. She admits that she used often to make mistakes in interpreting such symbolic images, until she grew familiar with the modes of symbolization used by the various communicators. (This may be compared with the growing ease with which one solves cross-word puzzles when one begins to get used to the mental habits of the person who sets them.)

Finally, it should be noted that the Feda-persona says that she finds it particularly difficult to get *proper names* from the communicators, and that they find it peculiarly difficult to get them across to her. She says that such names sometimes pop up suddenly in her mind when she is not specially trying to get them, but that any direct questions from the sitter tend to put her off. (It is perhaps worth while to compare this with the increasing difficulty which many people have, as they grow older, in recalling at will proper names which are perfectly familiar to them. Their memories in general may be excellent, and they can often give all kinds of accurate information about the person or place whose name they wish to recall. Deliberate effort only makes the blockage more hopeless; the only resort is to turn one's attention to other matters, and then sooner or later the name just pops up in one's consciousness or one finds oneself articulating it.)

(3) *The Feda-persona's Account of how she transmits Messages.* The Feda-persona's statements about how she transmits messages through the medium's organism to the sitter are obviously figurative. I find them very obscure. Moreover, both the John-persona and the Etta-persona say that she is in part mistaken in her beliefs about what she does.

The Feda-persona says that, when she has received an idea and wants to transmit it, she operates on the appropriate part of the medium's *brain*. She talks of fumbling, and of trying to find the right part of the medium's brain for conveying a given idea. She compares the mistakes, which she is liable to make at that point, to 'pushing the wrong spring'. She talks of 'holding an image up above the medium's brain', of waiting until it feels to her to have been 'drawn to the right place', and then 'holding it there until it is attached'. She says that she 'pushes it towards one part, then towards another, until it is taken'. But she admits that these statements are not to be taken literally, for she says that all this so-called 'pushing' and 'pulling' is done with the *mind*, and not with the hands.

These statements have been commented upon critically by both the Etta-persona and the John-persona. Etta says that what Feda describes in terms of *movement* from place to place in the brain really consists in presenting the same *idea*, now in one form and now in another, to the medium's *mind*, until the latter grasps it and expresses it in words. John says that Feda's belief that she operates directly on the medium's *brain* is mistaken. She really acts directly on the *embodied mind* of the entranced Mrs Leonard, putting ideas telepathically into it. It is this mind which directly controls the medium's body and causes the ideas to be expressed by appropriate movements of the vocal organs. He compares the Feda-persona's telepathic action on Mrs Leonard's embodied mind with his own telepathic action on the mind of the Feda-persona when he gives messages to her. But he says that the telepathic action between the Feda-persona's mind and that of Mrs Leonard in trance is so immediate that Feda hardly realizes what is happening.

I think that it is worth while to remark at this point that none of us has any immediate knowledge of how in detail his body comes to express by speech or by writing the ideas which he wishes to record or to convey. The process is voluntary and deliberate, in the sense that one would almost certainly not be saying or writing what one does at a given time unless at that time one wished to express certain ideas. But it is certainly neither voluntary nor conscious, in the sense that one deliberately and wittingly does something to the appropriate parts of one's brain, as one deliberately and wittingly strikes the appropriate keys on a typewriter. There is continual interaction, in both directions, between the thoughts and the movements of the vocal organs, or of the hands and the pen, which express them. But one does not perceive or think of (and most of us know nothing about) the essential intermediate processes in brain and nerves. It is, therefore, hardly surprising that the Feda-persona should give a confused and confusing description of what she does when she tries to make Mrs Leonard's body express a certain idea in speech to the sitter.

Suppose we were to accept the account which the Feda-persona gives of herself, and which the John-persona and the Etta-persona give of her, viz. that she is an individual existing in her own right independently of the medium, and that she possesses the medium *habitually*, as John and Etta do *occasionally*. Then, it seems to me, it would be a complete mystery why the peculiar *voice* which is associated with the Feda-persona should issue from Mrs Leonard's lips when Feda is in control. If Feda conveys her ideas telepathically to Mrs Leonard's embodied mind, and the latter in the ordinary way (whatever that may be) causes Mrs Leonard's vocal organs to express those ideas, why do we not get Feda's thoughts expressed in Mrs Leonard's ordinary voice and verbiage?

(4) *The Utterances as they reach the Sitters.* Certain tentative conclusions, as to the way in which the Feda-persona receives ostensible communications, can be inferred from certain features of the medium's utterances when in trance.

The Feda-persona will often make statements or ask questions about someone or something, which she claims to have been *seeing* repeatedly for many months, which show plainly that she cannot have been seeing that object in the ordinary sense of the word. She might, e.g., claim to have been seeing a certain deceased person at a number of sittings, and might have given a description of his appearance which was on the whole highly characteristic and substantially correct. Yet, at quite a late stage in such a series of sittings, she might state for the first time that he wore a beard, or might raise the question whether he wore one. The inference drawn by both Una Lady Troubridge and Mrs Salter is that the Feda-persona gets a series of scrappy impressions, visual and of other kinds, telepathically; that she gradually pieces them together; and that she expresses the final synthesis in terms of 'seeing'. This agrees with the wholly independent statement made to Mr Drayton Thomas by his two ostensible communicators. But, if we are to quote them in support, we must also in fairness remember that they allege that Feda does often have experiences which are *not* of telepathic origin, but do consist of something analogous to sense-perception by means of her own 'sense-organs'.

The Feda-persona will often ask the ostensible communicator to repeat a word or sentence. When she is in control, the medium's body is in an attitude as of listening. Often the whole dramatic form of the process is as of something being dictated to her and of her repeating it. Moreover, she not infrequently makes mistakes, where the correct word is quite obvious to the sitter from the context, and where the nature of the mistake is precisely as if she had slightly misheard a word spoken to her. This happens most often when it is a question

285

of a proper name which is unknown to her, or a word of which she does not know the meaning. The following is a trivial example. She said, in the course of a communication: 'Week after week for *fears*', and then, after a long pause, corrected it to: 'Week after week for *years*'.

When the Feda-persona makes mistakes of this kind the ostensible communicator will often immediately afterwards correct her. The most dramatic cases of this are when the criticism or correction comes, as it sometimes does, in the ostensibly independent voice of the communicator, apparently from a point in space some distance from the medium's body. I will quote two good examples of this from Mr Drayton Thomas's paper. The Feda-persona said: 'It's like being put in charge of a department of *boars*'. Evidently puzzled, she asked the ostensible communicator: 'Do you mean *pigs*?', and then continued with the remark: 'Boars is an *institution*'. At once the ostensibly independent voice of the ostensible communicator said: '*Borstal*'. It is obvious here that something had come to Feda in the form of the spoken words: 'Borstal institution'; and that this, being unfamiliar to her, had been misheard as: 'Boars in an institution'. The other example is this. Feda said: '*Willy*? Who's he? *Willy* Somebody—I can't get his other name. Willy Somebody is *compelling* you'. The ostensibly independent voice thereupon said, rather crossly: 'It's not that at all'. Feda then continued: '*Willy-nilly*? Is that right? Willy-nilly you are being compelled'.

XII

THE PHENOMENOLOGY OF
MRS WILLETT'S MEDIUMSHIP

IN this chapter we shall be concerned with the phenomenology of a medium of a very different kind from Mrs Leonard, viz. the lady who is known in the literature of the subject as 'Mrs Willett'. She died in 1956, and an obituary notice of her appeared in the S.P.R. *Journal*, Vol. XXXIX, No. 694. From this I cull the following details.

Her maiden name was *Pearce-Serocold*, and she married in 1895 Charles Coombe-Tennant, a landed proprietor, of Cadoxton Lodge, Neath. Her husband's sister was wife of F. W. H. Myers, one of the founders of the S.P.R. and the author of *Human Personality and its Survival of Bodily Death*. Mrs Coombe-Tennant was a person of manifold interests and considerable practical ability, and took a prominent part in public affairs, particularly in South Wales. She became Chairman of the Arts and Crafts Section of the National Eisteddfod in 1918. In 1920 she was made a Justice of the Peace for Glamorganshire, being the first woman to hold that office there. She was also the first woman to be appointed by the British Government as a delegate to the Assembly of the League of Nations. That appointment was made in 1922.

I think it is important to mention these facts, in order to correct the common, and quite mistaken, opinion that persons with medium-istic gifts are invariably mere belfries hung with bats. Two other very noteworthy counter-instances were Mrs Verrall and her daughter Mrs Salter, both women of the highest practical ability, who did valuable public work and successfully held responsible offices.

DESCRIPTION OF MRS WILLETT'S MEDIUMSHIP

Myers died in 1901. Soon afterwards Mrs Coombe-Tennant became an associate member of the S.P.R. But she was not greatly interested

287

in such matters at the time, and she resigned in 1905. In 1908 she suffered a severe and sudden family bereavement. As a girl she had made some attempts at automatic writing, but had given it up. She now began trying again. At that time she knew of Mrs Verrall as an automatist, but had only a very slight personal acquaintance with her. She decided, however, to consult Mrs Verrall about her automatic writing. The history of the matter is as follows.

In August and September 1908 Mrs Coombe-Tennant read, in the S.P.R. *Proceedings*, Miss Alice Johnson's paper entitled 'A Report on Mrs Holland's Script'. (The name 'Mrs Holland' was the pseudonym of Mrs Alice Macdonald Fleming, a sister of Rudyard Kipling, living in India.) Mrs Holland too was a non-professional automatist. She found herself producing automatic script, which formed an important part of the so-called 'cross-correspondences', which I shall describe in more detail later. Mrs Coombe-Tennant, on reading this *Report*, felt an impulse to try for herself. She described these attempts in a letter of October 8th, 1908, to Mrs Verrall. The scripts which she then produced purported to come from Myers. Mrs Coombe-Tennant was not much impressed with them, and she destroyed them.

Early in 1909, however, an important development took place, which I will describe later. Thereafter the mediumship of Mrs *Willett* (as I will henceforth call her) was in fairly regular operation over a long period of years. The earlier scripts were sent for record, analysis, and collation to Sir Oliver Lodge, and the later ones to G. W. Balfour (afterwards the second Earl of Balfour), both of whom were prominent and active members of the S.P.R. The materials with which we shall be mainly concerned were produced by Mrs Willett from early in 1909 to the end of the first quarter of 1912. They form the subject of a long and important paper by Lord Balfour in Vol. XLIII of the S.P.R. *Proceedings*, entitled 'The Psychological Aspects of Mrs Willett's Mediumship'. Balfour's account is based on a prolonged and careful first-hand study of Mrs Willett's trance-utterances.

Certain parts of what follows would not be intelligible unless it were prefaced by a few words about the so-called 'cross-correspondences', which were in 1908 and for many years afterwards being reported, analysed, and commented upon in the S.P.R. *Proceedings*. These scripts came through the hands of a number of non-professional automatists, several of whom were personally strangers to each other and living in various parts of the world. They purported to come from the surviving spirits of F. W. H. Myers, Edmund Gurney, Henry Sidgwick, and certain of their friends. It was claimed, in the scripts themselves, that these persons, after their deaths, had devised and were using a method of communication which would rule out telepathy from the living as a possible explanation of the out-of-the-way and characteristic bits of information displayed in the automatic writings.

In essence the method was this. In the script of each automatist there would be fragmentary and allusive items, without special significance for the person in whose script they occurred. But these were highly significant for any investigator, acquainted with the personalities, interests, and acquirements of the alleged communicators, who might compare and put together the contemporary scripts of the various automatists in the group.

Mrs Willett, as we have seen, was related by marriage to Myers, and had known him personally. She had not known Gurney or Sidgwick; but she had seen photographs of them, and it must be assumed that she had often heard tell of them. Apart from this, one can say only that she was a cultivated and intelligent woman of good general education, moving in good society, but not specially interested in or familiar with psychological or philosophical literature. I think we must assume that she had seen, and had at least fluttered the pages of, *Phantasms of the Living* by Gurney, Myers, and Podmore, and Myers's *Human Personality*, which was published posthumously in 1903. That she had made any elaborate study of those works is most unlikely.

Mrs Willett's scripts were of two kinds. Some are clear and consecutive; others are scrappy and disjointed, and full of literary and other allusions. It is the scrappy allusive scripts which form the basis of the cross-correspondence phenomena. Recondite literary puzzles were a special feature of such scripts, and Balfour edited two famous instances in his papers 'The Statius Case' and 'The Ear of Dionysius' in Vols. XXVII and XXIX respectively of the S.P.R. *Proceedings*. We shall be directly concerned here only with the clear consecutive scripts. But we may have to refer to some of the scrappy allusive ones, in so far as these contain statements, purporting to come from Gurney or Myers, as to the methods by which the clear consecutive scripts are produced.

In what follows I shall use the word 'utterances' to cover both the sentences spoken by Mrs Willett's lips and those written by her hand in the course of a sitting. I shall speak of the 'Myers-persona', the 'Gurney-persona' and so on, and I shall refer to them as 'ostensible communicators'. When I say, e.g., that a certain utterance of Mrs Willett's was 'an ostensible communication from the Myers-persona', I mean neither to suggest that it did, nor that it did not, originate from a source other than Mrs Willett's mind or some part of it. Nor do I mean to suggest that, *if* it did so, the external source was, or that it was not, the surviving spirit of the late F. W. H. Myers or some part of it. I mean simply to record the fact that it was couched in the form of a communication from the surviving spirit of Myers.

(1) *Stages in the Development of the Mediumship.* Mrs Willett's mediumship developed in four successive phases, which Lord Balfour describes as 'lone scripts', 'silent daylight impressions', 'spoken daylight impressions', and 'deep trance'. I will first briefly describe each of these phases, and then give an account of the course of their development.

When producing 'lone scripts' Mrs Willett was sitting by herself. Her state of consciousness was almost normal, but her handwriting was far from normal. The words ran into each other, there were no stops, and any word that was wrong was not erased but was simply left standing. At no moment of the process did she anticipate the *meaning* of what she was just about to write, but she did know at each moment what *word* she was just about to write. It is uncertain how much she remembered of what she had written by the time she had finished writing on each occasion. In most of the lone scripts the ostensible communicator was Myers.

The name 'daylight impressions' occurs in the scripts themselves, as a phrase used by the Myers-persona. The conditions in which Mrs Willett received '*silent* daylight impressions' were the same as those in which she produced lone scripts, viz. she was by herself and in a practically normal state of consciousness. In this phase, however, she received impressions which contained, as an essential part, *definitely worded messages.* She also had experiences in which she seemed to herself to be directly aware of *a certain identifiable person*, e.g. Myers on some occasions and Gurney on others, who seemed to be addressing her. She often seemed to herself also to be directly aware of his emotional reactions, e.g. amusement, impatience, etc.

It will be worth while to consider these silent daylight impressions in rather more detail. (i) Her impressions of the words of such a message were in no sense *visual.* She did *not* see them 'in her mind's eye' as written letters. The experience was *auditory*, in the sense in which one often has auditory images of the sounds of words as one is reading them in a book or writing them down. But the experience was not auditory in any stronger sense. She 'heard them in her mind's ear', as one might put it, and had no *quasi*-perceptual hallucination as of hearing an external voice speaking the words. (ii) In these silent daylight impressions Mrs Willett's experience as of being in the presence of a certain identifiable person seemed to be devoid of all sensory, *quasi*-sensory, or imaginal content. She did *not*, e.g., seem to herself to *see* Myers or Gurney or to *hear* them speaking, nor did she have a picture of them 'in her mind's eye'. She seemed to

290

herself just to know intuitively that such and such a person was now located at a certain place outside her body. In the same direct, but non-sensuous and non-imaginal, way she seemed to herself on certain occasions to know that that person was amused or that he was angry. She did *not* seem to herself to *see* him smiling or frowning, or to *hear* him laughing; nor did she have any visual or auditory image of that kind. The experience resembled sense-perception only in so far as it was direct and non-inferential and was concerned with a particular existent in a particular temporary state. It differed from sense-perception in that it had no sensory or *quasi*-sensory content.

We come next to '*spoken* daylight impressions'. From the point of view of Mrs Willett as recipient these did not differ much from the silent ones. But in other respects there were important differences. In the first place, her state of consciousness was not quite normal. She tended to pass into a hazy, dreamlike state. The ostensible communicators carefully distinguish this from *trance*, but Lord Balfour says that it became very definite trance in the later developments of this phase. Secondly, the spoken daylight impression came when Mrs Willett was giving a seance, with some other person, e.g. Sir Oliver Lodge or Lord Balfour, as sitter. She then spoke her daylight impression to the sitter, who thereupon recorded in writing what she had said. From the sitter's point of view it was as if Mrs Willett were holding a conversation on the telephone with a certain person, whom he could neither see nor hear, and as if she were reporting what she was hearing as she received it.

The last phase to be considered is 'deep trance'. It should be noted that the *communicators* refused to call even this state 'trance'. Their reason seems to have been that they wanted to distinguish it carefully from the condition, already well known under the name of 'trance', in which Mrs Leonard, Mrs Piper, and many other mediums have made their utterances.

Even when Mrs Willett was in deep trance she did not lose control of her body, as if she were asleep or in a swoon. She would sit up and talk in a natural way and in the first person singular. There was no appearance of her body being used by a personality, such as Feda in Mrs Leonard's case, other than that which expressed itself through it in normal waking life. But, when she regained normal consciousness after a period of deep trance, she remembered little, if anything, of what had been happening.

Deep trance occurred only at a seance, with another person as sitter to watch over Mrs Willett and record what she said. But her utterances in deep trance were not only oral. In this phase, as in the lone script phase, Mrs Willett produced automatic writing, both of the connected and of the allusive kind. When in deep trance Mrs

Willett's handwriting became *normal*; the words were kept separate, sentences were marked off with stops, and wrong words were erased and the right ones substituted for them. The proportion of written to spoken daylight impressions, and the relative importance of the content of the two, varied from one sitting to another.

It should be noted that those experiences of Mrs Willett's, in which she seemed to herself to be in presence of certain communicators and to be aware of their emotions, altered in character as she went more and more deeply into the trance-state. In deep trance she might have complete sensory hallucination, i.e. she might seem to herself to be *seeing* Myers or Gurney, to be *hearing* him speak, to be *seeing* him smile or frown, and so on. This may be compared to one's own experiences in vivid dreams.

Between this extreme, which occurred only in deep trance, and the completely non-sensory and non-imaginal awareness of presence, characteristic of silent daylight impressions, there were several intermediate phases. These seem to be correlated with the different degrees of departure from normal consciousness. There was, e.g., a phase of *semi*-sensory hallucination. At that stage she did *not* seem to herself to be seeing a human body with her eyes or to be hearing a human voice with her ears, as we seem to ourselves to do in dreams. She had visual and auditory experiences which she recognized to be *imaginal* and not sensory. Nevertheless, they seemed to her to be initiated from *outside her body*. Lastly, there was an intermediate stage where, although she had neither a *quasi*-sensory hallucination nor this peculiar kind of outwardly referred imaginal experience, she yet seemed to herself to have an immediate awareness of the *position* of the communicator in relation to her body. She would talk of him, e.g., as being 'near' or 'far off', 'approaching' or 'going away', and so on.

(2) *Course of Development of the Four Phases.* I will now describe the way in which these four phases of Mrs Willett's mediumship developed out of each other. As I have said, it all began in 1908 with lone scripts purporting to come from Myers. Early in January 1909 she received, in the course of such a script, an ostensible communication in which the Myers-persona told her to stop writing, to try to apprehend directly the ideas that would be given to her, and to record them either at once or at some convenient later time. The Myers-persona gave the name 'daylight impressions' to the ideas thus conveyed. It was said in the scripts that Gurney was also involved in the experiments which were now to be made with Mrs Willett.

The next stage was that the Myers-persona and the Gurney-persona expressed a wish in their ostensible communications that

Mrs Willett should sit in the presence of certain other persons, and should dictate her daylight impressions to them. The first person whom they proposed as a sitter was Sir Oliver Lodge, the eminent physicist, who had been an active member of the S.P.R. from its early days and had known and collaborated with Gurney during his lifetime.

At first Mrs Willett strongly resisted this proposal, for she disliked the idea of holding a sitting, and perhaps losing normal consciousness, in the presence of a complete stranger, as Lodge then was to her. However, she eventually consented, and had many sittings with him. It was the Gurney-persona who asked that Lord Balfour should be introduced as a sitter. That wish was expressed again and again in communications purporting to come from Gurney during the earlier part of 1911. Mrs Willett resisted this proposal too at first, for she did not relish facing yet another stranger. But she finally consented, and Balfour had his first sitting with her on June 4th, 1911.

Two points are worth noting here. Gurney had been a close friend of Balfour's and they had co-operated in psychical research up to the time of Gurney's death in 1888. We must assume that Balfour would be fully acquainted with Gurney's published views, and with others which he may have thrown out in conversation but never written down. The other point is this. The Gurney-persona said that his reason for wanting Balfour to become a sitter with Mrs Willett was that Balfour would be interested in the *processes* involved in communication rather than in the *products*. As we shall see, most of the ostensible communications received in Balfour's presence did deal with that topic. Balfour was, in fact, a man of keen philosophic interests and of wide reading in philosophy. In his Presidential Address to the S.P.R. in 1906 he had developed a rather elaborate speculation as to the structure of human personality, in terms of a hierarchy of several minds connected with the same organism and interacting telepathically with each other (S.P.R. *Proceedings*, Vol. XIX).

The phase of deep trance first appeared (though it was not recognized as such at the time) at a sitting with Lodge on September 25th, 1910. But it was not until May 24th, 1911, that deep trance began to be maintained throughout the sittings, both for the production of script and for the dictation of spoken daylight impressions. After that it became the normal procedure, though there were variations in detail. At the earlier stages the more important ostensible communications all occurred in the *spoken* daylight impressions, but gradually the content of the *scripts* became equally important. The earlier scripts were all of the consecutive coherent type. The first disjointed allusive scripts occurred on February 4th and February

10th, 1910, and they formed part of the *Lethe* cross-correspondence material, which is described in S.P.R. *Proceedings*, Vol. XXV.

It should be noted that the Myers-persona and the Gurney-persona asserted repeatedly in their ostensible communications that they were deliberately experimenting with Mrs Willett, and were trying to develop in her a peculiar kind of mediumship for their own purposes. They did *not* want her to become a trance-medium of the usual kind, such as Mrs Piper or Mrs Leonard. They were anxious that her mind should remain in normal control of her body, while they were communicating through her, and that they should affect what she spoke or wrote *only indirectly*, by putting ideas and impulses into her mind. They said, too, that they wanted to keep Mrs Willett as a medium for their own use, and not let her become a medium for all and sundry. In this connexion they compared her to a bit of land which they personally had reclaimed and meant to cultivate for themslves.

(3) *Some further Details about Mrs Willett's Mediumship*. Before considering the contents of Mrs Willett's consecutive utterances, I will add a few further details about her mediumistic experiences.

In the first place, I would mention her experiences of *impulses* and *inhibitions*. Her commonest impulse was simply to sit down and produce script. This might happen on inconvenient occasions, and it might sometimes be misinterpreted by her. Thus, on a certain occa-sion she had a feeling which she took to be an impulse to write; but, when she tried to do so, she received an ostensible communication from the Myers-persona forbidding her. She thereupon had an impulse to look through certain S.P.R. reports. When she had read in them the words SYRINGA and LETHE, in association with the name DANTE, she felt that she had hit the nail on the head, though she had no idea why. The impulse then ceased. Now those words, in relation to each other, had an important meaning for the persons who were investigating the *Lethe* cross-correspondence case. On another occasion she felt a strong inhibition against looking at certain papers enclosed by Sir Oliver Lodge in a letter to her, and a strong impulse to hand them over at once to her husband and to get him to forward them without delay to Mrs Sidgwick. She acted accordingly. The papers in fact contained notes made by Lodge, which would have given to Mrs Willett certain information which it was undesirable, from the point of view of the experiment then in progress, that she should have at the time.

This brings us to Mrs Willett's own description of her state of consciousness. She ascribed these impulses and inhibitions to a part of herself which she called 'Mind No. 1'. She talked of her mind, as she knew it in ordinary life, as 'Mind No. 2'. At the conclusion of an impulse or an inhibition she would have an experience which she described as 'the two minds flashing together'. (I suppose that this metaphor is taken from an electric discharge.) Presumably Mind No. 1 was generally connected in some way with Mind No. 2, and was a subliminal part of Mrs Willett's total personality. Mind No. 2 would presumably be the ordinary self-conscious introspectable part of the total personality. It would, however, be in a slightly abnormal state on those occasions when Mind No. 1 was producing impulses or inhibitions in it.

Sometimes Mrs Willett talked as if she had a number of different selves, all connected more or less closely with Mind No. 1. Thus, she spoke on one occasion of 'a whole chain of me's', and on another occasion of 'a number of me's whirling round and fitting together'. These expressions recall to my mind certain bewildering experiences which I have occasionally had in dreams, especially when I have had an abnormally high temperature. They are hard to describe in any phraseology which does not sound self-contradictory, for our ordinary language is not adapted to deal with such conditions.

Again, Mrs Willett sometimes felt as if her mind were *blended with* that of one or other of the ostensible communicators. Thus, she said on a certain occasion, in reference to the Myers-persona: 'I seem to be almost becoming *him*.' She also used the following curious phrase after such an experience in connexion with another ostensible communicator: 'I seem to be coming together, and the bits don't fit.'

It would seem that the ostensible communications often reached the medium's consciousness in the form of auditory images of spoken words. As with Feda, she sometimes *failed* to catch the intended word, though it might be perfectly plain to the sitter. Thus, in her attempt to convey the, to her, unfamiliar classical name DEUCALION, she eventually spelled it out as DEW-K-LION.

When she found special difficulties, e.g. with technical philosophical terms or with classical quotations, the ostensible communicators often adopted either or both of the following supplementary devices. One method was to produce visual images of the letters of the word in sequence. Mrs Willett, e.g., on one occasion gave the familiar Old Testament name ABSALOM, which was quite meaningless and inappropriate in the context. Thereupon she received in sequence visual images of the letters A-B-S-O-L-U-T-E. This is a characteristic technical term in the Hegelian philosophy, which was unfamiliar to Mrs Willett, though a household word to the sitter, Lord Balfour, and familiar enough to the ostensible communicator, Gurney, in his lifetime. The other method was to accompany the auditory image of a word with one or more visual images which symbolize its

295

meaning. These symbolic images often involved something which had special associations for the ostensible communicator, and was easily interpretable by the sitters who had known that individual, but was quite meaningless for Mrs Willett, who had not. For example, when the late Professor Butcher was ostensibly communicating, Mrs Willett would experience an hallucinatory smell as of roses. This was quite meaningless to her, but had a very definite and characteristic association with certain incidents in Butcher's life which were well known to the sitter.

THE CONTENTS OF MRS WILLETT'S UTTERANCES

I come now to the *content* of the continuous scripts and the accompanying daylight impressions. In the main they consist of ostensible communications in which the Myers-persona and the Gurney-persona try to describe and explain to the sitters the following three things. (I) The *conditions* under which they work in communicating through Mrs Willett. (II) The *processes* involved in such communication in general, and the special procedure involved in conducting a cross-correspondence experiment. (III) Their views on certain *philosophical questions*, about the nature of human personality, its survival of bodily death, and the relation of the human individual to the Absolute.

One remark may be made at the outset about all these ostensible communications. They are plainly the product of a highly intelligent and cultured mind or minds, with a keen interest in psychology, psychical research, and philosophy, and with a capacity for drawing subtle and significant distinctions. Whatever the source or the sources of these utterances may be, they show a pretty thorough acquaintance with the theories and the terminology of Myers's posthumously published book *Human Personality and its Survival of Bodily Death*. All this would, of course, have been perfectly familiar to Lodge and to Balfour, the main sitters. It is known that Mrs Willett had read (with what degree of attention is uncertain) the *abridged* edition of that work; and it is asserted confidently by Balfour that she had *not* read the complete edition in two large volumes, which alone contains the philosophical theories. It is obviously impossible to exclude the possibility that she may at some time or other have skimmed the relevant pages.

The doctrines developed in the ostensible communications are in the main in agreement with Myers's speculations in that book. But the ostensible communicators develop some points in greater detail, and express views which conflict in certain points with those of the book. I do not find the statements made by the ostensible communi-

296

cators altogether clear or coherent. But I have not always found complete clarity or coherence in the statements of philosophers or psychologists who enjoyed the advantage of speaking or writing through their own physical bodies, instead of having to use post-humously the mind and the body of another person. On the whole, I think we may say that the obscurities and ambiguities are such as one might expect to find in the utterances of an intelligent philo-sophical psychologist, trying to describe and explain very complex and unfamiliar processes which he himself only partly understands, in language that is very imperfectly fitted to express his ideas, and under conditions which make all communication difficult. The style is never pompous or hieratic, and the ostensible communicators often insist on the limitations of their own knowledge.

Lastly, there is no question of a mere one-sided outpouring of theories, which the sitter must passively record and accept. Nor, on the other hand, is there any question of passive acceptance by the ostensible communicators of theories held by the sitter. In the seances in which Balfour was sitter and the Gurney-persona was ostensible communicator there was constant give and take. Balfour would read over at his leisure the record of a sitting, would reflect on points which seemed to him to be obscure or inconsistent, and would then at the next sitting make criticisms and suggestions and ask for explanations. The Gurney-persona would then deal with the points raised, try to clear up the obscurities and answer the criticisms, and would sometimes accept and sometimes vigorously reject Balfour's suggestions and interpretations. It was, in fact, as if Balfour were holding a conversation on psychological and philo-sophical topics over the telephone with a highly intelligent friend, who had emigrated to a foreign land where conditions of life were very strange and unfamiliar, and with Mrs Willett's body and mind acting as the receiving and transmitting apparatus for both parties.

(I) *Conditions under which the Ostensible Communicators claim to work*

Both the Myers-persona and the Gurney-persona say that, when they renew contact with human beings still living on earth and with their surroundings (as they do when communicating through the medium), they find it difficult to keep a grip on their own self-consciousness. It is only through the *medium*'s awareness of *them* that they can remain fully aware of themselves. A characteristic utterance, in this connexion, is: 'I know I'm real through *her* recognition of my reality.'

They say also that, in order for the medium to *receive* information from them, the subliminal part of her mind must be attuned to *their* conditions. But, on the other hand, in order to make her body *utter* the information received, the subliminal part of her mind must be in touch with the supraliminal part, and to that extent with the ordinary conditions of bodily life on earth. It is hard, they say, to keep the balance between these two desiderata, and this is one of the hindrances to successful communication.

There is a very interesting statement made by an ostensible communicator whom Mrs Willett always refers to as 'the Dark Young Man'. (It is quite plain from the context that this is the *persona* of Francis Maitland Balfour, a brother of Lord Balfour, a very distinguished Cambridge biologist and a keen mountaineer, who was killed at a fairly early age in an accident on the Alps.) Mrs Willett had never met him; but she had seen a photograph of him, and may well have heard talk of his brilliant promise and performance and his tragic death, which took place in 1882. In an ostensible communication from the Dark Young Man he stated that he had given to Mrs Willett a very vivid dream of being with him on the Alps. Mrs Willett had in fact had and described a very striking dream-experience, in which she seemed to herself to be *blended* with the Dark Young Man, to participate in his accident, and even to feel the pain which he suffered as a result of his fall. About four months later, in a spoken daylight impression, the *persona* of the Dark Young Man made the following statement through Mrs Willett. He said that, in order for him in his present condition to realize fully memories of experiences which he had had before his death, he had first to *convey telepathically to the medium* his thoughts of them. Then she, in her sleep, clothed those thoughts in appropriate visual, tactual, and kinaesthetic imagery, and gave them the appropriate emotional colouring of pain, fear, etc. Then he in his turn *got back* these concretized experiences telepathically from her. And, finally, it became almost like an experience of actual sense-perception for him.

(II) *Processes said by the Ostensible Communicators to be involved in Communication*

This is a long and complicated story, which must be divided into a number of headings.

(1) *Telergic and Telepathic Control.* The ostensible communicators draw a sharp distinction between the way in which *they* use Mrs Willett, and the processes which go on in communicating through a trance-medium of the more usual kind. They describe the process which takes place in the *latter* case as 'telergic', and they say that the result of it is that the medium's body is temporarily *possessed* by the communicator. They describe the process which they use with Mrs

Willett as 'telepathic' and not telergic, and as *not* leading to possession.

The distinction which they have in mind seems quite clear. Mrs Willett's normal mind is to remain in normal control of her body, and the communicators are to operate telepathically upon it. Her mind then expresses, by the ordinary control which it exercises over her speech-organs and her fingers, the ideas which it has received from the communicators. In telergy and possession, on the other hand, the medium's mind is ousted from control of her speech-organs and her fingers by another personality, which thereupon uses them directly to express its own ideas in speech or writing. It may be remarked that the word 'telergy' was introduced into psychical research by Myers himself, and that it never 'caught on'. Its first appearance in the text of *Human Personality* is on p. 197 of Vol. II. It is there defined as *direct* action on a person's *brain and nervous system* by the mind of some *other* person. In his published works Myers placed possession (which he takes to be a particular case of telergy) *above* telepathy. But the Myers-persona, who ostensibly communicates through Mrs Willett, takes a different view. He refers to telergy as 'a clumsy, creaking process', and puts control by telepathic action on the medium's mind above it. It seems that we die and learn.

(2) *Telepathy.* The Gurney-persona made some very interesting statements about telepathy. In the first place, he distinguishes it from another process, also involved in communication, which he calls 'telaesthesia'. Secondly, he distinguishes a number of different processes under the head of telepathy proper. I will proceed in the reverse order, and begin with his statements about telepathy proper.

(i) Telepathy is always a *direct* relationship between *one mind and another mind, not both animating the same body.* The ostensible communicators explicit refused to give the name 'telepathy' to interaction between *different parts of the same mind*, e.g. the subliminal and the supraliminal parts of it. It would also seem (though this is not, perhaps, quite clear) that they would refuse to describe as 'telepathy' interaction between two different minds animating the same organism, such as seems *prima facie* to happen in certain cases of multiple personality. According to them, this is not a mere question of nomenclature. They regard such processes as different in kind from the direct action of one mind on another, when the two do not animate the same organism. It is interesting to note that Lord Balfour, the sitter, himself favoured the view that the interaction between minds animating a common organism is fundamentally *akin* to the telepathic action between minds not animating the same

299

organism. The Gurney-persona strongly and explicitly dissented from Balfour on this point.

(ii) Generally the ostensible communicators speak of telepathy as *interaction* between mind and mind. But sometimes they describe it as a *blending* of two minds. They do not seem to realize the extreme difference which there is *prima facie* between these two views.

(iii) The Gurney-persona distinguishes two main forms of telepathy, and he subdivides the second of them into two sub-species, thus giving three forms in all.

(a) The first form of telepathy is described as a process analogous to aiming a projectile at a target. I take it that this would be deliberately generating a certain *quasi*-sensation or image or idea or impulse or emotion in another person's mind. (b) He describes the second form of telepathy in the following metaphorical terms. It begins by the communicators 'coming very close to the medium'. Thereupon, he says: 'a shutter is let down' (i.e. presumably, *opened*) 'between the two'. At this stage either of two things may happen, thus giving rise to the two sub-species of the second form of telepathy. (α) One alternative is that the communicator may *deliberately* do something which is described as 'shutting off or switching on a certain impression'. (β) The other alternative is that there may be what is described as 'a leak'. In that case certain information may get through from the communicator's mind to the medium's, without or against the communicator's will. In the first form, and in the first sub-species of the second, i.e. in (a) and in (b,α), the process is deliberate and intentional *throughout* on the part of the communicator. In the second sub-species of the second form, i.e. in (b,β), the process is deliberate and intentional on the part of the communicator *only at the preliminary stage*. Thereafter it is beyond his control. In all three kinds of telepathy the *medium*'s mind is represented as being purely *passive and receptive*; there is no question of deliberate selective attention or of search on her part.

It is obvious that all these descriptions are highly metaphorical. The metaphor is in terms of *light and vision*, in general, and it seems sometimes to be in terms of *electric light*, in particular. I think that the following analogy may illustrate the difference alleged to exist between the two sub-species of the second form of telepathy. Suppose that a photographic camera were set up in a dark room, and were focused on to a wall, on which is hung a sheet with various pictures and written sentences on it. One might selectively illuminate certain pictures and words, by means of directed beams of light focused upon them, and leave the rest in darkness. On the other hand, it might happen that there were some cracks in the shutters or some holes in the curtains of the room, so that certain words or pictures were illuminated, without or against one's will. The photographs which would appear on the plate in these two cases would correspond respectively to the results in the medium's mind of the first and of the second sub-species of the second form of telepathy.

I propose to call the first form of telepathy 'Telepathic Imposition', because the communicator here *imposes* a definite idea or impulse or emotion on the medium's mind. I will call the second form 'Telepathic Exposition', because here he, so to speak, *exposes* to the medium's mind certain parts of the content of his own. I will call the first sub-species of Telepathic Exposition '*deliberately* selective', and the second sub-species of it '*fortuitously* selective'.

(3) *Telaesthesia*. Let us now consider the process which the Gurney-persona distinguishes from telepathy proper under the name of 'telaesthesia'. I will begin with some quotations from the records of the sitting with Balfour on October 8th, 1911. 'Telaesthesia', says the Gurney-persona, 'is the power of acquiring knowledge without the intervention of discarnate mind. . . . Telepathy is one thing, viz. thought-communication. Telaesthesia is *knowledge*, not thought, acquired by the subliminal when operating normally in the met-etherial.' He continues this statement by describing what he does with the medium when he wishes her to acquire certain information by telaesthesia. He says that he takes the medium 'into a room', and screens off any action of his mind on hers. Her subliminal self then 'takes stock' of the 'room' and its contents. When she regains normal consciousness, there is (he says) 'lying in her subliminal, knowledge of certain objects perceived, not as the result of the action of my mind, but as a result of the telaesthetic faculty'.

There are several obscurities here. What precisely does the Gurney-persona mean when he contrasts 'communication of thought' with 'acquirement of knowledge without the intervention of discarnate mind'? Again, his talk of 'taking the medium into a room' plainly is, and is meant to be, metaphorical; but how should the metaphor be interpreted?

As regards the first point, I would make the following suggestion. I feel pretty sure that part at least of what the Gurney-persona means by his distinction between 'communication of thought' and 'acquirement of knowledge' is this. In the former, as we have seen, the medium's mind is held to be purely *passive and receptive*. It might be compared to that of a hypnotized subject receiving suggestions from the hypnotist. The activity is all on the side of the communicator, who either deliberately imposes certain thoughts on her mind or deliberately exposes to it certain of the contents of his own mind, and, as it were, illuminates some of them and leaves others in shadow.

301

In the latter, i.e. in telaesthesia, the medium's mind is active, attentive, and selective. It *deliberately selects* for special attention certain items from a wider field, and ignores others to which it might equally well have attended. It is like the difference between passively receiving and responding to hypnotic suggestions, and actively scanning or listening for oneself.

The question still remains: 'What are the contents of the field which the medium's mind selectively inspects in telaesthesia?' This would seem to be equivalent to the question: 'What is the cash-value of the Gurney-persona's metaphor of the *room*?' Balfour interrogated him closely on this point, but he never managed to get a clear, consistent answer. Balfour thinks that the phrase 'the contents of the room' means certain contents of the *communicator's mind*, including some of his conscious thoughts and some of his latent memories, which the communicator has selected beforehand as an appropriate field in which the medium's mind can range and rummage, and in which it can selectively attend to certain items. He interprets the phrase: 'I screen off any action of my mind on hers' as follows. Once the communicator has selected this field from the contents of his own consciousness and has exposed it as a whole to the medium's mind for telaesthetic inspection, he leaves it to the medium to explore it, to select for attention those items which interest her, and to ignore the rest.

On this interpretation telaesthesia is a process which has sometimes been called 'mind-reading'. There would be two points of resemblance, one positive and the other negative, between telaesthesia, on this view of it, and what I have called the fortuitously selective sub-species of telepathic exposition. The positive resemblance is that in both cases the total field available to the medium's mind is *a certain part of the contents of the communicator's mind*, which he has deliberately pre-selected for her use. The negative resemblance is that in neither case does the communicator's volition determine which of the items within that field the medium shall become aware of, and which of them she shall ignore. The *difference* is that, in the case of telepathy, the medium's selection within that field is *not* determined by her volition, whilst, in the case of telaesthesia, it *is* so determined.

On January 21st, 1912, Balfour questioned the Gurney-persona about the meaning of his metaphor of the 'room'. The latter now made a complicated statement, in which for the first time he distinguished a number of different 'layers' in the subliminal self. He now talked as if the 'room' itself and its contents exist in a certain intermediate stratum of *the medium's subliminal self*, which he symbolized by H_1, instead of in *the communicator's mind*, as Balfour had understood him to allege. According to this account, the contents of the 'room' are determined beforehand by some kind of agreement between the communicator and the *deepest layer*, H_0, of the medium's subliminal self; and not, as Balfour had understood, by the communicator alone. This implies that in telaesthesia both the knower and the objects known are confined to different strata of *the same self*, viz. the medium's. Now, on Balfour's interpretation of the Gurney-persona's earlier statements, the knower was the medium (or some part of her), whilst the objects known were part of the contents of the *communicator's* mind.

It is plain that these two accounts cannot be reconciled with each other. Balfour was inclined to think that the Gurney-persona must have been trying to describe a different process on the second occasion. If so, one can only say that the Gurney-persona must either have been very confused in his answers or have seriously misunderstood the question. For he was explicitly asked by Balfour, on the second occasion, to explain the metaphor of the 'room', and the nature of its relations to the medium and the communicator. And he had introduced that metaphor himself in his earlier attempt to describe *telaesthesia* as contrasted with telepathy.

The only other comment that I will make is this. The word 'telaesthesia', like the word 'telergy', was introduced by Myers and has not 'caught on' among psychical researchers. It is defined by him, in the Glossary, p. xxii, Vol. I of *Human Personality*. He defines it there as direct sensation or perception of objects or conditions, independently of the recognized channels of sense, occurring under such circumstances that *no known mind*, other than the percipient's, can be suggested as the source of the knowledge thus gained. He contrasts it with telepathy, where the intervention of some mind, other than that of the percipient, *is* an essential condition for the percipient's paranormally acquired knowledge. It is plain from this, and also from Myers's discussion under the heading 'clairvoyance' in the Glossary, p. xv, Vol. I of *Human Personality*, that he invented the word 'telaesthesia' as a generic term to cover such more specific popular terms as 'clairvoyance', 'clairaudience', etc.

Now, whoever and whatever may be the real source of the Gurney-persona's ostensible communications, it is plainly very familiar with Myers's thought and terminology. That makes me doubtful of the interpretation put by Balfour on the Gurney-persona's earlier statements, in so far as that interpretation implies that the only possible objects of telaesthesia are the contents of a *mind* other than the medium's. This, as I have said above, would make telaesthesia to be simply *identical with* 'mind-reading'. Now it is just possible that Myers intended 'telaesthesia' to *cover* mind-reading, as well as clairvoyance, clairaudience, etc.; though I think it would be hard to reconcile this with the definition paraphrased above. And it is possible to suppose that the Gurney-persona meant to suggest that, in these particular experiments with Mrs Willett, the medium's telaesthetic faculty was exercised almost exclusively on the contents of the communicator's mind. But I think that to *identify* telaesthesia with mind-reading not only involves a complete breach of Myers's own usage, but also requires us to put a very strained interpretation on certain of the Gurney-persona's statements. Take, e.g., his statement: 'Telaesthesia is knowledge . . . acquired by the subliminal when operating normally in the metetherial', and his phrase: 'knowledge of certain objects perceived . . . as the result of the telaesthetic faculty'. There is no doubt that 'the metetherial'—another phrase invented by Myers—is meant to indicate the whole environment in which minds, not animating ordinary human or animal bodies, are supposed to exist and perceive and operate (see *Human Personality*, Vol. I, Glossary, p. xix). I see no reason to think that the ostensible communicators meant to assert or imply, either that this consists of nothing but minds and their contents, or that nothing but these can be objects of telaesthetic awareness.

(4) *Excursus.* The ostensible communicators say that, *before* either telepathy from them to the medium or telaesthesia by the medium under their direction can take place, a certain preliminary process must be completed. This they call 'Excursus'. (It may be noted that this word does *not* occur as a technical term, if it occurs at all, in *Human Personality*.)

Excursus is described as a deliberate act, by which a mind, that is still animating a physical human body, seeks to get loose from the restrictions which that relationship involves, and to enter into communication with minds which are no longer incarnate in physical bodies, and with the environment in which they live. The communicators say that that environment—presumably what they elsewhere call the 'metetherial'—is the natural habitation of a certain part of every human mind, even when it is still animating a physical body. Excursus is said to require a certain *passivity* on the medium's part; but it also involves a definite *act* on her part, and is not a mere condition of lethargy. It is not itself a state of communion with the spirits of the dead, but it is a necessary precondition of it.

If the excursus is successful, it results in the temporary establishment of a certain relationship between a certain stratum of the medium's mind and the mind of one or other of the communicators. Communication may then take a form in which *telaesthetic mind-reading* by the medium of the contents of the communicator's mind is predominant. Or it may take a form in which *telepathic imposition* or *exposition*, exerted by the communicator, is predominant. Generally the two coexist or alternate with each other. It is said that, in the case of mind-reading, the process is performed by the subliminal part of the medium's mind, and is a perfectly normal activity which it regularly practises. It is only from the standpoint of the medium's ordinary everyday consciousness that the knowledge thus acquired seems paranormal.

It may be remarked that the communicators do not positively assert that the medium's mind ever exerts a reciprocal *telepathic* influence on that of the communicator. But they do not explicitly rule out that possibility. On the other hand, they do definitely assert that the *mind-reading* is to some extent mutual. Not only does the medium explore the contents of the communicator's mind, but the communicator also explores that of the medium's mind. (There is, of course, a good deal of independent evidence which suggests that a medium often reads the mind of the *sitter*, and even those of *certain other persons still living*, who are connected with the sitter, but are not present at the seance.)

(5) *Mutual Selection*. According to the Gurney-persona, excursus is followed by a process in which the medium and the communicator each select material from the mind of the other. He says that the communicator can select from *any* part or level of the medium's mind, but that the medium's field of choice is much more limited. She can select only from that part of the communicator's mind whose contents and structure are analogous to those of an ordinary incarnate human mind. There is, however, they say, another part of the communicator's mind, which works on different principles and uses different categories from those which pertain to incarnate human minds. That part is inaccessible to the medium. The Gurney-persona compares the part of a discarnate mind which *is* accessible to the medium to the *supraliminal* part of an incarnate human mind. He compares the part of a discarnate mind which is *inaccessible* to the medium to that part of an incarnate human mind which occasionally manifests itself in the products of literary or musical or mathematical genius.

It is alleged that, at the end of such a process of mutual selection, the medium's mind contains a mass of selected content in which two parts can be distinguished. One of them consists of the material which the *medium* has gathered by selecting from the communicator's mind. The other consists of that part of the original content of the medium's mind which the *communicator* has selected. The whole of this selected material, of both kinds, may remain latent in the medium's mind until the communicator chooses to bring it to the surface by telepathic influence. Then, and not till then, the whole or a part of it emerges into the medium's normal consciousness and is uttered by her in speech or in automatic writing.

There is one comment that I will make on this. It evidently implies that what has been called 'selection' by the communicator of certain parts of the content of the medium's mind, produces some kind of modification in the selected contents; and that this persists after the process of mutual selection is over and during the period of latency which follows. The contents selected by the communicator remain, so to speak, 'ear-marked' in some way that distinguishes them from the rest of the contents of the medium's mind. And they are in some way specially linked with the contents which she has acquired by her own selection from the communicator's mind. These two interlinked parts form a single mass of outstanding subliminal content, on which the communicator operates telepathically at some convenient future time, and thus brings to the surface of the medium's consciousness.

(6) *The Production of Cross-correspondence.* At a sitting on February 9th, 1911, with Sir Oliver Lodge as sitter, Lodge put a question to the Gurney-persona as to how the communicators produce the various interlocking scripts, written by different automatists, which together constitute a cross-correspondence. In sittings held with Lodge during the next few months the Gurney-persona repeatedly expressed the wish that *Balfour*, who had not as yet been a sitter, should be present. The reason given was that he would be interested in the *process* rather than in the *product*. (It should be noted that Balfour, a distinguished classical scholar with strong philosophical interests, had had much to do with the interpretation of the cross-correspondences. Somewhat later he published elaborate accounts of two of the most complex and impressive of these cases, viz. the 'Statius Case', S.P.R. *Proceedings*, Vol. XXVII, and the 'Ear of Dionysius Case', S.P.R. *Proceedings*, Vol. XXIX.)

Balfour had his first sitting with Mrs Willett on June 4th, 1911. At this sitting the Gurney-persona made a long statement about the way in which the scrappy allusive scripts, which contain the materials for cross-correspondences, are produced. He said that he found it very hard to describe the process clearly, and that at the end he felt uncertain whether and to what extent Balfour had understood him. He amplified his first statement at a later sitting on October 8th, 1911. The gist of what he said at these two sittings is as follows.

The original theme of a cross-correspondence is chosen by the communicator. It is not known to any of the automatists concerned, and it is through the communicator's influence that the relevant ideas reach their respective minds and are expressed in their several scripts. At this stage the communicator has in his own mind a mass of interconnected ideas, appropriate to the theme which is to form the subject of the cross-correspondence.

The communicator then does something which is metaphorically described as 'bringing the medium into a room'. This seems to mean performing on her some kind of telepathic action which puts her into a position to read this part of the communicator's mind. The medium then becomes aware telaesthetically of this part of the content of the communicator's mind, without further interference or guidance on his part. At the same time the communicator rummages about telaesthetically in the medium's mind, takes note of certain of her pre-existing ideas and associations which are relevant to his theme, and somehow 'earmarks' them from the rest.

This stage is followed by a period of *incubation*, which may last for some time. During this a subliminal process, which the Gurney-persona describes by the metaphorical term 'weaving', goes on in the medium's mind. The result of this would seem to be to link up the relevant material which she had acquired telaesthetically by reading the part of the communicator's mind which he has laid open to her, with the relevant material which was already in her mind and had been selected and earmarked by the communicator. A further result of the weaving process is to clothe this linked material in a symbolic and allusive guise. The process as a whole is said to be indispensable but risky. One of its alleged dangers is that the medium may lose, in the course of the weaving process, some of the knowledge which she has acquired telaesthetically from the communicator. Another danger is that the symbolization may distort the theme, or be misunderstood by those who are to collate the scripts and interpret them.

Finally, at the time when the script is to be produced, the communicator acts telepathically on the medium. He selects certain items from the mass of woven material in her subconsciousness, and by telepathic action tries to ensure that these, and only these, shall rise to her normal consciousness and be expressed in her automatic script. At much the same time, in another automatist taking part in the same cross-correspondence experiment, the communicator will select different, but complementary, items from the mass of woven material in *her* subconsciousness; and will cause *them* to rise to consciousness and to be expressed in *her* automatic script.

The above is alleged to be the *main* way in which cross-correspondences are produced. But the Gurney-persona said that it may be supplemented on occasion by the use of what I have called 'telepathic imposition'. Here the communicator deliberately imposes certain particular ideas on the medium's mind telepathically, as a hypnotist might do by verbal suggestion. The Gurney-persona gave an instance of a cross-correspondence which was, he said, produced by telepathically imposing a certain idea on the mind of medium *A*, and at the same time making the complementary idea emerge in the script of medium *B* by telepathically guiding it to the surface from the (in part) telaesthetically acquired mass of woven material in her subconsciousness.

(III) *Views of the Ostensible Communicators on certain Philosophical Topics*

I pass now to the views expressed by the ostensible communicators on certain topics which may loosely be called 'philosophical'. The most important sittings in which such topics were discussed were those of October 8th, 1911, January 21st, 1912, and March 5th, 1912. Balfour was the sitter. It should be borne in mind that he was greatly interested and very well read in philosophy. His own position may be described as predominantly, though not uncritically, Hegelian, like that of most of his academic philosophical contemporaries in England and the U.S.A. The Gurney-persona was the ostensible communicator, but he professed to be speaking on behalf of Myers rather than expressing his own views. There was also a sitting on May 11th, 1912, in which the *persona* of the philosopher Henry Sidgwick (Balfour's deceased brother-in-law) participated, though the main communicator claimed to be Gurney.

It is interesting to note the attitude of Mrs Willett, both in her trance-state and in her normal waking state, to these ostensible communications. It may fairly be described as one of boredom and bewilderment. In the course of the sitting on January 21st, 1912, e.g., when the Gurney-persona was discussing in technical language certain difficult philosophical problems, she exclaimed: 'Oh, Edmund, you do *bore* me so!' In the sitting of May 11th, 1912, she had enormous difficulties in getting the technical word 'interaction' (in reference to the relation of mind and body in the human individual) through, though it was obvious to the sitter that this must be what was meant in the context. She drew in the air with her finger what she described as 'a plait, of woven strands', and said: 'It's like that!' Finally, she wrote the four words INT UR AC SHUN; whereupon the Gurney-persona made a pun about 'Ur of the Chaldees', and remarked that the substitution of UR for ER would make Myers, who is sensitive to niceties of sound, shudder.

It looks as if the subliminal part of Mrs Willett was so bored with the whole tedious business that it became mulish, and refused to write or to speak a word which must have been quite familiar to her in other contexts. When these philosophical scripts were shown to Mrs Willett for the first time, many years later, she reacted in a way which would do credit to a present-day member of the fashionable 'Common-Language School' of philosophy. She exclaimed: 'It's all so much Greek to me!', and said that it left her utterly bored and bewildered.

Balfour says that the philosophy of the ostensible communications seems to be neo-Kantian or Hegelian, and is much more idealistic (in the technical philosophical sense) than that of Myers in *Human Personality*. A typical sentence is one that occurred at the sitting of May 24th, 1911, viz. 'The Absolute labours to attain self-consciousness through the myriad self-created sentient beings.' Mrs Willett, on being shown this script at a much later date, said that she had not the faintest idea where these thoughts came from.

The philosophical topics discussed fall under the following headings: (1) the problem of the interrelations of mind and body in a human individual; (2) the structure of the human self; and (3) the relation of the human self to the Absolute. I will now consider very briefly what the ostensible communicators have to say under each of these headings.

(1) *The Mind–Body Problem*. Nothing very illuminating was said on this topic. As we have seen, the medium was particularly recalcitrant to expressing the ideas which the ostensible communicators sought to convey through her. I will content myself with quoting the penultimate remark of the Gurney-persona on this subject. 'You can't make parallelism square with the conclusions to which recent research points. *Pauvres parallélistes!* They're like drowning men clinging to spars. But the epiphenomenalist bosh, that's simply blown away! It's one of the blind alleys of human thought.' Sidgwick is reported by the Gurney-persona as saying (with characteristic judiciousness) of the theory of interaction: 'Thread the maze, but don't lose the strand. There is a lot of confused thinking suggested by that word to many minds. You've all of you been fingering at the outsides of the theory, but it's there where the gold lies!'

So we may at least conclude that the ostensible communicators accept *some* form of interactionism, though none that has as yet been formulated, and that they definitely reject the rival theories of parallelism and epiphenomenalism.

(2) *The Structure of the Human Self*. The main points which the Gurney-persona makes under this head are the following:

(i) In the self of an ordinary human being one must distinguish three factors, viz. the *supraliminal*, the *subliminal*, and the *transcendental*. (ii) The subliminal part has several layers; but the transcendental self is something different from even the deepest stratum of the subliminal. (iii) Though it is common, and may often be convenient, to talk of the supraliminal 'self' and the subliminal 'self' of one individual, e.g. of Mr Smith, that is not strictly correct. They are *not* two selves, as, e.g., the selves of the two individuals, Mr Smith and Mr Jones, are. They are two parts or aspects or strata of a single self, which interact continuously with each other in a way quite different from the *telepathic* interaction which may take place between two genuine complete selves. (iv) Ordinary cases of dissociated personality, such, e.g., as the Beauchamp case, are pathological. They are due to organic disturbance in the individual's body. It is misleading to use them to interpret the normal relationship between the supraliminal and the subliminal parts of the self of an ordinary healthy individual. (v) All three factors, viz. the supraliminal, the subliminal, and the transcendental, contribute contents which persist after bodily death. But the following changes then take place. (*a*) Some elements of the contents of the supraliminal part of the *ante mortem* self vanish altogether, whilst the rest blend with the contents of its subliminal part. (*b*) The subliminal part of the *ante mortem* self, together with these additions from its supraliminal part, becomes the *supraliminal* part of the *post mortem* self. (*c*) The transcendental part of the *ante mortem* self becomes the *subliminal* part of the *post mortem* self.

It would appear from all this that the ostensible communicators hold that the *ante mortem* embodied self of a human individual is a triadic or three-storied system, and that it becomes a dyadic or two-storied one after the death of the body. It must be confessed that they give no clear account of the nature and functions of the *transcendental* part of the human self. (It is perhaps worth remarking that a distinction between the so-called 'transcendental' and 'empirical' selves plays an important part in Kant's philosophy in general and his metaphysic of morals in particular.)

Before leaving this topic of the reported structure of the human self, I would revert to a matter which I have already touched upon when dealing with what the Gurney-persona has to say about *telaesthesia*. It will be remembered that he made to Balfour, on January 21st, 1912, a complicated statement, in which he distinguished several different levels in the medium's subliminal self. What I wish to add here is this. In the first place, Balfour says that this statement differed in verbal form from all similar utterances of comparable length. Such utterances were generally punctuated by frequent repetitions of the phrase 'he says', as if the communicator paused after delivering each sentence to the medium, while she quoted it to the sitter. But the ostensible communication at present under discussion was uttered *continuously*, as if the medium were repeating it as she heard it, without attempting to understand the words and sentences.

Passing now to the content of this statement, the gist of it, so far as I can attach any clear meaning to it, seems to be as follows. In the medium's subliminal self we must distinguish at least three strata, which may be denoted by H_0, H_1, and H_2. H_0 is the deepest, i.e. the one which is most remote from the medium's normal everyday consciousness. It is this which telaesthetically acquires knowledge from the mind of the communicator. H_2 is the most superficial stratum, and it is this which is immediately responsible for the emergence of ideas in the form of words and sentences uttered by the medium. H_1 is a stratum intermediate between H_0 and H_2.

So far the doctrine is comparatively clear. But now comes a very obscure statement. It is alleged that the information acquired telaesthetically by the stratum H_0 cannot be transmitted in its original form either to H_1 or to H_2. It has first to undergo a process which is said to be analogous to *crystallization*. This seems to consist in breaking up the information, which exists in an unanalysed and unverbalized form in H_0, into various items, and in then associating each item with a concrete symbol.

This process of 'crystallization' is said to be performed *jointly* by H_0 and the communicators, who decide between them which are the most suitable ways of itemizing the information and symbolizing it, in order to get the message uttered. It would seem that the 'crystals' are produced in the intermediate stratum H_1 of the subliminal part of the medium's mind. And it would seem that it is the collection of these 'crystals' of itemized and symbolized information, originally acquired telaesthetically, which form the contents of the so-called 'room', about which we have heard so much. Nor is even this the whole story. It is said that finally there occurs a process which is described as 'binding'. This consists in H_1 passing on to H_2 in 'crystallized' form certain parts of the information which has been transmitted to it from H_0. H_2, which has control of the medium's organs of speech and writing, thereupon utters these items in automatic talk or script.

It is idle to pretend that this statement is at all clear in itself, or that one can discover its precise relation to earlier statements on the same topic which I have already summarized. Is 'crystallization', e.g., just another metaphorical name for the process formerly described as 'weaving'? Are 'crystallization' and 'binding' perhaps two processes, which were not before distinguished, but were lumped

311

together under the one name of 'weaving'? However that may be, there seems to be an inconsistency between the present statements and the earlier ones on the same topic. For it is now alleged that the material to be conveyed in the message is chosen *jointly* by the communicator and H_0, the deepest layer of the medium's subliminal stratum; whilst the earlier statements alleged that it is chosen *entirely by the communicator* without the medium's knowledge. Possibly the solution is that the earlier statement refers to the *initiation* of a message, and the later one to subsequent processes involved in conveying the material to the medium and getting her co-operation in uttering it.

Admitting all that can fairly be said about metaphor, obscurity, and *prima facie* inconsistency in this part of the ostensible communications, we must not be too hard on the ostensible communicators. Is there much less metaphor, obscurity, and *prima facie* incoherence in, e.g., Freud's account of the Id, the Ego, the Superego, the Censor, and their interrelations? Or, to take another instance, in Kant's account in the *Critique of Pure Reason* of the various factors alleged to be involved in the ordinary human awareness of self and of external objects? At any rate, it may fairly be said that the Gurney-persona is pellucidly clear, even in his darkest utterances, in comparison with, e.g., Hegel or Whitehead at their not infrequent worst.

(3) *Relation of the Human Self to the Absolute*. The main points here, so far as I can understand them, are the following:

(i) It seems to be suggested that the *transcendental* part of a human self stands to the Absolute in a relation which is roughly analogous to that in which the supraliminal part of an incarnate human mind stands to its subliminal part. (Since it has never been made clear to us what the ostensible communicators understand by the 'transcendental' part of a human self, or what they understand by 'the Absolute', this is not particularly illuminating. No doubt the Gurney-persona might fairly assume that Balfour and his philosophical contemporaries would be familiar with both these terms from their studies in Kant and in Hegel, and that they would associate appropriate ideas with them.) (ii) Finite selves are said to originate through a process of self-limitation on the Absolute's part, by means of which it attains to self-consciousness. (This doctrine is characteristic of Hegel, though it has no doubt been held, in one form or another, by many thinkers of an idealistic type.) (iii) It seems to be suggested that finite selves also, no less than the Absolute, attain to self-consciousness by a process of self-limitation.

TENTATIVE APPRAISAL OF THE UTTERANCES

I will end this chapter with a few words on the weight to be attached to the content of these ostensible communications through Mrs Willett.

I think it must be admitted that what the ostensible communicators tell us on the metaphysical problems which they handle does not add anything, either in content or by way of elucidation or support, to what so many mystics and idealistic philosophers have so obscurely adumbrated. As Dr Johnson remarked, when he compared a woman's preaching to a dog's walking on its hind legs: 'It is not done well, but you are surprised to find it done at all.' Surely it *is* very surprising indeed that anything of this kind should come from a lady so completely uninterested in and ignorant of philosophy as Mrs Willett was, and that it should be couched in language and dramatic form so characteristic of the persons ostensibly communicating.

Leaving the ostensible communicators' contributions to *philosophy* with a smile or a sigh, what are we to say of their detailed and fairly coherent statements about the conditions under which they have to work, about the processes involved in communicating in general and in producing cross-correspondences in particular, and about the *ante mortem* and the *post mortem* structure of the human mind?

As of the philosophical statements, the *least* that one can say is this. The mere utterance, by the lips and the pencil of a woman of Mrs Willett's normal range of interests and knowledge, of a long coherent series of statements of this kind, in the form of conversations by the deceased Gurney and Myers with the living Lord Balfour, about topics which had been the main interest in life of the ostensible communicators, is a fairly startling fact.

Suppose we altogether rule out the suggestion that Myers and Gurney in some sense survived bodily death and were the deliberate initiators of these utterances. We shall then have to postulate in some stratum of Mrs Willett's mind rather remarkable powers of acquiring information from unread books or the minds of living persons or both; of clothing it in phraseology characteristic of Myers and of Gurney, whom she had never met; and of working it up and putting it forth in a dramatic form which seemed to their friend Balfour to be natural and convincing.

Suppose, on the other hand, that we admit at least the possibility that Myers and Gurney may in some sense have survived bodily death, and that these utterances may *really* originate in them, as they *ostensibly* do. Then they will have the added interest that they may contain information 'straight from the horse's mouth' on topics about which the communicators should be well informed. Even on that hypothesis, there should be no question of swallowing the statements uncritically. Henry Labouchere once remarked, with reference to his parliamentary colleague Bradlaugh, that the mere fact that a man does not believe in God is not a sufficient reason for taking his opinion on more important matters for Gospel. Similarly, the mere fact (if it be a fact) that a man has survived bodily death is not a sufficient reason for supposing him to have become omniscient or infallible, or in general any wiser than he was before the death of his body. But it would not be unreasonable to think that he might have first-hand information, not directly available to us, about the *post mortem* conditions in which he and his friends exist and operate, about his own relations with persons still living in the physical body, and so on.

Suppose, further, that the ostensible communicator were, as he claims to be, identical with a certain person who was, in his earthly life, specially interested in the problems of human personality in general and of mediumship in particular. Then it would not be unreasonable to think that he might have first-hand information about the processes involved and the difficulties encountered in communicating through a medium.

Ostensible communications on these topics, coming from ostensible communicators who claim to be Gurney, Myers, Sidgwick, etc., and who speak and act in character, should therefore be treated with respect as possibly containing first-hand and expert information. In view of the admitted limitations of the ostensible communicators' own knowledge, and of the difficulties which they very plausibly allege to exist in getting their thoughts across to the medium and in getting her to express them without omission, addition, or distortion, we should be most unwise to treat these ostensible communications as oracles. But it would also be unwise merely to record with astonishment the *fact of their occurrence*, and to attach no weight to their *specific content* as containing possibly first-hand information from experts about the topics with which they deal.

314

XIII

SALTMARSH'S INVESTIGATION OF
MRS WARREN ELLIOTT'S
MEDIUMSHIP

IN the present chapter I shall give a fairly full account of what I regard as a model investigation of a case of trance-mediumship. The medium was Mrs Warren Elliott, a professional. The investigation was conducted in a series of sittings with her by the late Mr H. F. Saltmarsh of the S.P.R. towards the end of the 1920s. His report is to be found in S.P.R. *Proceedings*, Vol. XXXIX.

GENERAL ACCOUNT OF THE EXPERIMENTS

I will begin by giving a general account of the nature of the experiments and of the characteristic features of Mrs Warren Elliott's mediumship.

(1) *The Use of 'Relics'*. Like a good many other mediums, Mrs Elliott finds it helpful or even necessary to have presented to her at the seance some article, e.g. a ring, a lock of hair, a letter, etc., which has been connected with the dead person with whom she is to try to make contact. We may call such an object a 'relic'. There is no plausible theory, so far as I know, as to how relics function. But it is a fact that the handling of an inanimate object does sometimes enable a medium in some way to make statements relevant to events in the life of some person or persons who are or have been connected, either directly, or indirectly through the intervention of some third party, with that object.

Now the sittings in this investigation fall into two groups, according to the way in which the relic was presented to the medium. (i) In one group the person who owned the relic would take it along with him or her to a sitting with the medium, would hand it to her

315

at the beginning, and would receive it back from her at the end. These may be described as 'Owner-present sittings'. I will denote them, for short, by the phrase 'O-P sittings'. (ii) The other group of sittings were conducted in the following way. A number of persons were asked to send one relic apiece to the Secretary of the S.P.R. at the Society's offices. On receipt of any such relic the Secretary would put it into an envelope, write a number on the outside, put the envelope with its contents into a certain locked cupboard, and enter the number (together with the sender's name and address) in a certain book. On the day on which a sitting of this kind was to be held, the person from the S.P.R. who was to sit with Mrs Elliott would choose one of these envelopes at random, take it along to the seance, and hand it to the medium, just as the owner would have done at an O-P sitting. At the end the sitter would receive it back from the medium and return it at once to the Secretary of the S.P.R. Such seances as these may be described as 'Owner-absent sittings', and denoted for short by the phrase 'O-A sittings'. In two and only two cases the same relic was used at two O-A sittings.

Sometimes Mrs Elliott would open the packet, and sometimes hold it unopened in her hand. This seemed to make no significant difference to the degree of relevance or accuracy of her utterances. In *all* the sittings the owner's name was unknown to the medium. In the O-A sittings it was unknown to the sitter also. In the O-P sittings the owner was the sitter, and was accompanied by a shorthand-writer supplied by the S.P.R., who took down everything said by either the owner or the medium. In the O-A sittings the only sitter was the note-taker. Altogether four persons were employed as note-takers, but most of the note-taking was in fact done by two only of these. The names of the note-takers, with one exception, were unknown to the medium, though she knew that they came from the S.P.R. In the O-A sittings the owner of the relic was quite unaware that a sitting was being held at which the relic submitted by him or her to the S.P.R. would be handed to the medium.

(2) *Recording and Marking*. Mrs Elliott had a control who called herself 'Topsy'. In *all* the O-P sittings the medium went into a trance, and the ostensible communications were through the Topsy-persona. That holds for *most* of the O-A sittings also. But in some of these Mrs Elliott, apparently in her normal waking state, would simply dictate her impressions to the note-taker. There was no significant difference in degree of relevance or of accuracy of the information conveyed at O-A sittings by these two methods.

After each sitting the shorthand record was typed out, and a copy was sent to the owner of the relic which had been used. (This would, of course, be identical with the sitter in the case of an O-P sitting.) The owner was instructed to annotate it, and then return it with the annotations to the S.P.R. Mr Saltmarsh would then go through each record and would note the various items mentioned in it. To each of these he would assign a reference number. Thereafter the annotated record was put into an envelope, on the front of which was written a complete list of the items referred to, with their reference numbers.

It was found that certain items tended to repeat themselves in the various records with abnormal frequency. Saltmarsh describes these as '*clichés*'. He noted about one hundred of these, and entered them into a card-index. (An example of a *cliché* was the abnormally frequent mention of an injury to the leg or foot.)

Saltmarsh divided the ostensible communications into '*ante mortem*' (A-M) and '*post mortem*' (P-M), according as they referred to events alleged to have happened *before* or *after* the death of the ostensible communicator. He sub-divided each of these classes into 'physical' (ϕ) and 'non-physical' (non-ϕ). A reported event or circumstance was counted as *physical*, if and only if it were such that an ordinary observer, coming suddenly on the scene at the time and place referred to, would have witnessed it if it had existed or happened there and then. We thus have four ultimate sub-divisions in respect of subject-matter, viz. (A-M)-ϕ, (A-M)-(non-ϕ), (P-M)-ϕ, and (P-M)-(non-ϕ).

We come now to the scoring of the records. This was done in every case by Saltmarsh himself, on the basis of the comments made on the record by the owner of the relic employed at the sitting. For purposes of scoring Saltmarsh divided the statements into three groups, viz. 'vague' (V), 'definite' (D), and 'characteristic' (C). A V-statement is one of a thoroughly commonplace character, likely to fit a large proportion of persons. A D-statement is one which, while it might fit a fair proportion of persons, is not so commonplace as to be as likely as not to be true of any person chosen at random. A C-statement is one which would be most unlikely to be true of a person chosen at random. Saltmarsh assigned to any *true* statement 1 mark, if he judged it to be *vague*: 5 marks, if he judged it to be *definite*; and 20 marks, if he judged it to be *characteristic*.

The maximum possible score for a record was calculated by supposing that *all* the statements in it had been *true*, marking them in accordance with the above scale, and then adding the marks. The actual score would, of course, always be considerably less; for some of the statements would be false, and these would get no marks. Some records contained very few definite or characteristic statements. In such cases Saltmarsh made a deduction of 10 per cent from the gross actual score. The resulting nett score was the one finally assigned in such cases. The mark eventually assigned to any record is the *ratio* of the nett actual score to the maximum possible score, measured as a percentage.

Saltmarsh admits that simple addition is almost certainly an unsatisfactory way of combining the marks assigned to the various items in a record. He points out, too, that we must not regard the ratio of the actual nett score to the maximum possible score for a record as representing the *absolute* value of the communications at the sitting in question. At best such percentages furnish a means of *comparing* the values of the communications received at different sittings and under various conditions. That was in fact the only use which Saltmarsh made of them.

The question naturally arises: How far can we rely upon the owners' annotations? Saltmarsh instituted the following check on them. He sent copies of the records of certain selected O-A sittings to persons quite unconnected with the owners of the relics used on those occasions. Each such person was asked to imagine that the record which he was to annotate was that of a sitting at which a relic contributed by himself had been used, and to annotate it on that assumption. Saltmarsh then marked these records, on the plan explained above, in accordance with the annotations of the pseudo-owners. He then compared the percentage scores thus obtained with those which he had assigned to the same records on the basis of the annotations made by the actual owners of the relics employed.

Two checks of this kind were carried out. In the first of them, all the records related to one and the same ostensible communicator, who claimed to be a certain airman killed in action. There were 53 records referring to this individual. Saltmarsh chose for the pseudo-owners six persons, all of whom he knew to have lost a son or a brother, of about the same age as the ostensible communicator, in rather similar circumstances to those in which he had died. He divided up the records among these six. The results were as follows. The aggregate of the scores for these records, derived from the annotations made by the actual owners was 4,107, whilst the aggregate derived from the annotations of the pseudo-owners was 452. The aggregate maximum possible score was 5,642. So the percentage score based on the annotations by the actual owners was 72·8 per cent, whilst that based on those of the pseudo-owners was only 8 per cent. If, however, we consider *individual* markings, we find that, with *two* of the pseudo-owners, the percentage scores based on their annotations do not differ so significantly from that based on the annotations of the actual owners. In the case of both these pseudo-owners, as it happened, the percentage score assigned on the basis of their annotations was the same, viz. 17 per cent. The scores assigned on the basis

318

of the annotations of the actual owners were in one case 64 per cent and in the other 80 per cent.

The other check was conducted as follows. Saltmarsh had copies made of the records of 19 O-A sittings which had scored *high* percentage marks on the annotations of the actual owners. He made use of 15 pseudo-owners. He selected at random sets of 5 records out of these 19, and sent such sets to the pseudo-owners to be annotated. Of the pseudo-owners two annotated two sets of 5 apiece, whilst the remaining 13 each annotated one set of 5. Thus Saltmarsh received back in all 20 + 65 = 85 annotated copies of records of these 19 O-A sittings. Owing to his random selection of sets of 5, a set sent to one pseudo-owner on one occasion might overlap a set sent to another on another occasion. Thus, e.g., the record of one of the 19 O-A sittings was annotated by no less than 9 pseudo-owners, whilst the records of some others were annotated only by one pseudo-owner.

The aggregate maximum possible score for these 19 records was 5,554, and the aggregate actual score assigned by Saltmarsh on the basis of the annotations by the actual owners was 3,226. The percentage was therefore 58·1 per cent. Saltmarsh does not make it quite clear to me how he proceeded to get a comparable aggregate figure on the basis of the annotations made by the pseudo-owners. It seems obvious that, in the case of any record that had been annotated by *more than one* pseudo-owner, it would be necessary to take the average of the marks assigned to it on the basis of the annotations of each pseudo-owner to whom a copy of that record was submitted. In the case of any record that had been annotated by *only one* pseudo-owner, Saltmarsh would simply take the marks which he would assign to it on the basis of that person's annotations. The comparable aggregate score would then be the sum, for all 19 records, of the *average* scores assigned in cases of the first kind and the *actual* scores assigned in cases of the second kind. Whether Saltmarsh in fact proceeded in this way or not, the aggregate score that he gives in respect of the 85 annotations by his 15 pseudo-owners is 487. This is only 8·75 per cent of the maximum possible score of 5,554, as compared with the percentage of 58·1 per cent on the basis of annotations by the actual owners.

Here again, however, the aggregate result masks certain individual cases where the percentage score on the basis of annotation by a pseudo-owner came much nearer to that based on those of the actual owner. Thus, in the case of three pseudo-owners, each of whom annotated five records, the percentage scores based on their annotations were 23 per cent, 28 per cent, and 33 per cent, whilst those based on the annotations of the real owners were respectively 52 per cent, 59 per cent, and 46 per cent. Such differences seem hardly significant, though they are all in the same direction.

Everyone must decide for himself, on the basis of such figures as I have given, whether it is or is not reasonable to hold that the amount of agreement between the medium's statements and the relevant facts, as stated by the owners of the relics submitted to her, was significantly greater than might be expected through chance-coincidence. Saltmarsh admitted the crudity of the tests and the uncertainty of any inferences drawn from them. Later he and Dr Soal devised a much better general method of estimation, which, after being submitted to Sir Ronald Fisher and amended in certain respects by him, was published, under the title 'A Method of Estimating the Supernormal Content of Mediumistic Communications', in Vol. XXXIX of the S.P.R. *Proceedings.* The problem has been attacked since then by several experts in the U.S.A. The reader may be referred to the following papers: Pratt, 'Toward a Method of evaluating Mediumistic Material' *(Bulletin of the Boston S.P.R.,* 1936); Pratt and Birge, 'Appraising Verbal Test-material in Parapsychology' *(Journal of Parapsychology,* 1948); and Schmeidler, 'Analysis and Evaluation of Proxy Sessions with Mrs Caroline Chapman' *(Journal of Parapsychology,* 1958). For a startling example of how a complete stranger, when asked to annotate a mediumistic communication which seemed extremely appropriate to the peculiar circumstances of the actual sitter, *may* find it no less appropriate to himself and his own circumstances, the reader may be referred to a contribution by Mr Denys Parsons to S.P.R. *Proceedings,* Vol. XLVIII, entitled 'On the Need for Caution in assessing Mediumistic Material'.

(3) *The main Statistical Results.* We can now pass to the main statistical results of the investigation. These may be roughly summarized as follows. (i) The percentage of true statements in O-P sittings is about *half as much again* as in O-A sittings (76·3 : 52 per cent). (ii) The number of *post mortem* and of *ante mortem* statements in the whole lot of sittings is roughly the same (P-M 1619, A-M 1592); but the former contain a somewhat higher percentage of *true* statements than the latter (P-M 74 per cent, A-M 66·3 per cent). (iii) The physical statements are considerably more numerous than the non-physical (ϕ 2470, non-ϕ 741). But they contain a *lower* percentage of *true* statements than the latter (ϕ 66 per cent, non-ϕ 84·5 per cent). Among the *ante mortem* statements those about the ostensible communicator are much more numerous than those about the sitter; but among *post mortem* statements the opposite is the case.

SALTMARSH'S CONCLUSIONS AND REFLEXIONS

The results of the sittings can be considered from two points of view, viz. from the light which they throw on the *psychological* processes involved, and with regard to the question: Do they require us to postulate anything *paranormal*, and, if so, *what*? I am concerned here primarily with the former aspects of the case.

(1) *'Fishing'*, *Groping*, etc. It might well be thought that a medium, making a number of statements under the conditions described, would indulge in a certain amount of *deliberate invention*, and might further try to discover, by means of *'fishing'*, what statements would be likely to be appropriate.

Saltmarsh found no evidence for deliberate invention. At most there are the *clichés*, already mentioned; the occurrence later in a sitting of statements which would be easy inferences from what had gone before; and the occurrence of many commonplace statements which would fit most people.

As to 'fishing', this was of course impossible in the O-A sittings, since the sitter had no relevant normally acquired information for the medium to fish from. As regards the O-P sittings, Saltmarsh's comment is: 'Topsy does not *fish*, but she does *grope*'. What he means is this. Whatever may be the source of the information, it is certain that it comes to Topsy by means of *visual symbols*, which she has to interpret as best she can. Often she does not understand the symbolism, and then she is liable to offer alternative interpretations of it. Even when she has in fact hit on what seems to be the correct interpretation, she does not always realize that she has done so.

The Topsy-persona has certain mental or verbal habits, which show themselves in her utterances. (i) She gives certain names and initials much more frequently than they occur in contemporary England. Saltmarsh instituted a comparison between the frequency with which various male Christian names occurred in the communications and the frequency with which those names had occurred over the previous thirty-five years among the boys at a large public school. There were very great discrepancies, sometimes in excess and sometimes in defect. (ii) She has a habit of giving names that begin with the sound ROJ or ROD. (iii) She gives many highly fantastic names, and these tend to begin with the letter O. (It may be relevant that Mrs Elliott's maiden name was *Ortner*.)

In many sittings there is a great deal of completely unverifiable material given. Saltmarsh tried, as a check, a certain number of sittings at which the article handed to the medium as a relic was in fact something *completely new*. In all these sittings there was plenty

321

of ostensible communication, similar in style and character to that given when there was a genuine relic. These utterances were completely irrelevant to the person contributing the pseudo-relic, and seem to have been wholly 'in the air'. It is, however, of some interest to remark that in most of these cases the Topsy-persona alleged, with regard to the ostensible communicator, that he or she was *not* connected with the object that had been handed to her. The successive items in the utterances on such occasions had very little interconnexion with each other. Saltmarsh was inclined to compare them to a series of hypnagogic images, rising from some stratum in the medium's subconsciousness. He suggests that these images are probably generated from traces left on the medium's mind by incidents at previous sittings or in her ordinary daily life. Such internally generated images form the *matrix* in *all* the sittings. In a successful sitting, with a genuine relic, the veridical matter (however it may originate) is imbedded in this matrix of reminiscent fantasy.

(2) *Influences which might be operative.* We can now consider various influences which might conceivably affect the results, and ask ourselves whether they in fact do so. Saltmarsh discussed in turn the *owners of the relics*, the *note-takers*, the *nature of the relic* submitted, and the *condition of the medium* at the time of the sitting. I will follow that order.

(i) *Influence of Owners.* We can divide the owners into three classes, viz. (*a*) bereaved persons strongly affected emotionally, (*b*) bereaved persons not strongly affected, and (*c*) non-bereaved persons. Each of these classes can then be sub-divided into three sub-classes, viz. (α) those convinced of survival, (β) those with an open mind on the subject, and (γ) those convinced of non-survival. The results of the sittings can be classified as *good, moderate,* or *poor.* The question is whether there is any significant association between belonging to such and such a class of sitters and getting results of such and such a degree of goodness.

Now we must begin by allowing for the fact that a bereaved person whose emotions are strongly affected, or a person who is convinced of survival, will be likely, in annotating the record of a sitting which concerns himself, to stretch points which seem to favour the view that a deceased friend or relative has survived and is communicating. This applies both to O-A and O-P sittings. But we must remember, further, that at O-P sittings the owner is also the sitter. Now sitters of the two kinds just mentioned would be likely to give *more encouragement* to the medium, even if they do not inadvertently give away information; and that may suffice by itself to secure better

322

results. Moreover, such sitters *may* also give hints by gestures or changes of facial expression. These would not get recorded by the note-taker, though *verbal* indiscretions would appear on the record and could be allowed for. After taking all this into account, Saltmarsh found *no* significant association, positive or negative, between an owner being of any one of his nine categories and the results with his relic falling into any one of his three grades.

The following negative fact is of some interest. No less than seven of the owners claimed to have some kind of 'psychic' gifts. There was *no* significant association, positive or negative, between this alleged characteristic of an owner and the goodness, indifference, or badness of the results claimed with his or her relic.

(ii) *Influence of Note-takers*. It will be remembered that most of the note-taking was done by a certain two of the four note-takers. It happened that one of these had contributed a relic, and that some of the best results obtained were at sittings at which that relic was used. Now at some of the sittings at which this person was note-taker, and relics belonging to *other persons* were used, it looks as if *her* special ostensible communicator 'intruded'. By this I mean that communications purporting to refer to *that* individual tended to mingle with those that purported to refer to the deceased person associated with the relic that was being used at the time. Apart from this, it was found that the Topsy-persona quite often referred to the contemporary circumstances of the person who was acting as *note-taker*, and that her references were often so apposite as to suggest sporadic telepathy from the latter.

(iii) *Influence of the Relic*. The question here is whether the medium could have been influenced in her utterances in a perfectly normal way by what she could see or feel of the relic. The answer appears to be decidedly in the negative. In some sittings the package was not opened by the medium at all. In others the sitting began with the package unopened, and later on the Topsy-persona, finding that she was not getting on well, would open it. There was no significant difference in the results in the two cases.

(iv) *Influence of the Medium's Condition*. Some of the most successful sittings took place when the medium was tired or disturbed by external noises. As already stated, she was in trance at all the O-P sittings, but not at all the O-A sittings. If one compares the results of the O-A sittings in which she was in trance with those of the O-A sittings in which she was in her normal state, there is *no* significant difference either in the proportion of true statements or in the distribution of the statements into vague, definite, or characteristic. If Mrs Elliott liked the sitter, the chances of a good sitting were increased; but such liking was no guarantee of a good sitting.

(3) *Certain General Features of the Sittings.* The following general remarks may be added about certain features in the sittings:

(i) It was of no use to put *direct questions* to the Topsy-persona, for it was seldom that any relevant and definite answer was given. She jumps about from one topic to another, and it was seldom possible for the sitter at the time, or for the experimenter reflecting at leisure afterwards, to discover the links between successive topics. That is true also, though to a lesser extent, of those O-A sittings at which Mrs Elliott was in her normal state.

It appears, therefore, that the links between successive topics are not those of obvious association. There may, of course, be associative links private to the Topsy-persona or to Mrs Elliott, as the case may be.

(ii) In this connexion it may be of interest to consider the *clichés*, i.e. words and ideas which recur with abnormal frequency, which are not mere commonplaces, and which yet have no obvious relevance to the owner of the relic or to the note-taker. Saltmarsh compares them to the recurrent dreams which many people have. He notes also that, in persons who have hypnagogic imagery, such imagery tends to be recurrent and typical of the individual concerned. He suggests that the *clichés* may originate partly in symbols whose meaning is not clear to the medium or to her control, partly in reminiscences of other sittings, and partly from normal associations due to certain conjunctions of experiences peculiar to the medium in her daily life.

(iii) A third feature to be considered is the so-called 'intrusions', which happen at certain O-A sittings. The essential point is that on such occasions communications appear to be coming from, or to be about, a certain recognizable communicator, but one who is altogether unconcerned either with the relic which is being used, or with its absent owner, or with the note-taker who is present and may be regarded as the sitter.

There were two fairly persistent intruders. One purported to be Mrs *Dora Irving*, the deceased wife of the Rev. W. S. Irving, a member of the S.P.R. who had had frequent sittings with Mrs Leonard, at many of which that medium had been ostensibly possessed by the Dora-persona. (We have already made her acquaintance in Chapter XI, in connexion with Whately Carington's psychological and statistical work on Mrs Leonard's mediumship.) The other purported to be the deceased airman 'A', already referred to in the present chapter. Excellent ostensible communications, purporting to come from him, had been received at thirteen O-P sittings and seven O-A sittings in the present series, where a relic associated with him was used. He appeared as an 'intruder' in six other sittings, in which relics associated with other persons were used, and in which neither the owner nor the note-taker had any connexion with him. It may be remarked that both these intruders had shown themselves to be plausible and persistent ostensible communicators, in conditions where they were *not* intruding, e.g. in sittings with Mrs Leonard. Probably an ostensible communicator of whom that was not true would have failed to establish his or her identity sufficiently to be recognized if he or she were to intrude.

It is of interest to note that the Topsy-persona or normal Mrs Elliott, as the case might be, often recognized when the ostensible communicator was *not* connected with the relic submitted at the time. She had a characteristic symbolic experience on such occasions, viz. a visual image or a *quasi*-sensory visual hallucination as of the purporting communicator 'waving aside' the relic.

(4) *The Nature of the Symbolism.* This brings us to the general topic of the symbolism employed in Mrs Elliott's mediumship. Besides the example just given, we may adduce the following illustrations. Family relationship, or absence of it, between ostensible communicator and sitter is repeatedly symbolized for the Topsy-persona by ostensibly seeing the former as *close beside* (or, respectively, as *remote from*) the latter. Again, when she became aware somehow that two persons connected with a certain relic had been, as she put it, 'nearly married and then not married', she did so through the ostensible communicator showing her a wedding-dress and then letting it fall.

Sometimes the Topsy-persona is uncertain of the meaning of a symbol, which is presented to her in visual imagery or in *quasi*-sensory visual hallucination, and says so, giving two or more alternative possible interpretations. The following is an interesting case. It was characteristic of a certain ostensible communicator that the person whom he purported to be had had in this life a passion for *rice pudding*. He had been heard to say that he would willingly have one both at lunch and at dinner; and on one occasion he had said: 'You can give me more rice, I am never tired of it.' Now the Topsy-persona eventually got on to this singular taste of the ostensible communicator, but she did so in the following roundabout way. In the sitting at which the relic connected with this individual was used she approached this topic by an irrelevant and incorrect reference to 'India, or some hot place over the water, where there's lots of dark people'. Then came: 'Remember palms!' Then: 'He laughs, and says "Where bananas grow" '. Then: 'He laughs, and shows Topsy a lot of rice. There must be a joke about lots of rice—"more rice, never tired" '. No doubt rice was associated in Mrs Elliott's mind with India. This called up by association dark people and palms and bananas and finally rice. And then at last came the correct interpretation of rice as a favourite article of diet with the ostensible communicator.

The symbolism generally depends on very natural, or very widely accepted conventional, associations of ideas, rather than on associations peculiar to the medium. Thus *spatial nearness* typifies close blood-relationship; *black* is a symbol for worry or sorrow or death; the *waving away* of a relic by the hallucinatory figure of an ostensible communicator is a sign that he is not connected with that relic; and so on.

The dramatic form of a sitting with Mrs Elliott controlled by the Topsy-persona differs in the following way from that of a sitting with Mrs Leonard controlled by the Feda-persona. Feda presents the communications as if she obtained them by *listening* to communicators who are seldom visible to her, and then reported them to the sitter. Topsy presents the communications as if she obtained them by *watching* communicators, who are inaudible to her but make gestures and exhibit visual symbols, which she describes and tries to interpret. The difference, of course, is not absolute. Feda claims sometimes to see the communicators, and Topsy claims sometimes to hear them.

The Topsy-persona always talks as if she literally *saw* the communicators, though not of course with her physical eyes, and as if they deliberately *showed* her this or that visible (though non-physical) object or scene, as a symbol of the information which they wish to convey. If this were accepted literally, it would imply that the communicators have 'astral' bodies; that the Topsy-persona herself has one, provided with the 'astral' equivalent of physical eyes; and that there are 'astrally' visible objects and scenes, to which the communicators can direct her attention. Saltmarsh is not prepared to accept this, but thinks it much more likely that the Topsy-persona is at such times subject to some kind of *quasi*-sensory hallucinatory perception of the visual kind, analogous to a vivid dream had by a normal person when asleep.

He thinks that the *immediate* source of these experiences is in *every* case some stratum of the medium's subconscious self, and that all the raw material of the hallucinations comes from there. But he admits that, in *certain* cases, we may have to suppose, in order to account for the relevance and the veridicality of the information conveyed by

326

the symbolism, that the *stimulus*, which evokes and guides the phantasmogenic process, comes from some source *other than* any level of the medium's personality.

In support of his view that the *immediate* source of the symbolic experiences lies within the medium, Saltmarsh alleges that the Topsy-persona uses one and the same system of symbolism in ostensible communications from many different ostensible communicators. He alleges that that is true of the Feda-persona also, though the two use different symbols for the same idea. He argues that, if the symbols pre-existed in an 'astral' world and were literally shown to the control by the communicators, or if they were *directly* generated in her by the communicators as hallucinatory *quasi*-percepts, we should expect to find characteristic differences between the symbolism used when different ostensible communicators communicate through the same medium. Conversely, we should expect to find similarity between the symbolism used when one and the same ostensible communicator communicates through different mediums. (It should be remembered that several of the ostensible communicators in the sittings with Mrs Elliott had also ostensibly communicated at sittings with Mrs Leonard.)

It seems to me that the first prong of this double argument is somewhat blunted by Saltmarsh's statement that the symbolism used in the Elliott communications is based on *natural*, or *very widely accepted* conventional, connexions of ideas, rather than on associations peculiar to the medium. If that be so, the use of a common symbolism by a number of different ostensible communicators through Mrs Elliott might be due simply to the fact that the basis of the symbolism is common to almost everyone, including the medium, the sitters, and all the ostensible communicators.

(5) *Saltmarsh's Theory of the Processes involved.* However that may be, let us suppose, for the sake of argument, that the amount and quality of the veridical material in the ostensible communications makes it reasonable to postulate some remote source, other than any stratum of the medium's mind, as providing an evoking and guiding stimulus to her subconscious phantasmogenic powers. How are we, then, to think of the processes involved?

If we make this postulate, it is plain that we must assume that there is a certain stratum of the medium's mind which is the *immediate* recipient of this foreign influence. Saltmarsh calls this the 'Receptor Stratum'. We can then raise the question: What are the immediate products, in the Receptor Stratum, of the influence on it of sources of information foreign to the medium? Suppose we accept Saltmarsh's view that it is something *in the medium herself* which is directly responsible for the particular images or hallucinatory *quasi-perceptions* that eventually well up in the Topsy-persona or in normal Mrs Elliott and express in symbolic form the information received. Then we must suppose that such information is received and registered by the Receptor Stratum in some *other* form.

At this point we must distinguish between (i) information as to the emotions or bodily pains or pleasures of the ostensible communicator, and (ii) information as to *physical* states of affairs or as to experiences *other than* emotions or bodily feelings. The first case seems fairly simple, for the symbolism required is so obvious and natural. All that is needed is that the medium shall actually feel a kind of phantom bodily sensation, e.g. of pain in a certain part of the head, of suffocation, of palpitation, and so on, and that she should take this as a symbol of a corresponding affective experience in the ostensible communicator, of whom she is having an hallucinatory *quasi*-perception of the visual kind. There is considerable evidence that that *was* in fact the way in which such information was received.

But the mode of reception of information of the second kind raises much greater difficulties. Saltmarsh argued that such information must be supposed to be received and registered by the Receptor Stratum in some way which is altogether independent of formulation in audible or visible sentences, and of symbolization by imitative or metaphorical visual imagery or *quasi*-sensory hallucination. He summarizes this view in some extremely obscure sentences, which I will quote: '. . . The impression received by the Receptor Stratum is received as a *meaning*, i.e. the process is a purely *psychical* one, not expressed in language or other sensory impressions . . . The Receptor Stratum lies below or beyond the point at which differentiation into various senses occurs; i.e. a meaning would not be visual, auditory, olfactory, sapid, or tactual, but just *plain meaning*' (the italics in this quotation are mine, and not Saltmarsh's).

I cannot pretend to feel at all certain that I understand what positive doctrine Saltmarsh intended to convey by these sentences. But I suggest that what may have been at the back of his mind is something that could be put as follows. It is a fact that a whole indefinitely large class of sentences, spoken, written, or merely imaged by various persons and on various occasions, may all *have the same meaning*. And it is a further fact that certain gestures, pictures, dances, etc., may express *symbolically* the same meaning as those sentences express *verbally*. We may therefore talk of '*the* [common] meaning' of all those sentences and symbols. So far we are on safe ground.

But it is very natural to take the following step, viz. to take for granted that there must be a certain one peculiar entity, *other than* all the sentences and symbols which 'have the same meaning'; something which exists in its own right, and to which they all stand in a certain common relation, in respect of which *it* is what *they* all mean. We may use the word 'proposition' to refer to such supposed independently existent entities, provided we remember that this no more commits us to the belief that there are propositions, in that sense, than the use of the word 'dragon', to refer to supposed fire-breathing serpents, commits us to the belief that there are, have been, or will be such creatures. The step from the fact to the theory can be seen to be most precarious, when one contemplates it critically instead of taking it unwittingly. Yet I cannot help suspecting that, when Saltmarsh talks of the Receptor Stratum receiving information from an external source in the form of 'a meaning', and when he talks of 'just plain meaning', he is committed (though perhaps unwittingly) to this very theory. He is committed, I suspect, to the view that what is received is literally awareness of *propositions*, in the sense explained above, unmediated by any verbal or symbolic vehicle, whether sensory, *quasi*-sensory, or imaginal.

Now, quite apart from a strong feeling of doubt as to whether there are such entities as 'propositions', in the sense explained, I find it very difficult to swallow Saltmarsh's theory. Perhaps the following concrete example will bring out the difficulty that I feel. Suppose I wanted to convey to a certain individual on a certain occasion the information that some prominent public personage or other had lately died in England. If there were any language which I could speak or write and he could understand, I might utter in his presence or to him over a telephone, or write and have put before his eyes, a sentence in that language signifying that an event of that kind had happened. Failing that, if he and I were together in any town in England at the time, I might point out to him flags flying at half-mast on public buildings. If he were familiar with the relevant very widespread convention, he would equally well receive the information in that way.

Now, suppose that I had the power of evoking *telepathically* in his mind, without speaking to him directly or over a telephone, without putting any writing before his eyes, and without pointing to any symbolic object in his presence, a vivid image or hallucinatory *quasi*-perception as of that spoken or written sentence or as of a flag at half-mast on a building. Then there is no difficulty *in principle* in seeing that he could receive from me that particular bit of information on that occasion. The only difficulty would be in conceiving or imagining the process by which I could evoke telepathically in him the appropriate images or *quasi*-sensations. Given that I could do

329

so, there is no difficulty in understanding how he would thereupon come to think of, and perhaps to believe, that some prominent public personage or other had lately died in England.

But what I find very hard to understand is how a person could, on a given occasion, come to think of, and perhaps to believe, something specific, although at the time there was *not* present to *any* stratum of his mind, even in the form of an image or an hallucinatory *quasi*-perception, *any* verbal formulation of it in a language that he understands, or *any* concrete symbol for it in a convention that is familiar to him. Yet that seems to be what Saltmarsh wishes us to try to contemplate, in the reception of information about physical facts or about non-affective experiences by Mrs Elliott's Receptor Stratum. If that was not what he had in mind, I cannot guess what was.

Perhaps all that we really need to suppose is something on the following lines. May it not be that the direct effect of the foreign source upon the medium is simply to set the relevant parts of her *brain and nervous system* in such incipient states as *would*, if they were to develop normally, lead to her uttering *sotto voce* certain sentences in her native tongue, or to her having auditory images of those sentences as spoken or visual images of them as written? And may it not be that those incipient brain-states do *not* in fact develop in her in that normal way? May it not be that they act, instead, merely as stimuli to some phantasmogenic stratum of her mind, which thereupon generates visual images or hallucinatory *quasi*-perceptions as of persons and things and scenes, which symbolize, in a way characteristic of the medium and her habitual associations, those ideas and beliefs which *would* have been verbalized if those incipient brain-states *had* developed in the normal manner?

In this connexion the following remark of Saltmarsh's should be noted. Suppose we regard the Topsy-persona, as he is inclined to do, as a kind of secondary personality of Mrs Elliott. Then we cannot identify the stratum or department of the medium's mind which generates the symbols with the stratum or department which functions as Topsy. For the latter often confesses herself uncertain as to the right interpretation of those symbolic images or *quasi*-sensory hallucinations which present themselves to her. (Compare the following fact. When one has a dream, as of oneself doing and suffering such and such things in such and such scenery, one's dream-personality at the time is just as ignorant as is one's waking personality later, of the sources and the possible significance of the dream-scenery and the dream-drama. So far from the *dream-actor* creating the dream-scenery and the dream-drama, he and they are alike products of something in the individual, of which the dream-actor is quite unaware.)

330

I pass now to another part of Saltmarsh's speculations. He makes considerable play with a rather elaborate analogy to the physical phenomenon known as 'osmosis', and he supplements this with certain other physical analogies, not necessarily consistent with this or with each other. The essential points of the osmotic analogy are these. The medium's mind is likened to a tube, closed at one end with a semi-permeable membrane, and containing a solution of some substance, such as sugar, in some solvent, such as water. The solution in the tube is compared to the normal contents of the medium's mind. The lowest layer of it, immediately in contact with the semi-permeable membrane, is compared to the Receptor Stratum. The tube is supposed to be dipped, with the closed end downwards, into a vessel containing a weaker solution of the same substance in the same solvent. This vessel and its contents are likened, respectively, to a foreign mind (possibly, though not necessarily, the surviving mind of some deceased human being) and to its contents. The dipping of the tube into the vessel is likened to the establishment of some kind of *rapport* between these two minds. In the physical case solvent would diffuse from the liquid in the vessel, through the membrane, into the tube, and would mix with the contents of the tube. This is likened to the conveyance of information from the external source to the Receptor Stratum of the medium's mind.

Now, as a general rule, I am strongly against professional philosophers badgering honest working psychologists or psychical researchers with niggling criticisms on tentative theories expounded in analogies. If, on the whole, they find a certain analogy useful to co-ordinate the facts observed up to date and to suggest questions that can be investigated by experiment or further observation, I would turn a blind eye to the fact that absurdities arise if the analogy be pressed too far. But I am afraid that, in the present case, the absurdity is patent at the very first move. It is of the essence of the osmotic process that what turns up in the tube is *ipso facto* removed from the surrounding vessel. Every particle of solvent that is added osmotically to the contents of the tube is osmotically subtracted from the contents of the vessel. But that is radically unlike the conveyance of information from one mind to another. Mind B does not *ipso facto* lose any item of information which it conveys to mind A. When an alleged analogy breaks down so fundamentally in principle, one doubts whether it can be worth while to pursue it in detail.

I am inclined to think that the only valuable feature in Saltmarsh's osmotic analogy is this. It suggests that the conveyance of information from the external source to the Receptor Stratum of the medium may be a process which is quite *passive*, in the sense that it is not deliberately initiated or directed by either party. It is important to bear this possibility in mind; for the word 'telepathy' is liable to call up a picture of one mind deliberately *im*posing certain ideas on another or deliberately *ex*posing certain of its contents to the inspection of the other. And the word 'mind-reading' is liable to suggest one mind deliberately 'scanning' the contents of another mind. All these processes may, on occasion, take place. But it is well to have an analogy which allows for mere unintended and undirected 'leakage'; though, for the reasons given above, that analogy must not be pressed, and its *positive* associations must be firmly rejected.

It we must use a physical analogy, I think that *resonance* would be much better than *osmosis*. We might compare the medium's mind and that of the supposed external source of information to two stringed musical instruments; and we might liken the contents of a mind at any moment to the vibrations of those strings in such an instrument which happen to have been recently struck. Then, finally, we might compare the conveyance of information from the foreign mind to the medium's to the setting up by resonance, in certain strings of the former instrument, of vibrations similar to those at present going on in certain strings of the latter, through the two instruments being partially attuned to each other.

Saltmarsh makes several interesting suggestions which are quite independent of the osmotic analogy. One is that there would probably be a *double* process of *elimination* before the stage at which symbolic images or *quasi*-sensory hallucinations would arise in the consciousness of the control. The *first* elimination would take place at the level of reception; for it may well be that there is much in the content of the foreign mind to which the Receptor Stratum of the medium's mind cannot respond at all, or can respond only weakly or distortedly. The *second* would take place at the boundary between the Receptor Stratum and the phantasmogenic department of the medium's mind. Some of the content imparted to the Receptor Stratum might fit easily into the medium's innate mental structure or acquired habits and associations of ideas. Others might fail to do so, or might arouse positive resistance in her. The former would be likely to be represented with ease, and without much distortion, in symbolic images or *quasi*-sensory hallucinations. The latter might fail to get represented at all, or, if it were, might be represented by symbols so distorted that neither the control herself nor the sitters could guess what they meant.

Besides these gaps and distortions in the final product, due to this double process of elimination, there will inevitably be something which might be described as 'dilution' or 'contamination'. For any images or *quasi*-sensory hallucinations, which may have their ultimate origin in content imparted to the Receptor Stratum from a foreign mind, will certainly be accompanied, and often almost swamped, by dream-like fantasies, originating entirely within the medium from traces of her past experiences, as our ordinary nightly dreams and our waking reveries arise in us.

In view of the disconnected and fragmentary nature even of the information which turns out to be characteristic and true of a given ostensible communicator and to be outside the medium's range of normal knowledge and conjecture, and in view of the immense amount of padding in which it is imbedded, something like this account of Saltmarsh's seems to be a plausible picture of the psychological processes involved in Mrs Elliott's mediumship. Since a large proportion even of successful sittings with gifted mediums have the same characteristics, something like this view would seem to have a wide range of application to trance-mediumship. But, as Saltmarsh admits and emphasizes, there are *occasional* bursts of what look like deliberate coherent messages concerning specific and characteristic events or circumstances in the earthly life of the ostensible communicator or of some friend or relative of his or hers.

To fit such facts into the theory, we might have to suppose that, although the conveyance of information from the foreign mind to that of the medium is *for the most part* of the nature of 'leakage', or 'seepage', where such selection as takes place is automatic, yet that is *not always* the case. Occasionally, and for a short time, we might suppose, the foreign mind is able deliberately to determine that the Receptor Stratum of the medium shall respond to a certain selected coherent cluster of its own ideas. Even that will not suffice, unless the ideas thus evoked in the Receptor Stratum are such that the phantasmogenic mechanism of the medium's mind can readily produce such images or *quasi*-sensory hallucinations as will symbolize them in a way intelligible to the control or to the sitter. It may be that this is a condition over which the communicating mind has no control, and which it must just leave to luck. But it is also conceivable that it might occasionally and for a short time be able deliberately to influence this also.

333

XIV

THE
PICTURES PRESENTED THROUGH MRS LEONARD AND THROUGH MRS WILLETT COMPARED WITH EACH OTHER AND WITH THAT PAINTED BY SWEDENBORG

IT will now be worth while to compare and contrast the picture presented to us through Mrs Leonard by the John-persona and the Etta-persona, in sittings with Drayton Thomas, with that presented to us through Mrs Willett by the Gurney-persona and the Myers-persona in sittings with Lodge and with Balfour.

Before doing so, we should remind ourselves that we are dealing with two very different kinds of mediumship in the two cases. Mrs Leonard is a medium who has a *regular control*, the Feda-persona, and in whom ostensible *possession* (which the Gurney-persona and the Myers-persona ascribe to 'telergy') by this, that, or the other ostensible communicator, is a fairly frequent occurrence. The essential point is that, when she is giving a sitting, her normal personality is completely in abeyance. It is ousted, generally by the control Feda, and occasionally by the personalities of certain ostensible communicators, such as John or Etta Drayton Thomas, A.V.B., and so on.

Mrs Willett, on the other hand, had no regular control, analogous to Feda, and was never or hardly ever ostensibly possessed by Gurney, Myers, or any other ostensible communicator. Whilst giving a seance she was, of course, in a somewhat abnormal state, and this was at times one that might fairly be termed 'trance'. But even then there was nothing that could be described as a recognizably different and recurrent personality, temporarily in control of her organism. It will be remembered that this was stated explicitly by the Gurney-

334

persona to be the state of affairs which he and Myers were aiming at. They did not want Mrs Willett to become a trance-medium of the usual kind. To use their own terminology, they wanted to operate through her by means of 'telepathy' and 'telaesthesia', and *not* by means of 'telergy' leading to 'possession'. Since the final results are, and were intended to be, so different in the two cases, it will not necessarily be a sign of inconsistency if there should be a considerable difference in the processes alleged to be involved.

It is plain that we cannot expect to find, in the statements made to Balfour through Mrs Willett, anything comparable with the statements made to Drayton Thomas by the John-persona and the Etta-persona as to what happens when they take possession of Mrs Leonard's body. For Mrs Willett's body was *not* taken possession of by those who claimed to communicate through her, and the ostensible communicators explicitly said so. Nor can we expect to find anything comparable to the statements, as to the relations of the control Feda to Mrs Leonard's normal personality or to Mrs Leonard's body, which were made either by the Feda-persona about herself or by the John-persona and the Etta-persona about her. For in Mrs Willett's case there was nothing analogous to a regular control, such as Feda. Finally, we cannot expect to find, in the statements made to Drayton Thomas through Mrs Leonard, anything comparable with the elaborate account, given by the Gurney-persona to Balfour, of the processes involved in preparing and carrying through a cross-correspondence experiment. For Mrs Leonard's ostensible communicators were not concerned with such experiments.

What may fairly be compared are statements made by the two sets of ostensible communicators on each of the following topics: (1) The nature and structure of human beings in their *ante mortem* and their *post mortem* state. (2) The ways in which a human being, in the *post mortem* state, conveys information, for the purpose of communication to a sitter, to the mind which is at the time in control of the medium's body. Let us now consider these two matters in turn.

The Nature and Structure of the Human Individual. As to the *ante mortem* structure of the human mind, both parties agree in distinguishing a conscious or supraliminal *stratum* and a subconscious or subliminal *stratum*. That, however, may be regarded as a commonplace, accepted in some sense or other by practically everyone nowadays. It is also worth remembering that the word 'subliminal' and the notion of the 'subliminal self' play a very important part in Myers's writings, and therefore would be extremely familiar to those interested in psychical research during the period when these communications were being made. Lastly, it should be noted that the word 'subliminal' had a considerably different kind of emotional overtone, for Myers and those influenced by his writings, from that which the word 'subconscious' or 'unconscious' has for post-Freudian generations. Myers thought of the 'subliminal self' as something grander and more numinous than the poor old supraliminal; as the source of 'inspired' works of genius in literature, music, painting, mathematics, etc.; as the seat of paranormal faculties in this life, and as destined to live hereafter (and perhaps, in a sense, as living already) an incomparably higher and fuller life in the 'metetherial'. We, on the other hand, tend to think of 'the unconscious' mainly as it presented itself to the psychiatrists of Vienna in the intimate babblings of their neurotic patients, viz. as a sink (and a pretty dirty one, at that), into which the less reputable desires and sentiments of the 'conscious self' have been thrust, in which they continually ferment and infect our daily lives, and from which they occasionally well up in outbursts of overt craziness. No doubt 'the unconscious' somehow combines these two aspects, and both Myers and Freud were well aware of the fact. But Myers and those influenced by him were certainly inclined to emphasize its more admirable side and to play down its less respectable features. Freud and those influenced by him were inclined to go to the opposite extreme, and the current popular notion of 'the unconscious' is derived almost wholly from swallowing uncritically an over-simplified version of their teachings.

We may now note the following differences between the statements of the two sets of ostensible communicators. Whilst both parties agree in distinguishing a supraliminal and a subliminal part of the *ante mortem* human mind, the Willett-communicators allege that there is also a third factor, which they call 'the transcendental'. The Leonard-communicators make no mention of this.

Then, again, the Gurney-persona goes into much greater detail about the subliminal part of the *ante mortem* human mind than do the Leonard-communicators. He distinguishes at least three layers in it, and assigns various functions to these. It is the layer furthest removed from normal waking consciousness which acquires information telaesthetically from the minds of the communicators; it is in the intermediate layer that this is itemized and verbalized; and it is the layer immediately below normal consciousness which causes the medium's body to utter the information in speech or writing. The Leonard-communicators have nothing to say about all this, though they do not say anything obviously inconsistent with it.

We are given no explicit information as to what may be the cash-value of the spatial metaphor of higher and lower 'levels'. I suppose that one fairly obvious criterion would be this. An item belongs to a *lower* level than another item, if it influences the subject's conscious experiences and overt behaviour *less* frequently, easily, and obviously than does the latter; if *more* drastic psychological methods or physiological treatment (e.g. prolonged psychoanalysis, deep hypnosis, use of shock-treatment, etc.) are needed in order to make the subject aware of the former; and so on. Because of the associations attached to the word 'subliminal' in Myers's writings, there is always (I am inclined to think) a suggestion that what is 'deeper', in this purely neutral sense, must also be 'deeper', in the evaluatory sense of more spiritual more wonderful, and so on. If the 'subliminal' be such a fine thing, then (the suggestion is) the more 'sub' it is the better!

As to the *post mortem* structure of the human mind, both parties agree that there is some kind of shift between what was formerly supraliminal and what was formerly subliminal. But they differ very considerably in matters of detail.

The Leonard-communicators allege that the division into these two layers *vanishes* at death, and they presumably mean that everything that was subconscious becomes fully conscious. They add, however, that a similar division is temporarily reinstated when they take possession of the medium's body. The part then in possession functions like the *conscious* part of a human mind in its normal *ante mortem* state, and the rest functions like the *subconscious* part of such a mind. But, it is alleged, the part of the communicator's mind which is in temporary possession of the medium's body bears to the rest of his mind a very much smaller proportion than the conscious part of a human mind, in its normal waking *ante mortem* state, bears to the rest of that mind. I should think that the cash-value of these statements would amount to the three following assertions about the state of a person's mind after death: (i) He either is continually remembering, or at any rate can at any time recall at will, all his *ante mortem* and his *post mortem* experiences. (ii) When in temporary possession of the medium's body he is actually remembering, or can recall at will, only a part of his *ante mortem* and *post mortem* experiences. (iii) That part is much smaller than the fraction of his *ante mortem* experiences which a person still alive in the physical body actually remembers, or could recall at will, at any moment of his normal waking life.

The Willett-communicators take a somewhat different view, and this depends on their doctrine of a 'transcendental' part of the human mind, over and above its conscious and its subconscious parts. According to them, there *remains* after death a division in the mind of the deceased into what may properly be called a 'conscious' and a 'subconscious' part. But some of the contents of the *ante mortem*

337

field of consciousness vanish altogether, and the rest join up with the contents of the *ante mortem* subconscious to form the *post mortem* field of consciousness. The subconscious part of the *post mortem* self is supplied by the *transcendental* part of the *ante mortem* self. Without professing to understand precisely what is meant by this, one can see that the introduction of the 'transcendental' self makes it a different account from that put forward by the Leonard-communicators, and a considerably more complex one.

The Leonard-communicators assert explicitly that they have *sense-organs*, which they use for perception when they are not in possession of the medium's body. They state that they can use those organs even when in possession, but that they generally refrain from doing so and prefer to perceive by means of the medium's sense-organs. Similar statements are made by the control Feda. She, it must always be remembered, claims to resemble the communicators in being the surviving spirit of a deceased human being; and the communicators never question that claim. She alleges that she uses the medium's ears, e.g., for hearing ordinary physical sounds, and uses her own auditory sense-organs for hearing the voices of the communicators; and she insists that she is using 'hearing' in the same literal sense in both contexts. It is true that the kind of mistakes made by Feda have led attentive and critical sitters to conclude that she often cannot have been *seeing*, in anything like the literal sense, certain ostensible communicators whom she describes herself as 'seeing'. It is true also that the John-persona and the Etta-persona state that Feda sometimes says, and no doubt thinks, that she has been 'seeing' with her own visual organs, when the source of her information has been in fact telepathic. Nevertheless, they agree that she does from time to time literally 'see', with her own sense-organs, persons and things in their world. And they allege that she sometimes makes the opposite mistake of thinking that she has obtained information telepathically, when she has in fact gained it through actual 'vision'.

All this implies, of course, that the communicators and the control claim to have, and often to use, something analogous to sense-organs and vocal organs. Their statements about literally talking to Feda on some occasions, as contrasted with telepathically putting ideas into her mind on other occasions, fit in with this.

I think that we may fairly summarize the above by saying that the Leonard-communicators and the Leonard-control agree in holding a definitely *animistic* view of themselves and, by implication, of human nature in general. As such a view has become old-fashioned, and no longer moves in 'highbrow' circles, I propose to formulate it, as I understand it, in my own way.

According to animism, every human mind, whether in its *ante mortem* or its *post mortem* state, is essentially and inseparably bound up with some kind of extended *quasi*-physical vehicle, which is not normally perceptible to the senses of human beings in their present life. Let us call this the 'astral body'; and let us denote the relationship of the mind to it by saying that the mind of a human being 'informs' his astral body. The whole, composed of a human astral body informed by a human mind, constitutes an indivisible unit, which we may call a human 'soul'. In the *ante mortem* state a human being is a compound of two factors, intimately though temporarily interconnected, viz. his soul and his *physical* body. The relation of the soul to the physical body may be denoted by saying that the former 'animates' the latter.

So, on this view, the relation of a man's *mind* to his *physical* body is a complex one. For it is compounded of the relation of his mind to his *astral* body (which is an intrinsic, and perhaps indissoluble, union) and of the relation of his astral body to his *physical* body (which is an extrinsic and temporary one). At death the soul, i.e. the astral body with the mind which informs it, ceases to be connected with the physical body. The latter disintegrates. The former continues to exist and to operate in an environment composed of other souls and possibly of *quasi*-physical extended objects, analogous to astral bodies but not informed by minds. This view is certainly most unfashionable among those brought up under the influence of Western scientific ideas, and it may well be false; but it seems to me to be quite intelligible.

Now the Willett-communicators are plainly much less explicitly animistic than the Leonard-communicators. They never, I think, assert or imply that they have something analogous to bodies and sense-organs and vocal organs. They tell us nothing about the ways in which they communicate with each other; but the only ways in which they claim to communicate with Mrs Willett, and through her to the sitters, are by telaesthesia and by the various forms of telepathy which they distinguish. Of course, it is fair to add that they recognize possession and telergy, not merely as an abstract possibility, but as an alternative method of communication which they have considered and deliberately rejected. It may well be that the notion of possession, if thought out, would be found to imply something very like animism. But the Gurney-persona and the Myers-persona do not expound in detail their views about this rejected alternative and its implications.

It may be granted at once that the Willett-communicators hold what might be called a 'substantival dualist' view of the constitution of the human individual in the *ante mortem* state. That, after all, is

339

implied by their claim to be the surviving spirits of certain deceased human beings. For that claim would be meaningless on the supposition that a man's experiences and mental dispositions are a mere aspect of his physical body, or are in some other way one-sidedly dependent on its existence and functioning. But substantival dualism need not take the special form of *animism*, as I have defined it. For animism involves *two* dualisms, viz. that of soul and physical body (in the *ante mortem* state) and that of mind and astral body within the soul (in both the *ante mortem* and the *post mortem* states). Now the Willett-communicators might accept substantival dualism in its Cartesian form, viz. a *purely mental* substance, temporarily united in the *ante mortem* state with the physical body, and persisting after death without anything analogous to a body. I do not think that it is possible to infer with confidence from their statements whether they hold an animistic or a Cartesian form of substantival dualism. For statements which, if taken literally, might imply the animistic alternative, might be easily reconcilable with the Cartesian alternative if interpreted metaphorically.

It may be of interest, in this connexion, to refer, for what they may be worth, to Swedenborg's observations on this topic. Swedenborg, an extremely learned, intelligent, and practically efficient citizen of this world, had, from middle life onwards, experiences in which he seemed to himself to enter into the world of surviving spirits, to survey it at leisure, and to converse with many whom he met there. He states that, before he had had the empirical evidence thus obtained, he had thought that, *if* men should survive bodily death, they would do so as purely disembodied minds. That is to say, he had accepted the Cartesian alternative. But later he was surprised to find that this was a mistake. In the ordinary visible and tangible body of a man in his *ante mortem* state there is contained a more subtle kind of organism, which is extended, but lacks the mechanical properties, such as inertia and weight, which are characteristic of ordinary matter. After death this subtle organism persists and constitutes the body in the *post mortem* state.

Now Swedenborg relates that he met two classes of surviving human spirits, who were subject to opposite kinds of delusion on this point. He met a few (presumably the souls of men who had been convinced Cartesians) who persisted in believing themselves to be unextended and purely mental substances. He met many more who made an opposite kind of mistake. Finding that they still had sensations, and taking for granted that sense-perception is bound up with the existence and functioning of a *physical* body, they imagined that they still had such bodies. And, in that belief, they often refuse for a long time to admit that they are dead.

Swedenborg says that he had frequent conversations with surviving spirits on this question, and that some of them stubbornly refused to be convinced that they no longer possessed ordinary physical bodies and were no longer living an ordinary *ante mortem* life on earth. In particular, he relates how he attended the funeral of the great Swedish engineer Polhem, whose assistant he had been as a young man. He states that on that occasion he had a conversation with Polhem's spirit, and that the latter asked indignantly why they were burying him, seeing that he was still alive. Swedenborg states that the deceased grow out of this delusion in course of time. It may be added that there are on record quite a fair number of mediumistic cases in which the ostensible communicator, who had in fact died a sudden and violent death or had been insane, talks and behaves as if he believed himself to be still living and still undergoing the painful experiences associated with his last *ante mortem* moments.

The reader may regard these reports by Swedenborg of his experiences among the spirits either as travellers' tales or as the buzzing of bees in the bonnet of an elderly crackpot. Of a man who, on the one hand, continued to display up to the end of a very long life high scientific ability, excellent sense in the management of his own affairs, and great practical wisdom in affairs of state, and yet, on the other hand, devoted himself to giving an allegedly inspired symbolic interpretation of every word and sentence in the Mosaic scriptures, it is difficult to form a balanced judgement. Perhaps the best that one can say is that there may be many mansions in our Father's house which are not open to 'well-adjusted' worldlings, who would pass with distinction all the tests which psychologists have devised for the discovery and canonization of the commonplace. However that may be, I am content here to retail these sayings of Swedenborg as interesting and as *prima facie* relevant to the differences between the testimony of the Leonard-communicators and the Willett-communicators concerning the constitution of the human individual in this world and in the next.

The Processes involved in Communication. I pass now to the second topic on which the statements of the two sets of ostensible communicators may fairly be compared. This is the question: How does a person, who has survived bodily death, convey information, for the purpose of communication to a sitter, to the mind which is at the time in control of the medium's body?

In order to compare statements which are as nearly as possible *in pari materia*, we must take (i) statements by the Leonard-communicators as to how they convey information to Mrs Leonard's control Feda, and (ii) those of the Willett-communicators as to how they

341

convey information to the normal personality of Mrs Willett in the slightly abnormal state in which she is during the sittings. For it is to *Feda*, when in control of Mrs Leonard's body, and not to the normal personality of Mrs Leonard, that the John-persona and the Etta-persona claim to convey information directly. And it is to the *normal personality* of Mrs Willett (though in a somewhat abnormal state), and not to anything of the nature of a control, that the Gurney-persona and the Myers-persona claim to convey information. Plainly, the two situations are not *completely* parallel. For Feda claims to be the surviving spirit of a deceased human being; and, if we reject that claim, we must regard her as a secondary personality of Mrs Leonard's, analogous to the secondary personality Sally, e.g., in the case of Miss Beauchamp. On either alternative the parallel with Mrs Willett is incomplete.

Allowing for these differences, there is a good deal of similarity in the statements of the two sets of communicators. Both claim to convey information by telepathy; and both draw a distinction between deliberately injecting an idea into the mind which is in control of the medium's body, and her acquirement of certain ideas by 'reading' the contents of their minds.

The Willett-communicators go more into detail and draw more elaborate distinctions. They distinguish telaesthesia from telepathy; they divide telepathy into telepathic imposition and telepathic exposition; and they subdivide the latter into two species. We must remember that the Willett-communicators claimed to be the surviving spirits of Gurney and of Myers, who in this life had devoted much of their attention to the psychology of the subconscious and the phenomena of ostensibly paranormal cognition, and who were classical scholars accustomed to drawing subtle distinctions and coining appropriate names for them. The two Leonard-communicators with whom we are here concerned, claimed, on the other hand, to be the surviving spirits of a Wesleyan minister and of his middle-aged daughter; that is to say, persons of good general education, but with no special qualifications in the sphere of psychology or para-psychology or in the invention of technical terminology. The differences in detail, which I have pointed out, would be quite compatible with the view that substantially the same facts are being described, in the one case by more, and in the other by less, expert and sophisticated communicators.

Some alleged Observations by Swedenborg. I have now said all that I have to say about the agreements and disagreements between the Leonard-communicators and the Willett-communicators about comparable topics, concerning which they might be expected to have first-hand information, if they were what they claimed to be. I have already referred to Swedenborg, in connexion with the animistic view of the constitution of the human individual. Now he claimed also to have discovered, from personal observation and enquiry conducted in the world of departed spirits, a number of facts about how they communicate. His statements seem to me to be of considerable interest, both in themselves and in comparison with the ostensible communications on this topic which we have been considering. I shall therefore give a synopsis of them, which the reader may treat as he thinks fit.

Swedenborg distinguishes between an 'outer' and an 'inner' self, in persons in their *ante mortem* state. The outer self is the part of us which manifests itself in our dealings with external things and other persons. It is the *façade* which each of us puts up to other men, and it often becomes the *façade* which one puts up to oneself too. The outer self has often succeeded so well at its job during one's earthly life that one has come to assume that it is the whole, or the predominantly important part, of one's personality.

Immediately after his death a man is still dominated by his outer self and his outwardly directed interests. So too are most of the surviving spirits whom he meets at that stage. During that period, whenever he thinks of another person's face or of facts connected with that person on earth, the individual thought of seems to him to be present bodily before his eyes. While this phase lasts there are many apparent reunions between former friends and relatives. The duration of this stage varies from about a day to about a year of our time, according to the degree of dominance of the outer self at the time of death. (I would again remark that a good many ostensible communications through mediums, which purport to come from those who have died suddenly through accident or in battle, fit in rather well with what Swedenborg claimed to have observed for himself.)

At the next stage, according to Swedenborg, every surviving spirit has to act and to appear to himself and to others in accordance with his *inner* self, i.e. his ruling system of desires, emotions, sentiments, and valuations, unchecked by social and prudential considerations. The habitual outward propriety, which has been imposed by society on persons whose desires and emotions are evil, but who have managed to conform, now drops away from them, and they show themselves in their true colours. When a human spirit, at this stage, acts with evil intention, he automatically attracts predominantly evil spirits and puts himself into their power. They may induce in him the illusion that he has a physical body, and that it is being physically tormented in various ways. The details of the

343

torments are hallucinatory; but the *agony* is real, just as it is in a nightmare. Human spirits who are predominantly good undergo a painful process of purification at the hands of the evil spirits, to whose power the evil in them has subjected them, until, as Sweden-borg puts it, 'the falsities are vastated out of them'.

At the end of this second stage the spirits of predominantly bad men have had to give up all pretence of goodness. They gravitate to the society of infernal spirits (i.e. predominantly evil non-human rational beings), and such a society is the reality at the back of the popular notion of Hell. There are in fact many hells; but each of them is a group of like-minded egotists, doomed to exist in intimate social intercourse; and each such group seethes internally and interminably with mutual suspicion, envy, jealousy, and hatred. (Would it be unduly cynical to wonder whether Swedenborg had unwittingly extrapolated from observations and experiences of the less successful instances of *ante mortem* home-life?)

Swedenborg remarks that, at each stage of a person's evolution in the spiritual world, he finds it hard to imagine and still harder to believe that there is another stage. To pass from his present stage, whatever that may happen to be, seems to him to be death. In a sense he 'wants' to be in a higher state, but in another sense he does not 'want' to lose his present life.

Immediately after a man's death what Swedenborg calls his 'external' memory is alleged to be evanescent. By 'external memory' he means the power of recalling at will features in one's environment which one has explicitly noted and attended to. But *a little later* the external memory becomes very strong and obsessive, and the departed spirit is liable to think of himself as still in the physical body, still living in the same house, still owning the same clothes and furniture, and so on. On these vivid and obsessive memories of familiar external things and other persons, surviving spirits at this stage build a kind of private dream-world of *quasi*-sensory hallucinations. But, although their external memory thus acquires an hallucinatory degree of vividness, it is under very imperfect control. Spirits at this level can seldom recall what they happen to wish to recall at the time; though sometimes they can be enabled to do so if suitable reminders are supplied, as they were on occasion by Swedenborg during his intercourse with them.

Swedenborg distinguished from external memory two other kinds of memory, which he called 'inner' and 'inmost'. The contents of 'inner memory' are the traces of everything that has ever affected one's senses, whether it has been explicitly noted and attended to or not 'Innermost memory' consists of traces of every kind of *experience*, whether noted and discriminated at the time or not, which a person has ever had. It would thus include traces of one's most private and unexpressed and perhaps subconscious feelings and emotions and judgements.

Now Swedenborg alleges that he found that spirits have the power of ransacking the inner and the innermost memories of other persons, whether in the *ante mortem* or in the *post mortem* state. (This may be compared with the statements about 'mind-reading' made by both the Leonard-communicators and the Willett-communicators.) He states that the spirits with whom he was conversing would often tap his inmost memory. He claims to have noticed, further, that items which he had become aware of on *remotely successive* occasions, but which were closely associated in his mind, would be presented together, as if *simultaneous*, to a spirit who was tapping his memory. As a result, such a spirit would often give a lifelike impersonation of somebody whom Swedenborg had known well. He warns anyone who attempts communication with the dead to be particularly on his guard in this matter; for, he says: 'Impersonations are most common in the world of spirit'. (All this seems to me to fit in remarkably well with many features of ostensible communications from deceased friends and relatives which are the staple commodity at seances where unsophisticated sitters consult second-rate mediums.)

Swedenborg remarks that the souls of the departed, at any rate in the earlier stages of their *post mortem* development, are particularly liable to hold mistaken beliefs about themselves and their surroundings with intense conviction, because they lack the check which sense-perception imposes on fantasy in the case of a normal waking person in the *ante mortem* state. He noticed that they would often pick up items from his mind, without knowing whether these did or did not correspond to objective facts; would then believe them implicity; and would sometimes regard them as coming from their own memory. He alleges that spirits, at this stage of their development, are extremely susceptible to suggestions, whether good or bad. This provides them with appropriate, if transitory, heavens and hells. The scenes and the actors are hallucinatory, but the pleasures and pains are real enough.

Swedenborg makes some interesting statements about the modes of cognition and of communication employed by persons in the *post mortem* state. Their language, he says, does not consist, as ours does, of *conventional* signs. So far as I can understand, he alleges it to be a system of *visual* images, which convey their meanings through some *natural* intrinsic relationship, such as resemblance. Even in the *ante mortem* state, he asserts, we possess this natural pictorial language, and Swedenborg holds that it lies at the basis of all conventional spoken or written language. When a man in this life talks

345

to his fellow-men, these natural symbols express themselves automatically in the auditory conventional signs of the language with which he is familiar. When the surviving spirit of a man communicates with a man still living in this world, the spirit's pictorial ideas are conveyed telepathically to the man, and they then fall automatically into the appropriate spoken or written words of that man's native language, just as his own ideas do.

Spirits often alleged that they *literally spoke* to Swedenborg. But he pointed out to them that they were mistaken. In the first place, he reminded them, *they* had no vocal organs capable of setting the air in motion; whilst *he* could hear, in the literal sense, only if his ears were stimulated by such vibrations. Moreover, as he pointed out to them, what he ostensibly heard them saying was always in *Swedish*, as if that were their native tongue, though in some cases they were the surviving spirits of *contemporary foreigners*, and in others those of men who had lived on earth long before modern Swedish had come into existence.

He remarked that he never ostensibly heard them as speaking any language with which he was not himself familiar. Sometimes, indeed, they sought to prove to him that they were literally speaking, by making him ostensibly hear them as talking Latin or Greek. But he did not let them 'get away with' that argument. He pointed out that they were merely ransacking his memory of those languages, and then causing the pictorial ideas, which they conveyed telepathically to him, to express themselves in the verbal forms which he had learned as a schoolboy or an undergraduate. What normally happened was this. The spirit transmitted ideas *telepathically*, and not orally, to Swedenborg, and those ideas would then fall automatically into auditory images of spoken Swedish sentences, which Swedenborg would 'hear', as we might put it, 'in his mind's ear'. The communicating spirit would observe this, and, being confused, would think that he himself was uttering sentences in his own language and that Swedenborg was literally hearing them with his ears and understanding them.

The spirits of the recently dead continue for some time to go through the motions of communicating with *each other* by speech. But that is an illusion, bound up with the illusion that they still have physical bodies. Eventually they grow out of both, and thereafter communicate with each other wittingly and deliberately by telepathically conveyed visual imagery. (All this seems to me to form an illuminating critical commentary, all the more interesting through being prospective and unintended, on the claims of the Feda-persona and the Leonard-communicators literally to talk and to listen to each other.)

A spirit can communicate only a small part of his knowledge and of his experiences to a person still in the *ante mortem* state. For much of it will not fit into imagery derived, as ours is, from normal sense-perception, nor can it be expressed in the words and linguistic forms of human speech. (This may be compared with a statement made by the Gurney-persona in reference to 'Mutual Selection', and summarized above under that heading in Chapter XII. He asserts, it will be remembered, that there is a part of a discarnate human mind which works on different principles and uses different categories from those which pertain to human minds in the *ante mortem* state. And he alleges that the contents of that part of a discarnate human mind are, for that reason, inaccessible to a medium.)

Finally, Swedenborg states that the influence between human beings in the flesh and spirits in the *post mortem* state is *mutual*. The latter are often as little aware of our influence on their thoughts and feelings as we are of their influence on ours. Swedenborg himself claimed to live in this world and to have a latchkey into the spirit-world, and thus to enjoy an advantage over both the ordinary man in the flesh and the ordinary spirit out of it.

What are we to say to all this? We can, if we like, simply dismiss it as the delusions of a man who was mad in a few respects, though conspicuously sane in all others. If so, we must at least admit that his delusions had a high degree of internal coherence. We must admit that, granted that he uncritically accepted these abnormal experiences as *in principle* veridical, his reflexions *in detail* upon them were highly intelligent and critical. But I think we shall have to go rather further than that. We must admit, I think, that what he tells us, on the alleged basis of his personal experience and observation, coheres with and supplements in a reasonable way the contents of the relevant ostensible communications through Mrs Leonard and Mrs Willett.

On the basis of his alleged observations, Swedenborg would probably have said that both sets of ostensible communicators are substantially correct in their account of communicating through telepathy and telaesthesia. He would have said that the Leonard-communicators are correct in realizing that they still have something of the nature of an extended organism, and are not purely mental unextended substances. But he would probably have held that, when they claim to have and to use sense-organs and vocal organs, and literally to speak and to hear, they are still under a kind of delusion which is almost universal among the spirits of the recently deceased. He might have added that it is not surprising that the more sophisticated Willett-communicators should have got over that delusion, if they ever had it, and therefore should not describe their situation in such terms.

347

I think that there is yet another feature of many mediumistic communications into which Swedenborg's account of the alleged facts fits rather well. One notes that the Willett-communicators have nothing to say, and the Leonard-communicators very little, about their environment and activities *between* the sittings, when, on the hypothesis that they are surviving spirits of the deceased, they must presumably be living their own lives and pursuing their own business. One contrasts this with the wealth of trivial and homely detail on such topics which is often lavished, through mediums, on unsophisticated sitters by ostensible communicators claiming to be the spirits of their Uncle John or their Aunt Maria.

Swedenborg would probably have said that this is just what one might expect. Granted that Uncle John and Aunt Maria have survived, each is living in a private dream-world of *quasi*-sensory hallucination, based on their memories of their life on earth and on their predominant earthly interests. And, granted that they are communicating, all that they can tell us is details about it. But we may fairly suppose that the Leonard-communicators, and *a fortiori* the Willett-communicators, have got beyond that stage. And, in proportion as they have done so, there will be less and less in their experience which can be fitted into the imagery and the language of *ante mortem* life.

XV

A SET OF MEDIUMISTIC COMMUNICATIONS WHICH SEEM TO INVOLVE PARANORMAL COGNITION

THE foregoing chapters of this section have been mainly confined to what may be called the 'phenomenology' of trance-mediumship. But, of course, what *primarily* interests the psychical researcher is the question whether ostensible communications through mediums include verifiable statements, which are highly specific and relevant to the ostensible communicator, and which plainly fall outside the range of the medium's normal knowledge or conjecture.

For practical purposes there are two alternative modes of procedure here. One is to give fairly brief synopses of a large number of cases, the other is to give a fairly detailed account of a few or of a single one. The former method has the advantage of showing the wide *variety* of such cases, of enabling them to be arranged in some kind of systematic order, and of showing that no single simple explanation will cover them all. I should regard the careful study of such a collection of synopses, followed by a reading of the original reports of at least some of the cases summarized, as an essential preliminary to any reasonable judgement on the question at issue. Fortunately, there exist three admirable recent works of this kind, to which the reader may be referred. One of them is Professor Gardner Murphy's 'Three Papers on the Survival Problem'. These appeared originally in the *Journal* of the American S.P.R. for January, July, and October, 1945, and have lately been made available by that Society in a single brochure. Another is Professor Hornell Hart's book *The Enigma of Survival* (Rider, 1959). The third is Mr W. H. Salter's *Zoar* (Sidgwick and Jackson, 1961).

For this and other reasons I shall here take the latter alternative. I shall give a fairly full account of a recently reported case, which seems to be well attested and to be highly relevant to the question at issue. It may be described as 'The Vandy Case'. The report of it occupies No. 691, Vol. XXXIX, of the S.P.R. *Journal*, which is dated March 1957. It was sent to the S.P.R. by Mr George Vandy, and it concerns sittings held by him and his brother Harold, with various mediums in 1933, shortly after the death of their brother Edgar on August 6th of that year. The reports in question and other correspondence and papers connected with the case had been locked away for many years, owing to conditions arising from the Second World War. They came again into the possession of George Vandy in 1953, and he submitted them to the S.P.R. shortly afterwards.

THE KNOWN FACTS ABOUT EDGAR VANDY AND HIS DEATH

I will begin by stating the main relevant facts which are known about the deceased Edgar Vandy and his death. He was a brilliant engineer and inventor, 38 years old, who lived in London with his mother and two sisters. His father was dead. Two brothers, George and Harold, were living, besides the two sisters already mentioned. One brother had died in infancy, and one sister, Millie, had died some five years before 1933. Edgar was unmarried. He was occupied in working out the details of a complex machine which he had invented. References to this play an important part in the case, and I shall describe it later.

Edgar Vandy had a friend, Mr N. J. This man owned two cycle-shops, and Edgar had first become friendly with him through buying materials for his work at one of these shops. On the morning of Sunday, August 6th, 1933, Mr N. J. called in his car, with his mother, at the Vandys' house and took Edgar with him for a drive to visit a private estate near N. in Sussex. N. J.'s sister was secretary to the owner of this estate, who was away at the time. On arriving at this house, Edgar and N. J. were joined by this sister at about 11.30 a.m. There was a private swimming-pool near the house, and the two men decided to bathe, as the day was very hot. The pool was 4 feet deep at the shallow end and 7 feet deep at the other end, with an edging of crazy-pavement. The bottom was cemented. The pool was fed by an underground stream, the water was rather cloudy, and there was a certain amount of slime on the shelving cement floor, but there were no weeds. Edgar was a poor swimmer and could not dive, but he had bathed on the previous Thursday with his brother Harold at the Regent Street Polytechnic. He had not thought of bathing when he set out on the present occasion, and had no suit with him. So he borrowed one from Miss J., which did not fit him very well.

It is stated by N. J. that he and Edgar did not use the cubicles, but undressed in the bushes adjoining the pool. Edgar's clothes were in fact found afterwards about 200 feet away in a wood. N. J. stated that Edgar was ready before he was, and that he did not see him enter the pool because his view was obscured by the bushes. It is not known whether Miss J. remained in the neighbourhood of the pool or not. George Vandy states that recent attempts to trace her (presumably made some time in the 1950s) have failed.

Edgar Vandy was found dead in the swimming-pool, and an inquest was held, which was reported in the *Sussex Gazette* and in some other local papers, but not, so far as can be ascertained, in any of the London papers. The main witness was N. J. His sister was not asked to give evidence, and was not present at the inquest. (This struck Harold Vandy as strange, especially in view of the fact that she had certainly come on the scene at a later stage and had made an effort to recover the body from the pool.)

N. J.'s evidence at the inquest was as follows: They had gone to bathe at about 12 noon. He had never bathed there before, nor had he ever bathed anywhere with Edgar before this. Edgar had entered the water, unseen by N. J., who did not complete his undressing and reach the pool until two or three minutes later. When N. J. first saw Edgar in the water the latter was lying on the surface, face downwards, with his arms stretched out and fluttering his hands. Edgar began splashing, and N. J. realized that something was amiss. He thereupon jumped in. By the time he reached Edgar the latter was beginning to sink. N. J. caught hold of him, but could not keep his grip. Edgar sank, and N. J. then went to seek for help.

The body was first recovered at 13.15, in presence of the police and a doctor. The pool had had to be dragged and partially drained before this could be done. Artificial respiration was tried, but in vain. Afterwards the body was placed in a garage.

The medical evidence was as follows. There were no abnormalities in the bodily organs which could account for the death. There were two slight abrasions under the chin, one on the right shoulder, and one on the left side of the body. The tongue had been bitten through. Death was undoubtedly due to drowning, but there was less fluid in the lungs than is usual when death is so caused. The doctor was inclined to think that Edgar had been stunned before being drowned. He thought that the bruises on the body suggested that the victim had fallen. He put forward the theory that Edgar had dived in, struck his jaw and lost consciousness, and had then been drowned.

Harold Vandy stated at the inquest that he had bathed with Edgar at a London swimming-bath a week or so before the accident. He asserted that Edgar could not dive, and could only just swim across the bath. He therefore thought it most unlikely that Edgar would have attempted, whilst still alone, to dive into a pool which was completely strange to him.

Edgar's cousin Ted (an expert swimmer and life-saver), who visited the site some time later with George Vandy, put forward the following theory. He thought that Edgar must have entered the pool from the shallow end, that he had 'suddenly stepped down on the ramp', and had been thrown into deep water. (I do not understand the phrase 'stepping down on the ramp'. I suppose it must refer to a spring-board for diving. No doubt the phrase was intelligible to those familiar with the scene.) Another theory, mentioned by George Vandy, is that Edgar was attempting to climb out of the pool at a point where he could not touch bottom; that he had got half-way out, and had then slipped and hit his chin against the edge; and that he was thus stunned and afterwards drowned.

CONSULTATIONS WITH MEDIUMS

The outcome of the inquest was unsatisfactory to Edgar's two surviving brothers, George and Harold. There remained a certain amount of mystery as to the precise details of the death, and, in particular, as to the failure to rescue the drowning man in time to save his life.

George Vandy had no belief in survival of bodily death, nor did the results of the sittings to be described below suffice to alter his opinion. But he had been a member of the S.P.R. for some years at the time of the tragedy, and he was aware of the evidence alleged for various kinds of ostensibly paranormal cognition. He thought it possible that trance-mediums might possess such powers, and that they might by means of them be able to throw some further light on his brother's last moments.

In Chapter XI of this book, when dealing with the phenomenology of Mrs Leonard's mediumship, we had occasion to refer to Mr Drayton Thomas and certain of his work with Mrs Leonard, in which the two ostensible communicators were his deceased father John and his deceased sister Etta. At this point in the Vandy Case another line of investigation pursued by Mr Drayton Thomas becomes relevant. This is what are known as 'proxy-sittings'. The essential features of a proxy-sitting are the following. The experimenter (in the present case Mr Drayton Thomas) receives in writing from some person, often a complete stranger to him, a few distinctive facts about a certain recently deceased individual, also completely unknown to the experimenter. The specified facts are such as would suffice to enable the experimenter to recognize with some probability that the medium was referring to the individual in question, if she should happen to do so during his next sitting with her. The normal procedure was then the following. The experimenter would write down the information which the stranger had sent him about the unknown deceased individual, so as to impress it on his memory; would read it over to himself in private; and would then seal it up and post it to an officer of the S.P.R., to be filed without being opened. Before going to the sitting at which he would try to make contact with the individual in question, Drayton Thomas (who was himself fully convinced of survival and of communication with the dead through mediums) would spend a little time in his study in meditation, endeavouring mentally (as it seemed to him) to get in touch with the deceased and to ask for his co-operation. After that he would visit the medium (in this case Mrs Leonard) and have a sitting with her. She would be told nothing of the contents of the filed paper, or of the reason for that particular sitting, though she was aware of the general idea of 'proxy-sittings'. Sometimes, under such conditions, the medium ostensibly makes contact with someone who answers to the description submitted to the sitter of the deceased individual, and proceeds to supply further specific details which are found to be highly characteristic of that person and very unlikely to apply collectively to anyone else.

George Vandy had never met Drayton Thomas personally, but he had heard him give a lecture on proxy-sittings. He therefore wrote to Drayton Thomas, asking him (i) whether he would undertake a proxy-sitting with Mrs Leonard on his behalf, and (ii) whether he could mention the names of some other mediums with whom the writer might himself have sittings. The only fact relevant to Edgar which he stated in his letter was that 'he wanted to obtain information about a brother who had died recently, and that there was some doubt in the minds of relatives as to the cause of the death'. No names or other details were given, and, in particular, it was not mentioned that the death was due to other than natural causes. The writer mentioned that there was a sister and another brother still living. Drayton Thomas answered on August 15th, 1933. He recommended three mediums, Miss Campbell, Mrs Mason, and Miss Bacon. He promised to take a proxy-sitting with Mrs Leonard for George Vandy as soon as opportunity should arise, but mentioned that there might be some delay.

George Vandy thereupon made arrangements for either himself or his brother Harold or both to have sittings with the three mediums recommended by Drayton Thomas. The following precautions were taken against the possibility that the mediums might gain relevant information beforehand by normal means, and against unwitting conveyance of information by leading questions, etc., in the course

353

of the sittings. (i) In making an appointment with a medium the intending sitter always gave a fictitious name and address. (ii) All correspondence making appointments, etc., was carefully preserved for future reference. (iii) To each sitting the sitter took with him an experienced shorthand-typist, chosen by himself and unknown to the medium. The name was never mentioned to the medium, and the person employed was not always the same. The shorthand writer took down a verbatim report of everything that was said either by the medium or by the sitter from the beginning to the end of a sitting. These notes were then typewritten and sent to the sitter, who annotated them immediately after receiving them.

A synopsis of the relevant details of the arrangements at these sittings is given in the table below:

Date	Place	Medium	Sitter	Sitter's Pseudonym	Note-taker
24/8/33	Medium's home	Miss Campbell	George V.	'Felton'	Mr N. J.
30/8/33	,,	,, ,,	Harold V.	'Greenbaum'	Miss Jolivard
15/9/33	Coll. of Psychic Science	Mrs Mason	George V.	'Felton'	,, ,,
19/10/33	,,	Miss Bacon	Harold V.	'Greenbaum'	,, ,,
11/11/33	,,	,, ,,	George V.	'Calvert'	Mr Foster

In referring to sittings I shall for convenience use the following notation. I shall place *first* the initial of the *medium* and *second* that of the *sitter*, joining the two with a hyphen. Thus, e.g., 'L-T' means the sitting at which Mrs Leonard was the medium and Mr Drayton Thomas the sitter; 'C-G' means the sitting at which Miss Campbell was the medium and George Vandy the sitter; and so on.

The following observations may be made on the entries in the above table. (i) It is stated that there is no obvious likeness between the brothers George and Harold, and therefore no obvious normal reason why Miss Campbell or Miss Bacon, with each of whom both had a sitting, should connect the two sitters, whose pseudonyms and fictitious addresses were different. But one cannot ignore the possibility, for what it is worth, that the medium may in each case have somehow sensed a connexion between the two sitters. (ii) It will be noted that George Vandy took with him, as note-taker at his first sitting with Miss Campbell, Mr N. J., i.e. the man most intimately concerned with the circumstances surrounding Edgar's death. N. J. happened to be a competent shorthand writer. He was not introduced by name to Miss Campbell, but his presence may well have influenced the course that the communications took. (iii) Miss Jolivard, the note-taker at three of the sittings, was a trained short-hand-typist employed in Harold Vandy's office. She had twice in her life seen Edgar, on occasions when he had called on Harold at the office. She knew nothing of the invention on which Edgar was work-ing at the time of his death. (iv) It will be noted that two of the sit-tings at which George Vandy was sitter were held at the rooms of the British College of Psychic Science, viz. one on September 15th, 1933, with Mrs Mason, and another on November 11th of the same year with Miss Bacon. In view of this he took particular care on the second occasion to avoid all chance of being identified with the 'Mr Felton', in whose fictitious name he had had a sitting in the same building with Mrs Mason some two months earlier. He used the new pseu-donym of 'Calvert', wrote from a different fictitious address in mak-ing the appointment, and took with him a different note-taker, viz. Mr Foster. The latter was an expert shorthand-writer, who knew very little about Edgar and nothing about the machine on the perfecting of which Edgar was at work at the time of his death.

THE CONTENT OF THE OSTENSIBLE COMMUNICATIONS

For the present purpose I shall confine myself to the two most important topics which are mentioned in detail in the various sit-tings, viz. (A) Edgar Vandy's death, and (B) the machine which he had invented and on which he was working at the end of his life.

(A) EDGAR VANDY'S DEATH

In reference to the circumstances of Edgar's death we may divide the sittings into two groups, viz. (I) the proxy-sitting L-T, and (II) the five non-proxy sittings entered in the above table.

(I) *The Proxy Sitting L-T.* It will be remembered that Drayton Thomas, in his reply of August 15th, 1933, to George Vandy's letter, had promised to have a proxy-sitting with Mrs Leonard as soon as a convenient opportunity should arise. On September 6th, 1933, i.e. shortly after the sittings which George and Harold Vandy respec-tively had had with Miss Campbell, Drayton Thomas happened to be having a sitting with Mrs Leonard. This was *not* intended as a proxy-sitting on behalf of the Vandys. Drayton Thomas had not been thinking of George Vandy's letter immediately beforehand, and had not gone through his normal process of 'meditation' in reference to the person referred to. He was, of course, completely unaware of the fact that the two brothers had each lately had a sitting with Miss

355

Campbell. In fact this sitting of Drayton Thomas's with Mrs Leonard concerned himself and certain of his own deceased relatives.

At a certain point in this sitting, however, Mrs Leonard's control, Feda, said to Drayton Thomas: 'Do you know a man who passed just lately; it was quite sudden?' Feda stated that this person had been well and vigorous until quite recently, and she got an image first of the letter 'M' and then of the letter 'H' in connexion with him. (It will be remembered that a recently deceased sister was named 'Millie', and that one of the two brothers interested in the case was called 'Harold'.) Feda continued as follows: 'I seem to get a thought from someone, as if they were thinking of you. Keep a look out. This may be a proxy-case about someone who went out through falling.'

At that point it struck Drayton Thomas that this might possibly refer to the case indicated in George Vandy's letter to him of about three weeks ago. He therefore remarked to Feda that the present intervention might refer to a case which he had been asked about a few weeks earlier. He added, however, that he knew nothing about a *fall* in that connexion.

Feda then continued to the following effect. The person concerned was not a boy, but he was not old. She had the idea of a tragic accident involving a fall. She got the impression of giddiness and a sensation as of falling. She then remarked on certain financial and other practical consequences of his sudden death to surviving relatives and friends. I omit these remarks, in order to string together the references to the circumstances of the death.

Drayton Thomas now remarked to Feda that, if the communicator were the person whom he thought he might be, he would have two older brothers still living, one of whom had written to him to arrange a proxy-sitting. Drayton Thomas added that there appeared to be something mysterious in the circumstances of the death, and asked whether the communicator could throw light on these and help relieve the survivors' minds.

Feda thereupon continued as follows: 'It was not his fault, he says . . . There was a funny feeling in his head—a woolly head—muddled . . . It was something he had felt before . . . and feels even now when he thinks of his passing . . . He says: It was not *anyone's* fault, certainly not *his* . . . He says: Stepping out unconsciously . . . my mind not on myself at the moment. I was thinking of other things . . . an aberration . . . not planned, coming about in a way too much for me, not realizing what was going to happen . . . doing things automatically for a short time . . . I was holding, grasping something . . . I think I wanted to turn or twist or move something. I realized the importance of air . . . was very tired mentally . . . Am

356

sure I closed something . . . Think I let go. I remember saying to myself: I must be careful what I do with this . . . how I handle and turn
it. Then it seemed as if my mind became curiously blank . . . I can't
remember exactly what happened—thought I was falling down and
through something, as one does in sleep . . . It has nothing to do with
them at all, and they could not have helped me in any way at all. I
am sure they would have done, had it been possible . . . I'm so deeply
sorry about all the trouble . . . that . . . could not be avoided . . . at
the dragging something . . . or someone in . . . the malicious, stupid,
wrong interpretation given to certain proceedings . . . certain aspects
of the whole exaggerated . . . I ought to be here now on earth . . . I
am sure they think so too. I say again, blame no one, not even me . . .
I do not want them to think it was anyone's fault. Yet I do not want
them to think I was picked out by God, or some fate, or some
nonsense of that sort. Just a combination of circumstances were too
much; no one's fault.'

Shortly after this contact was lost with this ostensible communicator, and a little later Mrs Leonard awoke from her trance. Just
before that Drayton Thomas asked Feda whether she had been
seeing the communicator. She answered that she had not, but that
he had been *dictating* his message to her and she had merely been
transmitting it. She added that she had the impression of a man
labouring under a kind of anxiety, wanting to explain things, but
willing to do so only in his own way.

This intervention, coming out of the blue, was certainly singular
and impressive. Drayton Thomas concluded that it might well refer
to the deceased brother mentioned in George Vandy's letter. So he
sent the record of the sitting to George, who not unnaturally felt
that it fitted.

The following points are worth noting. (i) There is no explicit
reference to water or to drowning, but a strong suggestion of some
kind of fainting followed by a fall (as the communicator put it)
'down and through something'; (ii) the reiterated statement that the
deceased was grasping, handling, and turning something, which he
cast aside shortly before the end, cannot be confirmed and is almost
certainly false; (iii) it seems plain that the dramatic form of the communication is as if it came from a person anxious to refute two suspicions about the circumstances of his death, viz. (*a*) that it was due
to deliberate action or blameworthy carelessness on his own part,
and (*b*) that his life would have been saved if and only if certain other
persons had not failed to act as they should and easily could have
done. We shall find variations on this theme running through the
communications coming by way of the other mediums.

Before passing to these other ostensible communications, I would

357

emphasize the two following points. (i) The first is the extreme slenderness of the link between the deceased Edgar and the medium Mrs Leonard. The only *normal* link at the time when the sitting took place was that George Vandy, who was personally unknown to both Drayton Thomas and Mrs Leonard, had written to the former some three weeks earlier a letter, in which he had stated only that he had lost a brother under unspecified circumstances which were causing anxiety to him and to his surviving brother and sister, had asked for advice as to mediums whom he might consult, and had requested Drayton Thomas to make the matter the subject of a proxy-sitting.

(ii) The second point is this. I would not cite the present case as a typical or as a particularly impressive instance of the class of proxy-cases. It is not *typical*, in that Drayton Thomas had *not* made any of his usual preparations for a proxy-sitting on behalf of a particular applicant. He was not at the time consciously thinking of the contents of George Vandy's letter, and the sitting had been arranged with altogether different ostensible communicators in view. The communication, which was taken to refer to the deceased Edgar Vandy, was of the nature of an 'intrusion'. For that very reason it is not *particularly impressive*, taken by itself, from an evidential point of view. For the fact that the contents of the 'intrusion' in some ways fitted rather well into the circumstances of Edgar Vandy's death might well have been fortuitous.

The *main* strength of the Vandy Case is in the contents of the *non-proxy* sittings, and the proxy-sitting described above is of importance only when taken in concatenation with them. It should be added that the *best* proxy-cases are very impressive indeed, and are among the most remarkable performances of trance-mediumship. Any reader who may wish to pursue that topic further is recommended to study the following two papers by Drayton Thomas in the S.P.R. *Proceedings*, viz. 'A Proxy Case extending over Eleven Sittings with Mrs Osborne Leonard' (*Proceedings*, Vol. XLIII, Part 143) and 'A Proxy Experiment of Significant Success' (*Proceedings*, Vol. XLV, Part 159). The former may be referred to as the 'Bobby Newlove Case' and the latter as the 'Macaulay-Lewis Case'.

(II) *The non-Proxy Sittings.* The distinguishing mark of the non-proxy sittings is that at each of them the sitter was one or other of the two surviving brothers, George and Harold.

(1) *Way in which ostensible Contact was made with the Deceased.* Before making comparisons between statements made in two or more of the sittings, I will go through the five in chronological order, and

describe the way in which ostensible contact with the deceased Edgar Vandy first manifested itself in each sitting.

(C-G). The sitting began with *inaccurate* references to the sitter's mother, who was alleged to be 'in the spirit world', but was in fact alive. The medium then stated that the sitter was *one of five children.* He assented; but immediately afterwards the medium corrected the number to *six.* The sitter then recollected that a brother had died in infancy, and that the amended number was the right one. Thereupon the medium said explicitly: 'You have a *brother* in the spirit world, who passed over as the result of an *accident.*' She then proceeded to make various statements about him, which were in the main characteristic and correct.

(C-H). The sitting began with a brief and correct allusion to the sitter's *deceased father,* followed by some comments on the sitter's health. Directly after this the medium said: 'There is a man who passed over *very suddenly,* and he seems terribly anxious to communicate with you . . . He is in a very disturbed state, as if he is *suffering from shock,* as if he passed over feeling he would like to get back *to clear matters up.*' Almost immediately afterwards she said explicitly: 'He is your *brother,* he tells me. He says *brother.*' Thereupon she proceeded to make a number of statements concerning him and the manner of his death.

(M-G). The sitting began poorly, with what the sitter describes as a certain amount of 'fishing and fumbling'. Allusions were made to four persons, none of whom could be identified. Thereafter she mentioned the name 'Millie', and there were some vague communications purporting to come from the sister of that name who had died some five years earlier. At that stage the *sitter put the question*: 'Has she' [i.e. Millie] 'seen any other people yet?' The medium answered: 'She speaks of having seen her *brother,* passed out young. She passed out *before* him. There is a young man come in response to her call— I should think 34, or something like it.' After that the medium proceeded to make a number of statements about this young man and how he had met his death.

(B-H). The sitting began with a description of an *elderly man,* purporting to be the sitter's *father.* Nothing of evidential value came through until the *sitter handed to the medium a roll of paper,* which had been made by Edgar as one of the 'records' to be used in the machine on the construction of which he had been working. The sitter, of course, did not mention any of these facts to the medium, but merely showed her the roll and asked for her impressions. Thereupon she said: 'Whoever this belonged to, did he not pass out in a *very tragic* way?' 'Well, yes,' answered the sitter. Thereupon the medium launched out into a detailed description of the owner of the roll and the circumstances of his death. So far as I can discover, she *never* realized that this person was in fact a brother of the sitter.

(B-G). The sitting was a long one. The medium plunged at once *in medias res*. She immediately began to talk of a *young man*, who was obviously Edgar Vandy, gave a description of his appearance, and an account of the circumstances of his death. To the latter topic she repeatedly returned, elaborating the details. *All* the communications in this sitting concerned Edgar.

(2) *Themes common to Several Sittings*. I shall next compare the various sittings (including Drayton Thomas's sitting with Mrs Leonard) with a view to picking out certain themes which are common to several of them concerning Edgar and the circumstances of his death. Such common themes may be classified according to whether they occur in all six sittings, in exactly five sittings . . . and so on down to exactly two sittings. It should be remarked that a theme may be common to two or more sittings, but there may be variations in points of detail, and these may sometimes be inconsistent with each other.

(i) *Common to all Six Sittings*. There are two such themes, viz. (*a*) that Edgar *fell*, and in particular that *his head was hit and damaged*; and (*b*) that *one or more persons were present at the scene of the tragedy*, that it might be thought that they *could and should have saved Edgar's life and that they failed to do so through cowardice or incompetence*, and that *Edgar wishes to shield them*.

(*a*) *Fall and blow on the head*. The essential statements are as follows:

(C-G). Something *hit* him . . . He had some *blow to the head*. His head was *jerked back* so violently that he thought at first that his neck was broken. There were some *bruises* . . . (C-H). Did he get *hit on the head*, as if his head had touched something? But before his head had touched he had lost all sense. He must have known that he was going . . . Now he illustrates that he seemed to *double up and fall*. I think a *fall on the head* . . . (L-T). This may be a proxy-case of someone who went out through *falling* . . . I get the idea of a *fall*, an accident . . . I was *falling down through something*, as one does in sleep . . . (M-G). I get the *blow*. I get it he was *knocked unconscious* . . . He is giving me a pain right through here [touching the back of her neck] . . . I get *falling*, a feeling of *falling* . . . (B-H). He gives me such frightful pain. I don't know what happened—all over my body; it is just as though I had been *broken* . . . Would you understand why I get this awful pain in the body? . . . I seem to get a grasping sensation of some sort, as though I cannot hold on to the earth and had to let go . . . (B-G). As he stood near me I felt a distinct *blow or crack on the head*, and a pain in the back of the neck. I seem as if I had *fallen forward*.

It may be remarked that these various statements seem to be fairly consistent both with each other and with the facts revealed at the inquest. There is a minor inconsistency between C-H, in which it is stated that Edgar had lost all consciousness *before* getting the blow on the head, and M-G, in which it is stated that he was *knocked* unconscious.

(b) *Question of blame attaching to others*. The essential statements are as follows:

(C-G). He is now getting on to something he does not want to discuss . . . He does not care to speak about it now . . . His passing over involved *someone else*; I don't say directly, but *indirectly through neglect or incompetence* . . . He is not terribly keen on this enquiry. He *does not want you to enquire too deeply into the cause of the death . . .* There was *somebody else*. There was another person. [It should be noted, however, that it is stated in the same sitting that Edgar was *alone* when he *fell*. 'He had no one with him at the time . . . No one saw him fall.']

(C-H). One point he insists on, and that is that he was *talking to someone*, and he *deliberately does not give the name* . . . Your brother is very good-natured, and there is a lot of feeling behind his not giving the name . . . There is someone on this side [i.e. still living on earth—C. D. B.] it gives me a feeling he is *trying to protect*. I can't quite get it, but he is saying: 'She was *frightened and went away*'. . . It was an accident which was foolish; but it brings in another person, and that is a point which he seems to think you will find it difficult to digest . . . There was some other person present . . . Someone besides him was very frightened. He was *stupid with fear*, and did not know what to do . . . He [i.e. Edgar—C. D. B.] has *no anger* towards them, only sympathy and sorrow.

[It should be noted that the delinquent 'someone' is first referred to as a woman and later as a man. I suppose that this might be made consistent by assuming that both Mr N. J.'s sister and Mr N. J. himself were involved at different stages of the tragedy.]

(L-T). It has nothing to do with them at all, and they could not have helped me in any way. I am sure they would have done, had it been possible . . . I am so deeply sorry about all the trouble . . . at the dragging—I think he says 'dragging'—someone or something *in*. Sorry, but it could not be helped. The malicious, stupid, wrong interpretation given to certain proceedings, exaggeration—I say so—certain aspects of the whole exaggerated . . . I say again: Blame no one, not even me. I'll do my best to straighten things out for three people's sake . . .

(M-G). I feel that he could tell me more than he will tell me, but he might *implicate someone else*. That is what I feel, and he does not want to give it . . . (B-H). He seems to be very unwilling to assist me now . . . Whether he was sensitive on earth I cannot tell, but he certainly seems like it now . . . Is it true that you cannot get accurate information as to what happened . . . and that there is *something being hushed up*? . . . Someone was there and *knows what happened, but will not own up*. If the other person, who was with him, had not been *cowardly*, it would not have happened. The other man *knows about it and will not say*. I do not know if he was frightened and got out of the way and left him; he [i.e. Edgar—*C. D. B.*] is asking me to tell you that. [It will be noted that here the delinquent is definitely stated to be a *man*.]

(B-G). It is as if there were *someone else*—but no one listened to him calling out, no one heard him *except this man, who was rather worried*. . . He is telling me that he was *not alone*. There was somebody near him who *swam away or got out and did not wait to help him*. He distinctly said that there was another man there at the time he was hurt. He says: 'I don't altogether *blame him*'. . . I don't know whether he was suggesting that somebody *might have prevented his passing out*, or that there might have been a *questionable incident* about it. Was not somebody suspected? Well, he wants to make it quite clear that there was nothing *intentionally* done. It was merely done *through fear* on the part of *somebody else*, who went away without giving assistance. It was a *cowardly* act, but not intentional . . . [Here again it will be noted that the delinquent is a *man*.]

I think that the following comment may be made on all this. It is perfectly clear that we are concerned here with a quite definite and outstanding theme, common to all six sittings, and highly relevant to the circumstances of Edgar's death and to the suspicions in the minds of his surviving relatives. But there is a certain difference between the handling of it in the proxy-sitting, on the one hand, and in all the non-proxy sittings, on the other. In the proxy-sitting it is asserted that there was nothing that the other person or persons concerned could have done to help, and that their action or failure to act has been misinterpreted by third parties. In the non-proxy sittings the line taken is that help *could* have been given, and *would* have been were it not for extreme fear on the part of someone, whom *Edgar* on the whole does not blame and wishes to shield.

(ii) *Common to exactly Five Sittings*. There are two themes common to all five non-proxy sittings, but not occurring in the non-proxy one.

These are (*a*) references to *water* and *drowning*, and (*b*) that Edgar's death was a *strangely unlucky* event, which might easily have been avoided.

(*a*) *References to water and drowning.* The essential statements are as follows:

(C-G). He shows me *water*. Was there water in connexion with his death? . . . He shows me his arms and legs, he was dressed in a *short swimming-suit* . . . He keeps talking of a *struggle to get breath* . . . His clothes were at *some distance* from where he was. He was not accustomed to be dressed as he was then. [In reference to the above statements, it will be recalled that Edgar was dressed in a borrowed swimming-suit, which did not fit him very well, and that his clothes were in fact at some distance from the pool.]

(C-H). He shows me *water* . . . He *dived* naturally and was killed . . . [It should be remarked that it is most unlikely that Edgar would have dived, since it is known that he had never learned to do so.]

(M.G). He was *suffocated*, and that is why I get this pain—I can tell you that much . . . He is very rambling in his statements, showing me a scene as if he could have been near *water—not the sea*, a *little* amount of water . . . At the time of his passing he was rather near water. Was he *drowned*? [The sitter answered: 'Yes', and the medium then continued as follows] . . . Of course he was. I don't know how he came to get this *blow*, but he was *found in the water* . . . He certainly had a blow, and I am getting as though he were *semi-conscious when he was in the water* . . .

[It will be remembered that there was evidence at the inquest that Edgar had been stunned before being drowned, and that there were bruises on his body which suggested that he must have fallen. Mrs Mason got the impression of the fall and of an injury through some kind of blow before she got the idea of drowning. She was led to the latter by way of an impression of death taking place near a *small* bit of water, and *not* the sea. That was, of course, correct.]

(B-H). I feel as though I were going *under* somewhere, as though in some way I were losing contact in an extraordinary manner . . . I feel very *cold* . . . as though something had happened . . . Would you understand why I feel so *deadly cold*? [The sitter said: 'I could probably understand that', and the medium continued] . . . It seems to me that the one you want has only just recently passed out, and that you are not sure of the way he did so. [The sitter assented, and the medium continued] . . . I am getting a sensation of *floating out on water* . . . as though something happened, but *I am in water*. Is that wrong? [The sitter said: 'Not altogether', and the medium continued as follows] . . . It was an accident, and I do not know why, but it is so

363

wet at the time . . . [After some other statements she continued as follows] . . . He seems to show me a scene where he was found . . . He is showing me *two people bending over him* as though they were trying to help him . . . I get the impression of *wet and cold* . . . of being in the *water*, as though I had been *dropped into water*. [On awaking from trance the medium said *inter alia*: 'I feel as if I had been *drowned*.']

[The main comment to be made is this. The medium got repeated impressions of the death being by drowning, and of the body being leant over and picked up by a number of persons, whom she sometimes states to be two and at other times three. But she got the false impression—as appears if one reads the full report of the sitting—that the scene of the tragedy was a *large stretch of water*, and not a lake or a pool.]

(B-G). I don't know whether he was a *strong swimmer*—there is *sea* at the back of him. Whether he had been *swimming* I can't say . . . I am seeing him as if he went *into the sea or near the sea*. I am seeing him *on the shore about to go in*. I don't know what this means—whether he was not a strong swimmer and had an accident that way . . . I don't know if it was the *turn of the tide*. It is something like that; he got *caught under or in the turn of the tide* . . . He was *not alone* in the water—there were people beside the water . . . It looks *something like the sea* . . . It would seem strange, because he was *accustomed to going in the water*. It seems almost—I don't quite know—something beyond him—he seems to have been *caught under* . . .

[There followed a long communication about the machine which Edgar had invented, and after that the medium reverted to the subject of his death. The sitter interpolated the question: 'Can he tell us exactly what happened?' and the medium continued as follows] . . . He passed out through *water*. I don't think it was a *swimming-bath*. I am in a *private kind of pool*, and I am getting *diving* and things like that. Yes, I am *out of doors*, I am not enclosed—it is like a *private swimming-pool* . . . You know he had a *blow on the head* before he passed over. He *banged part of his scalp*. [The sitter asked: 'How did he do that?', and the medium continued] . . . Not *diving*. His foot slipped, and the bottom of the pool is not bricked-in . . . He is talking about *catching his foot in the bottom*, being *drawn under* . . . I am not sure if someone was diving at the time. There was a *diving-board*, and whether someone knocked him or not, I don't know . . . He remembers going under and feeling a distinct blow on the head. He could not come up, as he apparently *lost consciousness under the water*. The water should have been *transparent*, and it is very extraordinary that no one saw that . . . He has a sensation of being *drawn underneath*. I don't know whether the *bottom was bricked or tiled*, but it seems as though there were some *grass at the bottom*. It is an open-air pool, and he says he must have *fallen forward*, and *crashed in*, and *knocked his head*. He knows that there was *someone swimming there at the time*. He talks to me as if he were under the water some little time before he drowned . . . Whether he was *foolish enough to have dived* I don't know. It is the *first time he attempted it*. He did not die of suffocation, as a swimmer does . . . I will try to re-enact his passing, which he is trying to show me: 'I was sliding to the bottom of the pool in this very fainting condition, owing to pitching forward in some way and knocking my head just before' . . . Would this pool *belong to a certain place*? I don't know; it seems so extraordinary . . .

[The following comments may be made. (α) The medium begins, as in her sitting with Harold Vandy, with the mistaken impression that the accident took place while swimming in the *sea*. But now this is gradually corrected. She comes in the end, without any prompting from the sitter, to exactly the right view, viz. that it happened in a *private swimming-pool in the open air*, as opposed both to the sea and to an enclosed public swimming-bath. (β) She is mistaken in saying that Edgar was accustomed to going into the water to bathe. (γ) She is uncertain whether he did or did not dive, but is clear that it would have been a foolish thing for him to do, since it would have been a first attempt. (δ) It is almost certainly false that there was another person swimming there *at the time*, though there was, of course, another person, viz. N. J., who was *just about* to swim there. (ε) There was a *diving-board*, as stated. But that might fairly be guessed. The bottom of the pool was neither bricked nor tiled, as stated, but was *cemented*. There was no grass at the bottom, only a little *slime*. The water was not transparent, it was somewhat *cloudy*.]

(b) *The death a singularly unlucky and easily avoidable event.* The essential statements concerning this second theme are the following:

(C-G). He says that, *if he had altered his plans a little*, this would not have happened . . . (C-H). He is saying: '*It seems so silly. I ought to have been able to save myself, but it was not long before my heart just seemed to stop*' . . . (M-G). From what I see of the conditions, it is just as though it were *strange that he was drowned* . . . (B-H). I also sense that it was *quite an accident* . . . if plans had been changed . . . it would not have happened . . . He is saying that it was *such a mistake*, because he need not have been in that place at that time . . . (B-G). There were not many people about at the time; there seems to be only him and another man and no one else. If there had been, I feel sure *he could have been brought out and saved* . . . There was something very like anguish, as if he could have been saved. If help had been given, he *need not* have passed over . . .

[The only comment that I would make is this. There are two

365

different bits of ill-luck, and the second is contingent on the first. In the first place, Edgar's very presence on that occasion at the place at which he met his death was very much of a fluke. It depended on N. J.'s having called at the Vandys' house in his car, and on Edgar's having accepted N. J.'s invitation to take him for a drive. This is the point made in C-G and in B-H. Secondly, granted that Edgar bathed and met with the unlucky accident in the swimming-pool, it was bad luck that he was not rescued. This is the point made in C-H, in B-G, and probably in M-G.]

(iii) *Common to exactly Four Sittings.* There are two themes which are common to four and only four of the sittings. These are (*a*) that the death was *not due to suicide or to culpable carelessness on Edgar's part*, and (*b*) that there was a feeling of *dizziness* just before or in close conjunction with the accident.

(*a*) *Death not due to suicide or culpable carelessness.* The essential statements on this theme are as follows:
(C-G). He was not responsible for his own death. He did not *commit suicide*, and he says that he was *not foolish*, it was not his fault. (L-T). He says: 'It was *not my fault*' . . . He says: 'It was not anyone's fault, and *certainly not mine*'. . . (M-G). He did not *take his own life*. He definitely wanted to say that to you . . . (B-H). If anyone thought it was deliberate, I do not get it as so . . . It was *not his fault*. It seemed to be something that happened under very unusual conditions.
[The only comment that seems called for is this. Whilst there is not the least suggestion in any of the sittings that it was a case of *suicide*, there are conflicting statements as to whether it was due to *carelessness or rashness* on Edgar's part. C-G, L-T, and B-H all insist that it was not *in any way* Edgar's fault. But B-G takes a different view. When the medium reverted to the death, after the long interlude in which she had been talking of the machine, she began as follows: He says he feels very ashamed of the way he passed. It was so stupid, and such a crazy thing to do. He says: 'I feel I want to ask them to forgive me for doing such a crazy thing at the time; but I did not know that it was dangerous.']

(*b*) *Feeling of dizziness in conjunction with the accident.* The essential statements concerning this second theme are the following:
(C-H). There was a great *feeling of stupidity* . . . (L-T). There was a funny feeling in his head, a '*woolly head*', muddled . . . It was something that he felt before, while, and even now when he thinks of his passing . . . (M-G). He said he was with some other man, and he

366

adds: 'I came over queer. *Everything went black,* and I do not know . . .' (B-G). It is very strange why he went to the bottom, and he is talking of the sensation of falling and *dizziness* . . . He is *not* going through the agony of passing out as though of being drowned and fighting against it . . . I get a *numbness of the brain*; and I am *not* being choked at all, not like a swimmer fighting for breath . . .

(iv) *Common to exactly Three Sittings.* There are in fact three such themes, but only one of them is of enough interest to be treated here. This is a reference to a *scar*, which was already on Edgar's body and was not due to the fatal accident. The relevant passages are as follows:

(C-G). He shows me an *old scar*, and says: 'This is my identification-mark.' On his *face* . . . (B-H). I don't know whether it was as a child, but he had a *scar* on a certain part of his body, which still remains . . . He was as a *child* knocked on the *head or brow*, which left a scar . . . He is also saying that *under his arm* there is a distinct *mole* . . . (B-G). He has a *cut across his forehead* . . .

[As regards these remarks, Edgar's brothers state that he had a large scar on the right-hand side of his forehead, due to being thrown from a trap in childhood. Edgar had been heard by them to remark: 'This scar will always identify me.' The reference to the mole is also stated by the brothers to be correct.]

(3) *Relative Significance of various recurrent Themes.* I omit, as they are of no particular interest, the themes which are common to two and only two of the sittings, and pass now to the relative significance of the various recurring themes which have been noted above. Obviously none of them would be of any significance, unless it were highly specific and characteristic of the ostensible communicator, as distinct from the great majority of recently deceased persons. I think that each of the themes that I have mentioned fulfils that condition, and that the combination of all of them does so in a degree which makes the hypothesis of chance-coincidence quite incredible.

If that be granted, we may proceed to classify themes, from the point of view of relative significance, in the following way. (i) Those common to pairs of sittings in which *both* medium and sitter are *different.* (ii) Those common to pairs of sittings in which *the sitter is the same* but the *mediums are different.* (iii) Those common to pairs of sittings in which *the medium is the same* but the sitters are different. It is obvious that the first are *caeteris paribus* most strongly suggestive of something paranormal. I should myself be inclined to think that themes which occur in the second but not in the first category are more significant than those which occur only in the third.

367

I propose here to consider only themes which fall into the first and most significant category. In the first place, it is plain that any theme which is common to the proxy-sitting L-T and any of the non-proxy sittings fulfils these conditions. There are five such themes, viz. (*a*) that Edgar *fell*, and in particular that *his head was hit and damaged*; (*b*) that *one or more persons were present at the scene of the tragedy*, that *it might have been thought that they could and should have saved Edgar's life*, and that *Edgar wishes to shield them*; (*c*) that the death was *not due to suicide*; (*d*) that there was a *feeling of dizziness* just before or in close conjunction with the accident; and (*e*) that the deceased was a *young man, but not a boy*.

Secondly, any theme which occurs in *all five* of the non-proxy sittings necessarily occurs *inter alia* in pairs of sittings in which both sitter and medium were different, and therefore falls into the first category. This adds two further themes, viz. (*f*) references to *water and drowning*; and (*g*) that the death was *a strangely unlucky accident which might easily have been avoided*.

Finally, if we compare the following pairs of non-proxy sittings, viz. C-G and B-H, C-H and M-G, C-H and B-G, M-G and B-H, we find one additional theme, not already mentioned under previous headings, which falls into the first category. This is (*h*) the report of a *scar on the body*, which is common and peculiar to the pairs of sittings C-H and M-G.

There are, thus, in all eight themes, some of them highly specific and characteristic of the deceased and the circumstances of his death, which occur in sittings where both the medium and the sitter are different.

(B) EDGAR VANDY'S MACHINE

I pass now from Edgar Vandy's death, and the references to it, to the machine which he had invented and on which he was working at the time of his death.

The essential Facts about the Machine. It was called the 'Electroline' Drawing Machine, and it was intended to accomplish electro-mechanically results which had never before been produced except by skilled hand-work.

The function of the machine was to draw, more accurately and far more quickly than would be possible by hand, originals of lettering and decorative work, from which copies could be made either by lithography or by other methods of reproduction. The originals were drawn by the machine either (*a*) on sheets of aluminium or zinc, or (*b*) in black ink on white cards. The former could be used for planographic printing, known as 'lithography'. The latter could be photographed for line blocks for typographic or letterpress reproduction.

The essential movements of the machine were controlled by perforated 'records' on rolls of paper, rather like pianola-records. The letters of the alphabet were recorded on such a roll, a complete alphabet on each one. One and the same roll would then enable the machine to draw many thousands of designs of different sorts and sizes. The originals for reproduction in several different colours could all be drawn at one operation. The records worked by engaging small 'feelers', which fell into holes as the record unrolled, and thus picked up electric impulses. These impulses governed the motions of a moving 'bridge' and carriage, to which was attached the pen which drew the letters and designs.

The machine was about 6 feet square, and had a large drawing-board of 60 in. × 40 in. It was started by pushing a button. On the switchboard were two pilot lights, one red and the other bluish green, which would normally light up as soon as the machine was started. They indicated the presence of the two main currents, viz. one which charged the accumulators and the other which was used in the working of the machine. When the machine began to work a long metal 'bridge', carrying a pen-carriage, would start to move forward. The working of the machine was accompanied by a series of 'clicks', made by a number of electro-magnets and relays which controlled its movements. It was by the combined action of the bridge and the pen-carriage that the letters and designs were drawn.

Immediately before his death Edgar had finished designing and constructing an accessory, the function of which was to rule parallel lines in ink. In connexion with this work he had had the help of a lithographic artist named Macnamara, known familiarly as 'Mac', who instructed him in the technicalities of using a pen for ruling lines on lithographic originals. The pen is similar in construction to those supplied with compass-sets. In the apparatus it was balanced by an adjustable weight to ensure the correct pressure.

Only one model of the machine was ever made on a *commercial* scale. Most of the finance for this was provided by Edgar's cousin William, and it was built at the latter's premises in the city of London. The parts were made by various engineering firms, who were not told what they were intended for. When delivered they were fitted together in a private room on William Vandy's premises, set aside for that purpose. In this work Edgar had as his assistant a Mr John Burke. The commercial model never left the premises. It was partly dismantled after Edgar's death, and later on parts of it were destroyed in the air-raids on London.

As regards the *experimental model*, all the plans and calculations for it were made by Edgar at his own home, and the parts were constructed and fitted together in his own workshop there. After his death it was presented, in 1934, to the Science Museum at South Kensington. A photograph of the machine, with a description of certain numbered parts, is reproduced to face p. 32 of the S.P.R. *Journal* for March 1957.

Of those present at the sittings only the two brothers Vandy had any knowledge of the machine. The various note-takers knew nothing about it. Of the two brothers, George was a professional engineer, and knew much more about the technical details of the machine than Harold, who was an estate-agent.

It should be added that Edgar Vandy had a great interest in, and a technical knowledge of, *wireless telegraphy*, and that he was engaged in working out improvements in it. He and George had been founder shareholders in the British Broadcasting Corporation. Edgar was also frequently installing ingenious electrical and other gadgets in his own home and in the homes of some of his friends. Among the fairly numerous references to Edgar's electrical and mechanical interests, which occur in the various sittings, it is not always easy to separate specific references to the Electroline Machine from statements which might as well or better concern one or another of these simultaneous technical activities.

Apparent References to the Machine by the Mediums. For the present purpose we can eliminate the proxy-sitting, for there is nothing in it which looks in the least like a reference to the machine. Among the non-proxy sittings we can eliminate C-G. For, beyond a reference to Edgar's interest in wireless transmission, there is little or nothing in it about his mechanical or inventive activities. On the other hand, we must add to the four remaining non-proxy sittings, already considered in connexion with the circumstances of the death, a second sitting which Harold Vandy had with Miss Campbell on September 8th, 1933. For this contains a number of statements which seem *prima facie* to refer to the machine. I will denote it by the symbol $(C-H)_2$, and I will henceforth refer to Harold's first sitting with Miss Campbell as $(C-H)_1$. So the sittings now to be considered are $(C-H)_1$, $(C-H)_2$, M-G, B-H, and B-G. I will now go through them in that order.

$(C-H)_1$. At a certain stage in this sitting Harold explicitly put to the medium the question: 'What are his desires, and what was the nature of his work?' In answer there came the following string of statements . . . If you [Harold] tried to do his work, you could not . . . He shows me something he wants handed on to someone. It is a little thing that he wants utilized. It is *something he invented*. He says: 'I invented.' He tells me there are lots of notes of it in the book which is

370

missing, which can be used. But not by *you*; someone else can do something with it. It will be of commercial value, if it is properly done, and he wants it pushed . . . Is it anything to do with *air*? He is talking about something to do with *air-pressure* . . .

[At this point the following comments may be made. The medium correctly tumbled to the fact that the deceased was an inventor, keenly interested in mechanical and electrical technique, and that the sitter was *not* expert in such matters. But the details do *not* fit the Electroline. It was not a *little* thing, and *air-pressure* had nothing to do with it.]

I return to the medium's statements . . . The other thing is so simple in construction that it is a wonder that it was not thought of before. It is something that turns over. He laughs about something to do with a *burglar*. He says he is mixing things up. Now he is showing me something that stands so high [indicating the height with her hand]—three things in one—run in three ways. Very cheap indeed. I think he means cheap in comparison with what is now being used. It is not quite finished, it can't quite be used yet . . . There is another man who comes to the house too . . . There is another thing, a small point, and he worked on this one point a long time, but he got it. It has not been fitted, but he knows what he wants now. Can you place a *ship* in connexion with it? . . . You will be very careful how you use this thing of your brother's; it is something on the brink of being discovered and used. Your brother had it working all but one thing . . .

[This is a rich mixture, and the medium does not exaggerate when she says: 'He is mixing things up.' Harold Vandy thought that it was a conflation of references to the *Electroline* machine and to a new type of door-bell which Edgar was constructing for his friend N. J. This bell consisted of a small electric motor, which was to be set in motion by pulling a rope at the front door, and would then cause some pegs to strike against gongs formed by two brake-drums from an old car. The pull was to be a bit of rope with a knot in it to imitate the rope used in *a ship's bell*. N. J. had come to the house, only a week before Edgar's death, to bring the necessary parts. The apparatus had nothing to do with *burglars*, but might perhaps by association have suggested a burglar-alarm. It seems to me that very little weight can be attached to any of these speculations.]

To continue with the medium's babble . . . Do you know of something to do with a *machine*? . . . Do you know if he also knew how to *make sound in greater volume*? He is trying to show me a *fine mesh thing* attached to one of his inventions, very fine and sensitive, and picks up quickly. It comes up in *print*—that is the thing which is very good. It is different from the one I mentioned before . . .

371

[This looks rather more like a specific reference to the *Electroline*, and it is deliberately marked off from previous references by the phrase 'It is different from the one I mentioned before'. On the other hand, the remark about 'making sound in greater volume' is completely irrelevant. Harold thought that the 'fine mesh thing' might be the medium's impression of one of the perforated paper records. If the paper is held up to the light, the perforations make it look like mesh. It might fairly be described as 'very sensitive', and it might fairly be said that as a result of its operation something 'comes up in print', viz. the letters or the design which the pen proceeds to draw. It is this result which the medium describes as 'very good', and it was of course the whole point of the invention.]

My own feeling is that, if the statements in (C-H)$_1$ stood alone, it would be extremely rash to assert more than that they indicate a correct and remarkable impression, on the medium's part, of Edgar's very varied inventive interests and activities. It is only when they are taken in the context of statements made in other sittings that they perhaps acquire a more specific significance.

(C-H)$_2$. This contains very much more specific references than does (C-H)$_1$ ... Does he know a man called '*Mac*'? He is saying something that sounds like: '*Mac understands some work that I am doing.*' This man would understand, for he [i.e. Edgar] is saying: '*Press has not yet quite the right weight behind it*' ... Something heavy ... He holds on to a thing like—Has he got something *where two sides come together*?—*where you insert something in between*, and two things come together ...

[This is plainly a very palpable hit on the medium's part. It will be remembered that 'Mac' was the familiar name for Macnamara, the lithographic expert who was helping Edgar to construct an accessory which would enable the Electroline to rule parallel lines for reproduction by lithography. It will be remembered, too, that the pen resembled a compass-pen, in that the ink was inserted between two contiguous blades, which were then brought together. And finally it will be remembered that the pressure of the pen was regulated by means of an adjustable weight.]

The medium continued as follows ... He shows me a *red and a green light*, which I cannot understand the significance of. Did he, for some purpose of his own, change the electric bulb to a coloured bulb?

[To this Harold answered: 'No, I don't understand this.' But afterwards he recalled the two pilot lights, one red and the other bluish green, on the switchboard of the Electroline, and concluded that the reference was to them.]

The medium continued as follows ... He is trying to show me

climbing on a ladder, and something to do with a *light.* Again, he talks about a '*main current*'. He is very excited. This is something new in electricity, something which has been worked in a new method. Is it connected with *the house*? If you can only get it pushed, he is looking on it to advance things financially. It refers to something *outside,* something in a line of business, something that *works automatically* . . . He is a little impatient with me, he can't get me to see what he has drawn . . . This is *a fairly big thing* he is trying to show me, and has a *wooden board.* He *presses* something, and I get something *rolling forward,* and then a *click, click, click.* That is the thing he is trying to tell me about . . . He is *not* trying to write up something, but he is showing me *a lot of letters,* A, B, C, D, etc. He shuffles them about a bit with his hands. Then he shows me a funny thing, just like a thin *line.* Then an *arm* comes up and *projects about half a dozen letters* . . .

[It seems to me that this part of the medium's discourse begins pretty badly. One must, of course, allow for the extreme difficulty which a non-mechanically-minded person would find in giving a coherent verbal account of a series of impressions about one or more complicated bits of machinery, received apparently in the form of visual images, partly imitative and partly symbolic. But, allowing for this, the plain fact is that the reference to climbing a ladder is meaningless, that the Electroline cannot with any propriety be described as 'something new in *electricity*', and that it is not 'connected with the house'. But, after this bad start, the statements do seem to fit the Electroline and its method of working rather surprisingly well. It was a 'fairly big thing'; it did have a 'wooden' drawing-'board'; and, when it was started by 'pressing something', something did 'roll forward', there was a series of 'clicks', and an arm did in a sense 'come up and project letters'. The remark about 'not trying to write up something, but showing a lot of letters' means, I take it, that the letters and the operations with them are an integral feature of the apparatus and its working. And that is correct.]

The medium now proceeds to statements about the deceased Edgar's attitude towards his invention . . . In the next three months he wants that completed and cleared off, as if something of a business can be done with it. He says: 'I *had it working,* and yet it *won't work now.*' He is not satisfied. Whoever it is that is working this, it is not correct, as he [Edgar] had it working smoothly and easily . . .

[As regards this, Harold Vandy states that Edgar was the only person who had fully mastered the technique of working the machine. It had been used once since his death, in order to draw a chart by means of the new attachment which Edgar had only just completed. But the man who then used the machine was insufficiently skilled,

373

and the action was not as smooth as it had been when Edgar had used it.]

(M-G). I pass now to George Vandy's sitting with Mrs Mason. At a certain stage in this he put to her the following question: 'Can he' [i.e. the ostensible communicator] 'tell me something of his principal interests during the last ten years—his principal work?'

The medium began by explaining the way in which she was getting her impressions . . . First of all I will explain to you. This person is not talking to me . . . He shows me pictures and I interpret them.

She then continued as follows . . . I interpret that he was rather fond of *machinery* . . . He is putting up a lot of wires and machinery and wheels. I think from what I have seen of him that he would have been very clever at that sort of work—inventive brain—a *very good inventor* . . . He was making something to do with machinery when he died. He shows me something—all I see is a jumble of wheels . . . He shows me as if he *were going to patent it* . . . It seems as if it were an *engine kind of thing* . . . I can't tell exactly what it is, I wouldn't understand it . . . He is showing me as if he were pulling it to pieces—as though it had got to be just so . . . He says, if you will go on with it, he will help you to get it together and make it work properly . . .

[The only comment that seems called for is this. Mrs Mason quite obviously gets on to the fact that Edgar was an inventor, much concerned with machinery of various kinds, and engaged at the time of his death in developing a machine which he might have patented. She prudently excuses herself, on the ground of mechanical ignorance, from attempting to describe in detail the machine of which she gets vague visual impressions. She thus avoids ludicrous mistakes, but also fails to score palpable hits concerning the Electroline and its working.]

(B-H). At a certain stage in Harold Vandy's sitting with Miss Bacon he put to her the following question: 'Can he' [i.e. Edgar] 'describe the nature of his principal work?' She proceeded thereupon to make the following statements:

He was extremely clever at something he was doing, and it has upset him terribly because all his work on earth has stopped. That is his greatest grief . . . He shows me a room, and I don't know if it has to do with wireless or radio, but it is like machinery and machines going very rapidly, as though they were producing something. All this machinery seems to go up and down. I don't say that it is electrical, the machines are actually producing something . . . He seems to have something to do in tending them. I don't get it quite accurately. There is a terrific noise . . .

At this stage Harold asked: 'Were there several machines?' To this the medium answered as follows:

374

. . . Not in the room he was in. There are in *other parts*, but there seems to be *only one with him* . . . There were more machines, but he did a particular thing . . .

[It may be remarked that Edgar's commercial model of the Electroline was housed in a special room by itself on the premises of his cousin William, and that the rest of the building was occupied with other machines of various kinds employed in William's business.]

The medium continued as follows: . . . Would *lithography* or something of that sort come into it? He says '*lithography* or something to do with *printing*' . . . I don't know whether *photography* comes into it as well, but he is trying to show me *plates* or something . . . It seems to be *very fine work*, but in the room he is in I do not get many machines, but *one special machine*. In other parts of the building there are more, but he had a special thing. He was very accurate in it and took a great pride in it. They would have *a difficulty in doing the exact work after he passed*, because he was specially trained on it or had patented it . . . He seems to know you so well, and I feel as though the thing goes on or would go on. Was it not a *secret process*? He says you know about it. I don't know if a *medal* would have been given to him in an exhibition, or if he was going in for it. But it is a *new process*. Is 'lithography' a kind of printing? . . .

[The above is a very remarkable sequence of statements. The only part of it which seems definitely wrong is the reference to a *medal* and an *exhibition*. It is true that *photography* did not enter into the process. But the medium was very tentative in her reference to this; she referred to it only in connexion with the communicator 'showing her *plates* or something'. Now *plates*, though not photographic ones, did play an essential part. For one of the functions of the Electroline was to make drawings on sheets of aluminium or zinc to be used for reproduction by *lithography*. The specific use of the technical term 'lithography' by the medium seems to me to be remarkable. The fact that she interpolated the question: 'Is lithography a kind of printing?' suggests that she got the impression of the *word* without having any clear idea as to its *meaning*. It is true that the machine had nothing to do with *printing*, in the very specific sense of setting type, inking it, and reproducing copies by pressure. But the word is commonly used in a much wider sense, as when we talk of making 'prints' on sensitized paper from a photographic plate or film. Now the Electroline *was* essentially concerned, not indeed with printing in the sense of *reproducing copies*, but in the sense of making originals from which copies were to be 'printed' by one means or another. Finally, the expression 'secret process' exactly describes the Electroline at the stage which it had reached at the time of Edgar's death. It had not yet been patented, and it was important that the details should not be divulged prematurely. Moreover, as already stated, no one except Edgar had really mastered the efficient working of the machine at the time of his death.]

At this point the sitter put to the medium the negative question: 'You cannot get hold of the nature of his work?', thus inevitably suggesting that what she had been saying on this topic had not been altogether satisfactory. She proceeded as follows:

. . . It would be a secret process, like paper would be done in a secret way not known outside. He is holding pages up to the light . . . It is a secret printing on this thing, and would be known only to himself. It would be a thing someone could not copy, a secret machine like if you were to hold up a bank-note you would see the watermark through it. It would be more like Bank of England notes . . .

[Here the medium is either getting an entirely false impression, or is putting a quite wrong interpretation on impressions which may themselves be relevant to the machine and its details. She seems to transfer the notion of secrecy, which applies only to *the machine itself* and its way of working, to its *products*. Perhaps the most charitable view would be to suppose that she had an impression of the perforated paper records, which played an essential part in the working of the machine—'he is holding pages up to the light'—and misinterpreting these as products of the machine, with a mark on them which could not be imitated 'like Bank of England notes'. But it is not our business here to be charitable, and all this is pure conjecture.]

(B-G). We come finally to the sitting which George Vandy had with Miss Bacon. This was a long sitting, and there was in it a great deal about Edgar's activities as an inventor. It is perhaps significant that the sitter was the one of the two brothers who was himself an engineer and had more detailed knowledge and appreciation of this side of Edgar's life and work. Unfortunately the record of the sitting is somewhat repetitious, for the medium tended to revert again and again to much the same topics, largely repeating herself yet giving a certain amount of new significant material. It is relevant to bear in mind that Edgar had been intensely interested in electrical technology in general and in wireless transmission in particular, and that he was engaged at the time of his death, not only on the Electroline machine, but also on improvements in wireless telephony. Some of the medium's statements seem to refer to the latter. It will be best for us to divide up the statements by reference to certain themes to which the medium keeps on returning.

(i) *Edgar's mechanical dexterity* . . . He would have been very clever with his hands, and he uses them in a very delicate way on some very fine work that he was engaged on at the time—something that he was specially proud of . . . He seemed to have a genius for something he did with his hands . . . Whether he inherited his gift I can't say . . . He is most clever with his hands producing something on a machine . . .

[These remarks, if fairly interpreted, would seem to refer at least as much to dexterity in doing something *by means of* a machine as to dexterity in *constructing* a machine. No doubt Edgar had both.]

(ii) *Regret at the cutting short of his work* . . . The work would mean a great deal to him in the future . . . He seems very upset. He was perfecting a process, or was working in a way for his own advancement —something he wanted to bring about, some idea . . . He was not satisfied with it, for I don't feel by the way he is talking that he had come to the end of his research on that . . . I don't know if this is right, but several other people would be interested in the invention besides himself, and would want to put money into it. I think it includes you [i.e. George Vandy], doesn't it? However, he is so upset, because it would have been something to revolutionize—and have meant a tremendous amount of success for everybody. He is terribly upset, because apparently people lent him money for this thing. He says: 'How can I ever pay them back? They put their faith in me. They put money into it, and however shall I pay the money back?' . . . He says: 'I am obsessed only with the idea of how to finish this —how to get it done' . . .

[The factual statements here are correct. George Vandy *was* himself one of several financially concerned. He says that the sentiments ascribed to Edgar in this matter are highly characteristic of him.]

(iii) *References to printing or to letters of the alphabet* . . . He is trying to reproduce something on machinery, and it would seem as if this machinery would not be where he was but in the place round him . . . There are a lot of tiny things like letters, they are all inked . . . I see a lot of block capitals . . . In some ways it looks like a printed thing, something beautifully printed. It came out of a thing in beautiful print— he is trying to show me as well as he can—in a very beautiful finished manner and process of duplication . . . I see him at this secret thing, and whether he printed it himself I don't know, but it is most beautiful work. I don't know what the printing was, it was not an ordinary book . . . I don't know if he was perfecting a process of secret printing; is it not printing that could only be read and understood by certain people? [George Vandy here dissented, saying: 'No, it could be read by anybody'] . . . Well, it is so fine. I can't explain—however, the letters looked different; they stood out. And the whole thing is so beautiful and well thought out. If it were produced, no one would be

377

able to copy it, and it could be used for documents and things like that . . . The secret was something—it was a peculiar way—I don't know what he is trying to show me. I don't know if he typed the letters. It is the peculiar way the letters are placed. Apparently they were placed in a little thing that he shows me, and it seems to simplify and do two or three things at once, as though, instead of four or five people having to handle it, it could be handled by one man and the whole thing completed . . . On this printing-machine—[here the medium remarked *sotto voce*: 'I'm sorry I called it that, Sir']—would he not have printed his own books on it? . . . It is something he . . . I don't know whether *folding* comes into it, a pushing in of paper— it seems automatically to do that and I see a lot of block capitals . . .

[Most of this seems to me pretty muddled. But there are certain points of interest in it. In the first place, it is to be noted that the medium, Miss Bacon, makes precisely the same fundamental mistake as she did in the latter part of the sitting B-H. She gets the mistaken impression that the machine was intended to print material in such a way that, *either* it would be intelligible only to one or a few chosen persons, like a *cypher*, *or* could not be copied or forged, like a *bank-note*. Secondly, it is interesting to note her *sotto voce* apology apparently to the ostensible communicator, for calling the apparatus a 'printing-machine'. Lastly, as to the references to *letters of the alphabet*, it should be remembered that in the Electroline these are recorded on perforated rolls of paper, each of which contains a complete alphabet, and which act like the records of a pianola. George Vandy states that the record which Edgar generally used, when demonstrating the machine to others, was one on which the alphabet was in *block capitals*. Now the medium said that she saw a lot of these. George Vandy considers that, when the medium says that 'the secret is the peculiar way the letters are placed. Apparently they were placed in a little thing that he shows me', she is obviously referring to the paper rolls. That does not seem in the least obvious to me. To give her her due, she was correct when she expressed wonderment at the fineness and beauty of the products of the machine, and she hit the nail on the head when she said that with the machine one man would be able to do the work that now needs several to do it.]

(iv) *References to 'plates'* . . . At times he holds a thing up, and it looks transparent. He is trying to show me this, and to say that no one could compete with him in what he was doing with this particular thing . . . I seem as though I were looking through glass plates with pictures on them . . . He showed me—he held up something in his hands to the light to look at. Whether it was part of photography— lithographs or photographs—I can't say . . . At times he holds up a thing and it looks transparent. He is trying to show me this, and to say that no one could compete with him in what he was doing with this particular thing . . .

[It is perhaps relevant to recall, in connexion with the above statements, that Edgar had been experimenting two or three weeks before his death with a method for using the machine to etch very fine parallel lines on *photographic plates*. The lines could be seen only when the plate was held up to the light. Apart from this, of course, the drawings made by the machine were executed either (*a*) on *plates* (though *not* transparent ones) for reproduction by *lithography*, or (*b*) on cards, which were to be *photographed* for line blocks. Those who are inclined to be charitable may say that the medium seems to be hovering around all these topics and producing a confused mixture of them.]

(v) *References to 'switchboards' and telegraphy* . . . He is showing me a bulb, batteries, and other things, near a switchboard . . . Whether he was connected with some telegraph or cable system, I don't know. You [i.e. the sitter] can't place that exactly can you? [George Vandy answered: 'Not exactly.'] . . . Either cable or telegraph work or something like that—the thing came into it . . . Whether this thing he is trying to show me is a certain kind of code, I don't know; but, if it had been finished, it would have made a great change in certain directions. I have got to ask you a certain question: whether he was connected at one time with cable or wireless or something like that. He seems to understand a switchboard, as though he were perfecting something to do with wireless or television. He was so clever at this . . . He is sitting at a switchboard, as though he knew all about it. Whether he transmitted messages, I don't know, because I can't describe it. He is trying to show me a picture of it . . .

[At this point the sitter asked: 'What does it look like?' In answer he got the statement, already quoted under the heading *References to printing*: 'In some ways it looks like a printed thing, something beautifully printed. It came out of a thing in beautiful print—he is trying to show me as well as he can—in a very beautiful finished manner and process of duplication.']

The medium then proceeded as follows: . . . I don't see any connexion between this printing and the switchboard—whether he did two things at one time. I see him at a kind of switchboard controlling valves, and then I see him at this secret thing, and whether he printed it himself I don't know, but it is most beautiful work . . . He was also engaged on other work at the time, so that the two things could be done at once . . . You [i.e. the sitter] have knowledge of one—of electricity—and of something else that he was actually engaged on . . .

At present you have only looked at the thing; you have touched it, but you have not gone on with it . . .

[Edgar Vandy's other main interest was in electricity in general and in wireless transmission in particular. Up to the time of his death he had been engaged on another important invention, viz. a certain device in connexion with *wireless telephony*. The medium was therefore correct in saying that he was interested in a certain invention besides that which had to do with printing. And she was correct in associating him closely with wireless transmission. But the repeated references to 'switchboards' are capable of two alternative interpretations. They might refer to the work on wireless telephony. But it is also true, as we have seen, that the Electroline machine was controlled by a switchboard, provided with two electric indicator-bulbs of different colours. So the reference might be to either or both of these topics. One has the impression that the medium herself is often confused (as well she might be) between them. Finally, it should be remarked that it was true that George Vandy understood Edgar's invention in connexion with wireless telephony, and that he had looked at the apparatus since Edgar's death, but had not gone on with it. He says that he had not ventured even to touch it.]

CONCLUDING COMMENTS ON THE CASE

I will first make some general comments on the case as a whole, and will then say something in detail about each of its two main features, viz. the references to Edgar Vandy's death, and the references to his invention.

Concerning the case as a whole, the most important point is this. It is quite incredible that the amount and kind of concordance actually found between the statements made by the various mediums at the various sittings should be *purely a matter of chance-coincidence*. It is, if possible, still more incredible that the amount and kind of agreement between the relevant parts of those concordant statements and the known or suspected facts about *either* (*a*) Edgar's death, *or* (*b*) his inventive activities, *taken severally*, should be wholly due to chance-coincidence. It would *a fortiori* be ridiculous to offer that explanation of the agreement between the two parts of the mediums' concordant statements and the two sets of known or suspected facts about Edgar Vandy *taken together*. It is enough to ask oneself these three simple questions: (i) What proportion of the male population of England are drowned *per annum* in open-air swimming-pools after mysteriously falling and getting a crack on the head? (ii) What proportion of the male population of England are skilled technicians, devoting themselves to inventions in general, and to designing and

380

perfecting machines for the mechanical reproduction of drawing and lettering in particular? (iii) What proportion of the male population of England fall into *both* these categories?

Here, as, e.g., in the case of Dr Soal's published results with Mr Shackleton and with Mrs Stewart, we are fairly faced with the following dilemma. Chance-coincidence must be rejected as an explanation. We must either suppose (without any direct evidence) elaborate fraud, in which the experimenter and the subjects must have collaborated; or we must admit the occurrence of modes of cognition which cannot at present be accommodated within the framework of accepted basic limiting principles. I leave each reader to accept that horn of the dilemma which he finds less uncomfortable.

References to Edgar Vandy's Death. Let us, for the sake of argument, reject the hypothesis of deliberate and elaborate fraud on the part of the two surviving Vandy brothers in collusion with the various mediums. Let us suppose, for the sake of argument, that the relevant details as to the circumstances of Edgar's death were obtained by some kind of paranormal process. We must then note one important *negative* fact. The brothers failed to get one grain of new and verifiable information about the question which was troubling them, and which had led George Vandy to consult Drayton Thomas and to initiate the series of sittings with the mediums recommended by the latter.

About this negative fact I would make the following remarks. (i) There was at least one living person, viz. N. J., who must have known a great deal about the relevant facts. He may well have been telling the truth when he said that Edgar was already in the water when he came on the scene. In that case he would not know about the circumstances under which Edgar had got into the water. But he must have known about what happened immediately afterwards. Now N. J. was *present as note-taker* at the first of the non-proxy sittings; and this took place about a fortnight *before* Drayton Thomas's sitting with Mrs Leonard, at which an ostensible communicator, who might be held to answer to the description of Edgar Vandy, intervened. As to the *sitters* at the non-proxy sittings, they had no normal knowledge of any of the relevant facts except those which had come out at the inquest. But they had, no doubt, formed theories and alternative conjectures of their own, and they must certainly have entertained emotionally toned suspicions towards N. J. and possibly towards his sister.

(ii) I think that the *minimal* paranormal hypothesis would be somewhat as follows. *All* the relevant information conveyed at the sittings came from the minds of persons still living on earth, and presumably in the main from those of N. J. and of the surviving brothers. Each medium became apprised of a more or less relevant selection of the contents of these persons' minds by some process of 'mind-reading' or 'resonance'; and then some stratum of her mind (analogous, perhaps, to that which produces our nightly dreams and our waking fantasies) wove together the ideas thus derived from various sources, under the stimulus of the emotional needs of the sitter, and presented the result to her consciousness in the dramatic form of communications from the surviving spirit of Edgar Vandy. While we are about it, we must not exclude the possibility of supplementary 'leakages' from the subconscious stratum of one medium's mind to that of another, or of mutual influences from each upon the psychological processes at work in the others.

If we take this view, we shall have to explain why an important part of the relevant content of N. J.'s mind *failed* to be revealed in the communications. For a good deal that N. J. must have known failed to come out. It may be that something in N. J. 'screened off' this from the 'mind-reading' of all the mediums. Or, alternatively, it may be that some influence (proceeding presumably from N. J.) acted upon the mind of each medium to prevent that part of the information which she had acquired from him emerging into her consciousness. Presumably we should then have to suppose that the repeated explicit statements by the mediums that Edgar wished to shield certain persons, and that he resented attempts to pry too closely into the circumstances of his death, are a transformation and a dramatization of inhibitions *felt by the mediums*, and really originating in *N. J.'s fear or shame*.

You may say that all this is a 'tall story'. It is indeed. But, granted the possibility of 'mind-reading' and of telepathic influence it is no 'taller' than the 'stories' which psycho-analysts daily tell, and which we have all become conditioned to swallow without much discomfort.

(iii) Passing now to the other extreme, I suppose that the *maximal* paranormal hypothesis would be that Edgar Vandy's personality had survived the death of his physical body; that the content of the communications originated, in part at least, in its persisting memories; and that it was in fact deliberately communicating some of its own thoughts and feelings telepathically to the various mediums. (It will be noted that there was no question, in this case, of ostensible *possession* by the communicator.)

I will conclude with two remarks on this hypothesis. (*a*) Unless one holds (as some intelligent and informed persons do) that the notion of survival of bodily death is either impossible *a priori* or antecedently so improbable as not to be worth serious consideration, this is *prima facie* much the simplest and most natural hypothesis. But, of course, that which is *prima facie* most simple and natural may not be the most satisfactory when *all* the very complex aspects of this and of other more or less parallel cases are taken into account.

(*b*) I do not think that the *negative* features in the information communicated are any serious objection to the hypothesis. As to the events immediately *after* death, which concerned certain other persons, the ostensible communicator gives a plausible reason for not divulging them. They were, or would be thought to be, discreditable to the persons concerned, whom he does not altogether blame and wishes in any case to shield. As to the events immediately *before* death, we must bear in mind that a person who has a fit or a concussion, and recovers from it, is often quite unable to recall what he had been doing or suffering immediately beforehand. Granted the hypothesis of survival, it would surely not be very surprising if a similar disability should exist in the mind of a person who had suffered a similar affliction, and, instead of recovering from it, had died but had survived the destruction of his physical body.

References to Edgar Vandy's Inventions. All that I need say under this head is the following. The references to Edgar's inventiveness and his interest and skill in mechanical, and particularly electrical, technique are repeated and unambiguous. But, when it comes to matters of detail, the ostensible communications are generally vague, ambiguous and incoherent. It should be remembered that Edgar was engaged constantly on a number of minor electrical jobs and gadgets, some in his own home and some for friends, besides the important and intricate invention which was his main concern in the latter part of his life. He was also engaged concurrently with another major invention concerned with wireless telephony.

It is often impossible to say whether a particular reference to electrical apparatus at a sitting refers to the Electroline machine, to the work on wireless telephony, or to one or another of the minor technical jobs. Nevertheless, *some* of the statements of *some* of the mediums may not unplausibly be referred to the main invention. On any hypothesis it is not easy to see how one could expect anything much more coherent. We are concerned here with a number of mediums, lacking all the necessary background of mechanical and electrical knowledge, struggling to describe one or a number of highly complex bits of apparatus, the purpose and workings of which they do not fully grasp, displayed to them in fleeting and fragmentary visual images. Whether their statements be derived paranormally wholly from the contents of the minds of living persons (in particular George Vandy), or in part at least from the surviving spirit of Edgar Vandy, we might fairly expect the hotch-potch that we actually find.

EPILOGUE

'Men fear death as children fear to go in the dark; and as that natural fear in children is increased with tales, so is the other.'

BACON, *Essay on Death*

HUMAN PERSONALITY, AND THE QUESTION OF THE POSSIBILITY OF ITS SURVIVAL OF BODILY DEATH

THE question of the possibility of a human personality surviving the death of the body with which it has been associated in earthly life is partly empirical and partly 'philosophical', in one sense of that term. It is empirical in the sense that, if it can be clearly formulated and shown to be an intelligible question, the only relevant way to attempt to answer it is by appeal to specific observable facts. In that respect it may be compared with the question: Does a bit of copper survive being dissolved in nitric acid? The relevant observable facts are some of those investigated by psychical researchers, and in particular certain phenomena of trance-mediumship. The question is 'philosophical' in that the phrase 'survival of bodily death by a human person' is by no means clear and unambiguous. Its ambiguities need to be noted, and the various alternatives which it covers need to be distinguished and clearly formulated. This is work for a person of philosophic interests and training. But it is idle for him to work in a vacuum, if he is to accomplish anything worth doing. He needs a background of knowledge of at least the facts of abnormal psychology and of the phenomena studied by psychical researchers, and he must carry out his analysis in the light of such knowledge. In this Epilogue I shall be concerned almost wholly with the task of clearing up the question and its implications.

If we are to understand what would be meant by, or involved in, the *survival* of a human personality, we must first be clear as to what we mean by a *human person*. I shall therefore begin by considering that question.

Let us use the name 'human being' (short for 'man or woman') to denote creatures like ourselves as we are in this life, i.e. beings with a certain characteristic kind of living physical organism, each of

387

whom speaks of himself as 'I' and is addressed or referred to by other such beings as 'You', 'Jack', 'Mr Jones', and so on.

Now, apart from and prior to all theory, it is a known fact that a human being is a *psychophysical* unit, having two mutually irreducible but most intimately interrelated aspects, viz. the bodily and the mental. In respect of the former he is a *physical object*, i.e. something of which it is significant to say that he weighs so much, is so tall, takes in and puts out so much energy in a given period, and so on. In respect of the latter he is a *psychical subject*, i.e. something of which it is significant to say that he is capable of *having experiences* of various kinds, e.g. pleasant or painful sensations, visual or auditory perceptions, etc., and that he is capable of being *aware of himself as doing so and as having done so*; and, moreover, something of which it is true to say that he does from time to time have such and such experiences and that he is from time to time aware of himself as doing so and as having done so. In respect of the former we speak of a human being as 'having a body'; he himself refers to this as '*my* body'; and others refer to it as '*your* body' or '*his* body' or '*Mr Jones's* body'. In respect of the latter we speak of a human being as 'having a mind'; he himself speaks of '*my* mind'; and others speak of '*your* mind' or '*his* mind' or '*Mr Jones's* mind'.

It is important to remember that this is quite a unique use of the possessive case, and that all other uses are probably derived from it. For there is always a temptation to treat such expressions as on all fours with 'Mr Jones's hat' and 'Mr Jones's nose'. If we do so, we may be led to make inferences which are certainly unjustified and may well be false or even absurd. We might be led, e.g., to take for granted that Mr Jones is something distinct from his mind and from his body and from the combination of the two; so that he might lose his body or his mind or both, as he might lose his hat or his nose or both, and still exist.

Since a human being is something which has both a physical and a psychical aspect, we can and should consider the question of the identity of a single human being, or the diversity of two human beings, under each of these two headings. Undoubtedly physical and psychical identity *generally* go together, and so do physical and psychical diversity. But it is *prima facie* conceivable that physical identity might be accompanied by psychical diversity, and it is *prima facie* conceivable that physical diversity might be accompanied by psychical identity.

The first of these two alternatives is not merely a theoretical possibility, but a recognized though rather uncommon actuality. There are certainly cases where one and the same human body is associated *in alternation* with two or more distinct personalities, and there are

388

cases in which it is alleged with some plausibility that two personalities are associated *simultaneously* with one and the same human
body. As to the second of these two alternatives, any of the millions
of human beings who accept the doctrine of reincarnation is committed to some form of the view that one and the same personality
is associated in course of time now with one and now with another
of a *sequence* of different human bodies. I do not know of any case
in which it is alleged that two or more *co-existing* human bodies,
e.g. that of a certain London banker and that of a certain contemporary Congolese chief, were associated either successively or
simultaneously with one and the same human personality. One could
conceive perhaps, in the abstract, that whenever the London banker
goes to sleep the Congolese chieftain wakes up, exhibiting the characteristic personal traits of the banker and remembering what the
banker had experienced and witnessed while awake, and *vice versa*.
It would be a wearing existence for both parties, and scarcely consistent with efficiency either in banking or in chieftainship; and I
doubt if one really can conceive the alleged possibility in concrete
detail.

In ordinary cases of alternating personality there is no suggestion
that any of the personalities which alternate with each other in
association with a certain one human body ever has been or ever
will be associated with any other human body. But, in cases where
a medium is ostensibly *possessed* for a time by the spirit of a certain
deceased human being, the personality associated with the medium's
body during the period in question claims to be identical with that
which was formerly associated with the body of that human being.
In some such cases there is certainly evidence which seems *prima facie*
strongly to support that claim, though there are perhaps none in
which the evidence is coercive.

Again, it is conceivable that there might be cases of ostensible
possession in which the personality temporarily associated with the
medium's body should claim that it *would in course of time* be associated with the body of a certain human being to be born at a certain
future date to certain parents in a certain place. I believe that there
are a few such cases. If the statements made were specific enough, it
would in principle be possible to verify or refute them. And, if they
should be verified, that would tend *prima facie* to support the claim,
though again the evidence for it would never be coercive. I know of
no cases which approach to fulfilling these conditions, but I am
here considering only various conceivable alternatives.

Let us begin, then, with the *physical* identity of a single human
being, i.e. the conditions under which we should agree that we are
concerned with one and the same living human body. We must

distinguish between what is *commonly understood,* or at any rate *tacitly presupposed,* in saying that a certain human body existing here and now is identical with a certain human body existing there and then, and a *criterion* for deciding whether this is or is not the case. A 'criterion' for human bodily identity may be defined as a characteristic, whose presence or absence can easily be detected, and with regard to which there is extremely strong empirical evidence that its presence is always associated with the presence of all that is commonly understood or tacitly presupposed in asserting such identity, whilst its absence is always associated with the absence of some essential element in the latter complex of properties.

A criterion for so-and-so may be no part of what is commonly understood or tacitly presupposed in asserting the presence of so-and-so. Thus, e.g., an extremely satisfactory *criterion* of human bodily identity and of human bodily diversity has been found to be the identity or the diversity, respectively, of the pattern in thumb-prints. But it is fairly safe to say that this is no part of what most people even nowadays do (or anyone before about 1890 did) commonly understand or tacitly presuppose when speaking of the identity of a certain human body in one set of circumstances with a certain human body in another set of circumstances.

There are fairly satisfactory criteria for the identity of a human being, in its *bodily* aspect, from its birth to its death; for the diversity of two *human bodies*; and for the distinction between a *living* human body and a dead one. That being assumed, we may now consider human beings in their *psychical* aspect, i.e. as persons.

I will begin by summarizing the essential facts about all the persons whom we have ordinary commonsense grounds for believing to exist. Each such person is something which combines in the most intimate way the following three features:

(1) It has an actual stream of experience of a certain special kind, though there may be numerous and longish gaps in this. Such a stream includes, besides *first-order* experiences (such as feeling a twinge of toothache, hearing a clock ticking, etc.), a running accompaniment of *second-order* and sometimes even of *third-order* experiences (e.g. feeling afraid on seeing a runaway horse, feeling ashamed of feeling afraid, feeling that it is rather silly to feel ashamed of feeling afraid, and so on). It includes ostensible rememberings, some purporting to be recollections of certain of one's own past experiences, and others purporting to be recollections of physical objects, states of affairs, or incidents as perceived by oneself in the past. Some of these ostensible rememberings may be partly or wholly delusive, but most of them may be presumed to be in the main veridical. It includes ex-

periences of making, initiating, carrying out, modifying, laying aside and taking up again, various plans, which have their place in a wider scheme of life. It includes, therefore, experiences of long-range expectation, which may be either categorical or merely conditional; and long-range emotions, prospective and retrospective. These may be either reflexive, such as remorse for one's own ostensibly remembered misdeeds, or anxiously toned anticipation of what one is about to experience in a forthcoming interview with one's headmaster; or they may be non-reflexive, such as anxious anticipation of the outcome of an operation to be undergone by a friend. Lastly, unless I am altogether exceptional, they include a continual accompaniment, during one's waking hours, of *sotto voce* 'talking to oneself'. Much of this takes the form of auditory imagery, rather than of whispered speech audible only to oneself. But I think that an essential factor in it is the actual occurrence of the relevant incipient movements in one's vocal organs or the muscles controlling them, and one's simultaneous awareness of these by actual sensation.

I shall describe any such stream of experience as 'personal'. There may well be streams of experience which lack some of these features and are below the personal level. It seems reasonable to suppose that the mental life of one of the higher mammals, such as a horse or a cow, would not include, e.g., experiences of long-range ostensible remembering or long-range expectation, and therefore would not include any of the emotions which presuppose such cognitive states. Let us describe such a stream of experience as 'animal'. It is hardly profitable to try to imagine the stream of experience which may accompany the life of a creature below the mammalian level, such as an oyster. It may be presumed to lack a great deal of what is characteristic of the mental life of a horse or a cow. The absence of highly specialized organs for perceiving various features of external things and states of affairs and events must involve a profound impoverishment in perceptual experience. One may fairly suppose, too, that such a creature as an oyster would lack even that power to recollect its *immediate* past and to anticipate its *immediate* future, which we can hardly avoid ascribing to a horse or a cow. Such a stream of experience might be described as 'biotic'.

Now a human being is not *only* a person. He is also a mammalian animal and a living organism. His personal stream of experience is grounded in his animal stream of experience, and the latter in turn is grounded in his biotic stream of experience; though the lower levels in this hierarchy may well be subtly modified by the higher ones. Moreover, there are periods in the life of a human being (e.g. when he is playing in a football match and actively engaged in running, tackling, etc., or when he is fighting hand-to-hand for his life) when the stream of experience associated with his body is almost confined to the animal and the biotic levels. And there may be periods (e.g. when he is in a state of coma or of dreamless sleep) when, if there be any stream of experience associated with his body, this is confined to the biotic level.

(2) So far I have been considering the mental or subjective aspect of a human being under what I will call 'the *occurrent* heading', i.e. in regard to the nature of the stream of *actual experiences* which constitute the mental life of such a being. I turn now to what I will call 'the *dispositional* heading'. The vast bulk of a person's memories, knowledge, beliefs, and skills exists at any moment only as *dispositions* to have such and such experiences or to perform such and such actions in such and such circumstances. The same is true, *mutatis mutandis*, of his desires, emotions, schemes, and ideals. Some of these dispositions are innate and common to human nature, others are peculiar to himself and have been acquired during his lifetime. They are organized in a special way, which is characteristic of himself and depends jointly on his innate constitution and on the training which he has received, the particular course of his experience, and so on, but which is a determinate form of the generic type of organization characteristic of human nature.

During any short period of his waking life only a few of these dispositions are manifesting themselves in actual experiences or actions. No doubt many more of them are in a state of incipient activity, which manifests itself in a felt readiness or a felt disinclination to act or to think in certain ways, and in such general characteristics of consciousness as selective attention, cheerfulness, or depression. Then, again, those which are in action on any given occasion are then manifesting themselves in that one of the many alternative possible ways which the circumstances of the moment call forth. During the numerous gaps in a personal stream of experience the *only* sense in which it is certain that a person exists is as the bearer of the potentialities summed up in such an organized set of dispositions.

(3) Every person, whom we have ordinary everyday reasons for believing to exist, is an *embodied* person. (i) There is one and only one body which manifests its existence and its internal states and processes to any one person in the following peculiar way, viz. by a fairly stable background of bodily feeling with occasional outstanding localized aches, tickles, feelings of strain, of nausea, and so on. Let us call this the '*organically felt* body'.

(ii) Let us ignore alleged cases of telekinesis. Then the following statement is true. The only events in the physical world which can be *directly* initiated or modified or inhibited by a person's experiences of *volition*, of putting forth and keeping up an *effort*, and so on, are certain events in certain parts of a certain one living body. There is good scientific evidence for saying that these physical events are in fact electrical changes in the brain of that body. These, and their immediate sequels in the motor nerves, are neither intended by volition nor represented by sensation in the stream of experience of the person in question. But the overt movements of the limbs, the articulate utterance of sounds, and so forth, which do in fact generally result from such changes in the brain, have been willed by the person in question and are certainly represented by organic sensations in his stream of experience. Let us speak of this body as the *'directly influencible* body'.

(iii) Let us ignore alleged cases of clairvoyance. Then the following statement is true. The only way in which a human person can become aware of any body or of any physical event or state of affairs is this. Appropriate sensations must occur in his stream of experience. In order for this to happen certain physical events must take place in the brain of a certain one body. That will in general happen only if the appropriate sensory nerve-endings of that body (whether extraceptive or proprioceptive) have been stimulated by a physical process of the appropriate kind, initiated from without or from within that body. Let us call this the *'directly influencing* body'.

(iv) The mere occurrence, in a person's stream of experience, of visual, tactual, auditory, and other sensations, initiated in the way just described, is by no means enough to constitute the experience of perceiving an external body or physical event or state of affairs. Many other conditions must also be fulfilled. But, when they are fulfilled and an ostensible perception (whether veridical or delusive) does occur in a person's stream of experience, its object is perceived as from a *centre* located within a certain one body. In visual perception or *quasi*-perception, e.g., it is perceived in a certain perspective, at a certain distance, and in a certain direction relative to that body. Let us call this the *'perceptually central* body'.

We may sum this up as follows, remembering that our statements are subject to the exclusion of alleged cases of telekinesis and of clairvoyance. Corresponding to any one personal stream of experience, and to the set of organized dispositions of which it is a manifestation, there is one and only one organically felt body, one and only one directly influencible body, one and only one directly influencing body, and one and only one perceptually central body.

Having listed these facts severally, we must now notice a most important additional fact, which is so familiar that it is liable to escape explicit mention. This is the fact that all these four descriptions apply, in all normal cases, to what is, by all ordinary physical criteria, *one and the same* body. It is *one and the same* body which alone manifests itself in a given person's experience by organic sensations; which alone can be directly influenced by his volitions, emotions, etc.; which alone can directly influence his stream of experience by initiating or modifying sensations in it; and which alone is the common centre about which the objects of all his ostensible perceptions are ranged.

So far as I can see, this fact is completely contingent. There is *prima facie* no purely logical absurdity in supposing that the organically felt body, the directly influencible body, the directly influencing body, and the perceptually central body, associated with a given personal stream of experience, should all be *different* bodies. A person might, e.g., get his organic and other sensations only through the stimulation of a certain human body in Cambridge; be able to speak and write only by directly influencing the brain of a certain human body in Stockholm; and perceive everything that he does perceive only as from a centre located in a certain human body in New York.

But, whatever the logical possibilities may be, and whatever occasional exceptions may occur, there is no doubt about what holds in ordinary human life. Corresponding to any personal stream of experience and to its dispositional background, for the existence of which we have ordinary everyday evidence, there is *one and only one* body which is at once its organically felt, its directly influencible, its directly influencing, and its perceptually central body. Moreover, each such body has the familiar appearance and behaviour of a living *human* body, and has the anatomical structure and physiological properties associated with a living *human* organism. It should be noted that there is no *logical* absurdity in supposing a personal stream of experience, with its dispositional basis, to be incorporated in a non-human body, e.g. that of a cat or a parrot. Finally, every living human body has *at least one* personal stream of experience and corresponding set of organized dispositions associated with it in the four ways described above. We commonly take for granted that it has *only one*, but that assumption is known to break down in cases of multiple personality. It should be noted that there would be no *logical* absurdity in supposing that there might be living organisms in human form, e.g. zombies or vampires, which incorporate *no* personal stream of experience and *no* associated set of organized dispositions. They might be expected to betray this defect, as zombies and vampires are alleged to do, by peculiarities in their observable behaviour, suggesting strongly that they are 'not all there'.

I have now stated what I take to be the essential features of an ordinary human person in this life. In order profitably to discuss the question whether it is possible that such a person should survive the death of his body, it is important first to consider the continuity, and the occasional breaches of continuity, within the stream of experience associated with a single human body *during its lifetime*. For the death and dissolution of a human body is a far more profound change than any that happens to it during its life; and it seems *prima facie* reasonable to suppose that it would involve either a complete cessation of the associated stream of experience, or, if not, an even more radical breach in its continuity than any that occurs during the life of the body.

I will begin by considering the normal alternation of sleep and waking, and will then pass to the abnormal (but not paranormal) phenomena of multiple personality uncomplicated by claims to mediumship. In considering the alternation of sleep and waking I shall at first exclude the experience of dreaming, and confine my attention to the case of a person who, on awaking, does not ostensibly remember any particular dream or even that he has been dreaming. We will consider first the evidence available to such a person *himself* of the occurrence of a gap within his stream of experience, and of his identity with the person to whom the earlier segment of experience belonged.

What is the evidence which a person A has, on awaking from an apparently dreamless sleep, that there has been a *gap* in his personal stream of experience, stretching back from the moment of waking to a certain moment in the past? Plainly an essential factor in it is a certain kind of combination of the presence and the absence of ostensible rememberings. On the one hand, ostensible rememberings either arise spontaneously or can be evoked voluntarily, which purport to be of experiences had or of things and events and states of affairs perceived up to and including a certain moment in the past. On the other hand, *no* ostensible rememberings either arise spontaneously or can be evoked voluntarily, which purport to be of experiences had or of things, events, or states of affairs perceived between them and the moment of waking.

Other important indicia available to a person in regard to himself are the following. (i) The surroundings which he perceives on awaking may seem to him familiar in all their main outlines, but certain details in them may have changed in exactly the way in which he knows from experience that they would be likely to have changed in a certain period of time (e.g. a candle may have burned down to a certain extent, the hands of his watch may have shifted by so much, and so on).

(ii) A very important indicium, available *only* to the person himself, is the basic familiarity of the massive background of bodily feeling, by which his body manifests itself to him in his personal stream of experience. Against this there may be a characteristic change in detail, e.g., the change from going to sleep feeling replete and waking up feeling hungry.

The importance of these two indicia will be seen, if we consider the following imaginary case. Imagine a human being going to sleep in familiar surroundings and expecting to awake in the same surroundings; and suppose that his body were gently moved during sleep into wholly strange ones. Imagine, further, that without his knowledge a certain drug were to be administered to him, which will operate during sleep so as to alter profoundly the whole background of organic sensation. Even if, on waking, there were plenty of ostensible rememberings, purporting to be of experiences had and of things and events perceived before the beginning of the period, it seems likely that the person who had just awoken would be extremely puzzled and confused as to his identity with, or diversity from, the person who had fallen asleep.

Let us now consider the evidence which a human being B can have as to the continuity or the discontinuity of the personal stream of experience associated with *another* human being A during a certain period. If we ignore for the present the possibility of telepathy and of clairvoyance, such evidence must consist entirely of external physical signs, circumstantial or narrative, noted and interpreted (wittingly or unwittingly) by B. And these must go back ultimately to causal ancestors in the overt behaviour, positive or negative, of A's body.

It is a *circumstantial* indicium for B that there has been a gap in A's stream of personal experience during a certain period, if he observes or is credibly informed that A's body did not make the normal responses to sensory stimuli, that its eyes were shut, that it was lying prone and breathing heavily, and so on. It is a *narrative* indicium for B, pointing in the same direction, if A afterwards tells him that, so far as he can remember, he was having no experiences during the period. These two kinds of indicia often point in the same direction, but sometimes they may conflict. A may tell B afterwards that he remembers having had certain dreams during the period in question. Or he may tell B afterwards that he remembers that he was continuously having experiences, of such and such kinds, during the period; but that he was stricken with temporary paralysis and aphasia, and so was unable to give any of the wonted external signs of consciousness.

So far I have deliberately excluded the experience of dreaming. I have dealt with this fairly fully in Chapter VI, and I may refer the reader to what I have said there. All that I need add here is this. Dream-experiences are important for our purpose in two quite different ways. In the first place they throw light on what is at present our main topic, viz. the limits of normal personal identity, continuity, and discontinuity. They form a convenient stepping-stone to cases of multiple personality, to which I propose to turn. Secondly, they show that a human being has within him the mechanism and the materials for producing an extremely elaborate, and often fairly coherent and sustained, sequence of hallucinatory *quasi*-perceptions, as of an environment of things and persons in which he is living and acting and suffering, although at the time he is not having the externally initiated sensations which are the basis of normal waking perception. This is relevant to the question of the possibility of survival. Since ordinary human beings can do this here and now, it is conceivable that, if a human person could and did survive the death of his present body, he might carry with him the mechanism and the materials for producing such internally coherent phantasmagoria, without needing external stimulation. If so, he might continue, even though disembodied, to live as it were in a kind of dream-world not so very unlike the world which he actually inhabited when embodied.

Deferring such speculations for the present, let us now consider the phenomenon of multiple personality uncomplicated with claims to mediumship. Such cases are *prima facie* of two kinds, viz. where one personality merely *alternates* with another in the same human being, and where one claims to *co-exist* with the other. We will begin with the former.

Let us suppose that two personalities, P_1 and P_2, alternate in the same human being A. Under what I have called the '*occurrent* heading', this means that there are two personal streams of experience, S_1 and S_2, associated with A's body in the ways already described. There are gaps in the stream S_1, as judged by the personality P_1, and as narrated by him to other human beings when he is in control of the body and able to use its speech-organs. The same is true, *mutatis mutandis*, of the stream S_2 and the personality P_2. But the gaps in either stream are occupied by segments of the other, and each segment influences and is influenced by the contemporary behaviour and circumstances of the body in the normal ways. So, to an external observer, A does not appear to have alternating periods of consciousness and unconsciousness, except of course for the normal alternations of sleep and waking.

That which comes under what I have called the '*dispositional* heading', i.e. the persistent set of organized traces and dispositions which underlies the personal stream of experience, changes sharply and characteristically whenever a segment of S_2 intervenes between two segments of S_1, and changes back again as sharply and characteristically whenever a segment of S_1 intervenes between two segments of S_2. The circumstantial indicia, e.g. handwriting, expressions of emotional reaction towards the same things and persons, range of acquired knowledge and skill displayed, and so on, change sharply when one personality alternates with the other. And these changes agree with the narrative indicia, coming from A's lips or pen, and reporting an interruption in one personal stream of experience and a reinstatement of the other.

Sometimes an interval may elapse between the ending of a segment of one such stream and the beginning of a segment of the other. This interval may appear as a gap in the stream of personal experience both to P_1 and to P_2, and during it A's body may show the normal indicia of suspended consciousness, e.g. of being asleep or in a swoon.

There is an obvious *prima facie* analogy between alternations of personality in the waking state and alternations between waking and dreaming experiences in normal human beings. But the unlikenesses are at least as noteworthy as the likenesses. (i) Generally each alternating personality professes and evinces complete ignorance of the experiences of the other. In some cases, however, one of them (and only one) claims to be (or to be able at will to become) aware in some peculiar way of the experiences of the other. But, even so, that one never speaks of those experiences as '*mine*', but always as '*his*' or '*hers*'. On the other hand, any dream-experience which a person is aware of having had is always referred to by him as '*mine*'.

(ii) In cases of alternating personality the experiences had by either personality, on successive occasions when it is in control of the body, link up with each other across the gaps during which the other personality was in control, as a normal person's waking experiences on successive days do, and as his dream-experiences on successive nights do not.

(iii) Lastly, the body is active and in receipt of the normal sensory stimuli from its surroundings when either of the two alternating personalities is in control and the other in abeyance.

It remains to say something about alleged cases of a plurality of *co-existing* personalities in a single human being. At the first move these resemble cases of merely alternating personality, such as I have just described. But now one of the alternating personalities (say P_1), when in control of A's body and therefore able to make statements in speech or in writing, claims to have persisted and to have had its own continuous personal stream of experience S_1 even during those periods when the other personality P_2 was in control of the body.

P_1 claims, e.g., to have been still getting the usual sensations through the stimulation of the body even when P_2 was in control of it; though he and P_2 may attend to very different selections from this common stock of sensory material, may put very different interpretations upon it, and may feel very different emotions towards what they both simultaneously perceive. Moreover, P_1 claims to be directly aware (or to be able to be so whenever he cares to take the trouble) of the thoughts, desires, and emotions which P_2 has when in control of the body. On the other hand, P_2 makes no corresponding claims. When he is in control and able to communicate by speech or by writing, he reports, with regard to the periods when P_1 is in control, that they are for him just complete blanks in his personal stream of experience. In fact, he knows nothing of P_1's existence, experiences, actions, or character except by hearsay or by inference.

There is one significant fact to be noted here. Sometimes P_2 claims that, in moments of relaxation or distraction, there occasionally well up in his personal stream of experience isolated images, which present themselves to him as referring to this or that specific *past experience*, or to this or that *past state of affairs* as it would have appeared to sight or to hearing, but do *not* present themselves as referring to any past experience of *his* or to any past state of affairs which *he* has witnessed. It is alleged that these curious experiences, which P_2 occasionally has, often correspond very strikingly to certain past experiences which P_1 in fact had, or to certain states of affairs which P_1 in fact witnessed, when in control of the body. If this be a correct account of such images, they cannot correctly be called ostensible *memory*-images in P_2. For a *memory*-image is essentially *autobiographical* in its reference. On the other hand, they resemble ostensible memory-images in being *retro*-referent. We might therefore describe them as 'non-autobiographical ostensible retrocognitions'.

This will be a convenient point at which to consider in rather more detail the part played by memory in personal identity itself, and in the awareness by a person at a certain moment of his identity with a certain person who existed at certain earlier periods.

We must begin by noting certain purely linguistic facts about the ordinary usage of the word 'memory' and associated words such as 'remember', 'recollect', etc. (1) If a person says 'I remember so-and-so', he may mean (i) that he is now in an actual state of remembering so-and-so. But he may mean only (ii) that he has a persistent capacity, acquired in the past, either to initiate such a state in himself at will or to get into such a state whenever he is suitably stimulated. We may call these respectively (i) the *occurrent*, and (ii) the *dispositional*, senses of 'memory'. Obviously 'memory', in the dispositional sense, presupposes 'memory' in the occurrent sense, and any ambiguities in the latter will affect the former.

(2) The phrase 'actual state of remembering' may be used to describe two very different kinds of state, though in practice one of them may often accompany the other. It may be used to denote (i) an *experience* of being aware retrospectively, and without inference by oneself or information from others, of some past experience had by oneself; or of some past external event or state of affairs which has been witnessed by oneself; or of some other person or some thing as he, she, or it was on one or more occasions in the past when witnessed by oneself. But it may also be used to denote an *application* of some kind of knowledge or skill acquired by oneself in the past. (Examples would be if a person were to say that he is now 'remembering' or 'calling to mind' the German for 'cherry', the first line of *Paradise Lost*, how to solve an equation of the second degree, the conjugation of τίθημι, and so on.) We may call these respectively (i) *experiences of recollecting*, and (ii) *states of applying* acquired knowledge or skill.

(3) When 'remembering so-and-so' is used to mean having an experience of recollecting so-and-so, it is used with the implication, or at least the very strong suggestion, that the experience is *veridical*. It would sound very odd to say: 'Smith is now remembering the sinking feeling that he had when about to interview his headmaster last Tuesday, but in point of fact he had no sinking feeling at the time.' And it would sound equally odd to say: 'Jones is now remembering the Master of X, as he looked when he fell into the river, but as a matter of fact the Master never fell into the river in his life.' One would be inclined to say that, if Smith did not have that feeling at the time in question, he cannot properly be said to be 'remembering' it now; and that, if the Master of X never fell into the river, Jones cannot properly be said to be 'remembering' the Master having done so.

It is, however, an important fact that there are experiences which, at the time when they occur, are indistinguishable to the experient from genuine experiences of recollecting so-and-so. If we are concerned with them merely in their phenomenological or psychological aspect, without regard to their veridicality or delusiveness, we tend to speak of them as 'experiences of recollecting so-and-so'. If, on the other hand, we explicitly consider them also in their epistemological aspect, and know or strongly suspect them to be delusive, we feel it inappropriate and misleading to apply that name to them.

We can avoid these linguistic ambiguities by introducing the technical term '*ostensible* recollecting' for any experience, whether it be veridical or delusive, which has the *purely phenomenological* features

400

of an experience of recollecting. We can then distinguish ostensible recollectings which are *veridical* and those which are *delusive*; and we can speak of 'a veridical ostensible recollecting of so-and-so', and of 'a delusive ostensible recollecting *as* of so-and-so'. What we have to bear in mind is that, when it is said without qualification that A is 'remembering' so-and-so, there is a very strong suggestion that A's experience of ostensibly recollecting is *veridical*, and that this suggestion may be completely misleading.

(4) It is part of the *meaning* of words like 'remembering' that they are *sui*-referential besides being *retro*-referential. To say that A is 'recollecting' so-and-so implies *ex vi termini* that so-and-so was either a past experience had by A *himself*, or was an event or state of affairs or person or thing perceived by A *himself* in the past. Again, to say that A is 'remembering' so-and-so (e.g. Euclid's proof that the angles at the base of an isosceles triangle are equal), in the sense of applying acquired knowledge or skill, implies *ex vi termini* that the set of organized dispositions, in which that knowledge or skill resides, was acquired or organized or both by A *himself* through something that *he* experienced or did or suffered in the past.

All this is a matter of linguistic usage. But that usage is no doubt bound up with the tacit unquestioned taking for granted of certain basic limiting principles which concern matters of non-linguistic fact. These may be formulated as follows: (i) The only *past events* that a person can ever be *directly* aware of (as distinct from becoming aware of them by inference, or by hearing and understanding the reports of others, or by perceiving and interpreting permanent records made by himself or by others) are either (*a*) *his own past experiences*, or (*b*) external events which *he himself has perceived*. (ii) A person can become *directly* aware at any moment (subject to the same explanations as above) of other persons and of things, as they were in the past, only in so far as *he himself perceived them* at the past time in question as being in the state in question. (iii) The only way in which a person can now be in possession of an organized set of dispositions to perceive or think or feel or behave in certain ways under certain circumstances, is either (*a*) through *inheritance* from his parents, or (*b*) through the influence of what *he himself* has done or suffered or experienced in the past.

The first two of the above principles may be more briefly, if less accurately, summarized as follows: The only kind of *direct retro-cognition* which a person can experience is *recollection*, i.e. a mode of retro-cognition, the objects of which are confined to *one's own past experiences* and to external events, things, and persons, *as perceived in the past by oneself*.

Now it is important to notice that there is no logical necessity in

401

these principles. It is not impossible, in the sense of self-evidently absurd, to suppose that a person might now be directly aware of a past event which was *not* one of his own past experiences and which had *not* been perceived by him when it happened. Nor is it impossible, in that sense, to suppose that a person might now be directly aware of some other person or of some thing, as it was in the past, though he had *not* perceived it or indeed been in a position to do so, at the past time in question. There is, in fact, a certain amount of quite decent *prima facie* evidence for the occurrence, in a few peculiarly gifted persons, of what I will call 'states of *direct* but *not ostensibly recollective retro-cognition*'. When such a person is presented by the experimenter with a certain thing (e.g. a ring, a fragment of pottery, and so on), which the subject has never seen or handled before, and about the history of which neither he nor the experimenter has any normal information, he may become ostensibly aware of certain highly specific incidents in which it seems to him that the thing was involved in the past. And subsequent enquiry may establish that the subject's statements as to such incidents are correct. Such experiences are not ostensibly recollective, for it does not seem to the subject that they refer to events or states of affairs which *he himself* has experienced or witnessed, either in his present life or in a former life in a different human body. (For examples the reader may be referred to a paper by G. Pagenstecher, entitled 'Past Events Seership', in Vol. 16 of the *Proceedings* of the American S.P.R.)

The following points should here be noted about ostensible recollecting of things, of other persons, and of external events and states of affairs. (*a*) In having such an experience one automatically takes for granted that one *must* have perceived at some time in the past an object such as one is now ostensibly recollecting. But one may have *no present recollection* of having done so. (*b*) In perceiving another person or an external thing or state of affairs one may have a characteristic kind of experience which we describe by saying that the object now perceived 'looks *familiar*', or 'sounds *familiar*', or 'feels *familiar*', and so on. In such cases one tends to take for granted that one *must* have perceived that object before, though one may have no ostensible recollection as of having done so. It is well known that such automatic *prima facie* 'takings for granted' may be quite misleading. There is sometimes overwhelming evidence for concluding that the person in question never did perceive such an object as he is now ostensibly recollecting, or that he never before perceived the object which he is now perceiving with a feeling of familiarity.

Let us now consider the bearing which the above remarks on 'memory' have on the question of 'memory' as a constituent in, or a criterion of, personal identity. (i) To say that everything that a person ever remembers is either an experience *had by himself* or something *witnessed by himself* is either tautologically true or materially false, according to the interpretation which one puts on the word 'remember'. If one uses it to mean what is meant by 'ostensibly and *veridically* recollect', the statement is a tautology. If one uses it to mean what is meant by 'ostensibly recollect, *whether veridically or delusively*', the statement is no longer tautological, but it is materially false. For there are certainly experiences of ostensibly recollecting, which are indistinguishable phenomenologically from veridical recollecting and lead the experient to precisely the same kind of 'taking for granted', but are *delusive*. What the person ostensibly recollects either never happened or never existed, or, if it did, it happened to or was witnessed by some other person. An example would be George IV's ostensible recollections, in his declining years, as of having fought in the Battle of Waterloo.

(ii) Consider next the statement that *only* that which a person recollects belongs to his own personal stream of consciousness. To begin with, this needs to be made more specific in respect of time. It is certain that at any given moment a person is actually recollecting only a very small selection from what he has experienced and what he has perceived. That selection varies very greatly from one moment to another, even within a short period of his life, according to his shifting interest and attention. Then, again, in the latter part of one's life one may *never* recollect many incidents in the earlier part of it which one may *often have recollected* when they were fairly recent. On the other hand, it is not unusual for very old people to have extremely vivid and detailed (and often veridical) recollections of scenes and experiences in their early life, and no recollections at all of experiences quite recently had or objects quite recently perceived.

In view of all this, the only form of the above statement which seems worth discussing is the following: *Only* that which a person recollects *at some time or other* belongs to his own personal stream of experience. But are we prepared to reject all that would be cut out by this principle? For my own part, I feel fairly confident that I must have had experiences and witnessed incidents which I did *not* recollect *even immediately afterwards*; which I have never recollected since; and which I am most unlikely ever to recollect in future, save possibly if I were to be hypnotized or psycho-analysed, which most likely I never shall be.

In this connexion I think it is relevant to mention the following kind of combination of recollecting and failing to recollect, which I have often noticed in myself and which is no doubt common in others too. At t_2 I may recollect, either spontaneously or by making a
403

special effort, that I *had*, immediately after awaking at t_1, a clear and detailed recollection as of a dream which I *had had* immediately before awaking then. But I may not be able, either at t_2 or on any subsequent occasion, to recollect the details of that dream. Moreover, I may at t_2 and possibly on subsequent occasions recollect that I tried, very soon after awaking at t_1, to *repeat* my detailed recollecting of the dream, and found that I could not do so. The occurrence of such *second-order* recollecting at any time is enough, even when one finds oneself quite unable to repeat the relevant *first-order* recollecting, to provide one with a *prima facie* case for believing that one did in fact have an experience of a fairly detailed and determinate kind at a certain time, though one can no longer recollect it in any detail.

It should be added that sometimes the following sequence of experiences may be had. At some time *after* t_2 (the latest moment at which one had tried in vain to recollect the details of the dream, but had recollected that one had recollected those details immediately after awaking at t_1) something may call up in one, by association, images which seem to one to bear on the forgotten dream. And at that stage, either spontaneously or by making a special effort, one may get a fairly detailed ostensible recollection of it. (I have often had this kind of experience myself, and it is not likely that I am singular in that respect.)

Now one's knowledge of the fact that this has happened in *some* cases has an obvious bearing on one's attitude towards those in which it has *not* happened. It tends to strengthen the conviction that, even in the latter cases, the mere occurrence of the second-order ostensible recollections (in the absence of any corresponding first-order ones) is *prima facie* evidence for one's having had in the remoter past a dream, which was *in fact* fairly detailed and determinate, but which one can no longer recollect in any detail.

In the above discussion I have been taking dreams as a striking example. But all that I have been saying of them would apply, *mutatis mutandis*, to cases where one ostensibly recollects having once upon a time had a clear and detailed ostensible recollection as of a certain *waking experience* in the then recent past, but is no longer able to get any detailed ostensible recollection as of that waking experience itself.

(iii) So far I have been considering 'memory' in its *occurrent* sense, and under that head I have been concerned rather with experiences of ostensible recollecting than with states of applying acquired knowledge or skill. I turn now to 'memory' in its *dispositional* sense, covering both the power to recollect such and such past experiences and such and such objects perceived in the past, and the power to think, talk, and act at present in certain ways which have been acquired in the past.

(*a*) It might seem plausible to say that *only* those experiences which a person *could* recollect belong to his personal stream of consciousness; and that *all* such experiences do so, even if there should be some of them which he never actually recollects. But there are ambiguities in both parts of this assertion.

In the first place, how much is supposed to be covered by 'could'? If we take it to mean no more than 'would, if he were to try and were to be supplied with normal reminders', we cut out many experiences which we should certainly wish to include in a person's stream of personal consciousness. If, on the other hand, we begin to extend the meaning of 'could' beyond this, it is hard to know where to stop. Is it to include what he would recollect if and only if he were treated by a skilled hypnotist or psycho-analyst? Or if and only if he were miraculously stimulated by God at the Day of Judgement? If we understand 'could' in so wide a sense as this, the proposition under discussion may exclude nothing that we should wish to retain, but it will be of no use as a criterion for what does or does not belong to a person's stream of consciousness.

Then, again, the question whether 'recollect' is understood to mean ostensibly *and veridically* recollect, or ostensibly recollect *whether veridically or not*, arises to bedevil the second clause in the statement under discussion. On the former interpretation that clause is true but tautological; on the latter it is informative but false.

(*b*) It is plain that the power to apply a certain skill, which we have good reason to believe can exist only after it has been gradually acquired, is an important element in, or criterion for, personal identity. Suppose that, during certain periods in the course of a certain human being's waking life he were to show the ability to understand and talk French, but no capacity to understand or to talk German; and suppose that during other periods, intermediate between the former, he showed the opposite combination of capacity and incapacity. That would be a strong indication (though not, of course, conclusive evidence) that two personalities alternated in control of that human being's body.

The fact is that, in the case of ordinary human beings in this life, there are many criteria for personal identity; and that ostensible recollecting is only one of them, though certainly a very important one. These various criteria usually support each other, but occasionally they may conflict.

We may illustrate this (*a*) in the case of an individual A judging about himself, without consulting others; and (*b*) that of an individual B judging about A without explicitly considering himself. Both these cases are, of course, artificial abstractions. Nearly everyone in this life is in constant social intercourse with many others, and is continually 'exchanging notes' with them.

(a) Suppose that A has regularly kept a diary for many years, and that he now reads it through. He will generally find all that is recorded to be more or less in character with his present personality, as he knows it, after allowing for a normal secular change with increasing age, and for normal occasional variations, such as temporary illnesses, falling in or out of love, and so on. Most of the recorded incidents will seem familiar; and, in regard to many, the reading of the record will call up more or less vivid and detailed ostensible recollections. He may well find, however, that some of the entries in his diary are altogether inconsistent with certain vivid and detailed present ostensible recollections, as of what he was experiencing and witnessing at the date in question.

This will not be likely to worry him. For his own experience, and what he has heard and read, will have convinced him that ostensible recollecting, though *in the main* trustworthy, as tested in various ways, is *occasionally* delusive in detail and even in outline. But suppose he were to find certain sets of entries in his diary, interspersed among the rest, with regard to which the actions described and the feelings recorded seemed to him quite 'out of character' and evoked no ostensible recollections whatever. Then he would be inclined to use some such linguistically paradoxical expression as: 'I suppose I *must* have had those experiences, or done those acts, or witnessed those events, but *I cannot have been myself* at the time.' Suppose, further, that he were to notice that, whilst all the *other* entries (among which these peculiar ones were interspersed) were in his own familiar handwriting, all the entries in question were in *a different and unfamiliar handwriting*, the same in all of them. He would then begin to consider very seriously the possibility that those entries all describe the experiences had, the objects perceived, and so on, by a certain person *quite literally other than himself*. Now it might be that he could confidently rule out the possibility that any *other human being* could from time to time have abstracted the diary from his writing-table and written those entries in it without his knowledge or consent. In that case he would almost be forced to the conclusion that the body which he generally controls is at intervals controlled by a *person other than himself*.

(b) For any human being B the identity and continuity of another human being A, in its *bodily* aspect, is a strong *prima facie* indication of A's identity and continuity in his or her *personal* aspect. But there may be such strong counter-indications in particular cases that B is forced to conclude that A's body is controlled at certain periods by one and at intervening periods by another, of two distinct personalities P_A and P_A', whose respective streams of personal experience have even less in common than the waking life and the dream life of a single embodied person. As I have said, the evidence available to B for such a conclusion may be both narrative and circumstantial. And the positive and negative facts about A's 'behaviour' (in the widest sense), which B can observe, may point in the same direction as the statements which A from time to time makes in speech or writing to B as to what is in principle private and unobservable by others.

I have now said as much as seems needful about the personalities of ordinary human beings, as revealed to themselves in self-observation and to their neighbours in speech, gesture, and action; about the gaps which regularly occur within a single personal stream of experience during sleep, and the dream-experiences which often occur within such gaps; about the rare but well attested cases, where two or more personal streams of experience are associated with one and the same human body, and the gaps in each are occupied by segments of the other; and about the part played by 'memory' (in the various senses of that ambiguous word which I have distinguished) as a factor in, or a criterion for, personal identity. I pass now to discuss, in the light of all this, the question of the possibility of a human personality surviving, in some sense or other, the death and destruction of the physical body with which it has been associated.

Before entering on this question it is necessary to distinguish the following alternatives. If a human personality could conceivably survive the death of the physical body with which it has been associated, it might be thought of as persisting either (1) *without any body*, or (2) in association with *a body of some kind or other*. The second of these alternatives divides into the following two sub-alternatives, viz. (i) that the body with which that personality is now associated is of a *peculiar non-physical kind*, or (ii) that it is just *another ordinary physical body, human or animal*, on earth or on some other planet. We may describe alternatives (1) and (2) respectively as 'unembodied' and 'embodied' survival; and we may describe the two sub-alternatives (i) and (ii) under alternative (2) respectively as 'survival with a non-physical body' and 'reincarnation'. It should be noted that reincarnation would not necessarily exclude *temporary* survival with a non-physical body or in an unembodied state. For suppose that there were an interval between the death of the human being A_1 and the conception of A_2, who is the next later incarnation of the personality which was associated with A_1's body. Then that personality must have persisted during the interval in some state other than that of physical embodiment.

As regards *unembodied* survival, I would make the following
407

remarks. The few Western philosophers in modern times who have troubled to discuss the question of survival seem generally to have taken for granted that the survival of a human personality would be equivalent to its persistence without any kind of physical organism. Some of them have proceeded to argue that the attempt to conceive a personal stream of experience, without a body as organ and centre of perception and action and as the source of a persistent background of bodily feeling, is an attempt to suppose something self-contradictory in principle or inconceivable when one comes down to detail. They have concluded that it is simply meaningless to talk of a human personality surviving the death of its body. Their opponents in this matter have striven to show that the supposition of a personal stream of experience, in the absence of any kind of associated organism, is self-consistent in principle and conceivable in detail. They have concluded that it is possible, at any rate in the sense of conceivable without inconsistency, that a human personality should survive the death of the body with which it has been associated.

Now I have two comments to make on this. One concerns both parties, and the other concerns the second group of them.

(a) Of all the hundreds of millions of human beings, in every age and clime, who have believed (or have talked or acted as if they believed) in human survival, hardly any have believed in *unembodied* survival. Hindus and Buddhists, e.g., believe in reincarnation in an ordinary human or animal body or occasionally in the non-physical body of some non-human rational being, such as a god or a demon. Christians (if they know their own business, which is not too common nowadays) believe in some kind of (unembodied?) persistence up to the General Resurrection, and in survival thereafter with a peculiar kind of supernatural body (St Paul's $\pi\nu\epsilon\nu\mu\alpha\tau\iota\kappa\acute{o}\nu, \sigma\tilde{\omega}\mu\alpha$) correlated in some intimate and unique way with the animal body, ($\psi\nu\chi\iota\kappa\acute{o}\nu \sigma\tilde{\omega}\mu\alpha$) which has died and rotted away. Nor are such views confined to babes and sucklings. Spinoza, e.g., certainly believed in human immortality; and he cannot possibly have believed, on his general principles, in the existence of a mind without some kind of correlated bodily organism. Leibniz said explicitly that, if *per impossibile* a surviving mind were to be without an organism, it would be 'a deserter from the general order'. It seems to me rather futile for a modern philosopher to discuss the possibility of human survival on an assumption which would have been unhesitatingly rejected by almost everyone, lay or learned, who has ever claimed seriously to believe in it.

(b) Suppose it could be shown that it is not inconceivable, either in principle or in detail, that there should be a personal stream of experience not associated with any kind of bodily organism. That would by no means be equivalent to showing that it is not inconceivable that the personality of a human being should survive, in an unembodied state, the death of his physical body. For such survival would require that a certain one such *unembodied* personal stream of experience stands to a certain one *embodied* personal stream of experience, associated with a human body now dead, in those peculiar and intimate relations which must hold if both are to count as successive segments of the stream of experience of one and the same person. Is it conceivable that the requisite continuity and similarity should hold between two successive strands of personal experience so radically different in nature as those two would seem *prima facie* to be? Granted that there might conceivably be unembodied persons, and that there certainly have been embodied persons who have died, it might still be quite inconceivable or overwhelmingly improbable that any of the former should be personally identical with any of the latter.

Speaking for myself, I find it more and more difficult, the more I try to go into concrete detail, to conceive of a person so unlike the only ones that I know anything about, and from whom my whole notion of personality is necessarily derived, as an unembodied person would inevitably be. He would have to perceive foreign things and events (if he did so at all) in some kind of clairvoyant way, without using special sense-organs, such as eyes and ears, and experiencing special sensations through their being stimulated from without. He would have to act upon foreign things and persons (if he did so at all) in some kind of telekinetic way, without using limbs and without the characteristic feelings of stress, strain, etc., that come from the skin, the joints, and the muscles, when we use our limbs. He would have to communicate with other persons (if he did so at all) in some kind of telepathic way, without using vocal organs and emitting articulate sounds; and his conversations with himself (if he had any) would have to be conducted purely in imagery, without any help from incipient movements in the vocal organs and the sensations to which they give rise in persons like ourselves.

All this is 'conceivable', so long as one keeps it in the abstract; but, when I try to think 'what it would be like' in concrete detail, I find that I have no clear and definite ideas. That incapacity of mine, even if it should be shared by most others, does not of course set any limit to what may in fact exist and happen in nature. But it does set a very definite limit to profitable speculation on these matters. And, if I cannot clearly conceive what it would be like to be an unembodied person, I find it almost incredible that the experiences of such a person (if such there could be) could be sufficiently continuous with those had in his lifetime by any deceased human being as to constitute together the experiences of *one and the same* person.

409

Passing next to survival with *some kind of non-physical body*, I would refer the reader to what I have said in Chapter IX (pp. 230–8) under the heading of *Extra-subjective Theories* of collective and reciprocal hallucinations, and to the discussion in Chapter XIV (pp. 342–8) under the heading *Some alleged Observations by Swedenborg*. I will content myself here with adding the following remarks:

(*a*) I think it is fair to say that some of those ostensible communicators through mediums who have given the most impressive *prima facie* evidence for their identity with certain deceased human persons, and who have displayed intelligence, good sense, and culture in their ostensible communications, have asserted explicitly that they have bodies and that they perceive by means of sense-organs, though they claim also to have other means of cognizing objects and events and of influencing things and persons. (I would cite Drayton Thomas's ostensible communicators and their statements as an example.) I think it is also fair to say that I know of no ostensible communicators who have *denied*, whether explicitly or by implication, that they have bodies.

Now it is of course possible to *accept* as veridical that part of the ostensible communications which points to the identity of the ostensible communicator with a certain deceased person, and to *reject*, as delusion on his part or as phantasy on the part of the medium, everything which asserts or implies that the ostensible communicator has a body of some kind and perceives by some kind of sense-organs. But I must say that that would strike me as a pretty high-handed and arbitrary way of dealing with evidence.

(*b*) Suppose it were possible to accept at anything like their face value any of the very numerous accounts of the production of 'ectoplasm' from the bodies of entranced mediums, and its formation into temporary 'materializations' as of this or that human form. Then that would, I think, strengthen the case for survival *with some kind of non-physical body*, if there be a case for *any kind of survival*. But I can attach very little weight to this line of argument. Physical mediumship in general, and that which is concerned with ostensible materialization in particular, reeks with and stinks of fraud. *Some* 'ectoplasm' is known to have been butter-muslin; much more of it may most reasonably be suspected of being composed of that or of some other equally homely material; and I know of no case where the evidence is good enough to build upon. But one ought, perhaps, to bear in mind the possibility that there may be 'one halfpenny-worth of bread to this intolerable deal of sack'.

(*c*) If survival be conceivable, then I cannot but think that the least implausible form of the hypothesis would be that, at any rate immediately after death and for some indefinite period later, the surviving personality is embodied in some kind of non-physical body, which was during life associated in some intimate way with the physical body. If so, I should think it quite likely that many surviving personalities would—as Swedenborg alleges that they do—at first, and for some considerable time afterwards, confuse this non-physical body with their former physical one, and fail to realize that they have died.

Passing finally to the alternative of *reincarnation*, I will make the following remarks:

(*a*) If one takes the world as a whole, belief in reincarnation is and has been perhaps the most widespread form of the belief in survival. It has not, however, been common in recent times in Western Europe, either among plain men or among philosophers or among those interested in psychical research. The most that can be said on the other side is that one very distinguished philosopher, McTaggart,[1] argued for it on metaphysical grounds in the early part of the twentieth century; and that among those interested in psychical research (other than Theosophists, who have acquired their doctrines from India) the doctrine has been taken much more seriously in France than in England.

(*b*) Such empirical evidence as has been adduced in favour of the view that the personalities of certain deceased human beings have been reincarnated in the bodies of certain other human beings, born after the death of the former, has recently been reviewed and critically discussed in two papers by Dr Ian Stevenson in the *Journal* of the American S.P.R., Vol. LIV, Nos. 2 and 3, entitled 'Evidence for Survival from claimed Memories of former Incarnations'. I would refer the reader to those two papers, and to the books and articles quoted in them. The evidence, even if it could be accepted at its face value, is far from coercive in any of these cases; but I think that it may fairly be said to be strongly suggestive of reincarnation in a few of the best of them.

(*c*) Such evidence as has been offered is always of the following kind. A certain member (generally a young child) of family X, residing at place Y, begins repeatedly to allege that he or she has lived on earth before as such and such a member of another family U at another place W, and has died there fairly recently under such and such circumstances. The young person in question (it is alleged) offers detailed accounts of the situation, external appearance, and internal arrangements of the house in which he or she claims to have lived and died; gives the names of various friends and relatives in the former life; describes certain outstanding incidents witnessed or taken

[1] *Some Dogmas of Religion*, Chapter IV; and *The Nature of Existence*, Vol. II, Chapter LXIII.

part in during that life; and so on. On being at last taken to the distant town in question, which neither the subject nor the present relatives have ever visited, the child in question (it is alleged) leads the way to the house without prompting, recognizes the former relatives, and so on, and then sometimes has further ostensible recollections which prove to be veridical. In some cases (it is claimed) certain circumstances about the house as a whole or one of the rooms have been changed. The subject at once recognizes this, and states that they were such and such when he or she used to live there; and these statements are found to be correct.

It is plain that evidence of this kind is open to many serious *prima facie* objections, and it may be doubted whether it would be prudent to accept any existing case at its face value. But, leaving that aside, it is of great interest to compare and contrast such cases with those in which an entranced medium is from time to time ostensibly possessed by a certain personality which claims to be identical with that of a certain deceased human being. Plainly the tests available for the veridicality or otherwise of such claims are *in principle* the same in both cases, though detailed procedures applicable in cases of the one kind may be inapplicable in those of the other.

(*d*) The principles taken for granted by those who would be inclined to regard evidence of the kind which I have been describing (provided it could stand up to criticism) as favourably relevant to the hypothesis of reincarnation, are the following. It is assumed that a present ostensible recollection by a person, as of a certain experience had or as of certain things, incidents, etc., witnessed, is *prima facie* evidence that, if such an experience *was* had and if such things, etc., *were* witnessed, then it must have been *that very same person* who had the experience or witnessed the scenes. Again, it is assumed that, if a person, on now perceiving certain things, persons, scenes, etc., feels them to be familiar, that is *prima facie* evidence that *that very same person* has perceived those same objects in the past. Now, by hypothesis, the ostensible recollections have proved to be *veridical*, in the sense that (whether or not they be *genuine recollections*) they agree with relevant facts about the past, of which the subject can have had no normal source of information. And, by hypothesis, the subject, *in his or her present body*, did not have and could not have had the experiences or witnessed the objects ostensibly recollected now, and has not previously perceived the objects which he or she now perceives with a feeling of familiarity. From these principles, and from these alleged facts, positive and negative, it is argued that the subject's present experiences are *genuine veridical recollections*, and therefore that the personality which is now associated with the subject's present body must have pre-existed and have been associated with a certain other human body which lived and died at an assignable place and time.

(*e*) If we would compare mediumistic phenomena with alleged cases of reincarnation, we might say that reincarnation would be a kind of *lifelong* 'possession' of the body of a living human being by the personality of one now dead, and that mediumistic possession would be a kind of *transitory and occasional* 'reincarnation' of the personality of a deceased human being in the body of the medium. The analogy cannot, of course, be pressed beyond a certain point. For the word 'possession' implies that the human being who is said to be 'possessed' has a *permanent independent personality of his own*, which is temporarily ousted or repressed by a *foreign* personality. The word 'reincarnation' has no such implications. The human being in whom the personality of a certain deceased individual is said to be 'reincarnated' is not supposed to have a personality of his own *other than* that which has been reincarnated in his body. Nevertheless, the analogy is not altogether futile; one could imagine, e.g., an intermediate case, where a human being evinced *multiple personality*, and where one (and not the other) of the two personalities claimed and appeared *prima facie* to be identical with that of a certain deceased human being. (Cf., e.g., the Roff-Vennum Case, discussed in Myers's *Human Personality*, Vol. I, pp. 360–8.)

(*f*) Even if there were cases where the evidence could stand up to reasonable criticism, and where it very strongly supported the hypothesis of reincarnation, it would be quite unjustifiable to jump from this to the conclusion that *all or most* human personalities are reincarnated sooner or later after the death of the bodies with which they have been associated. There is, plainly, not the faintest *empirical* evidence to suggest that reincarnation, if it happens at all, is anything but an extremely rare and exceptional occurrence. I say this, whilst fully realizing that there might be many cases where the relevant evidence has existed but was never recorded or followed up, and many cases where there would be no possibility of testing the statements which might be evidential if they could be verified.

(*g*) I will conclude my discussion of this topic with the following remark. I certainly cannot go so far as Hume, who said (in his *Essay on the Immortality of the Soul*): 'The *Metempsychosis* is . . . the only system of this kind, that philosophy can hearken to.' But I do think that the doctrine of reincarnation, as at any rate one conceivable form of human survival, is of sufficient theoretical interest and *prima facie* plausibility to deserve considerably more attention from psychical researchers, and from philosophers who concern themselves with the nature and destiny of human beings, than it has hitherto received.

413

Having now discussed in some detail the various alternative possibilities as to the *embodiment or non-embodiment* of a surviving human personality, *if* any such there should be, I pass finally to the main question: 'Is survival possible, and, if so, in what sense or senses?'

It seems to me that a *necessary*, though by no means a sufficient, condition for survival is that the whole or some considerable part of the *dispositional basis* of a human being's personality should persist, and should retain at least the main outlines of its characteristic type of organization, for some time after the disintegration of his brain and nervous system. The crux of the question is whether this is not merely conceivable, in the sense of involving no purely logical absurdity (whether explicit or implicit), but is also factually possible, i.e. not irreconcilable with any empirical facts or laws for which the evidence seems to be overwhelming.

To ascribe a disposition to anything is in itself merely to state a conditional proposition of a certain kind about it. In its vaguest form the statement is that, *if* this thing were at any moment to be in circumstances of a certain kind C, *then* an event of a certain kind E would happen in a certain kind of intimate relation R to it. In its ideally most definite form it would assert or imply a formula, connecting each alternative possible form of C with a certain one determinate specification of E and of R. This ideal is often reached in physics, but seldom or never in the case of biological or psychological dispositions.

But, whether the conditional proposition asserted be vague or definite, we do unhesitatingly take for granted that there must be, at the back of any such purely conditional fact, a *categorical* fact of a certain kind, viz. one about the more or less persistent *structure* of the thing in question, or about some more or less persistent *recurrent process* going on within it.

Now it is easy to imagine a persistent minute structure in a human being considered as a *physical object*. It is also easy to imagine recurrent processes, e.g. rhythmic chemical changes, changes of electric potential, etc., going on in the minute parts of a human being considered as a *physical object*. But it is very difficult to attach any clear meaning to phrases about persistent *purely mental* structure, or to the notion of *purely mental* processes, other than trains of experience of various kinds, with which each of us is familiar through having had them, noticed them, and remembered them. So it is not at all clear what, if anything, would be meant by ascribing to a human being, considered as a *psychical subject*, either a persistent purely mental structure or recurrent non-introspectable mental processes. Thus, it is almost inevitable that we should take for granted that the

414

dispositional basis of a human being's personality resides wholly in the minute structure of his *brain and nervous system* and in recurrent *physical processes* that go on within it. Not only is that supposition (unlike talk about '*mental* structure' and 'non-introspectable *mental* processes') intelligible and readily imaginable in detail. It is also in line with the view which we take without hesitation and with conspicuous success about the dispositional properties of purely physical objects, e.g. magnets, chemical compounds, etc. Moreover, it seems *prima facie* to be borne out by what we know of the profound changes of personality, as evidenced in speech and behaviour, following on disease in the brain or injuries to it, on the administration of certain drugs, on the disturbance of the balance of certain internal secretions, and so on.

Now, on this assumption, it seems plain that it is impossible for the dispositional basis of a man's personality to exist in the absence of his brain and nervous system; and therefore impossible for it to persist after the death and disintegration of his body.

Unless we are willing to drop the principle that every conditional fact about a thing must be grounded on a categorical fact about its persistent minute structure or recurrent internal processes, there seems to be only one view of human nature compatible with the possibility of the *post mortem* persistence of the whole, or any part, of the dispositional basis of a human being's personality. We must assume some variant of the Platonic-Cartesian view of human beings. This is the doctrine that every human being is some kind of intimate *compound* of two constituents, one being his ordinary everyday body, and the other something of a very different kind, not open to ordinary observation. Let us call the other constituent in this supposed compound a 'ψ-component'. It would be necessary to suppose that the ψ-component of a human being carries some part at least of the organized dispositional basis of his personality, and that during his life it is modified specifically and more or less permanently by the experiences which he has, the training which he receives, his habitual practical and emotional reactions towards himself and others, and so on.

Now there are at least two features in the traditional form of the Platonic-Cartesian doctrine which need not be accepted and which we should be wise to reject. (i) We need not assume that a ψ-component *by itself* would be a *person*, or that it would *by itself* be associated with a stream of experience even at the animal or the biotic level, such as that enjoyed by a cat or by an oyster. It might well be that personality, and even the lowliest form of actual experience, requires the association of a ψ-component with an appropriate living organism. The known facts about the intimate dependence of a human being's personality on his body and its states would seem strongly to favour that form of the doctrine.

(ii) We need not assume that a ψ-component would be *unextended* and *unlocated*, and have none of the properties of a physical existent. If we gratuitously assume this, we shall at once be in trouble on two fronts. (*a*) How could it then be supposed to have minute structure or to be the seat of recurrent internal processes, which is what is needed if it is to carry traces and dispositions? (*b*) How could it be conceived to be united with a particular living body to constitute an ordinary human being? If we are to postulate a 'ghost-in-the-machine' —and that seems to me to be a *conditio sine qua non* for the barest possibility of the survival of human personality—then we must ascribe to it some of the *quasi*-physical properties of the traditional ghost. A mere unextended and unlocated Cartesian 'thinking substance' would be useless and embarrassing for our purpose; something more like primitive animism than refined Cartesianism is what we need. (In this connexion I would refer the reader back to the discussion of Animism in Chapter XIV, pp. 338–41.)

Nowadays we have plenty of experience concerning physical existents which are extended and in a sense localized, which have persistent structure and are the seat of rhythmic modulations, which are not in any sense ordinary bodies, but which are closely associated with a body of a certain kind in a certain state. One example would be the electromagnetic field associated with a conductor carrying an electric current. Or consider, as another example, the sense in which the performance of an orchestral piece, which has been broadcast from a wireless station, exists in the form of modulations in the transmitting beam, in places where and at times when there is no suitably tuned receiver to pick it up and transform it into a pattern of sounds. Perhaps to think of what may persist of a human being after the death of his body as something which *has experiences and is even a person* is as if one should naïvely imagine that the wireless transmission of an orchestral piece exists, in a region where there is no suitably tuned receiver, in the form of *unheard sounds* or at any rate in the form of *actual sound waves in the air*. And perhaps to think that *nothing* carrying the dispositional basis of a man's personality *could* exist after the death of his body is as if one should imagine that nothing corresponding to the performance of an orchestral piece at a wireless station could exist anywhere in space after the station which broadcast it had been destroyed.

Any analogy to what, if it be a fact, must be unique, is bound to be imperfect, and to disclose its defects if developed in detail. But I think that the analogies which I have indicated suffice for the following purpose. They show that we can conceive a form of dualism, not inconsistent with the known facts of physics, physiology, and psychology, which would make it not impossible for the dispositional basis of a human personality to persist after the death of the human being who had possessed that personality.

Let us grant, then, that it is neither logically inconsistent nor factually impossible that the dispositional basis of a man's personality (or at any rate some part of it) might continue to exist and to be organized on its former characteristic pattern, for a time at least after the death of his body, without being associated with any other physical organism. The next question is whether there is any evidence (and, if so, what) for or against that possibility being realized.

The *persistence* of such a dispositional basis would presuppose, of course, that ordinary human beings have the dualistic constitution, which I have indicated, in this life. Now I think it is fair to say that, *apart from* some of the phenomena investigated by psychical researchers, there is *nothing whatever* to support or even to suggest that view of human beings, and a great deal which seems *prima facie* to make against it. If, like most contemporary Western philosophers and scientists, I were completely ignorant of, or blandly indifferent to, those phenomena, I should, like them, leave the matter there. But I do not share their ignorance, and I am not content to emulate the ostrich. So I pass on to the next point.

As to the bearing of the phenomena studied by psychical researchers upon this question, I would make the following remarks:

(1) To establish the capacity for telepathy, clairvoyance, or precognition in certain human beings, or even in all of them, would not lend any *direct* support to this dualistic view of human nature. At most it would show that the orthodox scientific account of the range and the causal conditions of human cognition of particular things, events, and states of affairs, needs to be amplified and in some respects radically modified. Since the orthodox scientific account of these matters is associated with a *monistic* view of the constitution of human beings, any radical modification in the former *might* involve rejecting the latter. But it is not obvious that it *must* do so. And, on the other hand, it is quite certain that to postulate a dualistic view of the constitution of man does not *by itself* provide any explanation for such paranormal feats of cognition. Except on the principle of *omne ignotum pro magnifico*, it is, e.g., no less odd on the hypothesis of animistic dualism than on that of materialistic monism, that certain persons should sometimes have detailed and correct cognition of future events and states of affairs which they could not possibly have inferred or guessed. At most the dualistic hypothesis might furnish a basis, which the monistic one fails to provide, for further theories explanatory of such paranormal phenomena.

417

(2) So-called 'out-of-the-body experiences' would appear *prima facie* to be favourably relevant to the dualistic hypothesis. Such experiences become important for the present purpose, only in so far as the subject's reported observations can be shown to be correct in matters of detail concerning which he could have had no normal knowledge or probable opinion, and where the details could have been perceived normally only by a human being occupying the position which the subject seemed to himself to be occupying at the time. Their importance is increased if, at the time in question, an apparition of the subject is 'seen' by one or more persons physically present in the place where the subject seems to himself to be present 'in the astral body'.

I would refer the reader to the discussion of such cases in Chapters VI and IX. Here I will only say that, if such experiences stood by themselves, it might be wiser to interpret them in ways that do not presuppose dualism; though that might involve stretching the notions of telepathy and clairvoyance far beyond the limits within which there is any independent evidence for them.

(3) From the nature of the case, much the strongest support for the dualistic hypothesis comes from those phenomena which seem positively to require for their explanation the persistence, after the death of a human being, of something which carries traces of his experiences, habits, and skills during life, organized in the way that was characteristic of him when alive. The phenomena in question are of at least two kinds, viz. cases of haunting, and certain kinds of mediumistic communication. The latter are the more important, being more numerous, more detailed, and better attested. I agree with Professor Hornell Hart ('Six Theories about Apparitions', S.P.R. *Proceedings*, Vol. L) in thinking that it is essential to consider the facts under headings (2) and (3) in close connexion with each other. For the two together give a much stronger support to the dualistic hypothesis than the sum of the supports given by each separately.

(4) If there be any cases in which there is satisfactory empirical evidence strongly suggestive of reincarnation, they would be favourably relevant to the dualistic hypothesis. For suppose that there were evidence which strongly suggests that a certain man B is a reincarnation of a certain other man A. The most plausible account would be the following. A was a compound of a certain ψ-component and a certain human body. When A died the ψ-component, which had been combined with his body, persisted in an unembodied state. When B was conceived, this same ψ-component entered into combination with the embryo which afterwards developed into B's body. There would then be a unique correlation between B's personality and A's, by way of the common ψ-component. For this is the dis-

positional basis of both personalities, and the modulations imposed on its fundamental theme by A's experiences, training, etc., may enter into the innate mental equipment of B. But there is no reason whatever why B should, under normal conditions, recollect any of A's experiences. Nor is there any reason why there should be even as much continuity between B's personality and A's as there is between the several personalities which alternate with each other in a single human being in certain pathological cases.

It may be remarked here that, with certain subjects under hypnosis, a skilled operator can by suitable suggestions evoke highly dramatic and detailed ostensible recollections, purporting to refer to one or more previous lives. (The best examples known to me are to be found in a book entitled *De hypnotiska hallucinationerna*, by the distinguished contemporary Swedish psychiatrist, Dr John Björkhem.) But, unless such ostensible recollections can be tested (which, from the nature of the case, is seldom possible), and shown to be veridical and not explicable by knowledge acquired normally, they provide no evidence for reincarnation.

Let us now take the persistence of the dispositional basis as an hypothesis, which admittedly has extremely little to recommend it in the light of all the known relevant *normal* facts, but derives an appreciable probability from such *paranormal* facts as I have enumerated above. We can then raise the following question: What are the alternative possibilities, as to the kind and degree of consciousness which might occur in connexion with the ψ-component of a deceased human being, during a period of dissociation from any living physical body?

In order to discuss this question it will be convenient to introduce the following terminology. I will describe a ψ-component as 'discarnate', if and when it is no longer associated in the normal way with the brain and nervous system of a living human body. This is meant to cover the two alternative possibilities (i) that it is *wholly unembodied*, and (ii) that it is *associated with some kind of non-physical analogue of a human body*, in a way somewhat analogous to that in which it was formerly associated with an ordinary human body. These two alternatives may be described respectively as (i) 'unembodied', and (ii) 'non-physically embodied', discarnation.

If I may 'stick my neck out', I would say that I find it useful to picture a ψ-component as a kind of highly complex and persistent vortex in the old-fashioned ether; associated (as a kind of 'field') with a living brain and nervous system and with events and processes in the latter; having imposed on it, by those events and processes, certain characteristic and more or less persistent 'modulations'; and capable of persisting (at any rate for a longer or shorter period) after the destruction of the brain and nervous system, as a vortex on the surface of a pond may persist after the dropping of a stone into the water. The notion of a ψ-component does not of course *presuppose* this, or any other, concrete specification. But I find it convenient to have one, and this is the one that I use.

We can now turn to our question. There seem to me to be at least the following four alternative possibilities:

(1) The discarnate ψ-component might persist *without any experiences* being associated with it, unless or until it should again become incarnated (occasionally or for a whole lifetime) in a physical organism, human or non-human.

(2) Either isolated experiences, or even a stream of more or less continuous experience, might occur in association with a discarnate ψ-component; but the several experiences might not be of such a nature, and the unity of the stream of experience might not be of such a kind and degree, that we could talk of *personality*. The consciousness might not reach the level of that of a rabbit or even that of an oyster.

(3) There might be a unified stream of experience associated with a discarnate ψ-component, and this might have some, but not all, the features of the experience of a full-blown personality. We might think of it by analogy with what we can remember of our own state when dreaming more or less coherently. Such a stream of experience, in order to be of the personal kind, would have to contain states of ostensible recollecting, and some or all of these might be veridical. But it might be that all of them were recollections of *post mortem* experiences, and that there were no states of ostensibly remembering any experience had by the human being in question *before* his death. In that case the *post mortem* discarnate personality would be as diverse from the *ante mortem* embodied one as are the alternating personalities of a human being suffering from dissociation.

On the other hand, it is conceivable that such a dream-like personal stream of experience might contain veridical ostensible recollections of certain *ante mortem* experiences, just as our dreams often contain such recollections of some of our earlier waking experiences. In that case it would be *as* legitimate to identify the *post mortem* discarnate personality with the *ante mortem* embodied one as it is to identify the dream personality and the waking personality of an ordinary human being.

(4) Finally, there might be a personal stream of experience associated with a discarnate ψ-component, which was as continuous and as highly unified as that of a normal human being in his waking life. Here again there would be two possibilities:

(i) The ostensible recollections, contained in this personal stream of experience, might all refer to *post mortem* experiences; or (ii) some

420

of them might refer to *ante mortem* experiences, and all or most of these recollections might be veridical. In either case there would be a full-blown personality connected with the discarnate ψ-component. In the former case this would be completely dissociated from the personality of the deceased human being in whom the ψ-component had formerly been embodied. In the latter case there would be the following two alternative possibilities. (*a*) The personality associated with the discarnate ψ-component might remember the *ante mortem* experiences had by the deceased human being in question, only as a human being in his waking state remembers isolated fragments of his dreams. (*b*) The discarnate personality might remember such *ante mortem* experiences, just as a human being in one of his later waking states remembers experiences had by him in his earlier waking states. In that case, and in that alone, we could say that the personality of the deceased human being had survived the death of his body, in the full sense in which one's waking personality is reinstated after each period of normal sleep.

We may sum all this up as follows. When a human being dies, at least the following alternatives (besides the obvious one that death is altogether the end of him) seem *prima facie* to be possible. (1) Mere persistence of the dispositional basis of his personality, without any accompanying experiences. (2) Such persistence accompanied by consciousness only at the *infra-personal* level. (3) Such persistence accompanied by a *quasi*-personal dream-like stream of experience, which may either (*a*) be completely discontinuous with the *ante mortem* experiences of the deceased, or (*b*) have that kind and degree of continuity with them which a man's dreams have with his earlier waking experiences. (4) Such persistence accompanied by a full-blown personal stream of experience. This might either (*a*) be completely discontinuous with the *ante mortem* experiences of the deceased; or (*b*) be connected with them only in the way in which one's later waking experiences are connected with one's earlier dream experiences; or (*c*) be connected with them in the way in which successive segments of one's waking experience, separated by gaps of sleep, are connected with each other.

Let us next consider the respective probabilities of these various alternatives, when viewed only in relation to admitted facts *outside* the region of psychical research.

The first thing to bear in mind is that the notion of a ψ-component is, by definition, the notion of something which carries the structural basis of that system of organized *dispositions* (cognitive, conative, and emotional) which is absolutely essential to anything sufficiently complex and stable and self-coherent to be counted as a personality. Now such dispositions will give rise to *actual experiences* if and only if they be appropriately stimulated from time to time; and the determinate form of experience or action to which a given disposition will give rise on any occasion will depend on the determinate form of the stimulus which it then receives. Moreover, a person can hardly be said to be *living* (as distinct from merely vegetating) unless he be continually *learning*, i.e. unless his experiences and his reactions to them affect the dispositional basis of his personality and modify it in detail, if not in its fundamental organization. Finally, it is an essential part of our notion of a person that he or she should have intentions and form plans, which can be realized (if at all) only in co-operation or in conflict with *other persons*, and by help of, or against the resistance of, independent surrounding *things*, with their characteristic properties and laws.

These elementary reflexions have an important bearing on the antecedent probabilities of the various alternatives under discussion. If we suppose that a discarnate ψ-component is *wholly unembodied*, then much the most likely alternative (excluding for the present purpose complete extinction) would be mere persistence without any kind of associated experiences. For we know that, when sensory stimuli acting on a man's body from without are reduced to a minimum, he tends to fall asleep. And we know that, when in addition sensory stimuli from within his body are reduced to a minimum, his sleep tends to be dreamless. Now a wholly unembodied discarnate ψ-component would presumably be completely free from both kinds of sensory stimulus. Yet ordinary human beings, who are, on the present hypothesis, compounds of a ψ-component with a living human body, do, in spite of that, have frequent periods of sleep which is to all appearance dreamless. The inference is obvious.

The least likely alternative, from the point of view which we are at present taking, would seem to be that the discarnate ψ-component should be associated with a full-blown personal stream of experience connected with that of the deceased in the way in which successive segments of his waking experience, separated by gaps of sleep, were interconnected with each other. For we know that certain variations, which occur within the body and its immediate environment during the lifetime of a human being, are accompanied by profound breaches in the continuity of his consciousness, e.g. falling asleep, swooning, delirium, madness, alternating personality, etc. Now the change involved in the death and dissolution of the body, with which a ψ-component has been united, must surely be more radical than any that happens during its incarnation. So it might reasonably be expected to involve at least as radical a breach in the continuity of consciousness as any that has been observed during the lifetime of a human being.

At this point the following question may be raised. As we know, some human beings have a *plurality* of personalities, which alternate with each other. In the case of such a human being we may ask ourselves the questions: If *any* of these personalities survive the death of their common body, *how many* of them do so? And, if not all do so, *which ones* do?

This leads me to the following general reflexion. The single personality of even the most normal human being is notoriously much less stable and comprehensive than it may seem to others or even to himself. The dispositional basis of it does not include by any means all of the dispositions inherited or acquired in his lifetime by that human being. It consists rather of a predominant selection from that whole, much more highly organized than the rest, and organized in a certain characteristic way. It might be compared to a single crystal, surrounded by a mass of saturated solution, from which it has crystallized and in which it floats. The total dispositional basis of a human being with two personalities, which alternate with each other, might be compared to a saturated solution which has a tendency to crystallize out, sometimes at one and sometimes at another of two centres, and in two different crystalline forms.

Suppose now that the dispositions of a human being are grounded in the structure and rhythmic processes of a ψ-component united with his body. And suppose that this ψ-component persists after his death and carries with it the structural and the rhythmic basis of those dispositions. It seems not unreasonable to think that the ψ-component, which had been united with the body of even the most stable and normal human being, would be liable, after its union with that body had been completely broken, to undergo a sudden or a gradual change of internal structure or rhythm, a disintegration or a reintegration on different lines.

Such considerations seem to me to reinforce those already put forward for holding that straightforward survival of the personality of a deceased human being is antecedently the least likely of all the alternatives under discussion.

Let us look back here for a moment to some of the characteristic features, enumerated above, of the personal stream of experience of an ordinary human being in this life, in order to see whether it is antecedently probable that they should persist, after the death of the body, in association with the discarnate ψ-component. Such a personal stream of experience has, as we have seen, the following characteristic features among others. (i) It contains a *core of bodily feeling*, due to processes constantly going on within the body. This generally changes but slowly in the course of one's life, and is plainly a most important factor in one's consciousness of self-identity.

(ii) Objects other than the body are perceived *as from the body as centre*, and as oriented in various directions and at various distances about it. (iii) It contains experiences of making, carrying out, modifying, dropping, and resuming various plans of action; and this involves initiating, controlling, and inhibiting movements of the limbs, and feeling the resistance and reactions of foreign bodies. (iv) In particular, it contains experiences of speaking and writing, of listening to the talk of others, engaging in conversation with them, reading their writings, and so on. An extremely important part of any embodied human personality is highly organized dispositions to have such experiences and to initiate and control such bodily movements.

Now, in the first place, it is not very easy to believe that a set of organized dispositions, so intimately connected in origin and in exercise with the physical body and its functions, can be located in something other than the body and only temporarily connected with it.

Let us, however, waive that difficulty. Let us suppose that a discarnate ψ-component does carry with it specific modifications of structure or rhythm answering to such dispositions. Let us suppose, in the first place, that it persists in a *wholly unembodied state.* Then it is plainly impossible that those dispositions should be manifesting themselves in *actual* speaking, writing, listening, etc. It is also plainly impossible that there should be at such times experiences of *actually* perceiving from a bodily centre; or of *actually* carrying out intentions by initiating and controlling bodily movements, of actually feeling the resistance and reactions of foreign objects, and so on. Nor is it possible at such times that there should be a core of organic sensation *actually* arising from the body and its internal states and processes.

At most we might admit the following possibilities. It would not be inconceivable that there should be a stream of *delusive quasi*-perceptual experiences, as of speaking, listening, reading, writing, doing and suffering, such as we have in our dreams. And it is not inconceivable that there might be some kind of imaginal replica of the core of organic sensation which one used to get in one's lifetime from processes within one's body. It seems very unlikely that such a dream-like life of imagery and hallucinatory *quasi*-perception would have as much continuity with the *ante mortem* personal stream of experience of the deceased as our dreams often have with our earlier waking experiences. For, when dreaming, one still has a body, and the same body as when awake; and one is still receiving actual organic sensations from processes within it, and still receiving occasional mild stimuli to one's sense-organs from without.

So much for what seems antecedently probable on the supposition that a ψ-component can persist in a *discarnate but wholly unembodied state*. If, on the other hand, we allowed that a ψ-component might persist in a *state of non-physical embodiment*, it would be easier to grant that it might have a stream of personal experience associated with it, and that this might be continuous with the deceased person's *ante mortem* stream of experience. For the 'astral body' might be supposed to play much the same part in the way of supplying actual organic sensation, actual *quasi*-sensory perception of external things, and so on, as did the physical body during its lifetime. And, if the 'astral body' is supposed to have been somehow 'interfused with' the physical body, during the lifetime of the latter, it might be plausible to think that the *post mortem* stream of experience and the *ante mortem* one would be fairly continuous with each other.

I have now said as much as seems necessary about the antecedent probabilities of the various alternatives, when considered *without* reference to the relevant phenomena studied by psychical researchers. Let us now introduce these into the background of our picture, and see what differences, if any, they make.

(1) I think that the fact that some human beings are capable of telepathic or clairvoyant cognition tends to weaken the otherwise strong probability that a discarnate and wholly unembodied ψ-component would merely persist without having any kind of experience associated with it. The appropriate stimuli for calling forth *normal* experiences in a human being are no doubt certain events in his brain and nervous system, initiated physically from within or from without his body. Such stimuli presumably could not act upon an unembodied ψ-component. But suppose we assume, for the sake of argument, a dualistic account of ordinary human beings; and that we accept, as we must, that they sometimes have telepathic or clairvoyant experiences. Then it would seem plausible to suggest that such experiences may be evoked by some kind of *direct* stimulation of an incarnate ψ-component by the action of other ψ-components, whether incarnate, discarnate but non-physically embodied, or wholly unembodied. On that supposition, this kind of action would not be mediated by the body even in the case of a physically embodied ψ-component; and so there would be no obvious reason why it should not continue to operate on a ψ-component which was discarnate and wholly unembodied. It might even operate much more freely under such conditions, since embodiment in general and physical embodiment in particular might tend to counteract it.

(2) Most of the few well attested cases of haunting suggest no more than the persistence and the localization of something which carries traces of a small and superficial, but for some reason obsessive,

425

fragment of the experiences had by a deceased human being within a certain limited region of space.

(3) Many mediumistic communications, which take the dramatic form of messages from the surviving spirit of a deceased human being, imparted to and reported by the medium's 'control', plainly do not warrant us in taking that aspect of them literally. Often they require no more radical assumption than telepathic cognition, on the medium's part, of facts known (consciously or unconsciously) to the sitter or to other living human beings connected with him.

In this connexion it is essential to bear in mind the well attested occurrence, even with mediums of undoubted honesty who have shown ample evidence of paranormal gifts, of the following two kinds of phenomena. (i) *Pseudo*-communications in the dramatic form of messages from a certain deceased person, who *is known to have never in fact existed*, but to have been deliberately suggested to the entranced medium by the sitter for experimental purposes. A famous example is the fictitious 'Bessie Beales', deliberately conjured up by Professor Stanley Hall in sittings with Mrs Piper in 1909 (see S.P.R. *Proceedings*, Vol. XXVIII, pp. 177–8). (ii) Ostensible communications, in correct dramatic form, purporting to come from a certain person, whom the sitter believes at the time to be dead, but who was (as is discovered later) *alive* and pursuing his normal avocations when the sitting took place. As an example I would mention the Gordon Davis case (S.P.R. *Proceedings*, Vol. XXXV, pp. 560–89). Here, in some sittings held by Dr Soal in 1922 with the medium Mrs Blanche Cooper, a former schoolfellow of his called Gordon Davis, whom Dr Soal at the time believed to have been killed in the First World War, not only ostensibly *communicated*, but ostensibly *possessed* the medium, speaking through her lips with the 'direct voice'. Afterwards, in 1925, Dr Soal ascertained that Mr Davis had survived the war, was living in London, and at the time of the sittings in question was engaged on his business as an estate-agent in Southend-on-Sea.

(4) Notwithstanding such cases as these, I think it very unplausible to claim that *all* well attested cases of ostensible possession of a medium by the spirit of a certain deceased human being can be explained by telepathy from persons still alive in the flesh and dramatization on the part of the entranced medium. I am thinking now of cases where the medium speaks with a voice and behaves with mannerisms which are recognizably reminiscent of the alleged communicator, although she never met him during his lifetime and has never heard or seen any reproduction of his voice or his gestures. (There are also cases in which it is alleged that a medium produces automatic script, purporting to be written under the control of the

spirit of a certain deceased human being, and undoubtedly in his characteristic handwriting, although she has never seen, either in original or in reproduction, any specimens of his manuscript. I do not know whether any such cases are well attested; but, if any such there be, they fall under the same category as the direct-voice cases, some of which certainly appear to be so.)

Now it seems to me that any attempt to explain these phenomena by reference to telepathy among the living stretches the word 'telepathy' till it becomes almost meaningless, and uses that name to cover something for which there is no *independent* evidence and which bears hardly any analogy to the phenomena which the word was introduced to denote. *Prima facie* the cases in question are strong evidence for the persistence, after a man's death, of something which carries traces of his experiences, habits, and skills, and which becomes temporarily united during the seance with the entranced medium's organism.

But they are also *prima facie* evidence for something more specific, and surely very surprising indeed. For they seem to suggest that dispositions to certain highly specific kinds of *overt bodily* behaviour, e.g. speaking in a certain characteristic tone of voice, writing in a certain characteristic hand, making certain characteristic gestures, etc., are carried by the ψ-component when it ceases to be incarnate, and are ready to manifest themselves whenever it is again temporarily united with a suitable living human body. And so strong do these dispositions remain that, when thus temporarily activated, they overcome the corresponding dispositions of the entranced medium to speak, write, and gesticulate in *her own* habitual ways.

(5) Nevertheless, it seems to me that *most* of the well attested mediumistic phenomena which are commonly cited as evidence for the survival of a deceased human being's personality, do not suffice to support so strong a conclusion. They fit as well or better into the following weaker hypothesis. Suppose that the ψ-component of the late Mr Jones persists, and that it carries some at least of the dispositional basis of his *ante mortem* personality, including organized traces left by his experiences, his acquired skills, his habits, etc. Suppose, further, that a medium is a human being in whom the ψ-component is somewhat loosely combined with the body, or in whom at any rate the combination does not prevent the body having a residual attraction for other ψ-components. (We might compare a medium, in this respect, to an unsaturated organic compound, such as acetylene.) When the medium is in trance we may suppose that the persisting ψ-component of some deceased human being, e.g. the late Mr Jones, unites with the medium's brain and nervous system to form the basis of a temporary personality. This might be expected

427

to have some of the memories and traits of the deceased person, together with some of those of the medium's own normal personality or of her own habitual 'control'. But, unless the persistent ψ-component has a personal stream of experience associated with it during the periods when it is *not* combined with the body of a medium, no evidence would be supplied at any sitting of *new* experiences being had, of *new* plans being formed and initiated, or of any *post mortem* development of the *ante mortem* personality.

Now it seems to me that the *vast majority* of even the best mediumistic communications combine these negative with these positive features. That is not true, I think, of quite all of them. Some few do seem *prima facie* to suggest the persistence of something which forms plans after death and takes measures to fulfil them between sittings. (The best of the cross-correspondence cases obviously fall under this heading. A useful collection of relevant instances has been published by Mrs Richmond in a little book entitled *Evidence of Purpose*.)

Of course, if the dispositional basis of a man's personality should persist after his death, there is no reason why it should have the same fate in all cases. In some cases one, and in others another, of the various alternatives which I have discussed, might be realized. It seems reasonable to think that the state of development of the personality at the time of death, and the circumstances under which death takes place, might be relevant factors in determining which alternative would be realized. Obviously there might be many other highly relevant factors, which our ignorance prevents us from envisaging.

Again, it would be rash to assume that those ψ-components of the deceased, for the persistence of which we have some *prima facie* evidence, are a fair selection of those which in fact persist. The nature or the circumstances, or both, of the very few which have manifested their continued existence, whether in haunting or through mediums, may well be highly exceptional. Plainly, in the case of the vast majority of those who have died, one or another of the following alternatives must have been fulfilled. Either they never had ψ-components; or their ψ-components have ceased to exist; or they have been reincarnated, either on earth or elsewhere, in human or animal bodies; or else they have lacked opportunity to communicate, or have failed (whether through lack of desire or of energy or of capacity) to make use of such opportunities as were available. For, if anything in this department is certain, it is that the vast majority of dead men have told no tales, and, so far as we are concerned, have vanished without trace.

In conclusion, I would say that I am inclined to think that those who have speculated on these topics have often made one or more of the following positive or negative mistakes:

(1) They have tended to ignore the discontinuities and abnormalities which are known to be frequent in the personalities even of normal human beings, and which are present to extremes in pathological cases.

(2) In dealing with traces and dispositions they have too often confined their attention to very crude and old-fashioned physical analogies. I suspect that they sometimes tend to think of the dispositional basis of a personality by the old analogy of a ball of wax, on which experiences make traces, as a seal might leave impressions. It is plain that this analogy *must* be inadequate and positively misleading, even on a purely anatomical and physiological view of the facts of memory, of association, of heredity, of personal identity, etc. *A fortiori* it must be hopelessly cramping to anyone who is trying to envisage a basis of dispositions which might persist after the death of a man's body.

(3) They have tended to take an 'all-or-none' view of the question of survival, and to assume that either *no one* survives or that *everyone* does so, and does so in *precisely the same sense*. Now I agree that there are very strong reasons for thinking that no one survives in any sense; since there are strong reasons against accepting the dualist view of human beings, which is a necessary condition for the possibility of any kind of survival. But suppose we think that these reasons are not conclusive, and that some of the phenomena studied by psychical researchers are good *prima facie* grounds for an animistic view of human beings. Then it is obviously possible that the ψ-components of *only some* human beings persist after the death of their bodies. And, as regards those that do, some may realize one and some another of the various possible alternatives which I have distinguished and discussed above.

(4) Those who have been inclined to accept the doctrine of human survival have nearly always taken a far too *anthropocentric* view of the situation. If the constitution of human beings be animistic, it is surely incredible that this should not also be true at least of the other higher mammals. And, if that be granted, it is hard to see where to draw a line within the animal kingdom. Now, if not only human beings but also monkeys, cats, and cows be compounds of a physical organism with a ψ-component, I cannot think of any good reason for holding that it is only in the case of human beings that the ψ-component ever persists after the death of the physical organism. If one finds that conclusion incredible, that may be a good reason for rejecting dualism in the case of human beings. But, before doing so on that ground, it would be as well to ask oneself whether one has any better reason than anthropocentric parochialism for finding the conclusion as to non-human animals incredible.

(5) Lastly, those who are convinced of human survival are much inclined to ascribe, quite thoughtlessly and mechanically, to discarnate human persons all kinds of semi-miraculous cognitive and active powers, not possessed by them when physically embodied. There seems to me to be no good reason *a priori* for any such assumption. Ceasing to be embodied *might* involve a setting free of powers which were inhibited by physical embodiment; it might equally involve an inhibition of powers which were formerly freely exercised. Obviously both these possibilities might be fulfilled. The proof of this, as of other puddings, is entirely in the eating.

Once we get outside the narrow sphere marked out by these tacit and illegitimate assumptions, we can envisage a number of interesting and fantastic possibilities. Suppose, e.g., that we think of a ψ-component as analogous to a persistent vortex in the ether, carrying modulations imposed on it by experiences had by the person with whose physical body it was formerly associated as a kind of 'field'. Then we can conceive the possibility of partial coalescence, partial mutual annulment or reinforcement, interference, etc., between the ψ-components of several deceased human beings, in conjunction perhaps with non-human psychic flotsam and jetsam which may exist around us.

There are reported mediumistic phenomena, and pathological mental cases not ostensibly involving mediumship, which would suggest that some of these disturbing possibilities may sometimes be realized. It is worth remembering (though there is nothing that we can do about it) that the world as it really is may easily be a far nastier place than it would be if scientific materialism were the whole truth and nothing but the truth about it.

To conclude, the position as I see it is this. In the known relevant *normal and abnormal* facts there is nothing to suggest, and much to counter-suggest, the possibility of any kind of persistence of the psychical aspect of a human being after the death of his body. On the other hand, there are many quite well attested *paranormal* phenomena which strongly suggest such persistence, and a few which strongly suggest the full-blown survival of a human personality. Most people manage to turn a blind eye to one or the other of these two relevant sets of data, but it is part of the business of a professional philosopher to try to envisage steadily both of them together. The result is naturally a state of hesitation and scepticism (in the correct, as opposed to the popular, sense of that word). I think I may say that for my part I should be slightly more annoyed than surprised if I should find myself in some sense persisting immediately after the death of my present body. One can only wait and see, or alternately (which is no less likely) wait and not see.

INDEXES

INDEX OF NAMES AND TITLES

433

435

S.P.R., its *Journal* (See *Journal*)
its *Proceedings* (See *Proceedings*)
Staley-and-Millbank station, 120
'Statius Case' (Balfour), 289, 306
Steel, Miss, 128–9, 204
'Stephen', Mr, 126–8, 201
Stevens, Mr W. L., 33
Stevenson, Dr Ian, 411
Stewart, Mrs G. (subject in Soal's experiments), 8, 11, 16
Soal's experiments with, 39–43, 381
Stockholm, 201, 202, 394
Strand Magazine, 119
Stratton, Prof. F. J. M., 169
'Study of Dreams, A' (Van Eeden), 162 *et seq.*
Sussex Gazette, 351
'Swanee River' (song), 254
Swedenborg, E., x, 411
on Animism and Cartesian dualism, 340–2
on the spirit-world, 342–8
on 'outer' and 'inner' self, 343
on 'external', 'inner', and 'innermost' memory, 344–5
on communication between spirits, 345–7
on mutual influence between incarnate and discarnate spirits, 347
estimate of his views, 347–8

'T', Mr (G. N. M. Tyrrell), 46
Tadcaster airfield, 133
Tait, Mr W. J., 175 *et seq.*, 204, 210
Ted (Edgar Vandy's cousin), 352
Theosophists, 411
Thigpen, Dr, 255
Thomas, Miss Etta, 258, 262, 273, 274, 284, 352, 410 (See *Etta-persona*)
Rev. C. Drayton, 7, 258, 261, 262, 272, 285, 334
his proxy-sittings with Mrs Leonard, 352–3
consulted by George Vandy, 353, 354
proxy-sitting in reference to Edgar Vandy, 355–8, 360, 381
Rev. John, 258, 262, 273, 274, 352 (See *John-persona*)
Thompson, A. J., his tables of 20-figure logarithms, 84
Thouless, Dr R. H., 261
on Whately Carington's work on trance-personalities, 268–9

Three Faces of Eve, The (Thigpen and Cleckley), 255
'Three Papers on the Survival Problem' (Gardner Murphy), 349
Tilley, Mrs, 122
Times, The, 123
Toksvig, Signe, ix
Topsy-persona (control), 316, 330
compared with *Feda*-persona, 326
'Towards a Method of evaluating Mediumistic Material' (Pratt), 320
Trinity College, Cambridge, ix, 29
Troubridge, Una, Lady, 261, 262, 274, 285
Tyrrell, G. N. M., 11, 24, 126, 161
his experiments with Miss G. Johnson, 46–57
psychological features of those experiments, 59–63
Mrs G. N. M., 46

'Uncle John', 348
University of California Press, ix
Ur of the Chaldees, 308
U.S.A., 6, 255, 256, 308, 320

'V', Mr (automatist), 23
Vandy, Edgar, 350–83
known circumstances of his death, 350–2
accident, leaving scar, in childhood, 367
communications concerning his death, 355–68, 381–3
description of his machine, 368–70
apparent references to his machine, 370–80, 383
his interest in wireless transmission, 380
George, 350, 351, 352, 354–5, 357, 358, 370, 383
consults Drayton Thomas, 353
sittings with Miss Campbell, 359, 360, 361, 363, 365, 366, 367, 368
with Mrs Mason, 359, 360, 362, 363, 366, 368, 374
with Miss Bacon, 360, 361, 362, 364–5, 366, 367, 368, 370, 376–80
Harold, 350, 351–2, 353, 354, 355, 358, 370

INDEX OF SUBJECTS